INTERSEX AND THE (NON)BINARY BODY IN CLASSICAL MUSLIM LEGAL, MEDICAL, AND LITERARY DISCOURSES

Edited by

Mehrdad Alipour & Indira Falk Gesink

LEIDEN UNIVERSITY PRESS

This book will be made open access within three years of publication thanks to Path to Open, a program developed in partnership between JSTOR, the American Council of Learned Societies (ACLS), University of Michigan Press, and The University of North Carolina Press to bring about equitable access and impact for the entire scholarly community, including authors, researchers, libraries, and university presses around the world. Learn more at https://about.jstor.org/path-to-open/.

Cover design: Andre Klijsen
Cover illustration: Indira Falk Gesink
Lay-out: Crius Group, Hulshout
Printer: Scanlaser bv, Zaandam

ISBN 9789087284992
e-ISBN 9789400605541 (e-PDF)
e-ISBN 9789400605558 (e-PUB)
https://doi.org/10.24415/9789087284992
NUR 630

Intersex and the (Non)Binary Body in Classical Muslim Legal, Medical, and Literary Discourses

IRANIAN STUDIES SERIES

The *Iranian Studies Series* publishes high-quality scholarship on various aspects of Iranian civilisation, covering both contemporary and classical cultures of the Persian cultural area. The contemporary Persian-speaking area includes Iran, Afghanistan, Tajikistan, and Central Asia, while classical societies using Persian as a literary and cultural language were located in Anatolia, Caucasus, Central Asia and the Indo-Pakistani subcontinent. The objective of the series is to foster studies of the literary, historical, religious and linguistic products in Iranian languages. In addition to research monographs and reference works, the series publishes English-Persian critical text-editions of important texts. The series intends to publish resources and original research and make them accessible to a wide audience.

Table of Contents

Notes on Transliteration and Dates

Transliteration in this study follows the IJMES system. The Arabic conventions are used throughout, while the Persian conventions are applied in Chapter Three. In Arabic passages, the *tāʾ marbūṭa* is rendered as *-a* (with one exception in an *iḍāfa* construction, where it appears as *-at* before a *hamzat al-waṣl*). In Persian passages, the *tāʾ marbūṭa* is likewise rendered as *-a*, except where it has been transformed into a *tāʾ* in the course of its adoption into Persian, in which case it is written *-at*. The Persian *iḍāfa* is represented as *-i* or *-yi*, as appropriate.

Dates throughout this work are presented as follows:

- Common Era (CE) and *hijrī qamarī* (Islamic lunar) dates: no special notation is used.
- *Hijrī shamsī* (Islamic solar) dates: marked with “sh”.

List of Tables and Figures

Acknowledgements

Mehrdad:
This book was made possible through the generous three-year VENI Talent research grant awarded to me by the Dutch Research Council (NWO) for my project *Beyond Binaries: Intersex in Islamic Legal Tradition* (2022–2025), hosted by the Department of Philosophy and Religious Studies at Utrecht University. I am grateful to my colleagues at Utrecht for their intellectual companionship, encouragement, and thoughtful conversations, which were invaluable in bringing this project to fruition.

As part of the project, I organised the international conference *Beyond Binaries: Intersex Body Politics in Premodern Islamic Legal, Medical, and Literary Discourses*, held at Utrecht University in June 2024. The event brought together distinguished scholars of gender, religion, and medicine, as well as intersex activist-researchers. I extend my sincere thanks to all participants and speakers whose contributions made the gathering so rich and thought-provoking. I am especially grateful to those who explored intersexuality beyond the Islamic tradition: Loren Schechter (Rush University), from a medical perspective; Susannah Cornwall (University of Exeter), from Jewish–Christian studies; and Mir Abe Marinus (NNID, the Netherlands' organisation for sex diversity), from an activist and human rights standpoint.

Special thanks to Indira Falk Gesink—who delivered the keynote lecture—for agreeing to serve as co-editor of this volume. With the combined support of my VENI grant and the generous hospitality of Baldwin Wallace University, where Indira is based, I was able to spend six months in Berea, Ohio. During this time, Indira and I worked closely on the preparation of this volume—an experience that proved both rewarding and intellectually invigorating. I am grateful to Swagata Banik, the former Dean of Graduate Studies & Research at Baldwin Wallace University, whose kind assistance made my visit to BW possible, and to the Department of History and its welcoming faculty, who warmly facilitated my stay and collaboration.

I also wish to thank my partner, Rishi Kalloe, whose love, patience, and unwavering support have carried me through this project.

Mehrdad and Indira:
The chapters included in this volume were selected for their thematic relevance and the authors' willingness to publish with us. In addition, several contributions were newly written for this collection rather than presented at the conference.

Accordingly, the volume should be regarded not as a proceedings collection, but as an expanded and deepened scholarly engagement with its central themes.

We extend our heartfelt thanks to all contributors for their patience, care, and commitment throughout the editorial process. We are also grateful to Ali-Asghar Seyed-Gohrab, editor of *The Iranian Studies Series* at Leiden University Press, for his encouragement and for welcoming this volume into the series. We would also like to thank the team at Leiden University Press, particularly Lisa van Vliet, Editorial Manager and Saskia Gieling, Managing Publisher, for their professionalism and for making the publication process smooth and efficient.

Indira:

I would like to thank my co-editor, Mehrdad Alipour, for extending this opportunity to me. The time we spent working together in 2024 was immensely enriching. As a professor at a relatively small liberal arts university, I rarely have the chance to work closely with others in the field of Islamic studies. I am truly grateful for the time we were able to spend in collaboration on this project. Thanks are also due to Paula Sanders, who has consistently supported our critiques of her research with grace and good humor. I would also like to acknowledge the financial support I received for this research from Baldwin Wallace University's Gigax fund and from the Consortium for Educational Resources on Islamic Studies (CERIS). And as always, I thank my husband Greg and my three very patient children for putting up with my late nights.

Contributors

Mehrdad Alipour is a scholar of Islamic legal and cultural history, examining the transformation of body politics, gender, and sexuality in Islamic contexts across the premodern and modern eras. He is the author of *Negotiating Homosexuality in Islam* (Brill, 2024) and "Navigating Body Politics in Shiʿi Legal Tradition" (*Islamic Law and Society*, 2025). Alipour is the recipient of the VENI Talent Grant (2022–2025) for the project *Beyond Binaries: Intersex Identity in Islamic Legal Tradition* (https://beyondbinaries.nl) and has previously held positions as a Research Fellow and Lecturer at Utrecht University and Goethe University Frankfurt.

Saqer A. Almarri is a Visiting Assistant Professor of Gender Studies and Literature and Creative Writing at New York University, Abu Dhabi. He has published scholarship on the intersections of the Arabic literary tradition in translation with the fields of Gender Studies and Body Studies. He was previously a Humanities Research Fellow for the Study of the Arab World at NYU Abu Dhabi. He may be contacted at saa9091@nyu.edu.

Ash Geissinger is an Associate Professor in the Religion Program at Carleton University (Canada). Geissinger's research is situated at the intersection of the study of the Qur'an and its exegesis, the Ḥadīth literature and its histories of interpretation, and gender. Recent publications include a book chapter on reading *ḥadīth*s through the lens of gender theory, and another book chapter that analyses two traditions, one of which credits Ḥafṣa bt. ʿUmar b. al-Khaṭṭāb with an economic role in early Medina.

Indira Falk Gesink is Professor of History and Director of the Core Curriculum at Baldwin Wallace University in Berea, Ohio. Her publications include *Islamic Reform and Conservatism: Al-Azhar and the Evolution of Modern Sunni Islam* (2009), *Barefoot Millionaire* (2013), and *Philosophies of History* (2018). Her work has also appeared in the *American Historical Review* and the *Journal of Middle East Women's Studies*.

Paula Sanders is Joseph and Joanna Nazro Mullen Professor in Humanities Emerita at Rice University. Her publications include *Creating Medieval Cairo: Empire, Religion, and Architectural Preservation in Nineteenth-Century Egypt*; *Ritual, Politics, and the City in Fatimid Cairo*; *A Mediterranean Society*, vol. 6 (with S. D. Goitein);

Oral-Scribal Dimensions of Scripture, Piety, and Practice: Judaism, Christianity, Islam (edited with Werner Kelber); and *Communities of the Qur'an: Dialogue, Debate, and Diversity in the 21st Century* (edited with Emran El-Badawi).

Ali-Asghar Seyed-Gohrab is Professor of Iranian and Persian Studies at Utrecht University in the Department of Philosophy and Religious Studies, and a member of the Royal Netherlands Academy of Arts and Sciences (KNAW). He has published extensively on Persian literature, mysticism, and religion. His publications range from Persian poetry to Sufism, including the role of religious and mystical motifs and metaphors in the Iran-Iraq War (1980–1988), and how peaceful religious injunctions are used to justify violence. He is currently the Principal Investigator (PI) of an ERC Advanced Grant entitled *Beyond Sharia: The Role of Sufism in Shaping Islam* (www.beyondsharia.nl), examining Islamic non-conformist movements.

Introduction

Mehrdad Alipour and Indira Falk Gesink

Every year, a significant number of infants are born with physical characteristics that do not fit within the typical binary of male and female. Estimates of the proportion of intersex people in the population range from 0.018% to 1.7%.[1] As historical documents demonstrate, such individuals have existed throughout history.[2] At present, these individuals are often described as *intersex*[3] or people with *variations of sex characteristics* (VSC).[4]

In a broad sense, the term intersex refers to variations in congenital sexual anatomy that are considered atypical for males or females. The UN Office for the Commissioner of Human Rights defines intersex as "an umbrella term used to describe a wide range of innate bodily variations in sex characteristics. 'Intersex' people are born with sex characteristics that do not fit typical definitions for male or female bodies, including sexual anatomy, reproductive organs, hormonal patterns, and/or chromosome patterns."[5]

One may be chromosomally intersex, with variations in genetic karyotype. Someone with 45X or 45XO (Turner) karyotype is usually assigned female at birth but has typically undeveloped or missing ovaries, and may not go through puberty. Someone with 47XXY (Klinefelter) karyotype is usually assigned male but may have sparse body hair and smaller genitalia, with feminization at puberty due to low testosterone. Someone could also be born with 45X/46XY or 45X/47XXY (mosaic) karyotype and have different cells of different karyotypes in different parts of the body.[6]

Intersex can also mean variations in gonadal sex. A fetus first develops internal structures that are potentially either male or female, which develop differently in most XY and XX individuals. Testes develop in the fetus at about eight or nine weeks, and ovaries by twelve weeks. A gene on the Y chromosome, SRY, activates another gene, SOX9, on an autosomal chromosome, which instigates development of testes development and other parts of the male reproductive tract. Genes on other chromosomes, FOXL2, RSPO1, and WNT4, are responsible for instigating development of ovaries. Testes and ovaries both produce estrogen and androgens (such as fetal testosterone), although in different quantities. The adrenal gland also produces estrogens and androgens, and the placenta and adipose tissue produce estrogens. Males need estrogens to produce sperm and for erectile function. Females need androgens for their ovaries and follicles to function. The testes also produce anti-Müllerian hormone, which causes the degeneration of female reproductive structures, while the testosterone spurs the development of male internal reproductive features. Variations in genes can cause a fetus to develop both an ovary and a testis, or an ovotestis, or partially developed gonads, or the retention of Müllerian structures in a fetus that is otherwise male.[7]

Variations in genes can also affect genital development. For example, mutations on the NR5A1 gene may cause hypospadias, in which the urinary meatus does not open at the tip of the penis but on the shaft or in the perineum, which could, according to classical Muslim jurists, result in someone being legally designated female or intersex.[8]

Hormones also influence development of external genitalia. Predominance of androgens (testosterone and dihydrotestosterone) produces male-appearing genitalia. Predominance of estrogens produces female-appearing genitalia. Some people with XY chromosomes are insensitive to androgens, so their bodies may have male gonads internally but female-appearing external genitalia (CAIS or PAIS). Some people with XY chromosomes produce less dihydrotestosterone (5α reductase deficiency), so they may be born with female-appearing external genitalia that cause them to be assigned female at birth. Some have hypospadias. However, they have testes that start producing more testosterone at puberty, so they may develop beards and experience phallus growth, vocal changes, and ejaculation.[9] A range of 56–63% of those with 5-ARD develop male gender identities.[10]

Genetic differences can alter hormones that affect sexual development. Mutations in the CYP21A2 gene affect the body's production of an enzyme that itself affects the body's levels of 21-hydroxylase, which is involved in the adrenal cortex's ability to produce androgens and cortisol (a hormone that affects the body's ability to maintain salt levels).[11] Mutations in the CYP17A1 gene change the body's ability to perform a sequence of steroid syntheses that produces dehydroepiandrosterone (DHEA), a precursor to steroid sex hormones.[12] Mutations in the CYP11B1 gene change the production of an enzyme, 11β-hydroxylase, that also affects steroid production.[13] All these genetic differences cause congenital adrenal hyperplasia (CAH), which can manifest differently in different individuals, but generally in people with XX chromosomes it instigates virilization of genitals, facial and body hair growth, and delayed or absent menstruation. CAH is also associated with development of male gender identity in people with XX chromosomes.[14] Rare CAH varieties are more prevalent in Middle Eastern and North African populations than in the global population,[15] and many studies suggest that the practice of consanguineous marriage in Middle Eastern and North African populations has concentrated specific genetic intersex variations in small geographical locales.[16]

In other words, there are a large variety of ways that a person can become intersex, and this variety helps to explain why researchers come up with such a wide range of figures for estimating the prevalence of intersex in the general population—the range depends on what variations one counts as intersex and where the sample is collected.

In classical Muslim discourse, individuals whose physical characteristics—particularly their sexual anatomy—did not conform to established definitions of male or female bodies were commonly referred to as *khunthā*.[17] This term, often invoked in legal, medical, and literary texts, was used to describe those whom we might today classify under the umbrella of intersex, particularly those with VSCs described above that result in ambiguous genitalia or apparent change of sex at puberty. Lexicographical sources reflect significant variation in how *khunthā* was understood. Al-Khalīl b. Aḥmad al-Farāhīdī (d. between 160/777–8 and 175/790–1), for instance, defined *khunthā* as an individual who is neither male nor female—suggesting the possibility of a third or indeterminate category, or perhaps a liminal state that resisted binary classification. In contrast, al-Jawharī (d. 393/1003) characterized the *khunthā* as someone who possesses both male and female genitalia, thus presenting *khunthā* as a composite of both sexes rather than as a distinct or ambiguous category.[18] Literary figures such as Muḥammad al-Muḥibbī (d. 1111/1699) and jurists such as al-Sarakhsī (d. 483/1090) also used the term to describe people who appeared to develop or change sex at puberty.[19]

These diverging definitions point to broader debates surrounding the conceptualization of *khunthā* in Arabic thought: Is the *khunthā* a male, a female, both, or neither? To what extent did lexicographers align with or challenge binary gender norms? How were such definitions negotiated, reinterpreted, or contested in medical, legal, and theological contexts? The contributors to this volume engage with such questions, tracing how classical definitions of *khunthā* informed and were shaped by wider discursive traditions. In doing so, they explore the intricate ways in which Muslim scholars and communities understood and responded to the presence of bodies that complicated dominant gender and sexual categories.

Despite growing visibility, intersex people continue to be overlooked—both by the broader society and, regrettably, even within some LGBTQ+ circles. As a marginalized group, intersex individuals share certain structural challenges with other LGBTQ+ communities yet also face specific forms of erasure and neglect. That said, scholarly attention to intersex topics has gradually emerged in the last few decades of the twentieth century. What was once confined largely to the medical domain—often marked by secrecy and pathologization—has now become the subject of broader academic inquiry. Researchers in sociology, gender studies, literature, religious studies, and other disciplines are now contributing to an expanding and interdisciplinary field of intersex studies.[20]

Furthermore, studies of animal biology have clarified that the world does not consist, as the ancient Greeks believed, of only male and female animals. Many species have multiple rather than binary chromosomal configurations that enable reproductive flexibility; some are hermaphroditic; some change sex within the course of their lifetimes and some several times a day.[21] This sexual variety is a biological fact, not a myth generated by "sex-change industry" or gender theorists.[22] This suggests that intersex should not be viewed as a "disorder" in which something has "gone wrong" in the course of fetal development. Rather, we should view it as one of the mechanisms by which species adapt and survive. Japanese spiny rats, for example, survive despite the complete disappearance of the Y chromosome in several species, because of the species' intersex adaptations. We don't know what function human intersex might serve in our species' evolutionary future, but the evolutionary history of other species suggests there may be one.

Within the field of Islamic studies, broadly defined, there has been little attention to changing attitudes in other fields like biology. With few exceptions,[23] scholars whose work focuses on Islam—particularly in relation to gender and sexuality—have largely overlooked intersex. Nevertheless, there are some scholarly engagements with classical Muslim legal traditions on intersex issues, alongside a smaller number of studies exploring Muslim medical discourses.[24]

A snapshot of the state of the field

Traditional Muslim scholars frequently portray Islam as intolerant of non-binary sex and gender categories.[25] This portrayal has reinforced orientalist narratives, suggesting that Islamic teachings on the male-female binary constitute a monolithic, inflexible code in which there is no space for dialogue and reinterpretation.[26] For example, Paula Sanders, in her well-recognized work, contends that classical Islamic legal texts enforce sex and gender dimorphism by defining males and females as true opposites; because classical Muslim jurists could not tolerate intersex ambiguity, they imposed a gender on ungendered bodies to protect against social disorder and preserve the male-dominated sexual hierarchy. Sanders based her conclusions on an examination of only four classical legal manuals, with special attention to *Kitāb al-mabsūṭ* by the Ḥanafī jurist Muḥammad b. Aḥmad al-Sarakhsī (d. 483/1090).[27]

Although Sanders's conclusions have been widely accepted by scholars in Islamic, Middle Eastern, and gender studies over the past three decades,[28] as she relates in Chapter One of this volume, she subsequently modified her earlier claims. Addressing Everett Rowson's thesis concerning the "penetrator" versus "penetrated" dichotomy in Arabic literary texts,[29] she wrote, "One of the most important conclusions resulting from this body of work is that male/female was not the only gender dichotomy in medieval Islamic societies; there was also male/not male."[30] Sanders recognized that Rowson's argument demanded a reassessment of Islamic legal texts on intersex people.[31]

Like Sanders's later view, Geissinger argued for the existence of a male/not-male binary in Muslim culture, asserting that the modern concepts of male and female as binary opposites are at odds with the classical Greek and medieval Christian ideas. Among the Greeks and medieval Christians, humans were not categorized in binary fashion but as a spectrum in which some were better or more complete humans than others. In this continuum, free males were regarded as the complete expression of humanness, physically, intellectually, and spiritually, followed by other types of people, including females, who represented lesser, imperfect degrees of humanity. According to this view, the bodies of females and males are different in degree but not in kind.[32]

Classical Muslim jurists, as noted by Geissinger, had a similar hierarchical understanding of gender, which determined a person's status in society. For this reason, individuals with ambiguous genitalia had to be categorized as either female or male, if possible. However, these jurists recognized other gender categories, such as effeminates (*mukhannathūn*), i.e., people who were not completely male and therefore imperfect. This classification was possible because classical jurists viewed gender on a spectrum that extended from being male to various degrees of not being male.[33]

Gesink argued that classical Muslim jurists viewed legal sex on a spectrum from all-male/protectors to all-not-male/protected. According to this view, intersex people occupy a "medial" category.[34] Based on her examination of several classical juristic texts, she challenged Sanders's argument on binary categories and argued that there are two strands of juristic thought on *intersex*, one that depicts sex as malleable until puberty and one that depicts sex as indefinitely malleable. According to her, "Intersex persons could be assigned or could adopt a legal sex of male, female or neither. Rather than 'protecting' male privilege, the authors of these texts largely served an individual's health and religious needs."[35]

Gesink adds that Sanders's earlier claim that Islamic legal discourse classifies intersex individuals exclusively within binary sex categories of male and female is based primarily on al-Sarakhsī.[36] Yet, other Muslim jurists recognized at least three legal sexes: male, female, and a "medial sex" comprising intersex people.[37] In the current volume, she expands this initial argument to account for jurists' needs to both accommodate non-binary bodies and remain faithful to scriptural texts that described human creation as male and female. Thus, while Sunni jurists did recognize three legal sex categories for the purposes of social accommodation, most still acknowledged only two ontological sex categories: male and female.

Current scholarship suggests that Muslim legal scholars in certain legal traditions were able to move beyond the rigid ontological binary of male and female. In a recent publication, Alipour offers what appears to be the first sustained argument that intersex individuals constitute a distinct ontological category of human beings in Shiʿi legal discourse—rather than merely forming a third legal or social category. He contends that Shiʿi jurists' primary concern was not always to assign a legal sex to intersex individuals, but rather to uncover their actual nature or sex. According to Alipour, their inquiries revolved around an ontological question: Are intersex individuals male, female, or do they constitute a distinct third human category? Through his analysis, Alipour demonstrates that from the fourteenth century onward, a notable group of jurists sought to establish intersex individuals as an ontological category beyond the binary of male and female.[38]

Yet other scholars have contributed to the discussion of intersex in Islamic contexts outside the discussion of binary or non-binary frameworks. Among these, Sara Scalenghe and Vardit Rispler-Chaim address the intersection of disability and intersex conditions. Scalenghe observes that, while Muslim medical, legal, and literary traditions often framed intersex individuals in narratives of marvel or wonder, such portrayals were generally not expressed with contempt or moral judgement. Scalenghe focuses primarily on the Andalusian medical authority Khalaf b. ʿAbbās al-Zahrāwī—also known as Abū l-Qāsim or Albucasis (d. 403–4/1013)—author of the thirty-volume medical encyclopedia *Kitāb al-Taṣrīf li-man ʿajaza ʿan al-taʾlīf* (*The Arrangement of Medical Knowledge for One Who is Not Able to Compile a Book for Himself*), commonly known as *The Method of Medicine*. She elaborates on how, in cases of anatomical ambiguity, Muslim physicians, particularly Albucasis, would sometimes intervene to surgically confirm a person's 'true nature' (sex or gender).[39]

On the other hand, Almarri explores the minority Ismaʿīlī Shiʿi perspective by focusing on al-Qāḍī al-Nuʿmān's *Daʿāʾim al-islām*. While adopting a binary approach aligned with early views expressed by Sanders, he provides a detailed analysis of the legal body and rights of intersex individuals in this tradition. He places special emphasis on an unusual narrative involving an intersex individual who submitted a petition to Shurayḥ (the well-known judge appointed in Kūfa by Imām ʿAlī) and to Imām ʿAlī himself. Almarri further develops this discussion in one of his contributions to this volume, arguing that the increased availability of online searchable libraries has made it possible for scholars to easily compare variant narratives, and suggesting a novel application of Russian literary analysis to narratives such as the aforementioned *khunthā* case that appear in a wide selection of texts.[40]

Sex and gender discourse

Before proceeding, it is important to make a point about the anachronistic application of modern "sex" and "gender" concepts to early Islamic documents. In other words, we need to establish whether the debates on binary/non-binary intersex in Islamic or Muslim cultures address sex or gender or both or neither. Currently, many studies of classical Islamic literature use these terms without defining them.[41]

Contemporary cultural and scientific discourses often characterize sex and gender as dichotomous. Most feminists and scholars of gender studies regard gender as a socially constructed phenomenon grounded in a "socialization approach," "masculine and feminine personality," or "feminine and masculine sexuality": Gender embodies the societal appreciation of what represents maleness and femaleness and the associated social or cultural implications and repercussions. By contrast, most of these modern scholars regard sex as a biological, genetic, and chromosomal trait.[42] Of course, not all feminists and scholars of gender studies agree with this distinction between gender and sex.[43] Yet, all such arguments and counter-arguments are part of the same modern discourses on sex and gender, one for which there was no equivalent in ancient Greek, Persian, or Mediterranean cultures; in medieval Christian Europe; or in classical Muslim Arab, Persian, or Ottoman societies. This distinction between gender and sex, as Judith Butler notes, challenges the presumption that such categories exist outside specific historical circumstances, cultural contexts, and power relations.[44]

Although there was no term in classical Arabic or Persian for either "sex" or "gender," Arabic and Persian do have binary concepts such as *marʾ/marʾa, dhakar/unthā, rajul/nisāʾ* in Arabic, and *mard/zan* in Persian, roughly man/woman or male/female. Most likely, these paired concepts refer to both the biological conditions and behavioral characteristics of the two groups. However, since classical Arab and Persian vernacular and scientific culture had no knowledge of the current discourse on sex and gender divisions, it is difficult to imagine that these terms signified either sex, gender, or both in any way aligned to our modern understanding.

Nevertheless, these classical cultures arguably were well acquainted with the differences between male and female biological features and behavioral characteristics. More accurately, they believed that there were women and there were men and there were others who were not quite men or women, but there was no word for that difference as such. For example, both Arabic and Persian literature often described certain individuals as effeminate men (*mukhannathūn*) and mannish women (*mutarajjilāt*) based on their behavior.[45] However, some authors perceived effeminate or mannish behavior as being shaped by biological variations and environment.[46]

Although there were no terms for "sex" and "gender," classical Muslim scholars did classify human beings in several ways. Muslim logicians, purportedly influenced by Aristotelian thought,[47] often assert that humans are a 'type' (*nawʿ*) of animal distinguished from other beasts by an 'essential' (*dhātī*) element known as 'differentia' (*faṣl*): being rational.[48] Thus, in their view, humans are rational animals. Building upon the 'accidental characteristics or attributes' (*'araḍiyyāt*) of humans, these logicians suggest a sub-taxonomy of humankind in which humans are divided into 'two groups' (*ṣinfayn*): male/man and female/woman.[49] In classical Qur'ānic exegesis (*'ilm al-tafsīr*), the term 'type' (*naw'*) is occasionally used.[50] In the Islamic legal tradition, jurists also used the following terms: 'nature' (*ṭabī'a*), 'category/division' (*qism*), 'genus' (*jins*), and 'creation/creature' (*khalq*).[51] In classical Islamic discourse, these concepts often encompassed not only biological conditions but also behavioral characteristics and variations in legal status.[52]

Islamic legal thought is especially sensitive to the sexed body and physiological differences of humans. On the one hand, in certain domains—such as ritual purification, prayer, fasting, pilgrimage, clothing, inheritance, criminal law, and people's roles in the public sphere—both Sunni and Shi'i law often depend on whether the legally responsible individual (*mukallaf*) is male or female, although there are several sub-categories of males and females whose status is refracted by intersectional categories such as free/slave.[53] On the other hand, these jurists, as will be noted later, primarily employ biological markers to assess individuals as male, female, or intersex. For this reason, they frequently base legal rulings on the physical sexual features of individuals, in preference to their behavioral characteristics. Indeed, jurists even recognize *mukhannathūn* (effeminate males) and *mutarrajjilāt* (mannish females) as males and females, respectively, because the *mukhannathūn* nor the *mutarrajjilāt* consider themselves to be men, do not consider themselves to be women, nor do Muslim society view them as anything other than male and female.[54] This is why both Shi'i and Sunni jurists often view *mukhannathūn* as males and *mutarrajjilāt* as females, based on their biological sex.[55] It makes sense that, for example, *mukhannathūn*, as the *ḥadīth*s suggest, are not allowed to enter the female quarter of a mosque for congregational prayers, and that *mutarrajjilāt* are not allowed to pray in the men's section of a mosque;[56] or that *mukhannathūn* and *mutarrajjilāt* are forbidden, respectively, to pursue female and male beautifications intended to resemble the opposite sex.[57] Moreover, in juristic contexts, these two groups are hardly ever treated as distinct categories with legal rights and responsibilities separate from those of men and women. When jurists or *ḥadīth* specialists do address them, it is to ensure that they are categorized as males or females. For example, jurists outline Islamic law regarding inheritance shares for various categories of people: while, as will be explored, they carefully delineate the inheritance rights of men, women, and intersex individuals (*khunthā*s), there is no mention of the specific inheritance shares of *mukhannathūn* and *mutarrajjilāt*. Similarly, in discussions about where individuals should stand in a mosque based on their nature/sex, jurists engage in detailed debates, typically asserting that men should stand at the front, women at the back, and intersex individuals in the middle.[58] However, there is hardly any discussion on the placement of *mukhannathūn* and *mutarrajjilāt* in congregational prayers. These examples suggest that, according to Muslim jurists, *mukhannathūn* and *mutarrajjilāt* were not perceived as distinct categories, but rather as part of the male and female categories, respectively.

Literary authors, however, often referred to *mukhannathūn* as a distinct social category. This may tempt us to employ the term "gender" to grapple conceptually with how *mukhannathūn* and *mutarrajjilāt* functioned in classical Islamic societies. Indeed, these were categories that were defined performatively: by behavior, dress, or even choice of musical instruments. This would nevertheless be an anachronistic application of that terminology, as the people of that time did not themselves recognize a distinction between categories that were defined by biology and categories that were defined by social performance or identity. As we have already said, there were men, there were women, there were *khunthā*s, and there were sub-categories of each of these. Some of those sub-categories had legal implications (such as "slave woman" or "virgin") and some did not (such as "*mutarajjil*" and "*mukhannath*").

With this in mind, the contributors to this volume occasionally use the term *sex* and *gender* to refer to the biological sex characteristics of intersex individuals and gender to address the social status or recognition of such individuals, aiming to make the discussion accessible to a contemporary readership. However, they often rely on more naturalized and historically grounded terms found in classical Arabic and Persian discourses, as discussed above. The use of *sex* and *gender*, therefore, is always undertaken with critical awareness of its semantic and epistemological implications.

The making of this volume

This volume has its origins in the international conference *Beyond Binaries: Intersex Body Politics in Premodern Islamic Legal, Medical, and Literary Discourses*, which Mehrdad Alipour convened at Utrecht University in June 2024, as part of his NWO Veni Talent project entitled "Beyond Binaries: intersex in Islamic legal tradition." The event brought together scholars from a range of institutions and disciplinary backgrounds to engage with emerging questions concerning the position of intersex individuals and identities in classical Muslim thought, particularly within legal, medical, and literary frameworks.

While several contributions to this volume originated as presentations at the conference, this is not a conventional proceedings collection. A number of chapters have been authored by scholars who did not participate in the event; their engagement with the project developed at a later stage. The selection of contributions has been guided not by participation alone, but by the intellectual coherence and scholarly significance of each piece in relation to the volume's overarching themes.

All chapters—whether first presented at the conference or subsequently commissioned—have undergone significant revision and anonymous peer review. The volume as a whole has been shaped by a sustained process of conceptual curation, editorial dialogue, and scholarly exchange, aimed at offering a coherent and original contribution to the study of intersex body politics in classical Islam.

To date, and to the best of our knowledge, no monograph or edited volume has addressed the subject of intersex individuals in Islam at book length. This volume thus represents the first sustained scholarly attempt to explore this topic in depth. We hope that it meets the expectations of both specialists and general readers interested in intersex studies, gender studies, religious and Islamic studies, as well as broader inquiries into the body, law, and culture. By bringing together a range of disciplinary perspectives and historical sources, the volume aims to open new avenues for scholarly reflection and foster a more nuanced understanding of how intersex lives and bodies have been conceptualized, regulated, and narrated within Islamic traditions.

Book chapters

In Chapter One, Paula Sanders reflects on the intellectual and disciplinary contexts that shaped her 1991 article on intersex individuals—then referred to as "hermaphrodites"—in medieval Islamic law. This retrospective piece traces the evolution of her scholarly engagement with gender, beginning with an early emphasis on sexual hierarchy within a women's studies framework and gradually shifting towards approaches informed by gender studies, queer theory, and biological understandings of sex. The central argument of her original essay—those Islamic legal texts sought to preserve a binary male-female framework marked by male dominance, thereby reinforcing a rigid sexual hierarchy through their treatment of hermaphrodites—is revisited in light of more recent scholarship. Sanders now argues that such interpretations were shaped by the academic paradigms of the time and did not fully account for the complexity or mutability of sex and gender in premodern Islamic legal and literary sources. By situating her earlier work within broader developments in gender theory and the historical study of Islam, Sanders both critiques and extends her previous scholarship, ultimately advocating for historically grounded research attuned to contemporary concerns around sex, gender, and embodiment.

Chapter Two, by Indira Gesink and Mehrdad Alipour, examines the conceptualization of intersex in Arabic lexicographical traditions and explores the representation of intersex individuals in Arabic literary sources. The chapter begins with a detailed analysis of how various Arabic dictionaries define and contextualize the term *khunthā*, exploring its linguistic roots and semantic range. Gesink and Alipour then turn to the presence of *khunthā* figures in Arabic prose and poetry. As scholars of Arabic literature have observed, intersex individuals appear far less frequently in literary texts than effeminate men (*mukhannath*s). Nonetheless, occasional references in literary and travel narratives provide important insights into how such bodies were perceived—often shaped by a blend of cultural interpretation, imaginative elaboration, and, at times, elements of fantasy. While these depictions often position intersex individuals within the traditions of *ʿajāʾib* (marvels) and *gharāʾib* (wonders), they are not necessarily characterized by contempt or negative moral judgement.

Chapter Three, by Ali-Asghar Seyed-Gohrab, expands the literary exploration of *khunthā* by examining representations of intersex figures in classical Persian poetry and prose. Seyed-Gohrab investigates how *khunthā* (intersex) and *mukhannath* (effeminate) figures are identified in classical Persian literature, beginning with the question of whether these two stock characters—often conflated in vernacular culture and popular readings as a single category—are in fact distinct categorical identities. Persian poets, the chapter argues, clearly differentiate between them: while *mukhannathūn* are sometimes linked to brothels and depicted pejoratively, they also function as moral counterpoints that convey ethical lessons, as seen in ʿAṭṭār's tale of Shiblī, where gender transgression becomes a path to spiritual refinement. Homoerotic desire in Persian court poetry, meanwhile, tends to favor masculine figures, and men exhibiting femininity are often stigmatized as *mukhannath*. In contrast, the *khunthā* appears metaphorically in Rūmī's *Masnavī* to critique worldly dualities, though his symbolic use of gendered metaphors—such as equating the mother with the base self—reflecting deeply ingrained cosmological hierarchies and a worldview far removed from contemporary sensibilities.

Saqer Almarri, in Chapter Four, investigates how classical Qurʾānic commentaries interpreted sexual difference and the category of the *khunthā* in relation to Qurʾān 4:1 and 92:3. It asks how these commentators reconciled the social reality of the *khunthā* with the Qurʾān's silence on it, focusing on their hermeneutic strategy which framed the *khunthā* as an ambiguity of human perception rather than an ontological reality. While this approach sought to restore a binary gender system based on the creation narrative of Adam and his mate, it paradoxically institutionalized the *khunthā* as a liminal, exceptional subject positioned between masculinity and femininity, requiring specialist legal interpretation. The chapter highlights the continuity of this exegetical hermeneutic over time and raises questions about its possible extension into modern and contemporary Qurʾānic commentaries, particularly regarding nonbinary, trans, and intersex subjects.

Chapter Five, by Ash Geissinger, examines how gender categories are constructed and contested within the Sunni *ḥadīth* corpus and its commentaries.

Focusing on *mukhannath* rather than *khunthā*—the central theme of this book—the author highlights that the *ḥadīth* corpus contains more narrative material and interpretive engagement concerning *mukhannath*s, making them a more productive subject for analyzing how classical *ḥadīth* scholars negotiated gender ambiguity. Nonetheless, the author links the two categories, noting that despite their differences, both *khunthā*s and *mukhannath*s occupied marginal and ambiguous positions within gendered frameworks, as some earlier studies have observed. While both categories reflect gender and sexual in-betweenness, *ḥadīth* literature treats them unequally, offering fewer and less detailed references to *khunthā*. The author explores how textual variants surrounding the *mukhannath* figure Anjasha reveal shifting gender classifications and broader concerns with preserving hierarchical structures of gender and authority. The study thus argues that *ḥadīth* traditions serve as dynamic sites for negotiating gender instability, with *mukhannath* offering a more nuanced lens than *khunthā* for understanding these interpretive processes.

In Chapter Six, Saqer Almarri engages with debates surrounding *khunthā* within Ismāʿīlī Shiʿi legal and *ḥadīth* discourse. Almarri revisits the question of a Fatimid legal code by examining a striking case in which a *khunthā* appears in court claiming to have fathered a child. While his earlier work suggested the uniqueness of this narrative, he has since identified additional material recounting a parallel case involving Shurayḥ, ʿAlī, and a *khunthā*. Although the sources remain limited and fragmented, Almarri demonstrates how digital humanities methods can be employed to trace and reconstruct these dispersed references across digital corpora. In doing so, he sheds light on a case where Shurayḥ is confounded by a *khunthā* who has fathered a child, and ʿAlī responds by annulling the *khunthā*'s marriage and declaring them a man. Drawing on digital philology, Almarri explores how this instance of early Islamic gender testing has been represented by different authors, each framing the episode according to particular legal or interpretive concerns. His synoptic reading brings these fragments together to reveal the varied emphases and functions of the narrative across different contexts.

Chapter Seven, by Mehrdad Alipour, investigates the discourse surrounding intersex individuals in early Shiʿi scriptural texts and the classical Twelver legal tradition, employing digital humanities methods to locate and examine early Shiʿi *ḥadīth* collections and how their compilers conceptualized the intersex body and its legal and social roles. The chapter traces the evolution from *ḥadīth* discourse to the juristic writings of scholars shaped by these narrations, highlighting that while intersex individuals appear across various domains of Islamic law, the most sustained legal engagement has centered on inheritance, owing to the predominance of inheritance-related *ḥadīth*s. However, Alipour also demonstrates that classical jurists addressed intersex-related matters in other legal areas, including marriage, (un)intentional homicide, congregational prayer, and funerary rites. Through a close reading of legal sources, the chapter explores constructions of intersex identity both in terms of anatomical signs or markers and, in certain contexts, through self-identification—although such forms of agency were limited and only occasionally acknowledged within juristic reasoning. Alipour further analyzes a range of legal cases to illuminate how jurists understood the legal personhood of intersex individuals, particularly in relation to their rights and responsibilities. The chapter culminates in a discussion of the binary–non-binary framework introduced by the jurist Ibn Idrīs al-Ḥillī (d. 1202 CE), a conceptual shift that sparked considerable debate among Shiʿi jurists from the fourteenth to the early twentieth century—a debate the author has explored in detail elsewhere.[59]

In Chapter Eight, Indira Gesink considers the historical evolution of Sunni legal discourse on intersex. She argues that the term "*khunthā*" was not present in the earliest juristic discussions but by the 1000s had become a fixed feature of Sunni legal manuals. Based on a selective survey of Shāfiʿī, Ḥanafī, and Ḥanbalī legal manuals, she outlines the different areas of concern as they developed over time among authors of different legal schools. As Shiʿi authors did, Sunni authors elaborated rules to accommodate non-binary people in circumcision, congregational prayer, inheritance, manumission, compensation for injury and death, marriage, and funerary rites. Unlike Shiʿi authors, Sunni jurists were ultimately unable to reconcile the binary framework of the Qur'ān with the social reality in which non-binary people lived, which forced many to insist that the epistemological category of *khunthā* was not also an ontological category, and that in fact a *khunthā*'s essential nature was either male or female. At the same time, they constructed a legal framework in which a *khunthā* was a medial being in between male and female.

In Chapter Nine, Mehrdad Alipour examines al-Rāzī's medical writings to explore how classical Persian medical discourse conceptualized sex and gender diversity. Focusing on categories such as *khunthā* (intersex person), *mukhannath* (effeminate), and *mutarajjil* (mannish), the study argues that al-Rāzī diverged significantly from the prevailing norms of his time—including those later upheld by physicians such as al-Zahrāwī and Ibn Sīnā—by neither pathologizing intersex individuals nor attaching moral judgement to gender non-conforming bodies. Instead, al-Rāzī offers a non-hierarchical and biologically grounded model of human variation, in which sex or biological characteristics and behavioral traits are seen as naturally determined and shaped by biology and environmental factors, rather than culturally constructed. He identifies five sex categories, including intersex, and approaches these classifications without recourse to a male-female binary or a spectrum that privileges masculinity. While al-Rāzī does medicalize certain behaviors, such as the receptive desire of some *mukhannath*s, his approach avoids surgical intervention and sensationalism. The chapter further demonstrates that, despite the prevalence of gendered norms in both medical and legal Islamic discourses, al-Rāzī's model stands apart in its refusal to enforce binary classification or attach legal hierarchy to sexed bodies. Ultimately, the study highlights al-Rāzī's distinctive contribution to Islamic and Persian medical thought and its implications for understanding the diversity of sex and gender in the premodern Islamic world.

Faith and intersex advocacy

This book belongs to the field of religious studies, particularly at its intersection with the study of sex and gender. This discipline offers a critical lens through which to interrogate how religious traditions—and in the case of this work, Islam—have historically shaped, regulated, or contested bodily categories and identities, including those that do not conform to prevailing binaries.[60] Given that religious studies is concerned not only with texts and doctrines but also with lived and cultural belief, ritual, and authority, it is particularly well positioned to analyze how intersex individuals and their families navigate religious teachings and institutions.

While legal, medical, and sociological frameworks have played a vital role in the advancement of intersex rights, the religious dimension remains significantly underexplored. Yet, across both the Global South and Global North, large segments of society continue to draw on religious traditions to make sense of sex, gender, and embodiment. The authority of religious discourse—whether in the form of official doctrines or the moral teachings of traditional scholars and preachers—can shape not only public opinion but also private decisions within families. In such contexts, intersex individuals and their parents may find themselves caught between securing rights and preserving religious commitments.

The problem, however, is not religion per se, but the limited range of interpretations that are made available. In the absence of visible, affirming theological alternatives, it is often the most conservative and pathologizing voices that come to define "the religious view." This restricts the imaginative and practical options available to religiously committed families and may even drive them to seek surgical intervention or to conceal the situation altogether, fearing stigma.

Religious studies, then, should not be marginal to intersex advocacy but understood as an integral and necessary part of it. Religious traditions are not fixed; they are contested, interpreted, and reimagined in different times and places. Without engaging these traditions critically and constructively, advocacy risks alienating precisely those communities where the stakes are highest. It also misses the opportunity to demonstrate that affirming intersex lives is not necessarily at odds with religious commitments.

To our understanding, intersex activists and scholars would benefit from recognizing the constructive potential of religious discourse to enhance and accelerate the negotiation for intersex rights. Finding allies from within religious institutions—churches, mosques, synagogues, temples, and others—would not only deepen the reach of advocacy efforts but could also help to challenge harmful interpretations from within. Building such alliances is not a detour from the struggle for justice; it is a necessary path towards making that justice more widely accessible and enduring.

Notes

1 Anne Fausto-Sterling suggests the higher number, counting as intersex "all live births that do not conform to a Platonic ideal of absolute sex chromosome, gonadal, genital, and hormonal dimorphism" (Anne Fausto-Sterling, *Sexing the Body: Gender Politics and the Construction of Sexuality* [New York City: Basic Books, 2000], 53). According to the Intersex Society of North America (currently inactive), "If you ask experts at medical centers how often a child is born so noticeably atypical in terms of genitalia that a specialist in sex differentiation is called in, the number comes out to about 1 in 1500 to 1 in 2,000 births (0.07–0.05%). But a lot more people than that are born with subtler forms of sex anatomy variations, some of which won't show up until later in life" (Intersex Society of North America, "How common is intersex?", Accessed March 2024: https://isna.org/faq/frequency/#). Other studies estimate the percentage of intersex not higher than 0.018%, arguing that chromosomal variants of 47,XYY and 47,XXX, vaginal agenesis, Turner syndrome (45,X), Klinefelter syndrome (47,XXY), and late-onset congenital adrenal hyperplasia (LOCAH), should not be counted as intersex conditions. This is because, in these cases, the chromosomal sex is consistent with the phenotypic sex, and the biological sex characteristics are observable and can be classified as either female or male (Leonard Sax, "How Common Is Intersex? A Response to Anne Fausto-Sterling," *Journal of Sex Research* 39, no. 3 (2002): 174–8). Others suggest that 0.37% is the accurate percentage of intersex people (Carrie L. Hull and Anne Fausto-Sterling, "Letter to the Editor," *American Journal of Human Biology* 15, no. 1 (2003): 112–6). Some intersex organisations agree with the higher estimate of 1.7% "in the absence of better internationally accepted data" to protect the whole population of individuals "who are stigmatized—or risk stigmatization—due to innate sex characteristics" (Intersex Human Rights Australia, "Intersex population figures", Accessed March 2024: https://ihra.org.au/16601/intersex-numbers/). Also see Alice Domurat Dreger, *Hermaphrodites and the Medical Invention of Sex* (Cambridge: Harvard University Press, 2000); Melanie Blackless, et al., "How Sexually Dimorphic Are We? Review and Synthesis," *American Journal of Human Biology* 12, no. 2 (2000): 151–66.

2 See Michelle M. Sauer, *Gender in Medieval Culture* (London: Bloomsbury Academic, 2015); Fausto-Sterling, *Sexing the Body*; Joan Cadden, *Meanings of Sex Difference in the Middle Ages Medicine, Science, and Culture* (Cambridge: Cambridge University Press, 1995); Ruth Mazo Karras, *Sexuality in Medieval Europe: Doing unto Others* (London: Routledge, 2012); Thomas Laqueur, *Making Sex: Body and Gender from the Greeks to Freud* (Cambridge, MA: Harvard University Press, 1992); Cary J. Nederman and Jacqui True, "The Third Sex: The Idea of the Hermaphrodite in Twelfth-Century Europe," *Journal of the History of Sexuality* 6, no. 4 (1996): 497–517; Miri Rubin, "The Person in the Form: Medieval Challenges to Bodily Order," in *Framing Medieval Bodies*, eds. Sarah Kay and Miri Rubin (Manchester: Manchester University Press, 1996): 100–22.

3 In the nineteenth and early twentieth centuries, it was common for English-speakers to refer to these people as "hermaphrodites," referring to the myth. However, medical specialists and activists almost unanimously avoid using the term "hermaphrodite," as it tends to stigmatise intersex people and confuse non-professionals, including those with intersex conditions and their families (see Charles Armstrong, "Intersexuality in Man," in *Intersexuality in Vertebrates including Man*, eds. Charles N. Armstrong and Alan J. Marshall [1964]: 349–93; John Dewhurst and Ronald R. Gordon, *The Intersexual Disorders* [London: Tindall and Cassell, 1969], 1–5; Alice D. Dreger, Cheryl Chase, Aron Sousa, Philip A. Gruppuso, and Joel Frader et al., "Changing the Nomenclature/Taxonomy for Intersex: A Scientific and Clinical Rationale," *Journal of Pediatric Endocrinology and Metabolism* 18, no. 8 [2005]: 729–33, at 732).

4 See Diamond and Beh, "Variations of Sex Development"; Elizabeth Reis, "Divergence or Disorder?: The Politics of Naming Intersex," *Perspectives in Biology and Medicine* 50, no. 4 (2007): 535–43; Stephanie A. Budwey, *Religion and Intersex: Perspectives from Science, Law, Culture, and Theology* (London: Routledge, 2023), 4.

5 OHCHR, *Background Note on Human Rights* (United Nations: Human Rights Office of the High Commissioner, 2019), 2, Accessed March 2024: https://www.ohchr.org/en/documents/tools-and-resources/background-note-human-rights-violations-against-intersex-people; Monro and colleagues briefly address the UN Office for the Commissioner of Human Rights' definition of intersex (Surya Monro et al., "Intersex: Cultural and Social Perspectives," *Culture, Health and Sexuality* 23, no. 4 [2021]: 431–40, at 433). Also see Dan Christian Ghattas, "Protecting Intersex People in Europe: A Toolkit for Law and Policy Makers," *OII Europe*, (2023[2019]), 9, Accessed March 2024: https://www.oiieurope.org/wp-content/uploads/2019/05/Protecting_intersex_in_Europe_toolkit.pdf. According to the Intersex Society of North America (ISNA), "Intersex is a general term used for a variety of conditions in which a person is born with a reproductive or sexual anatomy that doesn't seem to fit the typical definitions of female or male" (Intersex Society of North America, "What Is Intersex?" Accessed March 2024: https://isna.org/faq/what_is_intersex/). Although ISNA dissolved itself in 2008, its website remains available and its two successor organizations also host the same content: Accord Alliance, www.accordalliance.org and InterACT: Advocates for Intersex Youth, https://interactadvocates.org, "What Is Intersex?" It is worth noting that some clinicians diagnose intersex as "disorders of sex development" (DSDs), including anomalies of the sex chromosomes, gonads, reproductive ducts, and genitalia. See Ieuan A. Hughes et al., "Consensus Statement on Management of Intersex Disorders," *Journal of Pediatric Urology* 2, no. 3 [2006]: 148–62, at 554; Consortium on the Management of Disorders of Sex Development, *Clinical Guidelines for the Management of Disorders of Sex Development in Childhood* (Intersex Society of North America, 2006), 2, Accessed March 2024: https://dsdguidelines.org. The same guidelines also provide a comprehensive list of over twenty intersex conditions, 5–7. Some medically non-technical lists can be found in the following sources: American Psychological Association, "Intersex": https://dictionary.apa.org/intersex; Intersex Society of North America, "Intersex Conditions": https://isna.org/faq/conditions/; MedlinePlus, "Intersex": https://medlineplus.gov/ency/article/001669.htm#:~:text=Differences%20of%20sex%20development%20(DSD,an%20older%20term%20for%20DSD. The medical names of each condition often vary depending on the medical experts, type of studies undertaken, and language used. A large number of intersex and human rights activists caution against using the term *disorders of sex/gender development*. They object to the DSD terminology because, according to them, it stigmatises variations of sexual characteristics and ignores the plight of those who suffer from medical mismanagement and secrecy. See, for example, Marie-Noëlle Baechler, "Letter to the Editor: Children Are Not Disorders," *Archives of Disease in Childhood*, (2006), Accessed July 2024: https://adc.bmj.com/content/91/7/554.responses#children-are-not-disorders; David Cameron, "Letter to the

Editor: Re: Variations of Sex Development instead of Disorders of Sex Development," *Archives of Disease in Childhood*, (2006), Accessed July 2024: https://adc.bmj.com/content/early/2006/04/19/adc.2006.098319.responses?versioned=true#re-variations-of-sex-development-instead-of-disorders-of-sex-development; Milton Diamond and Hazel G. Beh, "Letter to the Editor: Variations of Sex Development Instead of Disorders of Sex Development," *Archives of Disease in Childhood*, (2006), Accessed July 2024: https://adc.bmj.com/content/early/2006/04/19/adc.2006.098319.responses?versioned=true#variations-of-sex-development-instead-of-disorders-of-sex-development). Also see the documents on the website of the Organisation Intersex International (OII): www.intersexualite.org/Disorders_of_Sex_Development.html. For a comprehensive overview of the controversies on DSD terminology, see Ellen K. Feder and Katrina Karkazis, "What's in a Name? The Controversy over 'Disorders of Sex Development'," *Hastings Center Report* 38, no. 5 (2008): 34–6.

6 Budwey, *Intersex and Religion*, 17; Cornwall, *Sex and Uncertainty*, 244–5; Viloria and Nieto, *Spectrum of Sex*, 48–55.

7 Budwey, *Intersex and Religion*, 17–18; Viloria and Nieto, *Spectrum of Sex*, 44; Vittorio E. Bianchi et al., "The role of androgens in women's health and wellbeing," *Pharmacological Research* 171, (2021): 105758. The SRY gene on the Y chromosome initiates testes development by triggering the expression of the SOX9 gene. SRY acts as a master switch, activating SOX9 in the genital ridge, which then leads to the differentiation of Sertoli cells and ultimately, the formation of testes.

8 Sally Tantawy et al., "Analysis of the gene coding for steroidogenic factor 1 (SF1, NR5A1) in a cohort of 50 Egyptian patients with 46,XY disorders of sex development," *European Journal of Endocrinology* 170, no. 5 (2014): 759–67.

9 Budwey, *Intersex and Religion*, 19–21; Valoria and Nieto, *Spectrum of Sex*, 42–7, 81–2.

10 Peggy T. Cohen-Kettenis, "Gender change in 46,XY persons with 5alpha-reductase-2 deficiency and 17beta-hydroxsteroid dehydrogenase-3 deficiency," *Archives of Sexual Behavior* 34, no. 4 (2005): 399–410. Babu and Shah say 53% of those raised as girls with 5-ARD report gender dysphoria. Choice to retain female gender identity may be culturally influenced; social prejudice against gender change may also prevent some assigned female at birth from choosing to change to male (Ramesh Babu and Utsav Shah, "Gender identity disorder [GID] in adolescents and adults with differences of sex development [DSD]: A systematic review and meta-analysis," *Journal of Pediatric Urology* 17, no. 1 (2021): 39–47.

11 Liliana Burdea, Lokesh Sharma, and Magda D. Mendez, *21-Hydroxylase Deficiency* (StatPearls Publishing, 2025), National Library of Medicine https://www.ncbi.nlm.nih.gov/books/NBK493164/; the cascade reaction from cortisol underproduction leads to "hyperplasia of the adrenal cortex, accumulation of cortisol precursors" and to production of excess androgens, which virilize 46XX infants (Ibid.). There is a "nonclassic" form of 21-HD that manifests in XX individuals with facial hair and infrequent menstruation. The "classic" form of 21-HD develops prenatally and can be detected in newborns. 75% of those with classic 21-HD have no enzyme activity and cannot maintain salt levels ("salt-wasting"); this is a life-threatening condition that requires medical intervention. 25% have the "simple virilizing" form that manifests in XX individuals with ambiguous genitalia. See Saroj Nimkarn, Prasanna K Gangishetti, Mabel Yau, and Maria I New, "21-Hydroxylase-Deficient Congenital Adrenal Hyperplasia," *GeneReviews National Library of Medicine* https://www.ncbi.nlm.nih.gov/books/NBK1171/.

12 Dianna Chormanski, Lokesh Sharma, and Maria Rosaria Muzio, *17-Hydroxylase Deficiency* (StatPearls Publishing, 2025).

13 Ahmed Khattab et al., "Clinical, Genetic, and Structural Basis of Congenital Adrenal Hyperplasia due to 11β-Hydroxylase Deficiency," *Proceedings of the National Academy of Sciences* 114, no. 10 (2017): E1933–E1940.

14 Cohen-Kettenis, "Gender Change," 399; Burdea, et al, *21-Hydroxylase Deficiency*.

15 Khattab, et al., "Clinical, Genetic, and Structural Basis of Congenital Adrenal Hyperplasia due to 11β-Hydroxylase Deficiency." 95% of people with CAH have 21-hydroxylase deficiency (21OHD), but because this VSC is genetic, geological pockets of rarer forms exist (Busra Gurpinar Tosun and Tulay Guran, "Rare Forms of Congenital Adrenal Hyperplasia," *Clinical Endocrinology* 101, no. 4 [2024]: 371–85), for example in Turkey (Z. Şiklar et al., "17α Hydroxylase/17, 20 Lyase Deficiency: Clinical Features and Genetic Insights from a Large Turkey Cohort," *Endocrine* 85, no. 3 [2024]: 1407–16). See also Babu and Shah, "Gender Identity Disorder."

16 Sara Scalenghe, *Disability in the Ottoman Arab World, 1500–1800* [Cambridge: Cambridge University Press, 2014], 125–9; Ze'ev Hochberg et al., "Clinical, Biochemical, and Genetic Findings in a Large Pedigree of Male and Female Patients with 5 Alpha-reductase 2 Deficiency," *Journal of Clinical Endocrinology and Metabolism* 81, no. 8 (1996): 2821–7; Nasir A. M. al-Jurayyan, "Ambiguous Genitalia, Two Decades of Experience: Clinical Management and Sex Assignment," *Journal of Taibah University Medical Sciences* 5, no. 1 (2010): 13–20, at 14; M. M. Lubani et al., "Prevalence of Congenital Adrenal Hyperplasia in Kuwait," *European Journal of Pediatrics* 149, no. 6 (1990): 391–2; Soheir et al., "Cytogenetic and molecular study in intersex," *Egyptian Journal of Medical Human Genetics* 13, (2012): 281–89, at 284; M. A. Abdullah et al., "Ambiguous Genitalia: Medical, Socio-cultural and Religious Factors Affecting Management in Saudi Arabia," *Annals of Tropical Paediatrics* 11, (1991): 343–8; Hüseyin Özbey et al., "Gender assignment in female congenital adrenal hyperplasia: a difficult experience," *BJU International* 94, no. 3 (2004): 388–91, at 389; Ivan Watson, "Rare gender identity defect hits Gaza families," CNN (17 Dec. 2009): https://www.cnn.com/2009/WORLD/meast/12/17/gaza.gender.id/index.html; Aslı Derya Kardelen et al., "A Rare Cause of Congenital Adrenal Hyperplasia: Clinical and Genetic Findings and Follow-up Characteristics of Six Patients with 17-Hydroxylase Deficiency Including Two Novel Mutations," *Journal of Clinical Research and Pediatric Endocrinology* 10, no. 3 (2018): 206–15, at 208. One study estimated prevalence of 5-alpha reductase deficiency in Gaza to be as high as 1:100 male births, 1% (G. Kohn et al., "Male Pseudohermaphroditism Due to 17 ß-Hydroxysteroid Dehydrogenase Deficiency (17BHSD) in a Large Arab Kinship. Studies on the Natural History of the Defect," *Journal of Pediatric Endocrinology* 1, no. 1 (1985): 29–37, at 31).

17 See Abū ʿAbd al-Raḥmān al-Khalīl b. Aḥmad al-Farāhīdī, *Kitāb al-ʿayn*, ed. Mahdī al-Makhzūmī and Ibrāhīm al-Sāmarrāʾī, 8 vols. (Baghdad: Dār al-Rashād, 1980), 4: 248; Abū Naṣr Ismāʿīl al-Jawharī, *al-Ṣiḥāḥ tāj al-lugha wa-ṣiḥāḥ al-ʿarabiyya*, ed. Aḥmad ʿAbd al-Ghafūr ʿAṭṭār, 6 vols. (Beirut: Dār al-ʿIlm li-l-Malāyin, 1407/1986–7), 1: 281; Muḥammad b. al-Ḥasan Ibn Durayd al-Azdī, *Jamharat al-lugha*, ed. Ramzī Munīr Baʿlbakī, 3 vols. (Beirut: Dār al-ʿIlm li-l-Malāyīn, 1987), 1: 418; Muḥammad b. Aḥmad al-Azharī, *Tahdhīb al-lugha*, 15 vols. (Beirut: Dār Iḥyāʾ al-Turāth al-ʿArabī, 2001), 7: 145; Aḥmad b. Muḥammad b. ʿAlī al-Fayyūmī, *al-Miṣbāḥ al-munīr fī gharīb al-sharḥ al-kabīr, 2 vols. (*Beirut: al-Maktaba al-ʿIlmiyya, 1994*)*, 1: 183; Muḥammad b. Mukarram Ibn Manẓūr, *Lisān al-ʿarab*, 15 vols. (Beirut: Dār Ṣādir li-l-Ṭibāʿa wa-l-Nashr, 1414), 2: 145; Muḥammad Murtaḍā al-Zabīdī, *Tāj al-ʿarūs min jawāhir al-Qāmūs*, ed. ʿAbd al-ʿAzīz Maṭar, 40 vols. (Kuwait: Maṭbaʿat Ḥukūmat al-Kuwait, 1414/1994), 5: 240–2.

18 Al-Jawharī, *al-Ṣiḥāḥ*, 1: 281.

19 Muḥammad al-Muḥibbī, *Khulāṣat al-āthar fī aʿyān al-qarn al-ḥādī ʿashar (*Beirut: Dār al-Ṣādir, 1111AH), 3: 315–6; Muḥammad b. Aḥmad al-Sarakhsī, *Kitāb al-mabsūṭ* (Cairo: Maṭbaʿat al-Saʿāda, 1906–1913), 30:105, 109, 112.

20 Parts of such studies have been published in special issues of journals, including *Chrysalis: The Journal of Transgressive Gender Identities* 2, no. 5 (1997–98); *GLQ: A Journal of Lesbian and Gay Studies* 15, no. 2 (2009); *Culture, Health and Sexuality: An International Journal for Research, Intervention and*

Care 23, no. 4 (2021); and *TSQ: Transgender Studies Quarterly* 9, no. 2 (2022). Other pioneering studies in this regard are Gilbert Herdt (ed.), *The Third Sex, Third Gender: Beyond Sexual Dimorphism in Culture and History* (Princeton: Princeton University Press, 2020 [1993]); Alice Domurat Dreger, *Hermaphrodites and the Medical Invention of Sex* (Cambridge, MA: Harvard University Press, 1998); John Colapinto, *As Nature Made Him: The Boy Who Was Raised as a Girl* (New York: HarperCollins, 2000); Anne Fausto-Sterling, *Sexing The Body: Gender Politics and the Construction of Sexuality* (New York City: Basic Books, 2000); *Hermaphrodites with Attitude* (Newsletter of ISNA), published from December 1994 until Spring 2003; Sharon E. Sytsma (ed.), *Ethics and Intersex* (*International Library of Ethics, Law, and the New Medicine* 29, 2006th edition); Sharon Preves, *Intersex and Identity: The Contested Self* (New Brunswick: Rutgers University Press, 2003); Alice Dreger (ed.), *Intersex in the Age of Ethics* (University Publishing Group, 1999); Suzanne Kessler, *Lessons from the Intersexed* (New Brunswick: Rutgers University Press, 1998); Morgan Holmes, ed., *Critical Intersex* (London: Routledge, 2009); Susannah Cornwall, *Sex and Uncertainty in the Body of Christ: Intersex Conditions and Christian Theology* (London: Routledge, 2010); idem, "British Intersex Christians' Accounts of Intersex Identity, Christian Identity and Church Experience," *Practical Theology* 6, no. 2, (2013): 220–36; Julie A. Greenberg, *Intersexuality and the Law: Why Sex Matters* (New York City: New York University Press, 2012); Megan K DeFranza, *Sex Difference in Christian Theology: Male, Female and Intersex in the Image of God* (Grand Rapids: Wm. B. Eerdmans, 2015); Hida Viloria and Maria Nieto, *The Spectrum of Sex: The Science of Male, Female, and Intersex* (London and Philadelphia: Jessica Kingsley Publishers, 2020); Leah DeVun, *The Shape of Sex: Nonbinary Gender from Genesis to the Renaissance* (New York: Columbia University Press, 2021).

21 See, for example, Bruce Bagemihl, *Biological Exuberance: Animal Homosexuality and Natural Diversity* (New York: Stonewall Inn Editions, 2000); Mary Jane West-Eberhard, *Developmental Plasticity and Evolution* (Oxford: Oxford University Press, 2003); Joan Roughgarden, *Evolution's Rainbow* (Berkeley: University of California Press, 2004); Malin Ah-King, "Queer Nature: Towards a Non-Normative View on Biological Diversity," in *Body Claims*, ed. Janne Bromseth, Lisa Folmarson Käll, and Katerina Mattson (Uppsala: Center for Gender Research, Uppsala University, 2009): 212–33; Malin Ah-King and Sören Nylin, "Sex in an Evolutionary Perspective: Just Another Reaction Norm," *Evolutionary Biology* 37, no. 4, (2013): 234–46; Janet L. Leonard, *Transitions between Sexual Systems* (Cham: Springer, 2018); and for general readers, Lucy Cooke, *Bitch: On the Female of the Species* (New York City: Basic Books, 2022; Audiobook, 2022), esp. chapter eleven, "Beyond the Binary."

22 See, for example, Ryan T. Anderson, *When Harry Became Sally: Responding to the Transgender Movement* (New York City: Encounter, 2018), which argues that media, medicine, and government policy produced a trend to depict gender as non-binary, contrary to science. See also the FAQs provided by the website "Sex Matters," which promotes binary gender, opposes the idea that one can change sex, and suggests that gender theorists are responsible for spreading myths about DSDs being a third sex: https://sex-matters.org/resources/sex-and-gender-faqs/#dsds.

23 See, for example, Abdelwahab Bouhdiba, *Sexuality in Islam*, trans. Alan Sheridan (Boston: Kegan Paul, 1985), 30–42; Paula Sanders, "Gendering the Ungendered Body: Hermaphrodites in Medieval Islamic Law," in *Women in Middle Eastern History: Shifting Boundaries in Sex and Gender*, eds. Beth Baron and Nikki Keddie (New Haven: Yale University Press, 1991): 74–95.

24 On Islamic legal discussions of intersex topics, see, for example, Ash Geissinger, "Islam and Discourses of Same-Sex Desire," in *Queer Religion: Homosexuality in Modern Religious History*, 2 vols., eds. Donald L. Boisvert and Jay E. Johnson (Santa Barbara: Praeger, 2012), 1: 69–90, at 72–3; Sara Scalenghe, *Disability in the Ottoman Arab World, 1500–1800* (Cambridge: Cambridge University Press, 2014), 124–62; Mehrdad Alipour, "Transgender Identity, the Sex-Reassignment Surgery Fatwās and Islamic Theology of a Third Gender," *Religion and Gender* 7, no. 2 (2017): 164–79, at 173–6; Saqer

A. Almarri, "'You Have Made Her a Man among Men' Translating the Khuntha's Anatomy in Fatimid Jurisprudence," *Transgender Studies Quarterly* 3, nos. 3–4 (2016): 578–86; idem, "Non-binary Sexual and Gender Identities in the Community: the *Khuntha* as an Isolated Being in the Mosque," *Body and Religion* 3, no. 2 (2020): 166–87; Indira Falk Gesink, "Intersex Bodies in Premodern Islamic Discourse: Complicating the Binary," *Journal of Middle East Women's Studies* 14, no. 2 (2018): 152–73; idem, "Intersex in Islamic Medicine, Law, and Activism," *in The Routledge Handbook on Islam and Gender*, ed. Justine Howe (London: Routledge, 2020): 116–29; Ani Amelia Zainuddin and Zaleha Abdullah Mahdy, "The Islamic Perspectives of Gender-Related Issues in the Management of Patients with Disorders of Sex Development," *Archives of Sexual Behavior* 46, (2017): 353–60. The following studies deal with Islamic medical and bioethical debates on intersex topics: Mohd Salim Mohamed and Siti Nurani Mohd Noor, "Islamic Bioethical Deliberation on the Issue of Newborns with Disorders of Sex Development," *Science and Engineering Ethics* 21, (2015): 429–40; Inas A. Mazen, "Clinical Management of Gender in Egypt: Intersexuality and Transsexualism," *Archives of Sexual Behavior* 46, (2017): 369–72; Nasir Malim and Aasim I. Padela, "Islamic Bioethical Perspectives on Gender Identity for Intersex Patients," *Journal of the British Muslim Medical Association* 5, no. 2 (2020): 19–25. On the correlation between the medicalisation of intersex people and Islamic *fatwās*, see Mehrdad Alipour, "The Nexus between Gender-Confirming Surgery and Illness: Legal-Hermeneutical Examinations of Four Islamic Fatwas," *Journal of Middle East Women's Studies* 18, no. 3 (2022): 359–86; Muhammad Afif Mohd Badrol, Abdul Bari Awang, and Sayed Sikandar Shah Haneef, "Intersex Gender Determination in Classical Islamic Law and Modern Medicine: An Analysis for Integration," *Al-Shajarah: Journal of the International Institute of Islamic Thought and Civilization* (ISTAC) 23, no. 2 (2018): 469–96; Taqwa Zabidi, "Analytical Review of Contemporary Fatwas in Resolving Biomedical Issues over Gender Ambiguity," *Journal of Religion and Health* 58, no. 1 (2019): 153–67. For general discussions of sex and gender in the Muslim world, including intersex topics, see Corinne Fortier, "Sexualities: Transsexualities: Middle East, West Africa, North Africa," *Encyclopedia of Women and Islamic Cultures* [EWIC] (2019); Basim Musallam, *Sex and Society in Islam: Birth Control before the Nineteenth Century* (Cambridge: Cambridge University Press, 1983); Vardit Rispler-Chaim, *Disability in Islamic Law* (Dordrecht: Springer Netherlands, 2007); Chantal Zabus, "Transing the Algerian Nation-State: Textual Transgender and Intersex from Pre-Independence to the Black Decade," *Acta Neophilologica* 52, nos. 1–2 (2019): 69–96; Dror Ze'evi, *Producing Desire: Changing Sexual Discourse in the Ottoman Middle East, 1500–1900* (Berkeley: University of California Press, 2006).

25 For *fatwās*, see Alipour, "The Nexus between Gender-Confirming Surgery and Illness," 359–86. On the views of Muslim preachers, see Assim al-Hakeem, "Gender Identity in Islam (Male, Female, Transgender, Intersex, No Gender)," *assimalhakeem*, Accessed October 2023: https://www.youtube.com/watch?v=pQoDE7tI7No; Amer Jamil, "The Muslim Perspective on Transgender Ideology (LGBT)," *@UstAmerJamil*, Accessed October 2023: https://www.youtube.com/watch?v=oWF-b_rXwpU; Yasir Qadhi, "Rulings on Transgenderism in Islam," *EPIC MASJID*, Accessed October 2023: https://www.youtube.com/watch?v=iCsUXGz1_6I.

26 Bouhdiba, *Sexuality in Islam*, 30–42; Sanders, "Gendering the Ungendered Body," 74–95.

27 The other three sources are *al-Mukhtaṣar* of al-Qudūrī (d. 428/1036–37), *al-Hidāya* of al-Marghīnānī (d. 593/1196), and *al-Mabsūṭ fī fiqh al-imāmiyya* of al-Ṭūsī (d. 460/1067). In addition to legal sources, Sanders refers to *The Canon of Medicine* (*al-Qānūn fī l-Ṭibb*) of Ibn Sīnā (d. 428/1037) (Sanders, "Gendering the Ungendered Body," 76). Gesink argues that Muslim medical discourse demonstrates flexibility concerning gender or sex categories; see Gesink, "Intersex Bodies," 160–3.

28 See, for example, Kecia Ali, *Sexual Ethics and Islam: Feminist Reflections on Qur'an, Ḥadīth, and Jurisprudence* (Oxford: Oneworld Publications, 2006), 114; Almarri, "'You Have Made Her a Man among Men'," 581; Elizabeth M. Bucar, "Bodies at the Margins: The Case of Transsexuality in Catholic

and Shia Ethics," *Journal of Religious Ethics* 38, no. 4 (2010): 601–15; Afsaneh Najmabadi, *Professing Selves: Transsexuality and Same-Sex Desire in Contemporary Iran* (Durham: Duke University Press, 2014), 177; Rispler-Chaim, *Disability in Islamic Law*, 70; Scalenghe, *Disability in the Ottoman Arab World*, 139–40; Zabidi, "Analytical Review of Contemporary Fatwas," 156; Ze'evi, *Producing Desire*, 9 and 23.

29 See Everett K. Rowson, "The Categorization of Gender and Sexual Irregularity in Medieval Arabic Vice Lists," in *Body Guards*, eds. Julia Epstein and Kristina Straub (New York: Routledge, 1991): 50–79; idem, "Gender Irregularity as Entertainment: Institutionalized Transvestitism at the Caliphal Court in Medieval Baghdad," in *Gender and Difference in the Middle Ages*, eds. Sharon Farmer and Carol Braun Pasternack (Minneapolis: University of Minnesota Press, 2003): 45–72.

30 Paula Sanders, "Hermaphrodites Revisited: A Reconsideration," (2008, unpublished), 4, Accessed October 2023: www.academia.edu/35003377 (site discontinued). Also, see Chapter One of this book.

31 Ibid.

32 Geissinger, "Islam and Discourses of Same-Sex Desire," 72–3. Also see idem, *Gender and Muslim Constructions of Exegetical Authority* (Leiden: Brill, 2015), 30–65; idem, "Applying Gender and Queer Theory to Pre-modern Sources," in *The Routledge Handbook of Islam and Gender*, ed. Justine Howe (London: Routledge, 2021): 101–15.

33 Ibid. Geissinger's main sources for this conclusion are Thomas Laqueur and Dror Ze'evi; we note that scholars have questioned the universality of Laqueur's thesis. This may be a productive area of new inquiry in Islamic studies: Did Muslim physicians and theoreticians of conception historically regard women as imperfect males? Did they regard non-males as less than fully human?

34 Gesink, "Intersex Bodies," 153.

35 Ibid

36 Ibid., 154.

37 Ibid., 153.

38 Mehrdad Alipour, "Navigating Body Politics in Shi'i Legal Tradition: Examining Sayyid Kāẓim al-Yazdī's Account of Non-Binary Intersex," *Islamic Law and Society* 32, no. 3 (2025): 262–315. Also, see Alipour, "Transgender Identity." It should be noted that recently, Yacoob has examined the binary perspective primarily from a Ḥanafī legal standpoint. She contends that in classical Ḥanafī law males and females are not the only legal entities. Although legal personhood is partially influenced by gender, other social factors such as age, enslavement, and social status are significant (Saadia Yacoob, *Beyond the Binary: Gender and Legal Personhood in Islamic Law* [Berkeley: University of California Press, 2024]).

39 Sara Scalenghe, *Disability in the Ottoman Arab World, 1500–1800* (Cambridge: Cambridge University Press, 2014), 132–6.

40 Almarri, "'You Have Made Her a Man among Men'."

41 Sanders uses these terms with the full understanding that it is anachronistic to apply a modern conceptualisation of "intersex" to classical Muslim legal literature. She uses the term "gendering" to define the way in which classical Muslim jurists "constructed the *khunthā mushkil*...as a social person" (Sanders, "Gendering the Ungendered Body," 79).

42 See, for example, Gayle Rubin, "The Traffic in Women: Notes on the 'Political Economy' of Sex," in *Feminist Anthropology: A Reader*, ed. Ellen Lewin (Oxford: Wiley-Blackwell, 2006 [1975]): 87–106; Kate Millett, *Sexual Politics* (New York: Columbia University Press, 2016), 28–31; Claire Renzetti and Daniel Curran, "Sex-Role Socialization," in *Feminist Philosophies*, eds. Janet Kourany, James Sterba, and Rosemarie Tong (Englewood, NJ: Prentice Hall, 1992): 31–47; Nancy Chodorow, "Family Structure and Feminine Personality," in *Feminism and Philosophy: Essential Readings in Theory, Reinterpretation, and Application*, eds. Nancy Tuana and Rosemarie Tong (New York: Routledge,

2018 [1995]): 199–216; Catharine A. MacKinnon, *Toward a Feminist Theory of the State* (Cambridge: Harvard University Press, 1989), chaps. 7 and 12. Also see Simone de Beauvoir, *The Second Sex*, trans. Constance Borde and Sheila Malovany-Chevallier (New York: Random House, 2011 [1949]); Judith Butler, "Performative Acts and Gender Constitution," in *The Performance Studies Reader*, ed. Henry Bial (London: Routledge, 2004 [1990]): 154–66; and idem, *Bodies That Matter: On the Discursive Limits of Sex* (London: Routledge, 2011 [1993]).

43 For example, some scholars critique studies of gender that ignore the influence of nationality, ethnicity, and race (Elizabeth V. Spelman, *Inessential Woman* [Boston: Beacon Press, 1988]; Butler, *Gender Trouble*, chap. 1). Others object to the classification of sex as a matter of biology without social or cultural meaning (Anne Fausto-Sterling, "The Five Sexes: Revisited," *The Sciences*, [July–August 2000]: 18–23). According to Fausto-Sterling, the binary notion of sex fails to include individuals with sex characteristics that do not fall into male and female categories (Anne Fausto-Sterling, "The Five Sexes: Why Male and Female Are Not Enough," *The Sciences* 33, [1993]: 20–24). Butler holds that, like gender, sex is culturally constructed, and thus the distinction between the two is not clear (Judith Butler, *Gender Trouble*, 10–11). Other scholars hold that the sex/gender distinction is useless (Toril Moi, *What Is a Woman?* [Oxford: Oxford University Press, 1999], chap. 1; Tomas Bogardus, "Evaluating Arguments for the Sex/Gender Distinction," *Philosophia* 48, [2020]; 873–92). There are other theories on sex and gender, including: sex/gender nominalism (Iris Marion Young, "Gender as Seriality: Thinking about Women as a Social Collective," in *Intersecting Voices*, ed. I. M. Young [Princeton: Princeton University Press, 1997]: 12–37), the positionality approach (Linda Alcoff, *Visible Identities* [Oxford: Oxford University Press, 2006], chap. 5); and the beyond-binary position offered by queer theorists (Robin Dembroff, "Beyond Binary: Genderqueer as Critical Gender Kind," *Philosopher's Imprint* 20, [2020]: 1–23). For a review of different positions and controversies on this topic, see Mari Mikkola, "Feminist Perspectives on Sex and Gender," in *The Stanford Encyclopedia of Philosophy*, eds. Edward N. Zalta and Uri Nodelman (Summer 2024 Edition).

44 Butler, *Gender Trouble*, chap. 1: 3–44.

45 Everett K. Rowson, "The Effeminates of Early Medina," *Journal of the American Oriental Society* 111, no. 4 (1991): 671–93; Mehrdad Alipour, *Negotiating Homosexuality in Islam: A Legal-Hermeneutical Examination of Modern Shiʿi Discourse* (Leiden: Brill, 2024), 107–13; idem, "Beyond Anachronism: Questioning Modern Gender and Sexuality Language in Classical Persian Literature," in *Gender and Sexuality in Persian Literary and Religious Traditions: Embodied Encounters*, ed. A.A. Seyed-Gohrab (Leiden: Leiden University Press, 2026): 181–206.

46 Franz Rosenthal, "Ar-Razi on the Hidden Illness," *Bulletin of the History of Medicine* 52, no. 1 (1978): 45–60, at 54–5.

47 Aristotle, "Politics," in *The Complete Works of Aristotle: The Revised Oxford Translation*, ed. Jonathan Barnes, trans. Benjamin Jowett (Princeton: Princeton University Press, 2016), Book I: 3, 1253a7–18. Also, see Kristin Andrews and Susana Monsó, "Animal Cognition," in *The Stanford Encyclopedia of Philosophy*, ed. Edward N. Zalta (Spring 2021 Edition), Accessed April 2024: https://plato.stanford.edu/archives/spr2021/entries/cognition-animal/. Kietzmann does not attribute this common definition of 'human' to Aristotle (Christian Kietzmann, "Aristotle on the Definition of What It Is to Be Human," in *Aristotle's anthropology*, eds. Keil, Geert and Kreft, Nora [Cambridge: Cambridge University Press, 2021]: 25–43).

48 According to this definition, "being animal" is also an essential element, referred to as 'genus' (*jins*), that humans share with other beasts. See, for example, Ibn Sīnā, *Dānishnāma-yi ʿalāʾī* (Hamadan: Dānishgāhi Bū ʿĀlī Sīnā, 1383sh), 26; Naṣīr al-Dīn al-Ṭūsī, *Asās al-iqtibās* (Tehran: Intishārāt-i Dānishgāh-i Tehran, 1367sh), 29.

49 al-Ṭūsī, *Asās al-iqtibās*, 30; Quṭb al-Dīn al-Shīrāzī, *Durrat al-tāj* (Tehran: Intishārāt-i Ḥikmat, 1369sh), 38; Muḥammad Riḍā al-Muẓaffar, *al-Manṭiq* (Qum: Mu'assasat al-Nashr al-Islāmī, 1430/1388sh), 96–7; 'Alī Kāshif al-Ghiṭā', *Naqd al-ārā' al-manṭiqiyya wa-ḥall*[u] *mushkilātihā*, 2 vols. (Beirut: Mu'assasat al-Nu'mān li-l-Ṭibā'a wa-l-Nashr, 1411), 1: 132–3.

50 See, for example, Abū Muḥammad 'Abd al-Ḥaqq Ibn 'Aṭiyya (d. 542/1147–48), *al-Muḥarrar al-wajīz fī tafsīr al-kitāb al-'azīz*, ed. 'Abd al-Salām 'Abd al-Shāfī Muḥammad, 6 vols. (Beirut: Dār al-Kutub al-'Ilmiyya, 1422/2001), 2: 4; Abū Bakr Ibn al-'Arabī (d. 543/1148–49), *Aḥkām al-Qur'ān*, 4 vols. (Beirut: Dār al-Kutub al-'Ilmiyya, 1424/2003), 4: 99; Muḥammad b. Aḥmad al-Qurṭubī (d. 671/1273), *al-Jāmi' li-aḥkām al-Qur'ān*, 20 vols. (Cairo: Dār al-Kutub al-Miṣriyya, 1384/1964), 5: 2. These exegetes (*mufassirūn*), relying on verses such as Q. 4:1 and Q. 92:3, often hold that the human race consists of two types: males and females. Thus, according to them, *khunthās* do not constitute a distinct type but belong either to the male type or the female type. The exegete Makkī b. Abī Ṭālib (d. 437/1045) also regards humans as either male or female and does not recognise a third category, although he does not use the term type (Makkī b. Abī Ṭālib, *al-Hidāya ilā bulūgh al-nihāya fī 'ilm ma'ānī l-Qur'ān wa-tafsīrih wa-aḥkāmih wa-jumal min funūn 'ulūmih*, 13 vols. [Sharjah: Kulliyyat al-Sharī'a wa-l-dirāsāt al-Islāmiyya–Jāmi'at al-Sharjah, 1429/2008], 2: 211). Nevertheless, the Māliki jurist and exegete Abū Bakr Ibn al-'Arabī presents a different opinion in this regard (see footnote 64). In the Shi'i context, classical exegetes, such as 'Alī b. Ibrāhīm al-Qummī (d. after 307/919), Muḥammad b. Mas'ūd al-'Ayyashī (d. perhaps 320/932), al-Shaykh al-Ṭūsī (d. 460/1067), and al-Faḍl b. al-Ḥasan al-Ṭabrisī (d. 548/1154), in their discussions of relevant verses about the creation of male and female, such as Q. 4:1, Q. 42:49, and Q. 92:3, do not address the category of *khunthā*.

51 On *qism*, see, for example, Muḥammad b. Aḥmad Ibn Idrīs al-Ḥillī, *al-Sarā'ir al-ḥāwī li-taḥrīr al-fatāwī*, 3 vols. (Qum: Mu'assasat al-Nashr al-Islāmī, 1410/1386sh), 3: 281; Yaḥyā b. Sharaf al-Nawawī (d. 676/1277), *al-Majmū' Sharḥ al-Muhadhdhab*, 20 vols. (Beirut: Dār al-Fikr, 1990), 2: 47. On *ṭabī'a*, see, for example, Shams al-Dīn Muḥammad b. Makkī al-'Āmilī, *al-Durūs al-shar'iyya fī fiqh al-imāmiyya*, 3 vols. (Qum: Mu'assasat al-Nashr al-Islāmī, 1417), 2: 379; Zayn al-Dīn b. 'Alī al-Juba'ī al-'Āmilī, *al-Rawḍa al-bahiyya fī sharḥ al-Lum'a al-dimashqiyya fī fiqh al-imāmiyya*, 2 vols. (Qum: Intishārāt-i Daftar-i Tablīqāt-i Islāmī, 1412/1373sh), 2: 332. On *khalq*, see, for example, Shams al-Dīn Muḥammad al-Ḥaṭṭāb al-Ru'aynī al-Māliki (d. 954/1547), *Mawāhib al-jalīl fī sharḥ Mukhtaṣar al-Khalīl*, 6 vols. (Beirut: Dār al-Fikr, 1412/1992), 6: 424. On *jins*, see, for example, Muḥammad b. Aḥmad al-Sarakhsī, *al-Mabsūṭ*, 30 vols. (Beirut: Dār al-Ma'rifa, 1414/1993), 13: 13.

52 For example, al-Rāzī alludes to both biological and behavioral characteristics to classify categories of humankind (Rosenthal, "Ar-Razi on the Hidden Illness," 54).

53 For example, jurists propose a taxonomy of males and females in which each category is divided into two groups: free males and enslaved males, and free females and enslaved females. This is followed by another subdivision, categorising each group of free and enslaved males, as well as free and enslaved females, as either Muslims or non-Muslims. These taxonomies can be extended by considering, for instance, whether or not a non-Muslim male or female can be identified as the People of the Book (*ahl al-kitāb*).

54 Geissinger, "Applying Gender and Queer Theory to Pre-modern Sources," 103.

55 Al-Sarakhsī, *al-Mabsūṭ*, 10: 158; Muwaffaq al-Dīn Abū Muḥammad Ibn Qudāma al-Maqdisī (d. 620/1223), *al-Mughnī*, 10 vols. (Cairo: Maktabat al-Qāhira, 1388/1968), 7: 104; Ḥasan b. Yūsuf al-Ḥillī ('Allāma), *Tadhkirat al-fuqahā'*, 2 vols. (Tehran: al-Maktabat al-Murtaḍawiyya li-Iḥyā' al-Āthār al-Ja'fariyya, 1388), 2: 574; 'Alī b. Ḥusayn 'Abd al-'Ālī al-Karakī, *Jāmi' al-maqāṣid fī sharḥ al-Qawā'id*, 13 vols. (Qum: Mu'assasat Āl al-Bayt li-Iḥyā' al-Turāth, 1414), 12: 36.

56 For the *ḥadīths* on this matter, see Alipour, *Negotiating Homosexuality*, 110, n87.

57 Ibid. Also, see Murtaḍā b. Muḥammad Amīn al-Anṣārī, *Makāsib al-muḥarrama*, 6 vols. (Qum: al-Majmaʿ al-Fikr al-Islāmī, 1420), 1: 173–5.

58 Ḥasan b. Yūsuf al-Ḥillī (ʿAllāma), *Taḥrīr al-aḥkām al-sharʿiyya ʿalā madhhab al-imāmiyya*, ed. Ibrāhīm al-Bahādurī, 5 vols. (Qum: Muʾassasat al-Imām al-Ṣādiq, 1422), 1: 129–30; Najm al-Dīn Jaʿfar b. Ḥasan al-Ḥillī (Muḥaqqiq), *Sharāʾiʿ al-islām fī masāʾil al-ḥalāl wa-l-ḥarām*, 4 vols. (Qum: Nashr-i Istiqlāl, 1409/1367sh), 1: 96; Aḥmad al-Muqaddas al-Ardabīlī, *Majmaʿ al-fāʾida wa-l-burhān fī sharḥ Irshād al-adhhān*. ed. Mujtabā al-ʿIrāqī, ʿAlīpanāh al-Ishtihārdī, and Ḥusayn al-Yazdī, 14 vols. (Qum, Iran: Muʾassasat al-Nashr al-Islāmī, 1422), 2: 446–7.

59 See Alipour, "Navigating Body Politics in Shiʿi Legal Tradition."

60 See, for example, Susannah Cornwall, "Bodily Rights and Gifts: Intersex, Abrahamic Religions and Human Rights," *Culture, Health and Sexuality* 23, no. 4 (2021): 533–47; Max Strassfeld, *Trans Talmud: Androgynes and Eunuchs in Rabbinic Literature* (Berkeley: University of California Press, 2022).

Bibliography

Abdullah, M. A., M. Katugampola, S. Al-Habib, N. Al-Jurayyan, A. Al-Samarrai, A. Al-Nuaim, P. J. Patel, and M. Niazi. "Ambiguous Genitalia: Medical, Socio-cultural and Religious Factors Affecting Management in Saudi Arabia." *Annals of Tropical Paediatrics* 11, (1991): 343–48.

Accord Alliance. www.accordalliance.org.

Ah-King, Malin and Sören Nylin. "Sex in an Evolutionary Perspective: Just Another Reaction Norm." *Evolutionary Biology* 37, no. 4 (2013): 234–46. https://doi.org/10.1007/s11692-010-9101-8.

Ah-King, Malin. "Queer Nature: Towards a Non-Normative View on Biological Diversity." In *Body Claims*, edited by Janne Bromseth, Lisa Folmarson Käll, and Katerina Mattson. Uppsala: Center for Gender Research, Uppsala University, 2009: 212–33.

Alcoff, Linda. *Visible Identities.* Oxford: Oxford University Press, 2006.

Ali, Kecia. *Sexual Ethics and Islam: Feminist Reflections on Qurʾan, Ḥadīth, and Jurisprudence.* Oxford: Oneworld Publications, 2006.

Alipour, Mehrdad. "Beyond Anachronism: Questioning Modern Gender and Sexuality Language in Classical Persian Literature." in *Gender and Sexuality in Persian Literary and Religious Traditions: Embodied Encounters*. ed. A.A. Seyed-Gohrab. Leiden: Leiden University Press, 2026: 181–206.

Alipour, Mehrdad. "Navigating Body Politics in Shiʿi Legal Tradition: Examining Sayyid Kāẓim al-Yazdī's Account of Non-Binary Intersex." *Islamic Law and Society* 32, no. 3 (2025): 262–315.

Alipour, Mehrdad. "The Nexus between Gender-Confirming Surgery and Illness: Legal-Hermeneutical Examinations of Four Islamic Fatwas." *Journal of Middle East Women's Studies* 18, no 3 (2022): 359–86.

Alipour, Mehrdad. "Transgender Identity, the Sex-Reassignment Surgery Fatwās and Islamic Theology of a Third Gender." *Religion and Gender* 7, no. 2 (2017): 164–79.

Alipour, Mehrdad. *Negotiating Homosexuality in Islam: A Legal-Hermeneutical Examination of Modern Shiʿi Discourse.* Leiden: Brill, 2024.

Almarri, Saqer A. "'You Have Made Her a Man among Men' Translating the Khuntha's Anatomy in Fatimid Jurisprudence." *Transgender Studies Quarterly* 3, nos. 3–4 (2016): 578–86.

Almarri, Saqer A. "Non-binary Sexual and Gender Identities in the Community: the *Khuntha* as an Isolated Being in the Mosque." *Body and Religion* 3, no. 2 (2020): 166–87. https://doi.org/10.1558/bar.15722.

American Psychological Association, "Intersex": https://dictionary.apa.org/intersex.

Anderson, Ryan T. *When Harry Became Sally: Responding to the Transgender Movement*. New York City: Encounter, 2018.
Andrews, Kristin and Susana Monsó. "Animal Cognition." in *The Stanford Encyclopedia of Philosophy*, edited by Edward N. Zalta (Spring 2021 Edition). Accessed April 2024: https://plato.stanford.edu/archives/spr2021/entries/cognition-animal/.
Al-Anṣārī, Murtaḍā b. Muḥammad Amīn. *Makāsib al-muḥarrama*. 6 vols. Qum: al-Majmaʿ al-Fikr al-Islāmī, 1420.
Armstrong, Charles. "Intersexuality in Man." in *Intersexuality in Vertebrates including Man*. edited by Charles N. Armstrong and Alan J. Marshall (1964): 349–93.
Al-Azharī, Muḥammad b. Aḥmad. *Tahdhīb al-lugha*. 15 vols. Beirut: Dār Iḥyāʾ al-Turāth al-ʿArabī, 2001.
Babu, Ramesh and Utsav Shah. "Gender Identity Disorder (GID) in Adolescents and Adults with Differences of Sex Development (DSD): A Systematic Review and Meta-analysis." *Journal of Pediatric Urology* 17, no. 1 (2021): 39–47. https://doi.org/10.1016/j.jpurol.2020.11.017.
Baechler, Marie-Noëlle. "Letter to the Editor: Children Are Not Disorders." *Archives of Disease in Childhood*, (2006), Accessed July 2024: https://adc.bmj.com/content/91/7/554.responses#children-are-not-disorders.
Bagemihl, Bruce. *Biological Exuberance: Animal Homosexuality and Natural Diversity*. New York City: Stonewall Inn Editions, 2000.
Barnes, Jonathan, ed. *The Complete Works of Aristotle: The Revised Oxford Translation*. translated by Benjamin Jowett. Princeton: Princeton University Press, 2016.
Bianchi, Vittorio E., Elena Bresciani, Ramona Meanti, Laura Rizzi, Robert J. Omeljaniuk, and Antonio Torsello. "The Role of Androgens in Women's Health and Wellbeing." *Pharmacological Research* 171, (2021): 105758. https://doi.org/10.1016/j.phrs.2021.105758.
Blackless, Melanie, Anthony Charuvastra, Amanda Derryck, Anne Fausto-Sterling, Karl Lauzanne, and Ellen Lee. "How Sexually Dimorphic Are We? Review and Synthesis." *American Journal of Human Biology* 12, no. 2 (2000): 151–66.
Bogardus, Tomas. "Evaluating Arguments for the Sex/Gender Distinction." *Philosophia* 48, (2020): 873–92.
Bouhdiba, Abdelwahab. *Sexuality in Islam*. translated by Alan Sheridan. Boston: Kegan Paul, 1985.
Bucar, Elizabeth M. "Bodies at the Margins: The Case of Transsexuality in Catholic and Shia Ethics." *Journal of Religious Ethics* 38, no. 4 (2010): 601–15.
Budwey, Stephanie A., *Religion and Intersex: Perspectives from Science, Law, Culture, and Theology*. London: Routledge, 2023.
Burdea, Liliana, Lokesh Sharma, and Magda D. Mendez. *21-Hydroxylase Deficiency*. StatPearls Publishing, 2025. National Library of Medicine https://www.ncbi.nlm.nih.gov/books/NBK493164/.
Butler, Judith. *Bodies That Matter: On the Discursive Limits of Sex*. London: Routledge, 2011 [1993].
Butler, Judith. *Gender Trouble: Feminism and the Subversion of Identity*. New York and London: Routledge, 1999.
Butler, Judith. "Performative Acts and Gender Constitution." *The Performance Studies Reader*. edited by Henry Bial. London: Routledge, 2004 (1990): 154–66.
Cadden, Joan. *Meanings of Sex Difference in the Middle Ages Medicine, Science, and Culture*. Cambridge: Cambridge University Press, 1995.
Cameron, David. "Letter to the Editor: Re: Variations of Sex Development instead of Disorders of Sex Development." *Archives of Disease in Childhood* (2006), Accessed July 2024. https://adc.bmj.com/content/91/7/554.responses#re-variations-of-sex-development-instead-of-disorders-of-sex-development.

Chodorow, Nancy. "Family Structure and Feminine Personality." in *Feminism and Philosophy: Essential Readings in Theory, Reinterpretation, and Application,* edited by Nancy Tuana and Rosemarie Tong. New York: Routledge, 2018 [1995]: 199–216.

Chormanski, Dianna, Lokesh Sharma, and Maria Rosaria Muzio. *17-Hydroxylase Deficiency*. StatPearls Publishing, 2025. https://www.ncbi.nlm.nih.gov/books/NBK546644/#:~:text=CAH%20is%20a%20group%20of,located%20on%20chromosome%2010q24%2Dq25.

Cohen-Kettenis, Peggy T. "Gender Change in 46,XY Persons with 5alpha-reductase-2 Deficiency and 17beta-hydroxsteroid dehydrogenase-3 Deficiency." *Archives of Sexual Behavior* 34, no. 4 (2005): 399–410.

Colapinto, John. *As Nature Made Him: The Boy Who Was Raised as a Girl.* New York: HarperCollins, 2000.

Consortium on the Management of Disorders of Sex Development. *Clinical Guidelines for the Management of Disorders of Sex Development in Childhood.* Intersex Society of North America, 2006. Accessed March 2024. https://dsdguidelines.org.

Cooke, Lucy. *Bitch: On the Female of the Species.* New York: Basic Books, 2022; Audiobook, 2022.

Cornwall, Susannah. "British Intersex Christians' Accounts of Intersex Identity, Christian Identity and Church Experience." *Practical Theology* 6, no. 2 (2013): 220–36.

Cornwall, Susannah. *Sex and Uncertainty in the Body of Christ: Intersex Conditions and Christian Theology.* London: Routledge, 2010.

De Beauvoir, Simone. *The Second Sex*. translated by Constance Borde and Sheila Malovany-Chevallier. New York: Random House, 2011 [1949].

DeFranza, Megan K. *Sex Difference in Christian Theology: Male, Female and Intersex in the Image of God.* Grand Rapids: Wm. B. Eerdmans, 2015.

Dembroff, Robin. "Beyond Binary: Genderqueer as Critical Gender Kind." *Philosopher's Imprint* 20, (2020): 1–23.

DeVun, Leah. *The Shape of Sex: Nonbinary Gender from Genesis to the Renaissance.* New York: Columbia University Press, 2021.

Dewhurst, John and Ronald R. Gordon. *The Intersexual Disorders*. London: Tindall & Cassell, 1969.

Diamond, Milton and Hazel G. Beh. "Letter to the Editor: Variations of Sex Development Instead of Disorders of Sex Development." *Archives of Disease in Childhood,* (2006), Accessed July 2024: https://adc.bmj.com/content/91/7/554.responses#variations-of-sex-development-instead-of-disorders-of-sex-development.

Dreger, Alice, ed. *Intersex in the Age of Ethics*. University Publishing Group, 1999.

Dreger, Alice Domurat, Cheryl Chase, Aron Sousa, Philip A. Gruppuso, and Joel Frader. "Changing the Nomenclature/Taxonomy for Intersex: A Scientific and Clinical Rationale." *Journal of Pediatric Endocrinology and Metabolism* 18, no. 8 (2005): 729–33.

Dreger, Alice Domurat. *Hermaphrodites and the Medical Invention of Sex*. Cambridge: Harvard University Press, 2000 (1998).

Al-Farāhīdī, Abū ʿAbd al-Raḥmān al-Khalīl b. Aḥmad. *Kitāb al-ʿayn*, edited by Mahdī al-Makhzūmī and Ibrāhīm al-Sāmarrāʾī. 8 vols. Baghdad: Dār al-Rashād, 1980.

Fausto-Sterling, Anne. "The Five Sexes: Revisited." *The Sciences* (July–August 2000): 18–23.

Fausto-Sterling, Anne. "The Five Sexes: Why Male and Female Are Not Enough." *The Sciences* 33 (1993): 20–24.

Fausto-Sterling, Anne. *Sexing the Body: Gender Politics and the Construction of Sexuality*. New York City: Basic Books, 2000.

Al-Fayyūmī, Aḥmad b. Muḥammad b. ʿAlī. *Al-Miṣbāḥ al-munīr fī gharīb al-sharḥ al-kabīr*. 2 vols. Beirut: al-Maktaba al-ʿIlmiyya, 1994.

Feder, Ellen K. and Katrina Karkazis. “What's in a Name? The Controversy over ‘Disorders of Sex Development.” *Hastings Center Report* 38, no. 5 (2008): 34–36.

Fortier, Corinne. “Sexualities: Transsexualities: Middle East, West Africa, North Africa.” in *Encyclopedia of Women and Islamic Cultures* [EWIC] (2019).

Geissinger, Ash. “Applying Gender and Queer Theory to Pre-modern Sources.” in *The Routledge Handbook of Islam and Gender*. edited by Justine Howe. London: Routledge, 2021: 101–15.

Geissinger, Ash. “Islam and Discourses of Same-Sex Desire.” in *Queer Religion: Homosexuality in Modern Religious History*. edited by Donald L. Boisvert and Jay E. Johnson, 2 vols. Santa Barbara: Praeger, 2012.

Geissinger, Ash. *Gender and Muslim Constructions of Exegetical Authority*. Leiden: Brill, 2015.

Gesink, Indira Falk. “Intersex Bodies in Premodern Islamic Discourse: Complicating the Binary.” *Journal of Middle East Women's Studies* 14, no. 2 (2018): 152–73.

Gesink, Indira Falk. “Intersex in Islamic Medical, Law and Activism.” in *The Routledge Handbook of Islam and Gender*. edited by Justine Howe (London: Routledge, 2020): 116–29.

Ghattas, Dan Christian. “Protecting Intersex People in Europe: A Toolkit for Law and Policy Makers.” OII Europe, 2023 [2019]. Accessed March 2024. https://www.oiieurope.org/wp-content/uploads/2019/05/Protecting_intersex_in_Europe_toolkit.pdf.

Greenberg, Julie A. *Intersexuality and the Law: Why Sex Matters*. New York City: New York University Press, 2012.

Al-Hakeem, Assim. “Gender Identity in Islam (Male, Female, Transgender, Intersex, No Gender).” *assimalhakeem*. Accessed October 2023: https://www.youtube.com/watch?v=pQoDE7tI7No.

Al-Ḥaṭṭāb al-Ruʿaynī al-Mālikī, Shams al-Dīn Muḥammad. *Mawāhib al-jalīl fī sharḥ Mukhtaṣar al-Khalīl*. 6 vols. Beirut: Dār al-Fikr, 1412/1992.

Herdt, Gilbert, ed. *The Third Sex, Third Gender: Beyond Sexual Dimorphism in Culture and History*. Princeton: Princeton University Press, 2020 (1993).

Hermaphrodites with Attitude (Newsletter of ISNA), published from December 1994 until Spring 2003.

Al-Ḥillī (Muḥaqqiq), Najm al-Dīn Jaʿfar b. Ḥasan. *Sharāʾiʿ al-islām fī masāʾil al-ḥalāl wa-l-ḥarām*. 4 vols. Qum: Nashr-i Istiqlāl, 1409/1367sh.

Al-Ḥillī (ʿAllāma), Ḥasan b. Yūsuf, *Tadhkirat al-fuqahāʾ*. 2 vols. Tehran: al-Maktabat al-Murtaḍawiyya li-Iḥyāʾ al-Āthār al-Jaʿfariyya, 1388.

Al-Ḥillī (ʿAllāma), Ḥasan b. Yūsuf. *Taḥrīr al-aḥkām al-sharʿiyya ʿalā madhhab al-imāmiyya*, ed. Ibrāhīm al-Bahādurī. 5 vols. Qum: Muʾassasat al-Imām al-Ṣādiq, 1422.

Hochberg, Ze'ev, Ralph Chayen, Nira Reiss, Zipora Falik, Amnon Makler, Mariana Munichor, Amicur Farkas, Olaf Hiort et al. “Clinical, Biochemical, and Genetic Findings in a Large Pedigree of Male and Female Patients with 5 alpha-reductase 2 Deficiency.” *Journal of Clinical Endocrinology and Metabolism* 81, no. 8 (1996): 2821–7. doi: 10.1210/jcem.81.8.8768837.

Holmes, Morgan, ed. *Critical Intersex*. London: Routledge, 2009.

Hughes, Ieuan A., Chris Houk, S. Faisal Ahmed, Peter A. Lee, and Lawson Wilkins Pediatric Endocrine Society. “Consensus Statement on Management of Intersex Disorders.” *Journal of Pediatric Urology* 2, no. 3 (2006): 148–62.

Hull, Carrie L. and Anne Fausto-Sterling. “Letter to the Editor.” *American Journal of Human Biology* 15, no. 1 (2003): 112–6.

Ibn al-ʿArabī, Abū Bakr. *Aḥkām al-Qurʾān*. 4 vols. Beirut: Dār al-Kutub al-ʿIlmiyya, 1424/2003.

Ibn Durayd al-Azdī, Muḥammad b. al-Ḥasan. *Jamharat al-lugha*, edited by Ramzī Munīr Baʿlbakī. 3 vols. Beirut: Dār al-ʿIlm li-l-Malāyīn, 1987.

Ibn Idrīs al-Ḥillī, Muḥammad b. Aḥmad. *Al-Sarāʾir al-ḥāwī li-taḥrīr al-fatāwī*. 3 vols. Qum: Muʾassasat al-Nashr al-Islāmī, 1410/1386sh.

Ibn Manẓūr, Muḥammad b. Mukarram. *Lisān al-ʿarab*. 15 vols. Beirut: Dār Ṣādir li-l-Ṭibāʿa wa-l-Nashr, 1414.

Ibn Qudāma al-Maqdisī, Muwaffaq al-Dīn Abū Muḥammad. *Al-Mughnī*. 10 vols. Cairo: Maktabat al-Qāhira, 1388/1968.

Ibn Sīnā. *Dānishnāma-yi ʿalāʾī*. Hamadan: Dānishgāhi Bū ʿĀlī Sīnā, 1383sh.

Ibn ʿAṭiyya, Abū Muḥammad ʿAbd al-Ḥaqq. *al-Muḥarrar al-wajīz fī tafsīr al-kitāb al-ʿazīz*. edited by ʿAbd al-Salām ʿAbd al-Shāfī Muḥammad. 6 vols. Beirut: Dār al-Kutub al-ʿIlmiyya, 1422/2001.

InterACT: Advocates for Intersex Youth, https://interactadvocates.org.

Intersex Human Rights Australia. "Intersex population figures," Accessed March 2024: https://ihra.org.au/16601/intersex-numbers/.

Intersex Society of North America. "How common is intersex?" Accessed March 2024: https://isna.org/faq/frequency/#.

Intersex Society of North America. "Intersex Conditions." Accessed June 2025: https://isna.org/faq/conditions/.

Jamil, Amer. "The Muslim Perspective on Transgender Ideology (LGBT)." @UstAmerJamil. Accessed October 2023: https://www.youtube.com/watch?v=oWF-b_rXwpU.

Al-Jawharī, Abū Naṣr Ismāʿīl. *Al-Ṣiḥāḥ tāj al-lugha wa-ṣiḥāḥ al-ʿarabiyya*, edited by Aḥmad ʿAbd al-Ghafūr ʿAṭṭār. 6 vols. Beirut: Dār al-ʿIlm li-l-Malāyin, 1407/1986–7.

Al-Jubaʿī al-ʿĀmilī, Zayn al-Dīn b. ʿAlī. *Al-Rawḍa al-bahiyya fī sharḥ al-Lumʿa al-dimashqiyya fī fiqh al-imāmiyya*. 2 vols. Qum: Intishārāt-i Daftar-i Tablīqāt-i Islāmī, 1412/1373sh.

Al-Jurayyan, Nasir A. M. "Ambiguous Genitalia, Two Decades of Experience: Clinical Management and Sex Assignment." *Journal of Taibah University Medical Sciences* 5, no. 1 (2010): 13–20.

Al-Karakī, ʿAlī b. Ḥusayn ʿAbd al-ʿĀlī. *Jāmiʿ al-maqāṣid fī sharḥ al-Qawāʿid*. 13 vols. Qum: Muʾassasat Āl al-Bayt li-Iḥyāʾ al-Turāth, 1414.

Kardelen, Aslı Derya, Güven Toksoy, Firdevs Baş, Zehra Yavaş Abalı, Genco Gençay, Şükran Poyrazoğlu, Rüveyde Bundak, et al., and Feyza Darendeliler. "A Rare Cause of Congenital Adrenal Hyperplasia: Clinical and Genetic Findings and Follow-up Characteristics of Six Patients with 17-Hydroxylase Deficiency Including Two Novel Mutations." *Journal of Clinical Research and Pediatric Endocrinology* 10, no. 3 (2018): 206–15.

Karras, Ruth Mazo, *Sexuality in Medieval Europe: Doing unto Others* (London: Routledge, 2012).

Kāshif al-Ghiṭāʾ, ʿAlī. *Naqd al-ārāʾ al-manṭiqiyya wa-ḥall^{u} mushkilātihā*, 2 vols. Beirut: Muʾassasat al-Nuʿmān li-l-Ṭibāʿa wa-l-Nashr, 1411.

Kessler, Suzanne. *Lessons from the Intersexed*. New Brunswick: Rutgers University Press, 1998.

Khattab, Ahmed, Shozeb Haider, Ameet Kumar, Samarth Dhawan, Dauood Alam, Raquel Romero, James Burns, et al. "Clinical, Genetic, and Structural Basis of Congenital Adrenal Hyperplasia Due to 11β-Hydroxylase Deficiency." *Proceedings of the National Academy of Sciences* 114, no. 10 (2017): E1933–E1940. www.pnas.org/cgi/doi/10.1073/pnas.1621082114.

Kietzmann, Christian. "Aristotle on the Definition of What It Is to Be Human," in *Aristotle's Anthropology*. edited by Geert Keil and Nora Kreft. Cambridge: Cambridge University Press, 2021): 25–43.

Kohn, G, E. E. Lasch, R. El Shawwa, Y. Litvin and A. Rosler. "Male Pseudohermaphroditism Due to 17 ß-Hydroxysteroid Dehydrogenase Deficiency (17BHSD) in a Large Arab Kinship. Studies on the Natural History of the Defect." *Journal of Pediatric Endocrinology* 1, no. 1 (1985): 29–37.

Laqueur, Thomas. *Making Sex: Body and Gender from the Greeks to Freud*. Cambridge: Harvard University Press, 1992.

Leonard, Janet L. *Transitions between Sexual Systems*. Cham: Springer, 2018.

Lubani, M. M., A-R. A. Issa, R. Bushnaq, Q. A. Al-Saleh, K. I. Dudin, P. C. Reavey, M. Y. El-Khalifa, D. S. Manandhar, Y. K. Abdul, AlE. A. Ismail, and A. S. Teebi. "Prevalence of Congenital Adrenal Hyperplasia in Kuwait." *European Journal of Pediatrics* 149, no. 6 (1990): 391–2.

MacKinnon, Catharine A. *Toward a Feminist Theory of the State*. Cambridge: Harvard University Press, 1989.

Makkī al-ʿĀmilī, Shams al-Dīn Muḥammad. *Al-Durūs al-sharʿiyya fī fiqh al-imāmiyya*. 3 vols. Qum: Muʾassasat al-Nashr al-Islāmī, 1417.

Makkī b. Abī Ṭālib. *al-Hidāya ilā bulūgh al-nihāya fī ʿilm maʿānī l-Qurʾān wa-tafsīrih wa-aḥkāmih wa-jumal min funūn ʿulūmih*. 13 vols. Sharjah: Kulliyyat al-Sharīʿa wa-l-dirāsāt al-Islāmiyya–Jāmiʿat al-Sharjah, 1429/2008.

Malim, Nasir and Aasim I. Padela. "Islamic Bioethical Perspectives on Gender Identity for Intersex Patients." *Journal of the British Muslim Medical Association* 5, no. 2 (2020): 19–25.

Mazen, Inas A. "Clinical Management of Gender in Egypt: Intersexuality and Transsexualism." *Archives of Sexual Behavior* 46, (2017): 369–72.

MedlinePlus, "Intersex": https://medlineplus.gov/ency/article/001669.htm#:~:text=Differences%20of%20sex%20development%20(DSD,an%20older%20term%20for%20DSD.

Megan K. DeFranza. *Sex Difference in Christian Theology: Male, Female and Intersex in the Image of God.* Grand Rapids: Wm. B. Eerdmans, 2015.

Mikkola, Mari. "Feminist Perspectives on Sex and Gender." *The Stanford Encyclopedia of Philosophy*. edited by Edward N. Zalta and Uri Nodelman (Summer 2024 Edition).

Millett, Kate. *Sexual Politics*. New York: Columbia University Press, 2016.

Mohamed, Mohd Salim and Siti Nurani Mohd Noor. "Islamic Bioethical Deliberation on the Issue of Newborns with Disorders of Sex Development." *Science and Engineering Ethics* 21, (2015): 429–40.

Mohd Badrol, Muhammad Afif, Abdul Bari Awang, and Sayed Sikandar Shah Haneef. "Intersex Gender Determination in Classical Islamic Law and Modern Medicine: An Analysis for Integration." *Al-Shajarah: Journal of the International Institute of Islamic Thought and Civilization* (ISTAC) 23, no.2 (2018): 469–96.

Moi, Toril. *What Is a Woman?* Oxford: Oxford University Press, 1999.

Monro, Surya, Morgan Carpenter, Daniela Crocetti, Georgiann Davis, Fae Garland, David Griffiths, Peter Hegarty, Mitchell Travis, Mauro Cabral Grinspan, and Peter Aggleton. "Intersex: Cultural and Social Perspectives." *Culture, Health and Sexuality* 23, no. 4 (2021): 431–40.

Al-Muqaddas al-Ardabīlī, Aḥmad. *Majmaʿ al-fāʾida wa-l-burhān fī sharḥ Irshād al-adhhān*, edited by Mujtabā al-ʿIrāqī, ʿAlīpanāh al-Ishtihārdī, and Ḥusayn al-Yazdī. 14 vols. Qum: Muʾassasat al-Nashr al-Islāmī, 1422.

Musallam, Basim. *Sex and Society in Islam: Birth Control before the Nineteenth Century*. Cambridge: Cambridge University Press, 1983.

Al-Muẓaffar, Muḥammad Riḍā. *al-Manṭiq*. Qum: Muʾassasat al-Nashr al-Islāmī, 1430/1388sh.

Najmabadi, Afsaneh. *Professing Selves: Transsexuality and Same-Sex Desire in Contemporary Iran.* Durham: Duke University Press, 2014.

Al-Nawawī, Yaḥyā b. Sharaf (d. 676/1277). *al-Majmūʿ sharḥ al-Muhadhdhab*. 20 vols. Beirut: Dār al-Fikr, 1990.

Nederman, Cary J. and Jacqui True. "The Third Sex: The Idea of the Hermaphrodite in Twelfth-Century Europe." *Journal of the History of Sexuality* 6, no. 44 (1996): 497–517.

Nimkarn, Saroj, Prasanna K Gangishetti, Mabel Yau, and Maria I. New. "21-Hydroxylase-Deficient Congenital Adrenal Hyperplasia." *GeneReviews* National Library of Medicine: https://www.ncbi.nlm.nih.gov/books/NBK1171/.

OHCHR. *Background Note on Human Rights* (United Nations: Human Rights Office of the High Commissioner, 2019) 2, Accessed March 2024: https://www.ohchr.org/en/documents/tools-and-resources/background-note-human-rights-violations-against-intersex-people.

Özbey, Hüseyin, Fayza Darendeliler, Hüyla Kayserili, Ümran Korkmazlar, and Tansu Salman. "Gender Assignment in Female Congenital Adrenal Hyperplasia: A Difficult Experience." *BJU International* 94, no. 3 (2004): 388–91.

Preves, Sharon. *Intersex and Identity: The Contested Self.* New Brunswick: Rutgers University Press, 2003.

Qadhi, Yasir. "Rulings on Transgenderism in Islam." *EPIC MASJID*, Accessed October 2023: https://www.youtube.com/watch?v=iCsUXGz1_6I.

Al-Qurṭubī, Muḥammad b. Aḥmad. *al-Jāmiʿ li-aḥkām al-Qurʾān*, 20 vols. Cairo: Dār al-Kutub al-Miṣriyya, 1384/1964.

Reis, Elizabeth. "Divergence or Disorder?: The Politics of Naming Intersex." *Perspectives in Biology and Medicine* 50, no. 4 (2007): 535–43.

Renzetti, Claire and Daniel Curran. "Sex-Role Socialization." in *Feminist Philosophies*, edited by Janet Kourany, James Sterba, and Rosemarie Tong. Englewood: Prentice Hall, 1992.

Rispler-Chaim, Vardit. *Disability in Islamic Law*. Dordrecht: Springer Netherlands, 2007.

Rosenthal, Franz. "Ar-Razi on the Hidden Illness." *Bulletin of the History of Medicine* 52, no.1 (1978): 45–60.

Roughgarden, Joan. *Evolution's Rainbow.* Berkeley: University of California Press, 2004.

Rowson, Everett K. "Gender Irregularity as Entertainment: Institutionalized Transvestitism at the Caliphal Court in Medieval Baghdad." in *Gender and Difference in the Middle Ages*. edited by Sharon Farmer and Carol Braun Pasternack. Minneapolis: University of Minnesota Press, 2003: 45–72.

Rowson, Everett K. "The Categorization of Gender and Sexual Irregularity in Medieval Arabic Vice Lists." in *Body Guards*, edited by Julia Epstein and Kristina Straub. New York: Routledge, 1991: 50–79.

Rowson, Everett K. "The Effeminates of Early Medina." *Journal of the American Oriental Society* 111, no. 4 (1991): 671–93.

Rubin, Gayle. "The Traffic in Women: Notes on the 'Political Economy' of Sex." in *Feminist Anthropology: A Reader*, edited by Ellen Lewin. Oxford: Wiley-Blackwell, 2006 [1975].

Rubin, Miri. "The Person in The Form: Medieval Challenges to Bodily Order." in *Framing Medieval Bodies*, edited by Sarah Kay and Miri Rubin. Manchester: Manchester University Press, 1996.

Sanders, Paula. "Gendering the Ungendered Body: Hermaphrodites in Medieval Islamic Law." in *Women in Middle Eastern History: Shifting Boundaries in Sex and Gender*. edited by Beth Baron and Nikki Keddie. New Haven: Yale University Press, 1991: 74–95.

Sanders, Paula. "Hermaphrodites Revisited: A Reconsideration." (2008, unpublished), 4, Accessed October 2023: www.academia.edu/35003377 (site discontinued).

Al-Sarakhsī, Muḥammad b. Aḥmad. *al-Mabsūṭ*. 30 vols. Beirut: Dār al-Maʿrifa, 1414/1993.

Sauer, Michelle M. *Gender in Medieval Culture.* London: Bloomsbury Academic, 2015.

Sax, Leonard. "How Common Is Intersex? A Response to Anne Fausto-Sterling." *Journal of Sex Research* 39, no. 3 (2002): 174–8.

Scalenghe, Sara. *Disability in the Ottoman Arab World, 1500–1800.* Cambridge: Cambridge University Press, 2014.

Al-Shīrāzī, Quṭb al-Dīn. *Durrat al-tāj.* Tehran: Intishārāt-i Ḥikmat, 1369sh.

Şiklar, Zeynep, Emine Çamtosun, Semih Bolu, Melek Yıldız, Ayşehan Akıncı, Firdevs Baş, Ismail Dündar et al., and Merih Berberoğlu. "17α Hydroxylase/17, 20 lyase Deficiency: Clinical Features and Genetic Insights from a Large Turkey Cohort." *Endocrine* 85, no. 3 (2024): 1407–16.

Soheir, S. Abou El Ella, Maha A.M. Tawfik, Dalia M. Ellahony, Nahla M. Anees. "Cytogenetic and Molecular Study in Intersex." *Egyptian Journal of Medical Human Genetics* 13, (2012): 281–89.

Spelman, Elizabeth V. *Inessential Woman.* Boston: Beacon Press, 1988.

Sytsma, Sharon E. ed. *Ethics and Intersex: International Library of Ethics, Law, and the New Medicine* 29. Princeton, NJ: Springer, 2006.

Tantawy, Sally, Inas Mazen, Hala Soliman, Ghada Anwar, Abeer Atef, Mona El-Gammal, Ahmed El-Kotoury, Birgit Köhler et al. "Analysis of the Gene Coding for Steroidogenic Factor 1 (SF1, NR5A1) in a Cohort of 50 Egyptian Patients with 46, XY Disorders of Sex Development." *European Journal of Endocrinology* 170, no. 5 (2014): 759–67.

The Organisation Intersex International (OII): www.intersexualite.org/Disorders_of_Sex_Development.html.

Tosun, Busra Gurpinar and Tülay Güran. "Rare Forms of Congenital Adrenal Hyperplasia." *Clinical Endocrinology* 101, no. 4 (2024): 371–85.

Al-Ṭūsī, Naṣīr al-Dīn. *Asās al-iqtibās.* Tehran: Intishārāt-i Dānishgāh-i Tehran, 1367sh.

Viloria, Hida and Maria Nieto. *The Spectrum of Sex: The Science of Male, Female, and Intersex.* London and Philadelphia: Jessica Kingsley Publishers, 2020.

Watson, Ivan. "Rare Gender Identity Defect Hits Gaza Families." CNN (17 Dec. 2009): https://www.cnn.com/2009/WORLD/meast/12/17/gaza.gender.id/index.html.

West-Eberhard, Mary Jane. *Developmental Plasticity and Evolution.* Oxford: Oxford University Press, 2003.

"What Is Intersex?", Accessed March 2024: https://isna.org/faq/what_is_intersex/).

Yacoob, Saadia. *Beyond the Binary: Gender and Legal Personhood in Islamic Law.* Berkeley: University of California Press, 2024.

Young, Iris Marion. "Gender as Seriality: Thinking about Women as a Social Collective." in *Intersecting Voices*, edited by I. M. Young. Princeton: Princeton University Press, 1997.

Al-Zabīdī, Muḥammad Murtaḍā. *Tāj al-ʿarūs min jawāhir al-Qāmūs*, edited by ʿAbd al-ʿAzīz Maṭar. 40 vols. Kuwait: Maṭbaʿat Ḥukūmat al-Kuwait, 1414/1994.

Zabidi, Taqwa. "Analytical Review of Contemporary Fatwas in Resolving Biomedical Issues over Gender Ambiguity." *Journal of Religion and Health* 58, no 11 (2019): 153–67.

Zabus, Chantal. "Transing the Algerian Nation-State: Textual Transgender and Intersex from Pre-Independence to the Black Decade." *Acta Neophilologica* 52, nos. 1–2 (2019): 69–96.

Zainuddin, Ani Amelia, and Zaleha Abdullah Mahdy. "The Islamic Perspectives of Gender-Related Issues in the Management of Patients with Disorders of Sex Development." *Archives of Sexual Behavior* 46, (2017): 353–60.

Ze'evi, Dror. *Producing Desire: Changing Sexual Discourse in the Ottoman Middle East, 1500–1900.* Berkeley: University of California Press, 2006.

CHAPTER ONE

"Gendering the Ungendered Body": A Brief Biography

Paula Sanders

Abstract

This retrospective piece places my 1991 article in the context of changing disciplinary and intellectual frameworks of women's studies and then gender studies, both rooted in the binary, which did not account for the mutability of sex and gender that a much wider range of sources and an approach that moves beyond the binary reveal. It then considers more recent works and approaches that may inform current concerns through a historical lens.

Keywords: gender, binary, historiography, biology, historical context

> "...I am still hoping to do history that matters, by which I mean not only history that might be useful for other historians, as theirs is so often for me, but also history that might bear somehow upon present day concerns, that might provide an interesting stance or perspective from which to view events in our own time."
>
> —Natalie Zemon Davis, "Doing History at 90"[1]

Context and change over time. They're the mantra of historians. We honor them when we study the past and when we study the way other people have written about the past. We rarely have the opportunity, however, to reflect in print on the contexts in which we framed our previous work and what we might do differently now.[2] The publication of this volume offers the rare opportunity to reflect on the essay on intersex persons in medieval Islamic law (at that time employing the conventionally used term 'hermaphrodites') that I published in 1991.[3] I think of this contribution as a biography of that piece in the context of changing institutional frameworks and disciplinary approaches to the study of women, gender, and sexualities in medieval Islamic societies as well as a reflection on the important role these studies might play in providing different perspectives on current cultural and political debates.[4]

In the late 1970s during my early years of graduate study at Princeton, two powerful intellectual, political, and cultural streams were intersecting: second-wave feminism as a political and cultural movement for social change, and women's studies as an emerging field of research in universities. In many universities, these streams converged as scholars began investigating historical topics from the point of view of women's studies, with particular attention to questions of social and cultural hierarchies of power. The mid-1970s through 1990s was also the era when some seminal works were published in the field of Middle Eastern and Islamic studies, particularly Leila Ahmed's *Women and Gender in Islam: historical roots of a modern debate*.[5] Ahmed describes what led her to write the book as a response to the Iranian Revolution, when she—having grown up in Egypt at a time when veiling was not the norm—began to question her own assumptions about the history of women in Islam as she saw Iranian women voluntarily veiling as a form of revolutionary protest.[6] Many other works, particularly on the complex history of veiling practices over time and place, also appeared at that time, with an emphasis on the variety of modern political, cultural, social, religious, and economic meanings of veiling. It was also the era when women scholars worked to recover the voices of women.[7]

At Princeton, one manifestation of these intersecting streams was the work of A. L. Udovitch, who was engaged in the large intellectual project of developing what he called an "archaeology of Islamic law"—influenced by the work of Clifford Geertz in cultural anthropology—to dig through the layers of legal texts to formulate and address problems of social, economic, and cultural history. It was in this context that I encountered the short chapter on the *khunthā* in al-Qudūrī's *Mukhtaṣar*, an eleventh-century abridgment of Ḥanafī law.[8] At that time, I translated the term as 'ambiguous hermaphrodite.' In keeping with current understanding, Indira Gesink translates the term more appropriately as 'medial sex.' I was intrigued and wanted to write about this text from the point of view of women's studies. Udovitch suggested that I take Natalie Zemon Davis's graduate seminar on the culture of the body in sixteenth century France to learn how to use both cultural anthropology and emerging feminist theory as a historian. Davis had come to Princeton in 1978, just a year before the seminar that made such an impact on my work. She brought with her—even at that early stage in the development of women's studies as an academic discipline—a history of innovation, having founded one of the first women's studies programs at the University of California, Berkeley, and published essays that placed both women and other marginalized groups at the center of her historical inquiries.

While it has been conventional for students of the medieval Islamic world to receive rigorous disciplinary training in history, anthropology, and literary criticism for some time now, that was not the case in 1979. But at Princeton, where I was formally a student in the History Department, there was an emphasis on asking new questions, framing the problems of Islamic history in broader contexts, and integrating different disciplinary methodologies into our philologically based training. In addition, what drove my interest in the text was not the case of the *khunthā* per se, but rather how I might use what I saw as an example of a marginal group to illuminate a central issue: the proper relationship between men and women as conceived of in Islamic legal literature.

The paper that I produced for that seminar focused on a topic that was then typical of projects in women's history, namely, sexual hierarchy.[9] I argued that classical Islamic jurists' handling of what I at that time saw as the extreme case of the *khunthā* revealed basic assumptions about how sexual hierarchy must operate in the world: men were always to be hierarchically superior to women and the male sphere was to be protected at all costs from intrusion by females from below. This approach is also evident in the conference paper I gave at the Berkshire Conference of Women's History in 1987, titled "Beyond male and female? Hermaphrodites and sexual hierarchy in medieval Islam."[10]

More than a decade later, I revised that old paper in light of new concerns that came out of the developing focus on gender studies. By this time—the mid- to late 1990s—many of the hundreds of women's studies programs in the United States were being reconceived and renamed as "Study of Women and Gender" or "Study of Women, Gender, and Sexuality," reflecting the expanding scope of our endeavors and framing studies with gender as the primary category of analysis. Less than a year after the Berkshire Conference paper, I was also moving towards gender as my central category of analysis when I presented "The importance of being gendered: hermaphrodites in medieval Islam" at the American Research Center in Egypt in Cairo in early 1988.[11] I was concerned with what the case of the *khunthā* could tell us about how societies construct categories of gender. No longer focused primarily on sexual hierarchy, I was now looking at the importance of gender as the primary point of entry into the social world. Still operating from the assumptions of the binary, I argued that strategies of medieval Muslim jurists worked to preserve the gendered integrity of the social world, which was founded upon a strict opposition of two true sexes, male and female.

Now some three decades removed from that 1991 article, additional methodologies and intellectual concerns provoke me to reconsider that piece and its assumptions once again. What have we learned in the last thirty years, what new considerations have arisen that warrant a different focus, a different argument, perhaps different conclusions to be drawn from these same texts on *hermaphrodites* that I first began to think about some forty-five years ago? Early studies of sex, sexuality, and gender were framed largely in terms of women's studies and feminist history. In spite of the relative dearth of textual material dealing explicitly with women, Islamicists concerned with gender remained preoccupied largely with female sexuality, representations of women and of femininity, and the male/female binary. We mirrored the concerns of gender and sexuality studies as a whole.

The development of new approaches within the emerging field of gender studies—the study of masculinity, gay studies, queer theory—once again expanded the focus and reshaped the inquiries of Islamicists. Everett Rowson's work stands out as particularly thought-provoking. In a pathbreaking series of articles published in the 1990s and early 2000s, Rowson argued persuasively on the basis of literary texts that the fundamental distinction in sexual identity in medieval Islamic societies was not between male and female, but rather between penetrator and penetrated.[12] The adult male was "sexually identified first and foremost as someone who penetrates,"[13] and this dichotomy (rather than sexual object choice) is the basis for understanding the continuum on which sexual identities were arrayed. One of the most important conclusions resulting from this body of work is that male/female was not the only gender binary in medieval Islamic societies: there was also male/not male.

While Rowson's analysis of a fundamental male/not male distinction is founded primarily on literary material, his insight required a reconsideration of the issues raised by the legal texts on the *khunthā*. In earlier work, I had used legal texts to provide a context in which to analyze the range of gendered social relations and assumed that the categories established in law would be consistent across other genres. The differences I observed in my admittedly casual perusal of literary materials were, I believed at the time, primarily a function of literary genre and social custom. I did not take them as evidence of a different set of gender categories that might simultaneously stand alongside the male/female dichotomy. What I failed to recognize and address was, as Marion Katz has succinctly put it, "gender and its attendant legal implications are deeply modulated by reference to other markers of personal and social status."[14] If the category male/not male aligns with penetrator/penetrated, then that question—which is founded upon the assumption of both the male/female binary and sexuality as determined by sexual object choice—no longer dominates our discourse.

Even in 1991, the same year that "Gendering the Ungendered Body" was published, the boundary between male and female was no longer seen as impermeable. In the decades that followed, new scholarly work dealt with gender ambiguities of various kinds which are not much discussed in legal sources. *Mukhannath*s (effeminates), like eunuchs, were permitted to interact with women; eunuchs filled a range of critical roles.[15] Women as political as well as economic and social actors were now becoming central to our understanding of Islamic societies across both time and place.[16] It seems to me that we talked mostly about *crossing* that boundary, not *blurring* it or simply abandoning it as a paradigm in a way that would give rise to the critiques of the binary and the reality of multiple sexes that would emerge over the next two decades.

In an even broader context, some biologists in the 1990s recognized sexual variation along a continuum. A key contribution to the conversations (and debates) was the 1993 article by the biologist Anne Fausto-Sterling, who argued that "if the state and legal system have an interest in maintaining a two-party sexual system, they are in defiance of nature. For biologically speaking, there are many gradations running from female to male; and depending on how one calls the shots, one can argue that along that spectrum lie at least five sexes—and perhaps even more."[17] Along with her clear explanation of the complex biology of sex, Fausto-Sterling also mentioned a small number of historical texts (for example, the Talmud and the Tosefta) that deal extensively with people of mixed sex and noted the European paradigm that has held since the late Middle Ages requiring one to choose—and stick with—only one sex. She also noted that the surgical approaches of twentieth century medicine are a "mode of discipline" and that "the medical community has completed what the legal world began—the complete erasure of any form of embodied sex that does not conform to a male-female, heterosexual pattern." However, her insights were not cited in the works of Islamicists or, indeed, by most other historians, who were largely working in isolation from biologists (as biologists were also working largely in isolation from historians). In my own piece, I mentioned only the medical opinions of John Money.[18] Had I been aware of—or looked actively for—biologists' work on this issue (as distinct from the work of medical practitioners), I might have thought differently. In 1993, as well, the Intersex Society of North America (ISNA) was founded as an advocacy organization for patients with variations of sexual characteristics (at that time, called "disorders of sexual development [DSDs]").[19] That organization was disbanded in 2008 and has been succeeded by Accord Alliance. These organizations continue to advocate primarily to improve the delivery of appropriate health care to intersex persons through advocacy and the development of new clinical guidelines.[20] In 2000, Fausto-Sterling noted optimistically (and prematurely) the distance traveled since 1993: "[M]odern society has moved beyond five sexes to a recognition that gender variation is normal," and engaged the critique that her schema "still gives genitals ... primary signifying status."[21]

The first quarter of the twenty-first century has seen an abundance of studies building on and moving beyond the scholarship of the 1970s, 1980s, and 1990s on gender and sexuality in the Islamic world. Pioneering research on intersex in Islamic societies began with disability studies, notably Vardit Rispler-Chaim's *Disability in Islamic Law* (2007) and Sara Scalenghe's *Disability in the Ottoman Arab World, 1500–1800* (2014), both of which included chapters on intersex considered as a socially disabling condition. New investigation of intersex and its implications for Islamic gender and queer studies began with Saqer Almarri's "You Have Made Her a Man Among Men" (2016) and Mehrdad Alipour's "Transgender Identity, the Sex-Reassignment Surgery Fatwās and Islamic Theology of a Third Gender" (2017).[22]

Building on the work of Rispler-Chaim, Almarri, and Scalenghe, the 2018 article by Indira Gesink offered a critique of the binary assumptions of "Gendering the

Ungendered Body" and traced the replication of its assumptions in subsequent scholarship.[23] Using an unusually comprehensive set of sources—juristic texts from all the major schools of law, as well as lexicography, biography, and medicine—she demonstrates that medieval Muslim writers in these genres recognized the mutability of sex and often positioned the *khunthā mushkil* (complicated intersex) as a medial sex. She argues further that protecting the male domain from intrusion was not a primary consideration (if a consideration at all) but rather that flexibility was key to ensuring the *khunthā mushkil*'s ability to fulfill religious obligations and navigate the social world. In other words, one of Gesink's key insights is that, far from being ungendered, the *khunthā mushkil* was *differently* gendered and could, in fact, be regendered depending upon any number of circumstances that she specifies.

More recently, Mehrdad Alipour's contributions have opened up new lines of inquiry that bring for the first time a deep engagement with a wide range of Shiʿi sources and that move beyond questions of legal, medical, and social accommodations to argue that in some Muslim contexts, intersex persons constitute a third ontological category.[24] Alipour's work demonstrates that as early as the fourteenth century, the male-female binary was being challenged by some Shiʿi jurists—sparking debates among Shiʿi jurists about whether there were, in fact, human beings who belonged to a third 'sex'. Using the legal writings of the Shiʿi jurist al-Yazdi (d. 1919), Alipour shows how jurists within a non-binary approach rebut binary arguments by deploying a range of technical arguments that are commonly employed in other contexts (e.g. underlying proofs that are universal and therefore apply to all humans, specific exceptions to general legal rulings, methods for resolving contradictions and doubts of various kinds) in order to reframe sex-specific legal rulings as evidence for the validity of the non-binary category of a third 'sex'.

***

The cumulative effect of the studies across time, place, and discipline demonstrate clearly that many societies have recognized and accommodated multiple sexualities and genders along a continuum. The current insistence (for political reasons) on true sex, the binary, on a 'normative' gender-and-sex system that privileges heterosexuality is, in fact, the outlier. Viewing the present through the perspectives of the past prods us to question what we thought were our givens. The U. S. State Department's 2025 prohibition of the "X" option for gender on the U.S. passport and the requirement that one's passport designate M or F to align with the (supposedly) true sex on one's birth certificate, provokes us to ask when this first occurred. Has it always been this way? What perceived needs did it meet? What's really at stake and for whom? The "X" was introduced as an option in 2022, but we'd do well to remember that including M or F as a marker of sex was itself introduced as an identifier in U.S. passports only in 1977, and was first recommended by a panel in 1972 because "in light of the increasing number of international air travelers and the rise in the early 1970s of unisex attire and hairstyles, photographs had become a less reliable means for ascertaining a traveler's sex."[25]

All of these things remind us that our own frameworks for interpretation are shaped by conventions bounded by time and place—many of which we believe to be of much longer and wider standing than is the case. These conventions are neither neutral nor necessary to a functioning society, and they demand explanation every bit as much as those things we deem (often wrongly) to be new, surprising, dangerous, and unconventional. The need to historicize conceptions of gender without defaulting to the male/female binary remains as urgent today as were the twentieth-century efforts first to include women in our histories and then to move them from the periphery to the center of our inquiries. A multitude of publications provide abundant evidence of the broad range of sexes and genders and of the fact that variation and accommodation are well documented in the past. Collective volumes like the four-volume *Cambridge World History of Sexualities* provide wide-ranging essays discussing sexualities in different historiographical, theoretical, and disciplinary frameworks (e.g., "The History of Sexuality and Women's History," "The History of Sexuality and LGBTQ+ History," "Trans and Gender Variant Sexualities in History").[26] However, even the essay "Scientific Sex in the Modern World" in the fourth volume on Modern Sexualities discusses the issue of intersex only briefly and does not engage the work of those biologists who contribute to our understanding of the complexities of gender, sex, and sexuality that have much to offer historians. Silences and omissions speak loudly. The 2024 essay in *The Cambridge History of Science* on "Embryology"[27] does not discuss the complex mechanisms of biological sex that are now well known—at least among biologists.

But more biology, it turns out, doesn't simplify matters for us. Consider this long post by biologist Rebecca R. Helm, which I cite here extensively because it is both so powerful and so delightful to read:

> If you know a bit about biology you will probably say that biological sex is caused by chromosomes, XX and you're female, XY and you're male. This is 'chromosomal sex' but is it 'biological sex'? Well ...
>
> Turns out there is only ONE GENE on the Y chromosome that really matters to sex. It's called the SRY gene. During human embryonic development the SRY protein turns on male-associated genes. Having an SRY gene makes you 'genetically male'. But is this 'biological sex'?
>
> Sometimes that SRY gene pops off the Y chromosome and over to an X chromosome. Surprise! So now you've got an X with an SRY and a Y without an SRY. What does this mean?

> A Y with no SRY means physically you appear female, chromosomally you are XY and genetically you're 'female' (no SRY). An X with an SRY means you're physically male, chromosomally XX and genetically male (SRY). But biological sex is simple! There must be another answer ...
>
> Sex-related genes ultimately turn on hormones in specific areas on the body, and reception of those hormones by cells throughout the body. Is this the root of 'biological sex'?
>
> 'Hormonal male' means you produce 'normal' levels of male-associated hormones. Except some percentage of females will have higher levels of 'male' hormones than some percentage of males. Ditto ditto 'female' hormones. And ...
>
> ... if you're developing, your body may not produce enough hormones for your genetic sex. Leading you to be genetically male or female, chromosomally male or female, hormonally intermediate, and physically intermediate. Well, except cells have something to say about this...
>
> Maybe cells are the answer to 'biological sex'?? Right?? Cells have receptors that 'hear' the signal from sex hormones. But sometimes those receptors don't work. Like a mobile phone that's on 'do not disturb.' Call and cell, they will not answer.
>
> What does this all mean?
>
> It means you may be genetically male or female, hormonally male/female/intermediate, with cells that may or may not hear the male/female/non-binary call, and all this leading to a body that can be male/intermediate/female.[28]

More biology doesn't provide easy answers for us now, and less biology (as our historical studies show) didn't prevent people in the past from making sense of and making room for the full range of human sex and sexuality in their midst. We should take our lessons from *both* biology and history as we move forward. As the following chapters in this volume demonstrate, when we engage a wide range of sources and move beyond conventional assumptions, the past does, indeed, provide us with new perspectives from which to view and understand our fellow human beings in our own time.

Notes

1 Natalie Zemon Davis, "Doing History at 90" in *H-France Salon* 11 (2019). Web (accessed in April 2025): https://h-france.net/Salon/SalonVol11no15.8.Davis.pdf.

2 I am grateful to the editors for so generously inviting me to do just that.

3 Paula Sanders, "Gendering the Ungendered Body: Hermaphrodites in Medieval Islamic Law," in *Women in Middle Eastern History: Shifting Boundaries in Sex and Gender*, eds. Nikki R. Keddie and Beth Baron (New Haven: Yale University Press, 1991): 74–95.

4 A 2002 article reports that there was a “rapid expansion [of women’s studies programs] from one integrated program in 1970 to 150 in 1975, 300 in 1980, 450 in 1985, and 600 in 1990.” Marilyn J. Boxer, “Women’s Studies as Women’s History,” *Women’s Studies Quarterly* 30 (2002): 42–51.

5 Leila Ahmed, *Women and Gender in Islam: Historical Roots of a Modern Debate* (New Haven: Yale University Press, 1992).

6 See “Revisiting ‘Women and Gender in Islam’ with Leila Ahmed and Kecia Ali, episode 12 of the Harvard Islamic Studies podcast at https://islamicstudies.harvard.edu/ep-12-revisiting-women-and-gender-islam-leila-ahmed-and-kecia-ali, October 4, 2022.

7 See, for example, “A Veiled Revolution”, Elizabeth Fernea, Producer. Marilyn Gaunt, Director. Icarus Films, 1982. Also, Fatima Mernissi, *Beyond the Veil: Male-Female Dynamics in Modern Muslim Society* (Bloomington: Indiana University Press, 1975. On recovering female voices, see Margot Badran, *Harem Years: The Memoirs of an Egyptian Feminist (1879–1924)* [New York City: The Feminist Press, 1987] and Margot Badran and Miriam Cooke, *Opening the Gates: An Anthology of Arab Feminist Writing* (Bloomington: Indiana University Press, 1990).

8 At that time, the *fiqh* texts we read in seminars on classical Islamic law were—as I recall—entirely Ḥanafī, despite the fact that we were all well aware of the other schools of law. I am not sure how to account for that except, perhaps, that there was a large focus on the Abbasid dynasty—which was closely associated with the Ḥanafī school—in those days.

9 There were a number of groundbreaking articles that addressed this question in different historical settings. One key example is Natalie Z. Davis, “Women on Top,” in *Society and Culture in Early Modern France: Eight Essays by Natalie Zemon Davis* (Redwood City: Stanford University Press, 1975): 124–51.

10 The so-called ‘Big Berks,’ held every three years, was the largest gathering of women’s historians in its time. Younger scholars may not know of its history and importance for women historians and for women’s history. For a brief history, see Carroll Smith-Rosenberg, “President’s Introductory Remarks, 1987 Berkshire Conference of Women’s History, Wellesley College—June 19, 1987,” in *Women’s Studies Quarterly* 16, (1988): 6–11.

11 The following year, a version of the newly refocused work was presented in what was almost certainly one of the earliest panels on gender for the Islamic section of the American Oriental Society. The panel at the 1989 meeting in New Orleans was titled Gender in Islamic Civilization, the papers given were “Men, Women, and Hermaphrodites in Medieval Islam” (Paula Sanders); “Demonizing the Queen of Sheba: Crossing Gender Boundaries in Jewish and Islamic literature” (Jacob Lassner); and “The Generous Eye and the Aesthetics of Oral Poetry” (Suzanne Pinckney Stetkevych). The commentator was Fedwa Malti-Douglas. Malti-Douglas would publish two of her most important books on women and gender in the next few years: *Woman’s Body, Woman’s Word: Gender and Discourse in Arabic-Islamic Writing* (Princeton, 1991) and *Medicines of the Soul: Female Bodies and Sacred Geographies in a Transnational Islam* (Berkeley, 2001). Lassner published *Demonizing the Queen of Sheba: Boundaries of Gender and Culture in Postbiblical Judaism and Medieval Islam* in 1993 (University of Chicago Press). Stetkevych’s work on Islamic poetics included at a very early stage questions of the intersection of gender and ritual in both pre-Islamic Arabic poetry and classical Arabo-Islamic poetry. See especially *The Mute Immortals Speak: Pre-Islamic Poetry and the Poetics of Ritual* (Ithaca, 1993).

12 See especially, Everett K. Rowson, “The Categorization of Gender and Sexual Irregularity in Medieval Arabic Vice Lists,” in *Body Guards: The Cultural Politics of Gender Ambiguity*, eds. Julia Epstein and Kristina Straub (New York: Routledge, 1991): 50–79; Everett K. Rowson, “Gender Irregularity as Entertainment: Institutionalized Transvestism at the Caliphal Court in Medieval Baghdad,” in *Gender and Difference in the Middle Ages*, eds. Sharon Farmer and Carol Braun Pasternack (Minneapolis: University of Minnesota Press, 2003), 45–72.

13 Rowson, "The Categorization of Gender," 54.

14 Marion H. Katz, "Gender and Law," in *Encyclopaedia of Islam Three Online*, eds. K. Fleet, G. Krämer, D. Matringe, J. Nawas and D. J. Stewart (Leiden: Brill, 2017). Katz says further in this EI3 entry "Despite the jurists' deep investment in defining and protecting clear gender identities and roles, in premodern legal texts gender categories are crosscut by differences in legal status related to age cohort, religious identity, social stratum, and slave or free status."

15 Everett Rowson, "The Effeminates of Early Medina," *Journal of the American Oriental Society* 111, no. 4 (1991), 671–93. On eunuchs and their roles at courts and association with women, see Shaun Marmon, *Eunuchs and Sacred Boundariess* (Oxford: Oxford University Press, 1995).

16 Jonathan Berkey demonstrates, for example, how the personal transmission by individual scholars to their students alongside a variety of institutional structures permitted broad access to religious knowledge, including women (Jonathan Berkey, *The Transmission of Knowledge in Medieval Cairo* [Princeton: Princeton University Press, 1992]). Leslie Peirce, *The Imperial Harem: Women and Sovereignty in the Ottoman Empire* (Oxford: Oxford University Press, 1993), shows that gender segregation was not an obstacle to the exercise of political power and documents—using archival materials—precisely how this worked in the Ottoman court of the sixteen and seventeenth centuries.

17 Anne Fausto-Sterling, "The Five Sexes: Why Male and Female Are Not Enough," *The Sciences* (March/April 1993): 20–24.

18 Money's work in the 1950s and 1960s created the medical protocols for sex reassignment surgery for infants born with ambiguous genitalia; it remained foundational to the delivery of medical care for the remainder of the twentieth century. For an interesting history of the modern conception of gender as distinct from sex beginning with Money's work, see Jemima Repo, *The Biopolitics of Gender* (New York, 2015), especially chapter 1, "The Birth of Gender: Social Control, Hermaphroditism, and the New Postwar Sexual Apparatus," 24–48.

19 The archived website is at *isna.org* (not to be confused with isna.com—the website of the Islamic Society of North America).

20 Accord Alliance, www.accordalliance.org.

21 Anne Fausto-Sterling, "The Five Sexes, Revisited," *The Sciences* (July/August 2000): 19–23.

22 Vardit Rispler-Chaim, *Disability in Islamic Law* (Dordrecht: Springer Netherlands, 2007); Sara Scalenghe, *Disability in the Ottoman Arab World, 1500–1800* (Cambridge: Cambridge University Press, 2014); Saqer Almarri, "You Have Made Her a Man Among Men: Translating the Khuntha's Anatomy in Fatimid Jurisprudence," *Transgender Studies Quarterly* 3, nos. 3–4 (2016): 578–86; Mehrdad Alipour, "Transgender Identity, the Sex-Reassignment Surgery Fatwās and Islamic Theology of a Third Gender," *Religion and Gender* 7, no. 2 (2017): 164–79.

23 Indira Gesink, "Intersex Bodies in Premodern Islamic Discourse: Complicating the Binary," *Journal of Middle East Women's Studies* 14, no. 2 (2018): 152–73.

24 Mehrdad Alipour, "Navigating Body Politics in Shiʿi Legal Tradition: Examining Sayyid Kāẓim al-Yazdī's Account of Non-Binary Intersex," *Islamic Law and Society* 32, no. 3 (2025): 262–315.

25 Cited in Samantha Allen, "How the Rise of Androgyny Changed Our Passports" in "The Daily Beast", October 13, 2018.

26 Merry Wiesner-Hanks and Mathew Kuefler, eds. *The Cambridge World History of Sexualities*, 4 vols. (Cambridge: Cambridge University Press, 2024). The chapters mentioned are all in Vol. 1. Authors in these volumes necessarily make choices given word limits as well as availability of scholarly studies in fields far from their areas of expertise, resulting in uneven coverage. This is in no way a criticism, but simply an acknowledgment of the role that the realities of academic publishing plays. The chapter by Serena Tolino in vol. 2, "Sexuality in Islamic Traditions," includes

discussion of medical as well as juristic sources, but does not address intersex. Vol. 3, subtitled "Sites of Knowledge and Practice," presents a wide variety of time-and-place-specific studies, but none on intersex in the Islamic world.

27 Nick Hopwood, "Embryology," in *The Cambridge History of Science*. Vol. 6, "The Modern Biological and Earth Sciences", eds. Peter Bowler and John Pickstone (Cambridge: Cambridge University press, 2009): 285–315.

28 Helm is a biologist at the University of North Carolina with research specialties in ocean surface ecology, developmental biology, and evolution. The complete thread is posted at https://bsky.app/profile/rebeccarhelm.bsky.social/post/3kzczd42uym26. I am grateful to Anita Persall Smith for bringing Helm's work to my attention.

Bibliography

Accord Alliance, www.accordalliance.org.

Ahmed, Leila. *Women and Gender in Islam: Historical Roots of a Modern Debate*. New Haven: Yale University Press,1992.

Alipour, Mehrdad. "Navigating Body Politics in Shiʿi Legal Tradition: Examining Sayyid Kāẓim al-Yazdī's Account of Non-Binary Intersex." *Islamic Law and Society* 32, no. 3 (2025): 262–315.

Alipour, Mehrdad. "Transgender Identity, the Sex-Reassignment Surgery Fatwās and Islamic Theology of a Third Gender." *Religion and Gender* 7, no. 2 (2017): 164–79.

Allen, Samantha. "How the Rise of Androgyny Changed Our Passports." *The Daily Beast*, October 13, 2018: https://apple.news/A5MIStbZYRPWkWQWVmnFx4A.

Almarri, Saqer. "You Have Made Her a Man Among Men: Translating the Khuntha's Anatomy in Fatimid Jurisprudence." *Transgender Studies Quarterly* 3, nos. 3–4: (2016): 578–86.

Badran, Margot and Cooke, Miriam. *Opening the Gates: An Anthology of Arab Feminist Writing*. Bloomington: Indiana University Press, 1990.

Badran, Margot. *Harem Years: The Memoirs of an Egyptian Feminist (1879–1924)*. New York City: The Feminist Press, 1987.

Berkey, Jonathan. *The Transmission of Knowledge in Medieval Cairo*. Princeton: Princeton University Press, 1992.

Boxer, Marilyn J. "Women's Studies as Women's History." *Women's Studies Quarterly* 30 (2002): 42–51.

Davis, Natalie Z. "Women on Top." in *Society and Culture in Early Modern France: Eight Essays by Natalie Zemon Davis*. Redwood City: Stanford University Press, 1975: 124–51.

Davis, Natalie Zemon. "Doing History at 90" in *H-France Salon* 11, (2019). Web. https://h-france.net/Salon/SalonVol11no15.8.Davis.pdf.

Elizabeth Fernea (producer) and Marilyn Gaunt (Director). *A Veiled Revolution*, Icarus Films, 1982.

Fausto-Sterling, Anne. "The Five Sexes, Revisited." *The Sciences* (July/August 2000): 19–23.

Fausto-Sterling, Anne. "The Five Sexes: Why Male and Female Are Not Enough." *The Sciences* (March/April 1993): 20–24.

Gesink, Indira. "Intersex Bodies in Premodern Islamic Discourse: Complicating the Binary," *Journal of Middle East Women's Studies* 14, no. 2 (2018): 152–73.

Hopwood, Nick. "Embryology." in *The Cambridge History of Science*. Vol. 6, "The Modern Biological and Earth Sciences." edited by Peter Bowler and John Pickstone. Cambridge: Cambridge University Press, 2009.

Katz, Marion H. "Gender and law." in *Encyclopaedia of Islam Three Online*. edited by K. Fleet, G. Krämer, D. Matringe, J. Nawas and D. J. Stewart (Leiden: Brill, 2017): https://doi-org.ezproxy.rice.edu/10.1163/1573-3912_ei3_COM_27397 Web.

Marmon, Shaun. *Eunuchs and Sacred Boundaries*. Oxford: Oxford University Press, 1995.

Mernissi, Fatima. *Beyond the Veil: Male-Female Dynamics in Modern Muslim Society*. Bloomington: Indiana University Press, 1975.

Peirce, Leslie. *The Imperial Harem: Women and Sovereignty in the Ottoman Empire*. Oxford: Oxford University Press, 1993.

Repo, Jemima. *The Biopolitics of Gender*. Oxford University Press, 2015, especially chapter 1, "The Birth of Gender: Social Control, Hermaphroditism, and the New Postwar Sexual Apparatus," 24–48.

"Revisiting 'Women and Gender in Islam' with Leila Ahmed and Kecia Ali," episode 12 of the Harvard Islamic Studies podcast at https://islamicstudies.harvard.edu/ep-12-revisiting-women-and-gender-islam-leila-ahmed-and-kecia-ali, October 4, 2022.

Rispler-Chaim, Vardit. *Disability in Islamic Law*. Dordrecht: Springer Netherlands, 2007.

Rowson, Everett K. "Gender Irregularity as Entertainment: Institutionalized Transvestism at the Caliphal Court in Medieval Baghdad." in *Gender and Difference in the Middle Ages*. edited by Sharon Farmer and Braun Pasternack. Minneapolis: University of Minnesota Press, 2003: 45–72.

Rowson, Everett K. "The Categorization of Gender and Sexual Irregularity in Medieval Arabic Vice Lists." in *Body Guards: The Cultural Politics of Gender Ambiguity*. edited by Julia Epstein and Kristina Straub. New York: Routledge, 1991: 50–79

Rowson, Everett. "The Effeminates of Early Medina." *Journal of the American Oriental Society* 111, no. 4 (1991): 671–93.

Sanders, Paula. "Gendering the Ungendered Body: Hermaphrodites in Medieval Islamic Law." in *Women in Middle Eastern History: Shifting Boundaries in Sex and Gender*. edited by Nikki R. Keddie and Beth Baron. New Haven: Yale University Press, 1991: 74–95.

Scalenghe, Sara. *Disability in the Ottoman Arab World, 1500–1800*. Cambridge: Cambridge University Press, 2014.

Smith-Rosenberg, Carroll. "President's Introductory Remarks, 1987 Berkshire Conference of Women's History, Wellesley College—June 19, 1987." *Women's Studies Quarterly* 16, (1988): 6–11.

Wiesner-Hanks, Merry and Mathew Kuefler, eds. *The Cambridge World History of Sexualities*, 4 vols. Cambridge: Cambridge University Press, 2024.

CHAPTER TWO

The Intersex Character (*al-khunthā*) in Classical Arabic Lexicography and Literature

Indira Falk Gesink and Mehrdad Alipour

Abstract

In classical Arabic language and literature as well as Muslim legal and medical discourse, the terms *khunthā* (roughly intersex person, someone possessing both male and female genitalia or neither) and *mukhannath* (effeminate) represent two distinct categories, despite their shared linguistic root, *kh-n-th*. This common root sometimes leads to confusion, with some mistakenly assuming the terms are synonymous. However, each term denotes a specific phenomenon within its own context. To clarify the distinctions between these terms and their associated phenomena, we will begin with lexicographical perspectives on *mukhannath*, followed by an exploration of *khunthā* in lexicons and in broader Arabic literature.

Keywords: *khunthā* in Arabic lexicography and literature, Khalīl b. Aḥmad, al-Jāḥiẓ, Abū l-Faraj al-Iṣfahānī, Ibn Ṭūlūn

Introduction

In classical Arabic language and literature, as well as in Muslim legal and medical discourse, the terms *khunthā* (commonly rendered as an intersex person—one who possesses both male and female genitalia, or neither) and *mukhannath* (typically denoting an effeminate male) constitute two distinct conceptual categories. Despite this distinction, their shared triliteral root—kh-n-th—has often led to confusion, with some erroneously assuming the terms to be interchangeable. In order to dispel this conflation from the outset, this chapter begins by briefly addressing the notion of *mukhannath*, before turning to its principal concern: the figure of the *khunthā* as understood within classical Arabic lexicographical and literary traditions.

Mukhannath

Takhannuth (effeminacy) is a category known to Muslim cultures since the early Islamic revelation. The anecdotal literature, such as the *Kitāb al-aghānī* of Abū l-Faraj al-Iṣfahānī (d. 356/967), early lexicographers' notes and observations, and *ḥadīth* sources convincingly suggest the existence of individuals called *mukhannath* (effeminate, pl. *mukhannathūn*) by the Muslim community in Medina at the time of the Prophet, as they existed before Islam.[1] The question is to what extent these individuals were effeminate, and whether they were considered as such in their behaviors and gender norms, biological sex, or sexual desires and preferences.

The words *takhannuth* and *mukhannath*, according to the Arabic lexicons, are derived from the root *kh-n-th*. The verb *khanatha* means to bend the opening of a waterskin for drinking as al-Farāhīdī (d. between 160/777–8 and 175/790–1) states: "I bent the mouth of the waterskin, thus it opened" (*wa-khanatht*[u] *fam al-qirbat*[i] *fa-inkhanathat*).[2] Abū ʿUbayd b. Sallām (d. 224/838) indicates that "a woman due to her languidness/elasticity was called *khunuth*."[3] Al-Jawharī (d. 393/1003) notes that '*inkhināth*' means suppleness (*tathannī*) and languidness (*takassur*) and the noun form of the verb is '*khunth*.'[4] Classical lexicographical dictionaries remark that a *mukhannath* was called as such due to his languidness, suppleness, and softness (*līn*).[5] Therefore, various terms derived from this root implies the idea of folding towards elasticity, delicacy, suppleness, and languidness.[6]

Al-Fayyūmī (d. ca. 770/1368), drawing from a group of his leading predecessors, states that a man who resembles or imitates a woman in the softness (*līn*) or pleasantness (*rakhāma*) of his voice is called *mukhannith*.[7] Al-Zabīdī (d. 1790), a post-classical/early modern lexicographer, explains that an effeminate man was called both *mukhannath* (in the form of 'passive participle' [*ism al-mafʿūl*]) and *mukhannith* (in the form of 'active participle' [*ism al-fāʿil*]) due to his languidness and softness.[8]

Al-Zabīdī recounts that his teacher, likely Muḥammad al-Ṭayyib al-Fāsī (d. 1170/1756), observed that some commentaries on *Ṣaḥīḥ al-Bukhārī* interpret the term as follows: if it refers to a man who mimics or resembles women in the languor of his limbs or the suppleness (*rakhāma*) of his voice, he is described by both terms, *mukhannath* and *mukhannith*. However, if the term denotes a man who engages in indecency or illicit sexual activity—specifically one who seeks penetration by other men—it should be used exclusively in the form *mukhannath*. Al-Zabīdī's teacher disagreed with this distinction, arguing that this understanding is a misrepresentation of the term, as effeminacy (*takhannuth*) in Arab culture does not suggest male passivity, which explains its absence in Arabic literature. He further asserts that the *ḥadīth* reports containing this term do not carry such a connotation.[9]

Some lexicons define the phrase "a man displaying effeminate traits" (*takhannath*[a] *l-rajul*) as "he performs the act of an effeminate" (*faʿal*[a] *fiʿl*[a] *l-mukhannath*).[10] Performing the act of an effeminate, as these lexical sources note, refers to behaviors characterized by a fluid or soft demeanor, as suggested by the languidness of their limbs and the suppleness of their voice. The lexicographical dictionaries, however, do not address the type of clothing typically worn by effeminates (*mukhannath*s). It also seems that the term was used in a broad sense, encompassing effeminacy in general, regardless of whether the behavior was voluntary or involuntary.[11]

Khunthā in Arabic lexicon

In Arabic lexicographical discourse, a group of people whose biological appearance and (often) sexual anatomy do not fit the definition of male or female bodies—those who are currently classed as intersex—were commonly referred to as *khunthā* (pl. *khanāthā* or *khināth*), as indicated, derived from the same root—*kh-n-th*—as *mukhannath*.[12] Al-Khalīl b. Aḥmad al-Farāhīdī defined *khunthā* as individuals who are neither males nor females.[13] This definition implies that such persons occupy a separate category from males and females, or that they may be a combination of both. By contrast, al-Jawharī described *khunthā* as male and female persons who have female and male sexual organs or genitalia altogether (*jamīʿan*).[14]

These definitions underscore the disputes regarding the conceptualization of *khunthā*: Does the term denote a male, a female, a blend of both, or neither? It appears that al-Jawharī's definition of the term, which prevailed among lexicographers,[15] does not address the nature or sex of a *khunthā*. It only implies that such a person possesses both male and female sexual organs. Thus, the question of what a *khunthā* is remains unanswered. However, al-Khalīl's definition has sparked extensive discussion in Islamic medical and juristic literature.[16]

According to al-Khalīl, *khunthā* is neither male nor female, which could mean that *khunthā*, in his understanding, is a category of human being that is different from both male and female categories. Thus, humans, given this approach, are divided into male, female, and *khunthā*. However, since al-Khalīl has not provided further elaboration on his approach, it can be interpreted in the following two ways: a *khunthā* simply is neither a male nor a female but entirely a different category of humanity; or a *khunthā* is not uniquely/exclusively a male or uniquely/exclusively a female but is a blend of both.[17]

Ibn Manẓūr (d. 711/1311–2) articulates the term somewhat similarly to al-Khalīl. According to him, a *khunthā* is a person who is neither exclusively male nor exclusively female. This point might implicitly indicate that a *khunthā* should be categorized as a different sex from an exclusively male individual as well as an exclusively female individual. Ibn Manẓūr also complicates this point in that the term can either be applied as an adjective, for example, one may speak of a "*khunthā* man," which means an individual who is legally and socially identified as male but has male and female sexual characteristics; or one may use the noun without qualification, namely using *khunthā* alone, which means a person who has physical markers of maleness and femaleness together, from sexual organs to other signs such as female breasts and beard, etc.[18] This last point might refer to jurists' distinctions between *al-khunthā al-mushkil* (complicated intersex) and *al-khunthā ghayr al-mushkil* (uncomplicated intersex). That is, when using the term *khunthā* without qualification, he might mean what the jurists call *al-khunthā al-mushkil*, a person whose sex cannot be determined, and when he uses the term *khunthā* man, he might mean *al-khunthā ghayr al-mushkil*, a person who has both male and female genitalia but also has other markers from which a jurist could assign male legal categorization.

Ibn Durayd notes that the term *khunthā*, like *mukhannath*, is derived from *kh-n-th* due to its resemblance with females.[19] Al-Azharī (d.370H/980) remarks that in Arab culture a female was occasionally called *khunthā* because of her softness and suppleness.[20] Nevertheless, despite the fact that both *mukhannath* and *khunthā* are rooted in *kh-n-th* and they might have been derived as such due to their gender ambiguity and the fact that they somewhat resemble females in softness, suppleness, elasticity, and so on, there seems no doubt that Arabic lexicographical dictionaries sharply discerned *mukhannath* people from *khunthā*. As demonstrated, the former was often identified based on their behavioral characteristics while the latter was defined by their physical markers such as sexual organs.

Khunthā in literature

While the *khunthā* appears with relative frequency in lexicography, it is rarely found in Arabic literature. Poets and biographers of the ʿAbbāsid era wrote frequently of the antics of *mukhannath*s, who figured significantly in moral critiques of the caliphs whose courts included *mukhannath* entertainers and courtiers. Joke manuals featured *mukhannath*s defending their sexual preferences, hilariously and often crassly. *Khunthā*s were not subject to moral condemnation and so provided fewer entertaining subjects for literary exploration. They were also evidently less visible in society than *mukhannath*s were, as the practice of assimilating to legal categorization of man or woman made a *khunthā* virtually invisible. Only the exceptionally rare *khunthā mushkil*, who had mixed genitalia, urinated from both sexual organs or lacked a dominant set of genitalia, had no mature sexual characteristics, and declined to assimilate to either sex would be marked out visually by standing in between lines of men and women at prayer in the mosque.

Nevertheless, where the *khunthā* does appear in literature, these mentions provide invaluable information about the cultural world in which the *khunthā*s lived. For example, the ʿAbbasid essayist al-Jāḥiẓ (d. 255/868–9) wrote prolifically and acknowledged eunuchs, *mukhannath*s, and women who loved women, and had sex with women but he rarely mentioned *khunthās*. Yet what he did say about them suggests that ʿAbbasid authors did not always expect their world to consist of just men and women, and that they brought these expectations with them to their interpretations of Qurʾān. Al-Jāḥiẓ composed a series of political letters during the reigns of ʿAbbasid caliphs al-Muʿtaṣim and al-Mutawakkil, some of which he addressed to al-Mutawakkil's minister, al-Fatḥ b. Khāqān. The stated purpose of these letters was to "bring together the hearts of those who make up the ʿAbbasid state."[21] In one letter, al-Jāḥiẓ discusses the value of the Turks, and he states that some writers think ethnic groups are distinguished by the characteristics of their names. He points out that names are more than just descriptors of actions, so while a "warrior" is "one who goes to war," the "mothers of Believers" were the Prophet's wives, not literally mothers. Furthermore, law made women "mothers" of children they only nursed, and "mothers" of their husbands' children by other women. This was God's will. And God would make whomever He wished an Arab, and whomever He wished a Persian, or Quraysh, or Zanj— "just as He would make whomever He wished male, female, *khunthā*, or something that was neither male, female, nor *khunthā*."[22] Here al-Jāḥiẓ is referencing verses of the Qurʾān 42: 49–50, which say "Unto God belongs sovereignty over the heavens and the earth; He creates whatsoever He will, bestowing females upon whomsoever He will, and bestowing males upon whomsoever He will. Or He couples males and females and causes whomsoever He will to be barren. Truly He is Knowing, Powerful."[23] In al-Jāḥiẓ's casual representation of this verse, God creates male children, female children, *khunthā* children who pair in one body male and female, as well as children who are something else altogether.

However, in the many volumes *Kitāb al-aghānī* (the Book of Songs) by Abū l-Faraj al-Iṣfahānī (d. 356/967), a massive work that is rich in anecdotes of eunuchs and *mukhannaths*, there is not one single mention of a human *khunthā*. Yet the work does acknowledge that such bodily conformations exist. Al-Isfahānī relates a story about the Battle of Yawm Jabala, one of the inter-tribal battles of sixth-century pre-Islamic Arabia. The account is as follows:[24]

> As for ʿAmr ibn ʿUdas, he managed to escape that day. The Banū Sulaym asserted that, on the Day of Jabala, horses were paraded before Mirdas ibn Abī ʿĀmir, who was the most knowledgeable among people about horses. A horse belonging to a young man from the Banū Kilāb was presented to him, and he said, "By God, no male or female will be able to fail it or overtake it; so, here is my cloak and twenty-five camels for it." When the people fled on the Day of Jabala, the Kilābī man set out on that very horse pursuing ʿAmr ibn ʿAmr. The Kilābī said: "I raced him the entire day on equal footing, and by God, I didn't sense that he was leading me by any measurable distance, yet he eventually gained and I lagged behind. So, I said, 'by God, it is the Moon of Mirdās.' ʿAmr then spurred his horse, striking it with a whip, and it was revealed to

> be *khunthā*—neither male nor female. I informed them [namely, the people of Banū Sulaym] that I had overtaken him. They said: '[do you mean] the Moon of al-Sulaymī?' I said no [, not really], then I reported them about the incident."
> Mirdās then said:
> "The chestnut horse stretched like a slender staff, thin and lean, for ʿAmr ibn ʿAmr, after being touched by hand. If not for the endurance of that *khunthā* and the distance to victory, its weakness in rising would have been truly constrained. It recalled the binding in Iraq and a sense of rest, while swords swayed above the warrior's head."

The anecdote continues, but the story of the horse does not come up again. The *khunthā* horse that is worth twenty-five camels and a cloak is exceptionally fast and enduring. All are positive traits. The text says explicitly that *khunthā* means "neither male nor female." This is an interesting way to put it, for it avoids the legal conundrum of something being *both* male and female. In a legal context in which rights and obligations were gendered, it was sometimes contradictory to be both. One could not, for example, wear both sewn and unsewn clothing on pilgrimage; one had to wear one or the other. One could not be both provider and maintained in marriage.

Yet most references to *khunthā* are to things that are of two natures. The vast majority of references to *khunthā* in literature prior to the eleventh century indicate a plant, the white asphodel flower.[25] A poem by Abū l-Ḥasan al-Duwayda lamented an inheritance too poor, a family that left him only barley bread, dates, yogurt, squash, and *khunthā*: "Were these things combined, even Adam would not have approached a woman."[26] *Khunthā* ends the hemistich in order to fill in the rhyming scheme: he is mourned (*yurthā*), squash (*quthā*), and woman (*unthā*). The roots of the asphodel flower were edible, and poor families consumed them, and they were also used for healing purposes. The flowers of this weed were a yellowish-white, its leaves gray, which led in Hellenic civilizations to its association with corpses and the underworld. Persephone wore a crown of asphodel, and mourners used it to cover graves. An inheritance consisting of asphodel would be poor indeed. The plant is hermaphroditic—self-pollinating, but its name in Arabic—*khunthā*—referred to its doubled nature, being both of the living world and of the dead.

Literature also helps us understand that not all *khunthā*s were defined by mixed genital features. In legal literature, even though jurists cite the formal definition of a *khunthā* as a person with both a penis and a vaginal opening or lacking any genitalia altogether, they often relate anecdotes or cases in which a person develops new sexual characteristics, usually at puberty, that are not in line with the formal definition. These anecdotes are the second most common reference to *khunthā* in literary sources.

During the Mamluk period, the market regulator and historian al-Maqrīzī (d. 845/1442) noted casually among long lists of notable deaths, floods, and practices causing inflation that occasionally people changed from female to male. He did not use the term *khunthā* but noted simply that these things were among the wondrous acts of God. For example, for the year 754, al-Maqrīzī recorded a note from the deputy of Tripoli, Amīr Aytmīsh, along with a document that he confirmed was from the *qāḍī* of Tripoli, that described a woman of Tripoli who had married three husbands, each of whom had been unable to take her virginity despite her willingness. When she reached the age of fifteen, her breasts withered and she slept day and night.[27]

> And something began to come from her vulva little by little, until it took the form of a small penis and two testicles. She kept the matter secret until a fourth man proposed to her, and all that remained was the marriage contract. She informed her mother of her situation, and it became well-known in Tripoli, and the Amīr Aytimīsh, the deputy, was informed of it, so he wrote a report about it and sent it to the Sultan.[28]

Al-Maqrīzī's account now switches pronouns and starts referring to the person with male gender. The person "came out among the people and took the name 'Abdallāh."[29] 'Abdallāh went to Damascus to explain his case to the deputy there, Amīr 'Alī, and he gave evidence to a chamberlain that he'd had three wet dreams in a period of six months. He developed a black beard and was inducted into the ranks of the soldiers.[30] "Nothing remained of the characteristics of women except his speech, for in him there was femininity (*unūtha*)...and this was one of the wonders of God's creation."[31] Al-Maqrīzī ends the account with a note that the Shaykh 'Imād al-Dīn Ismā'īl b. 'Umar b. Kathīr mentioned in his history that he had met 'Abdallāh.[32]

In a second, similar anecdote, al-Maqrīzī notes that on the first of Muharram in the year 776 (12 June 1374):

> A strange event happened, the like of which has happened before, which is that the Amīr Sharaf al-Dīn 'Īsā b. BābJak, the wālī (governor) of the Ashmūnīn, had had a daughter. When she reached the age of fifteen, her vagina became blocked and a penis and two testicles descended to her, and she had wet dreams as men do. This became well-known in al-Ḥusayniya—where he lived—and in Cairo, until it reached Manjak, so he summoned her and discovered the truth about her affairs. He ordered the removal of women's clothing from her and dressed her in men's clothing of the soldiers. He named her Muḥammad and made him a page among his servants and granted him a fief (*iqṭā'*), which everyone witnessed.[33]

Such evidence of God's miraculous creation was considered valuable. Al-Maqrīzī noted that in the year 768H, the ruler of Yemen sent as a gift to the sultan a horse that had neither penis nor testicles and urinated from a hole in its abdomen.[34]

One cannot generalize from a single source to all Mamluk society, of course. Nor is it possible to track a trajectory from these positive anecdotes to the tragic story of the Ṣūfī Muḥammad ibn Salāma as told by the late Mamluk historian Aḥmad b. al-Ḥimṣī (d. 934/1528). In b. al-Ḥimṣī's narration, Ibn Salāma was a respected Shāfiʿī ascetic who had, on 11 Ramadan 911 (14 February 1506), been beaten and killed because he had married "an obvious *khunthā* woman" (*imra'a khunthā wāḍiḥ*), consummated the marriage with her, and removed her virginity. The bride had previously rejected the suit of her paternal cousin from the Maghrib, and the cousin had complained about the couple to the Mamluk Amīr Tarabey. The Amīr fetched the newlyweds and had them beaten with clubs and whipped until they died, and the incident destroyed their reputations, yet still the people sorrowed greatly over Ibn Salāma's death.[35] The ordering of the events in this narration leads the reader to understand that the jealous cousin is to blame; he slandered the couple and caused Amīr Tarabey to abuse and kill them. Nevertheless, we are also to understand that the bride's status as *khunthā* also permits the violence to occur. It is something the Amīr can use to sanction his actions.

Ibn Ṭūlūn (d. 953/1546), a historian who was a near contemporary of Ibn al-Ḥimṣī, related the same story with more detail and different emphasis. Muḥammad b. Salāma al-Nābulsī al-Dimashqī, according to Ibn Ṭūlūn, was a young man, who posed as a mystic out of self-serving piety (*shābb*[an] *mutaṣawwif*[an] *mutamaṣliḥ*[an]). He traveled to Cairo, where he associated with Ṣūfī gazers who sought God in the faces of beardless youths, and he associated intimately with young boys (*murds*).[36]. He gained the affection of a group of self-serving pious individuals and became known among them for his pretensions to righteousness. Ibn Ṭūlūn did not approve. "His fame grew," wrote the historian, "until God wanted to make a demonstration of his condition."

In Ramaḍān of 1506, Ibn Salāma appeared at a marriage registration center (*markaz al-shuhūd*) in Cairo disguised as a girl—wearing a *niqāb* and a worn-out, patched *jilbāb*. He requested a marriage be contracted with him (as though he were a woman). The request was granted. After a few days, some neighbors began to suspect him. The witnesses grew afraid and informed Amīr Ṭarābāy, head of the guard rotation. The Amīr summoned him and investigated the matter. They found him to be a young man in women's clothing.

He claimed to be a *khunthā*, so women were assigned to examine him.[37] By conventional definition, a *khunthā* was defined by the presence of male and female genitalia, but we must keep in mind that many of the anecdotes feature people who change sex due to maturation with sexual characteristics that contradict the assumed legal categorization. Let us imagine for the moment that this person had been assigned male at birth but feminized at puberty. This would be plausible for a person with XX chromosomes and congenital adrenal hyperplasia. Ibn Salāma might have had a penis and no female vaginal opening. He would have been raised male and may even have developed a beard, which would confirm an external observer's impression of maleness. He might however have an internal sense of self as female and be attracted to men. In the modern world, such a person could have genetic and hormonal testing to confirm XY chromosomes and receive hormone treatment and become a fully functioning woman with normal reproductive capacity. In the 1500s, however, that person might never menstruate, and an imperforate vagina might never be discovered. Ibn Salāma was, in the eyes of the court, male.

The women who examined him saw only male genitalia, but the account says they could not be certain the bride was male, for "he had wounded himself under the penis and claimed that he menstruated." Another examination determined that he was not, in fact, menstruating. The Amīr ordered that he be flogged with whips and paraded publicly in Cairo, mounted on the back of a bull. He was flogged again and sent to the detention center (*maqshara*), where he died.

This, according to Ibn Ṭūlūn, caused the people to grow mistrustful of these people and to consider them false claimants to piety (*mutamaṣliḥūn*). Ibn Ṭūlūn further remarks that those who follow the true Sufi path have made clear that if the *walī* (true friend of God) is sincere, he must conceal his spiritual state. If he makes it public, he will be exposed to disgrace.[38]

Ibn Ṭūlūn's narrative signifies differently than that told by Ibn al-Ḥimṣī. Ibn al-Ḥimṣī's narrative expresses sympathy for a *khunthā* whom the governor kills. Ibn Ṭūlūn's narrative reinforces binary gender, as both the person killed and the Sufi gazing cults were transgressing the boundaries between male and female.

The Ottoman Damascene biographer Najm al-Dīn Muḥammad al-Ghazzī (d. 1061/1651) repeated the story almost a century later. Al-Ghazzī transmits Ibn al-Ḥimṣī's narration almost word-for-word and does not appear to be aware of Ibn Ṭūlūn's. There is no boy-masquerading-as-girl.[39] Yet al-Ghazzī's narrative context is somewhat different, because he makes a point elsewhere in his book to note his appreciation for Ṣūfī gazing: his narrative too exhibits sympathy for the couple.[40]

Nowhere in any of these accounts do the authors express distaste for the idea of *khunthā* marriage. They don't cite juristic texts about the legality or illegality of *khunthā* marriage. Nor do they stop to explain what a *khunthā* was. They assume their audience knows. Their audience is not interested in hearing about whether a *khunthā* should or should not marry; they are interested in hearing about abusive rulers who persecute poor ascetics or about men who disguise themselves as women.

Arabic literary production of the early Ottoman era reflects the same general acceptance that God's creation comes in more than just male and female. Muḥammad Amīn b. Faḍl Allāh b. Muḥibb al-Dīn b. Muḥammad al-Muḥibbī (d. 1111/1699) was a historian of Ottoman-era Syria and a Ḥanafī jurist. His book, *Tārīkh khulāṣat al-athar fī aʿyān al-qarn al-ḥādī ʿashar*, relates the biographies of notable people of the tenth and eleventh Islamic centuries. Some of his anecdotes note particular items of thematic interest that he encountered while gathering the evidence for the book. For example, al-Muḥibbī relates a number of anecdotes about *khunthās*, including one of those told by al-Maqrīzī that is related above.[41] In the year 953/1546, there came to the Dār al-Sulṭa in Constantinople from the city of Qunya a report about "a man with a large beard all the way to his chest" who asked the court to "free up his circumstances" because he was a woman. As evidence, he testified that he had a female vulva. The *ḥākim* of this city examined him and found him to be female with a vulva. The court shaved his beard and ordered him "to the *sitra*"—that is, to observe female legal obligations for dress. Al-Muḥibbī reported further that he had heard "she"—he changes the pronouns he uses for the *khunthā*—had married and had given birth vaginally.[42]

There is a similar story in *al-Kashkūl* by al-Bahā' al-Ḥārithī (Bahā' al-Dīn al-ʿĀmilī, d. 1030H/1621), who cites *Ḥayāt al-Ḥayawān* (Life of Animals), which in turn attributes the story to Ibn al-Athīr's *al-Kāmil fī-l-tārīkh* (Complete History), under the events of the year 623 AH (1226 CE). Ibn al-Athīr reports that he had a neighbor whose daughter was named Ṣafiyya. When she turned fifteen, she developed a penis and facial hair. Al-Bahā' adds that a comparable account was also recorded by the Persian historian Ḥamdallāh al-Mustawfī (d. ca. 744/1344) in his *Nuzhat al-Qulūb*. In the town of Qamīsha/Qumīsha (in the province of Isfahan), a girl was married, and on the wedding night experienced an intense itch in her genital region, after which a penis emerged, and she was then recognized as a man. This happened during the reign of Sultan Jān-Bulādh Khudābanda.[43]

Al-Muḥibbī also related from al-Qāḍī Akmal al-Dīn b. Burhān al-Dīn (d. 17 Dhū l-Ḥijja 1011 / 27 July 1603) the story of a young man from al-Qaymariyya in Damascus from the year 952 (1545–6). The young man was "a dark-skinned beardless youth of olive complexion called ʿAlī b. al-Rifāʿī." He was a bookbinder. A person named ʿAbd al-Raḥmān desired the beardless youth, and their relationship brought the beardless ʿAlī to the court of the Shāfiʿī judge Kamāl al-Dīn al-Biqāʿī. The account says that "the preponderance of evidence" suggested that ʿAlī was a *khunthā* and that in fact he inclined more to womanliness (*li-l-unūtha amyal*) than to manliness. Physicians ordered that he be examined. This examination determined that ʿAlī's pubic area had a genital opening with a small nipple (*ḥulma ṣaghīra*), above which there were three testicular-like swellings (*abkhāsh*). They removed those by surgical excision, revealing under the perforated spot a female vulva. This result enabled the Shāfiʿī *ḥākim* to rule that ʿAlī was female with the new name ʿAliya /ʿAliyya. The court then married her (again, note change of pronoun) to her lover ʿAbd al-Raḥmān. The account then notes that the two had sexual intercourse, that ʿAbd al-Raḥman found ʿAliya/ʿAliyya to be a virgin, and that she became pregnant by him "and bore him numerous children." Al-Muḥibbī asserts that most of the people of Damascus witnessed this.[44]

These accounts are related dryly. Al-Muḥibbī offers no judgment. He offers no commentary at all. *Khunthās* existed; people changed from one sex to another; it happens. The historian notes the events and moves on.

The impression literary accounts of the *khunthā* convey is that, simply, non-binary people existed. They were present. They were wonders of God's Creation. They were not monstrous, nor were they targets of moralizing tracts in the way that *mukhannaths* (effeminate men) were. As al-Jāḥiẓ pointed out, God made daughters, God made sons, and sometimes God made people who were either both daughter and son in one body, or neither. Who were we to question the acts of God?

Conclusion

This chapter has sought to delineate the conceptual distinction between *mukhannath* and *khunthā*, despite their shared Arabic root (*kh-n-th*). While the former generally refers to behavioral characteristics—typically associated with 'gender' presentation or perceived effeminacy—the latter concerns the biological classification of individuals born with physical characteristics that differ from those typically associated with male or female bodies. These two categories, although occasionally conflated due to their linguistic proximity, functioned distinctly within classical Arabic linguistic and literary frameworks.

As demonstrated, classical Arabic lexicographers devoted considerable attention to defining and describing the *khunthā*, constructing a vocabulary that attempted to contain the ambiguities of embodiment within existing binary paradigms. In contrast, Arabic literary sources tended to foreground the figure of the *mukhannath*, engaging in elaborate discussions that reflected broader societal anxieties about gender, performance, and propriety. The *khunthā*, by comparison, remained peripheral in such literary discourse—mentioned less frequently and rarely as a figure of narrative elaboration or symbolic investment.

What emerges from both lexicographical and literary texts is not a coherent binary model but rather a subtle recognition of the diversity of human embodiments. Although the modern notions of sex and gender did not exist, classical Arabic culture did not entirely erase such conceptual and categorical complexities. The presence of khunthās whose bodies did not fit neatly into male or female designations was acknowledged—often with curiosity or astonishment, but hardly with explicit contempt or hostility. The language used to describe them suggests a desire to understand rather than to condemn.

In sum, while the classical Arabic tradition did not explicitly theorize non-binary identity, its textual lexicographical and literary heritage offers evidence of a nuanced engagement with the fluidities and ambiguities of gendered and sexed embodiment. These engagements were not revolutionary in intent, but they nevertheless reveal a cultural and intellectual space where the limits of binary categorization were occasionally, if not deliberately, unsettled.

Notes

1 Everett Rowson has carefully compiled Prophetic *ḥadīth*s concerning effeminacy as transmitted in the Sunni *ḥadīth* collections (Everett K. Rowson, "The Effeminates of Early Medina," *Journal of the American Oriental Society* 111, no. 4, [1991]: 671–93). Likewise, several relevant *ḥadīth*s are found within the Imāmī *ḥadīth* compilations. Notably, almost all these Imāmī *ḥadīth*s are also attributed to the Prophet, closely mirroring the Sunni traditions on this topic. For further details on the Imāmī *ḥadīth*s related to this subject, see Mehrdad Alipour, *Negotiating Homosexuality in Islam: A Legal-Hermeneutical Examination of Modern Shiʿi Discourse* (Leiden: Brill, 2024), 110, 198.

2 Abū ʿAbd al-Raḥmān al-Khalīl b. Aḥmad al-Farāhīdī, *Kitāb al-ʿayn*, eds. Mahdī al-Makhzūmī and Ibrāhīm al-Sāmarrāʾī, 8 vols. (Baghdad: Dār al-Rashād, 1980), 4: 248.

3 Abū ʿUbayd al-Qāsim b. Sallām, *Gharīb al-ḥadīth*, ed. Muḥammad ʿAbd al-Muʿīd-Khān, 4 vols. (Ḥaydarābād: Dāʾirat al-Maʿārif al-ʿUthmāniyya, 1384/1964), 2: 283. Abū l-Faraj al-Iṣfahānī indicates the same point where he discusses a poet named Muhalhal (his name was ʿUday or Imrūʾ al-Qays b. Rabīʿa b. al-Ḥārith) who had languidness (*khunuth*) and softness (*līn*) and was often in the company of women (Abū l-Faraj ʿAlī b. al-Ḥusayn al-Iṣfahānī, *al-Aghānī*, 25 vols. [Beirut: Dār Iḥyāʾ al-Turāth al-ʿArabī, 1415/1994] 5: 41).

4 Abū Naṣr Ismāʿīl al-Jawharī, *al-Ṣiḥāḥ tāj al-lugha wa-ṣiḥāḥ al-ʿarabiyya*, ed. Aḥmad ʿAbd al-Ghafūr ʿAttār, 6 vols. (Beirut: Dār al-ʿIlm li-l-Malāyin, 1407/1986–7), 1: 281.

5 A number of lexicons only mentioned the languidness (see, for example, al-Khalīl b. Aḥmad, *Kitāb al-ʿayn*, 4: 248; Abū ʿUbayd b. Sallām, *Gharīb al-ḥadīth*, 2: 283); but others refer to both languidness and suppleness (See, for example, al-Jawharī, *al-Ṣiḥāḥ*, 1: 281); and yet others added elasticity or pliability as well (See, for example, Muḥammad b. Aḥmad al-Azharī, *Tahdhīb al-lugha*, 15 vols. (Beirut: Dār Iḥyāʾ al-Turāth al-ʿArabī, 2001), 7: 145; Muḥammad b. al-Ḥasan b. Durayd al-Azdī, *Jamharat al-lugha*, ed. Ramzī Munīr Baʿlbakī, 3 vols. (Beirut: Dār al-ʿIlm li-l-Malāyīn, 1987), 1: 418.

6 Muḥammad b. Mukarram b. Manẓūr, *Lisān al-ʿarab*, 15 vols. (Beirut: Dār Ṣādir li-l-Ṭibāʿa wa-l-Nashr, 1414), 2: 145; Muḥammad Murtaḍā al-Zabīdī, *Tāj al-ʿarūs min jawāhir al-Qāmūs*, ed. ʿAbd al-ʿAzīz Maṭar, 40 vols. (Kuwait: Maṭbaʿat Ḥukūmat al-Kuwait, 1414/1994), 5: 240–41.

7 Aḥmad b. Muḥammad b. ʿAlī al-Fayyūmī, *al-Miṣbāḥ al-munīr fī gharīb al-sharḥ al-kabīr, 2 vols.* (Beirut: al-Maktaba al-ʿIlmiyya, 1994) 1: 183. Also, see al-Zabīdī, *Tāj al-ʿarūs*, 5: 241.

8 Al-Zabīdī, *Tāj al-ʿarūs*, 5: 240–41.

9 Ibid., 5: 241. *Ṣaḥīḥ al-Bukhārī* is one of the six reliable Sunni *ḥadīth* compilations. The nature of the commentary addressed by al-Zabīdī's teacher is unknown to us.

10 Al-Khalīl b. Aḥmad, *Kitāb al-ʿayn*, 4: 248; al-Azharī, *Tahdhīb al-lugha*, 7: 145; Ibn Manẓūr, *Lisān al-ʿarab*, 2: 145.

11 Rowson, "The Effeminates of Early Medina," 673.

12 See al-Khalīl b. Aḥmad al-Farāhīdī, *Kitāb al-ʿayn*, 4: 248; al-Jawharī, *al-Ṣiḥāḥ*, 1: 281; Ibn Durayd al-Azdī, *Jamharat al-lugha*, 1: 418; al-Azharī, *Tahdhīb al-lugha*, 7: 145; al-Fayyūmī, *al-Miṣbāḥ al-munīr*, 1: 183; Ibn Manẓūr, *Lisān al-ʿarab*, 2: 145; al-Zabīdī, *Tāj al-ʿarūs*, 5: 240–42.

13 Therefore, Rowson's reading of al-Khalīl, in which he asserts that al-Khalīl upholds the word *mukhannath* as derived from *khunthā* due to their parallel forms of gender ambiguity, is inaccurate

(Rowson, "The Effeminates of Early Medina," 673). Rowson's interpretation appears to be based on the grammatical rule that the pronoun "hu" in *wa-min-hu ukhidh*[a] *l-mukhannath*[u] in al-Khalīl's book refers to the nearest noun mentioned, in this case, *khunthā*. While Rowson's reading may be grammatically plausible, in this instance, the pronoun does not refer to the closest noun. Rather, it points back to the earlier noun, namely the root *kh-n-th*, which means according to al-Khalīl, both *khunthā* and *mukhannath* are derived from the same root, i.e., *kh-n-th*. This understanding aligns with other lexicons, several of which have been cited here, whether composed near al-Khalīl's era or in later periods; these lexicons consistently indicate that both *mukhannath* and *khunthā* derive from the same root, *kh-n-th*. Consequently, none of these sources supports the view that *mukhannath* is derived from *khunthā*. Furthermore, given al-Khalīl's prominent role in the development of Arabic lexicography, it is likely that lexicographers would have noted and critiqued any such alternative view had they understood al-Khalīl to differ from their consensus.

14 Al-Jawharī, *al-Ṣiḥāḥ*, 1: 281.

15 For example, al-Azharī just repeats al-Jawharī's definition of *khunthā* (al-Azharī, *Tahdhīb al-lugha*, 7: 145). Al-Fayyūmī also describes a *khunthā* as a person who has both a vulva (*farj al-mar'a*) and a penis (*farj al-rajul*) (al-Fayyūmī, *al-Miṣbāḥ al-munīr*, 1: 183).

16 For medical discourse, see Muḥammad b. Zakariyyā l-Rāzī, *al-Ḥāwī fī l-ṭibb*, 7 vols. (Beirut: Dār Iḥyā' al-Turāth al-ʿArabī, 1422/2002), 3: 192; Ibn Sīnā, *al-Qānūn fī l-ṭibb*, 4 vols. (Beirut: Dār Iḥyā' al-Turāth al-ʿArabī, 2005), 3: 449; Abū l-Qāsim al-Zahrāwī [Albucasis], *Kitāb al-taṣrīf li-man ʿajaza ʿan al-taʾlīf: al-maqāla al-thalāthūn: al-Jarāḥa* (Riyadh: Maktabat al-Malik Fahd al-Waṭaniyya, 1422/2001), 306. Also, see Chapter Nine of the present book. For Sunni legal discussions, see Yaḥyā b. Sharaf al-Nawawī, *al-Majmūʿ sharḥ al-Muhadhdhab*, 20 vols. (Beirut: Dār al-Fikr, 1990), 2: 46–7; Muḥammad b. Aḥmad al-Sarakhsī, *al-Mabsūṭ*, 30 vols. (Beirut: Dār al-Maʿrifa, 1414/1993), 30: 91; Abū al-Ḥusayn ʿAlī b. al-Ḥusayn b. Muḥammad al-Sughdī, *al-Nutaf fī l-fatāwā*, ed. Ṣalāḥ al-Dīn al-Nāhī, 2 vols. (Amman: Dār al-Furqān/Beirut: Muʾassasat al-Risāla, 1404/1984), 2: 857–8; Abū l-Ḥasan ʿAlī b. Muḥammad al-Māwardī al-Baṣrī, *al-Ḥāwī l-kabīr fī fiqh madhhab al-imām al-Shāfiʿī*, 18 vols. (Beirut: Dār al-Kutub al-ʿIlmiyya, 1419/1999), 8: 108. However, several Sunni legal experts refer to *khunthā* as people with both male and female genitalia: see, for example, Abū Muḥammad ʿAbd al-Wahhāb b. ʿAlī al-Thaʿlabī al-Mālikī al-Baghdādī, *al-Maʿūna ʿalā madhhab ʿālim al-madīna "al-Imām Mālik b. Anas"*, ed. Ḥamīsh ʿAbd al-Ḥaqq, 3 vols. (Makka: al-Maktaba al-Tijāriyya, 1995), 3: 657; Abū l-Ḥusayn Aḥmad b. Muḥammad al-Qudūrī al-Ḥanafī al-Baghdādī, *Mukhtaṣar al-Qudūrī fī l-fiqh al-Ḥanafī*, ed. Muḥammad Muḥammad ʿAwīḍa (Beirut: Dār al-Kutub al-ʿIlmiyya, 1418/1997), 137; ʿAlī b. Abī Bakr b. ʿAbd al-Jalīl al-Marghīnānī, *al-Hidāya fī sharḥ Bidāyat al-mubtadī*, ed. Ṭalāl Yūsuf, 4 vols. (Beirut: Dār Iḥyā' al-Turāth al-ʿArabī, 2010), 4: 546). For Shiʿi legal discussions, see Jaʿfar Kāshif al-Ghiṭā', *Kashf al-ghiṭā'ʿan mubhamāt al-sharīʿa al-gharrā'*, 4 vols. (Mashhad: Maktab al-Iʿlām al-Islāmī, 1380sh), 1: 233–4; Muḥammad Jawād al-Ḥusaynī al-ʿĀmilī, *Miftāḥ al-karāma fī sharḥ Qawāʿid al-ʿAllāma*, 11 vols. (Beirut: Dār Iḥyā' al-Turāth al-ʿArabī, n.d.), 1: 113 and 3: 139; Muḥammad Ḥasan al-Najafī, *Jawāhir al-kalām fī sharḥ Sharāʾiʿ al-islām*, ed. ʿAbbās al-Qūchānī, 43 vols. (Beirut: Dār Iḥyā' al-Turāth al-ʿArabī,1981), 2: 6 and 3: 8; Murtaḍā b. Muḥammad Amīn al-Anṣārī, *Kitāb al-ṭahāra*, 5 vols. (Qum: Majmaʿ al-Fikr al-Islāmī, 1415), 3: 326; Mīr ʿAbd al-Fattāḥ al-Ḥusaynī al-Marāghī, *al-ʿAnāwīn al-fiqhiyya*, 2 vols. (Qum: Muʾassasat al-Nashr al-Islāmī, 1417), 1: 38; Sayyid Kāẓim al-Yazdī, *Ḥāshiyat Farāʾid al-uṣūl*, compiled by Muḥammad Ibrāhīm al-Yazdī, 3 vols. (Qum: Dār al-Hudā, 1426), 1: 225. The term *mamsūḥ* signifies "effaced," "rubbed up," and "smoothed." People who have no genitalia are called *mamsūḥ* because it was thought that due to the lack of genitals, the inner sides of their thighs would rub against each other and become smooth (Ibn Manẓūr, *Lisān al-ʿarab*, 2: 593–5). ʿAbd al-ʿAzīz Ibn al-Barrāj, *al-Muhadhdhab*, 2 vols. (Qum: Muʾassasat al-Nashr al-Islāmī, 1406), 2: 171–2. For further debates on classical Islamic legal tradition, see chapters seven and eight of this volume.

[17] Ibn Manẓūr, *Lisān al-ʿarab*, 2: 145.

[18] Ibid., 2:145

[19] Ibn Durayd, *Jamharat al-lugha*, 1: 418.

[20] Al-Azharī, *Tahdhīb al-lugha*, 7: 145.

[21] Al-Jāḥiẓ, *al-Rasāʾil al-siyāsiyya* (Beirut: Dār wa-Maktabat al-Hilāl, n.d.), 48, 487.

[22] Ibid., 488–9.

[23] The translation of Qur'anic verses is by Nasr, S. H., et al., *The Study Quran: A New Translation and Commentary* (New York: HarperOne, 2015).

[24] Al-Iṣfahānī, *Kitāb al-aghānī*, 11: 104–6.

[25] Mariame Najem, Laila Nassiri, and Jamal Ibijbijen, "Vernacular Names of Plants Between Diversity and Potential Risks of Confusion: Case of Toxic Plants Used in Medication in the Central Middle Atlas, Morocco," *Journal of Pharmacology and Pharmacognosy Research* 9, no. 2 (2021): 222–50, at 230.

[26] Quoted in Jamāl al-Dīn Abū Manẓūr, *Kitāb mukhtaṣar tārīkh Dimashq li-Ibn ʿAsākir*, ed. Rūḥiya al-Naḥḥās, Riyāḍ ʿAbd al-Ḥamīd Murād, Muḥammad Maṭīʿ (Damascus: Dār al-Fikr li-l-Ṭibāʿa wa-l-Tawzīʿ wa-l-Nashr, 1984), 28: 235.

[27] Aḥmad b. ʿAlī b. ʿAbd al-Qādir al-Maqrīzī, *al-Sulūk li-maʿrifat duwal al-mulūk*. ed. Muḥammad ʿAbd al-Qādir ʿAṭṭā, 8 vols. (Beirut: Dār al-Kutub al-ʿIlmiyyah, 1418/1997), 4: 182.

[28] Ibid

[29] Ibid

[30] Ibid., 4: 182–3.

[31] Ibid., 4: 183.

[32] Ibid

[33] Ibid., 4: 373.

[34] Ibid., 4: 297.

[35] Aḥmad ibn al-Ḥimṣī, *Ḥawādith al-zamān wa-wafayāt al-shuyūkh wa-l-aqrān* (Beirut: al-Maktaba al-ʿAṣriyya, 1999), 3: 99.

[36] Khaled El-Rouayheb, *Before Homosexuality in the Arab-Islamic World, 1500–1800* (Chicago: University of Chicago Press, 2005), 95–110.

[37] Shams al-Dīn Muḥammad ibn Ṭūlūn, *Mufākahat al-khillān fī ḥawādith al-zamān, tārīkh Miṣr wa-l-Shām*, ed. Muḥammad Muṣṭafā. 2 vols. (Cairo: al-Muʾassassa al-Miṣriyya al-ʿĀmma li-l-Taʾlīf wa-l-Tarjama, 1962–1964), 1: 297–98.

[38] Ibn Ṭūlūn, *Mufākahat al-khillān*, 1: 297–8.

[39] Najm al-Dīn Muḥammad b. Muḥammad al-Ghazzī, *al-Kawākib al-sāʾira bi-aʿyān al-miʾa al-ʿāshira*, ed. Ibrāhīm Sulaymān Yabbūr (Beirut: Dār al-Āfāq al-Jadīda, 1979), 1: 51.

[40] El-Rouayheb, *Before Homosexuality*, 83.

[41] All quotations are from Muḥammad Amīn b. Faḍl Allāh al-Muḥibbī, *Tārīkh khulāṣat al-athar fī aʿyān al-qarn al-ḥādī ʿashar* (Cairo: al-Maṭbaʿa al-Wahbiyya, 1867/8), 3: 315–6. Some words are obscured as if printed from old plates. Also, see two other editions: Muḥammad Amīn b. Faḍl Allāh al-Muḥibbī, *Khulāṣat al-athar fī tarājim ahl al-qarn al-ḥādī ʿashar* (Cairo: al-Maṭbaʿa al-Wahbiyya,1284/1867), 3: 315–6, which has the same text but somewhat clearer print than the 1867 edition; Muḥammad Amīn b. Faḍl Allāh b. Muḥibb al-Dīn b. Muḥammad al-Muḥibbī, *Khulāṣat al-athar fī aʿyān al-qarn al-ḥādī ʿashar* (Beirut: Dār al-Ṣādir, 1990), 3: 315–6, which has much clearer text and is available online and searchable. This particular anecdote is on 3: 316.

[42] Al-Muḥibbī, *Tārīkh khulāṣat al-athar*, 3: 315–6.

[43] Ibid., 3: 316.

[44] Ibid.

Bibliography

Abū Manẓūr, Jamāl al-Dīn. *Kitāb mukhtaṣar tārīkh Dimashq li-Ibn ʿAsākir*. edited by Rūḥiya al-Naḥḥās, Riyāḍ ʿAbd al-Ḥamīd Murād, Muḥammad Maṭīʿ. Damascus: Dār al-Fikr li-l-Ṭibāʿa wa-l-Tawzīʿ wa-l-Nashr, 1984.

Abū ʿUbayd al-Qāsim b. Sallām. *Gharīb al-ḥadīth*. edited by Muḥammad ʿAbd al-Muʿīd-Khān, 4 vols. Ḥaydarābād: Dāʾirat al-Maʿārif al-ʿUthmāniyya, 1384/1964.

Alipour, Mehrdad. *Negotiating Homosexuality in Islam: A Legal-Hermeneutical Examination of Modern Shiʿī Discourse*. Leiden: Brill, 2024.

Al-ʿĀmilī al-Ḥusaynī, Muḥammad Jawād. *Miftāḥ al-karāma fī sharḥ Qawāʿid al-ʿAllāma*. 11 vols. Beirut: Dār Iḥyāʾ al-Turāth al-ʿArabī, n.d.

Al-Anṣārī, Murtaḍā b. Muḥammad Amīn. *Kitāb al-ṭahāra*. 5 vols. Qum: Majmaʿ al-Fikr al-Islāmī, 1415.

Al-Azdī, Muḥammad b. al-Ḥasan b. Durayd. *Jamharat al-lugha*. edited by Ramzī Munīr Baʿlbakī. 3 vols. Beirut: Dār al-ʿIlm li-l-Malāyīn, 1987.

Al-Azharī, Muḥammad b. Aḥmad. *Tahdhīb al-lugha*. 15 vols. Beirut: Dār Iḥyāʾ al-Turāth al-ʿArabī, 2001.

El-Rouayheb, Khaled. *Before Homosexuality in the Arab-Islamic World, 1500–1800*. Chicago: University of Chicago Press, 2005.

Al-Farāhīdī, Abū ʿAbd al-Raḥmān al-Khalīl b. Aḥmad. *Kitāb al-ʿayn*. edited by Mahdī al-Makhzūmī and Ibrāhīm al-Sāmarrāʾī. 8 vols. Baghdad: Dār al-Rashād, 1980.

Al-Fayyūmī, Aḥmad b. Muḥammad b. ʿAlī. *al-Miṣbāḥ al-munīr fī gharīb al-sharḥ al-kabīr*. 2 vols. Beirut: al-Maktaba al-ʿIlmiyya, 1994.

al-Ghazzī, Najm al-Dīn Muḥammad b. Muḥammad, *al-Kawākib al-sāʾira bi-aʿyān al-miʾa al-ʿāshira*. edited by Ibrāhīm Sulaymān Yabbūr. Beirut: Dār al-Āfāq al-Jadīda, 1979.

Ibn al-Barrāj, ʿAbd al-ʿAzīz. *al-Muhadhdhab*. 2 vols. Qum: Muʾassasat al-Nashr al-Islāmī, 1406.

Ibn al-Ḥimṣī, Aḥmad. *Ḥawādith al-zamān wa-wafayāt al-shuyūkh wa-l-aqrān*. Beirut: al-Maktaba al-ʿAṣriyya, 1999.

Ibn Manẓūr, Muḥammad b. Mukarram. *Lisān al-ʿarab*. 15 vols. Beirut: Dār Ṣādir li-l-Ṭibāʿa wa-l-Nashr, 1414.

Ibn Sīnā. *Al-Qānūn fī l-ṭibb*. 4 vols. Beirut: Dār Iḥyāʾ al-Turāth al-ʿArabī, 2005.

Ibn Ṭūlūn, Shams al-Dīn Muḥammad. *Mufākahat al-khillān fī ḥawādith al-zamān, tārīkh Miṣr wa-l-Shām*. edited by Muḥammad Muṣṭafā. 2 vols. Cairo: al-Muʾassassa al-Miṣriyya al-ʿĀmma li-l-Taʾlīf wa-l-Tarjama, 1962-1964.

Al-Iṣfahānī, Abū l-Faraj ʿAlī b. al-Ḥusayn. *al-Aghānī*. 25 vols. Beirut: Dār Iḥyāʾ al-Turāth al-ʿArabī, 1415/1994.

Al-Jāḥiẓ. *al-Rasāʾil al-siyāsiyya*. Beirut: Dār wa-Maktabat al-Hilāl, n.d. https://shamela.ws/book/10709

Al-Jawharī, Abū Naṣr Ismāʿīl. *al-Ṣiḥāḥ tāj al-lugha wa-ṣiḥāḥ al-ʿarabiyya*. edited by Aḥmad ʿAbd al-Ghafūr ʿAttār. 6 vols. Beirut: Dār al-ʿIlm li-l-Malāyin, 1407/1986–7.

Kāshif al-Ghiṭāʾ, Jaʿfar. *Kashf al-Ghiṭāʾʿan mubhamāt al-sharīʿa al-gharrāʾ*. 4 vols. Mashhad: Maktab al-Iʿlām al-Islāmī, 1380sh.

Al-Maqrīzī, Aḥmad b. ʿAlī b. ʿAbd al-Qādir. *al-Sulūk li-maʿrifat duwal al-mulūk*. edited by Muḥammad ʿAbd al-Qādir ʿAṭṭā. 8 vols., Beirut: Dar al-Kutub al-ʿIlmiyyah, 1418/1997.

Al-Marāghī, Mīr ʿAbd al-Fattāḥ al-Ḥusaynī. *al-ʿAnāwīn al-fiqhiyya*. 2 vols. Qum: Muʾassasat al-Nashr al-Islāmī, 1417h.

Al-Marghīnānī, ʿAlī b. Abī Bakr b. ʿAbd al-Jalīl. *al-Hidāya fī sharḥ Bidāyat al-mubtadī*. edited by Ṭalāl Yūsuf. 4 vols. Beirut: Dār Iḥyāʾ al-Turāth al-ʿArabī, 2010.

Al-Māwardī al-Baṣrī, Abū l-Ḥasan ʿAlī b. Muḥammad. *al-Ḥāwī l-kabīr fī fiqh madhhab al-imām al-Shāfiʿī.* 18 vols. Beirut: Dār al-Kutub al-ʿIlmiyya, 1419/1999.

Al-Muḥibbī, Muḥammad Amīn b. Faḍl Allāh b. Muḥibb al-Dīn b. Muḥammad, *Khulāṣat al-athar fī aʿyān al-qarn al-ḥādī ʿashar*. 4 vols. Cairo: Dār al-Ṣādir, 1111h.

Al-Muḥibbī, Muḥammad Amīn b. Faḍl Allah. *Khulāṣat al-athar fī tarājim ahl al-qarn al-hādī 'ashar*. Cairo: al-Maṭbaʿa al-Wahbiyya,1284/1867.

Al-Muḥibbī, Muḥammad Amīn b. Faḍl Allāh b. Muḥibb al-Dīn b. Muḥammad, *Khulāṣat al-athar fī aʿyān al-qarn al-ḥādī ʿashar*. 4 vols. Beirut: Dār al-Ṣādir, 1990.

Al-Najafī, Muḥammad Ḥasan. *Jawāhir al-kalām fī sharḥ Sharāʾiʿ al-islām*. edited by ʿAbbās al-Qūchānī. 43 vols. Beirut: Dār Iḥyāʾ al-Turāth al-ʿArabī, 1981.

Najem, Mariame, Laila Nassiri, and Jamal Ibijbijen. "Vernacular Names of Plants Between Diversity and Potential Risks of Confusion: Case of Toxic Plants Used in Medication in the Central Middle Atlas, Morocco." *Journal of Pharmacology and Pharmacognosy Research* 9, no. 2 (2021): 222–50.

Nasr, S. H., et al. *The Study Quran: A New Translation and Commentary.* San Francisco: HarperOne, 2015.

Al-Nawawī, Yaḥyā b. Sharaf. *al-Majmūʿ Sharḥ al-Muhadhdhab*. 20 vols. Beirut: Dār al-Fikr, 1990.

Al-Qudūrī al-Ḥanafī al-Baghdādī, Abū l-Ḥusayn Aḥmad b. Muḥammad. *Mukhtaṣar al-Qudūrī fī l-fiqh al-Ḥanafī*. edited by Muḥammad Muḥammad ʿAwīḍa. Beirut: Dār al-Kutub al-ʿIlmiyya, 1418/1997.

Al-Rāzī, Muḥammad b. Zakariyyā. *al-Ḥāwī fī l-ṭibb*. 7 vols., Beirut: Dār Iḥyāʾ al-Turāth al-ʿArabī, 1422/2002.

Rowson, Everett K., "The Effeminates of Early Medina." *Journal of the American Oriental Society* 111, no. 4 (1991): 671–93.

Al-Sarakhsī, Muḥammad b. Aḥmad. *al-Mabsūṭ*. 30 vols. Dār al-Maʿrifa, 1414/1993.

Al-Sughdī, Abū al-Ḥusayn ʿAlī b. al-Ḥusayn b. Muḥammad. *al-Nutaf fī l-fatāwā*. edited by Ṣalāḥ al-Dīn al-Nāhī, 2 vols. Amman: Dār al-Furqān/Beirut: Muʾassasat al-Risāla, 1404/1984.

Al-Thaʿlabī al-Baghdādī, Abū Muḥammad ʿAbd al-Wahhāb b. ʿAlī. *al-Maʿūna ʿalā madhhab ʿālim al-madīna "al-Imām Mālik b. Anas."* edited by Ḥamīsh ʿAbd al-Ḥaqq. 3 vols. Makka: al-Maktaba al-Tijāriyya, 1995.

Al-Yazdī, Sayyid Kāẓim. *Ḥāshiyat Farāʾid al-uṣūl*. Compiled by Muḥammad Ibrāhīm al-Yazdī. 3 vols. Qum: Dār al-Hudā, 1426.

Al-Zahrāwī [Albucasis], Abū l-Qāsim. *Kitāb al-taṣrīf li-man ʿajaza ʿan al-taʾlīf: al-maqāla al-thalāthūn: al-Jarāḥa*. Riyadh: Maktabat al-Malik Fahd al-Waṭaniyya, 1422/2001.

Al-Zabīdī, Muḥammad Murtaḍā. *Tāj al-ʿarūs min jawāhir al-Qāmūs*. edited by ʿAbd al-ʿAzīz Maṭar. 40 vols. Kuwait: Maṭbaʿat Ḥukūmat al-Kuwait, 1414/1994.

CHAPTER THREE

Intersex and Effeminate Characters (*khunthā* and *mukhannath*) in Classical Persian Poetry[1]

Ali-Asghar Seyed-Gohrab

Abstract

Gender norms are discussed in classical Persian poetry in various literary genres and poetic forms such as *ghazal* ("love lyric"), *qaṣīda* ("panegyric") and *mathnavī* ("rhyming-couplets"). Whereas medieval Persian romances depict love relationships between male and female characters, emphasizing the protagonists' masculine and feminine traits, in other genres gender norms are more diffuse. As a rule, the *ghazal* depicts the beloved as a young man, evoking various aspects of homoerotic love. The prelude (*nasīb*, *tashbīb*) to many Persian panegyrics, likewise, is mostly homoerotic, usually showing the devotion of a male courtly poet to a king, a vizier, a political notable, etc. In addition, Persian poetry also introduces other gender categories, which allude to two social groups: effeminate males (*mukhannath*) and intersex individuals (*khunthā*). The homoerotic dimensions of Persian poetry create a sharp contrast to Islamic law. In a prodigious number of poems, their poets depict various dimensions of the homoerotic relationship without any apparent fear of or worry about religious injunctions and severe punishments. In this chapter, I shall focus on particularly the intersex references, discussing how these stock characters are depicted in the works of several Persian poets such as Sanā'ī, ʿAṭṭār and Rūmī.

Keywords: antinomianism; Islamic spirituality; *khunthā* and *mukhannath*, Farīd al-Dīn ʿAṭṭār; Jalāl al-Dīn Rūmī

Introduction

This chapter examines two distinct social categories in the medieval Persian-speaking world: *mukhannath* or "effeminate males," and *khunthā* or "intersex." These categories were clearly differentiated by society, which is crucial for understanding their roles. While much scholarly attention has been given to effeminate males, especially in the context of Persian amatory poetry, the distinction between these two social categories has often been overlooked. Furthermore, the term "effeminate males" is often used in a broad, uncritical way, sometimes associated with the category of male passivity. Before starting my analysis of these two categories, I will provide a brief overview of gender and sexuality in medieval Persia, a topic that certainly begs for systematic investigation. Gender relations in this period are frequently depicted in homoerotic contexts, which were an important aspect of Persian medieval culture and a significant part of people's gender identities. One central source for the study of the history of sexuality is Persian poetry which is uniquely rich in the way it depicts the amatory and professional relationships between courtiers.

From the outset of this poetic tradition, we see that homoeroticism is treated abundantly, especially as a courtly tradition. Persian courtly poetry is brimming with love stories between courtiers and soldiers, rulers and ministers, masters and enslaved people. As a rule, the ideal beloved in early Persian panegyric poetry (10th to 12th centuries) is an enslaved soldier who was ransomed from a region such as China, Central Asia or India.[2] The allusions to these ethnic identities in Persian love poetry reveal how such individuals, who usually appear as literary archetype and not recognizable individuals, were treated. These people, who were usually very young, were brought to Persia, and after training for a few years, they would work at different divisions of the court, from horsemanship to serving as pleasant companions at festivities, often functioning as servers of wine, playing music and singing.[3] Such a beloved was a page, who was also expected to be a mighty soldier on the battlefield. In other words, this beloved was equipped with the attributes of both masculinity and femininity, depending on the social context in which he appeared. During the wars he was a fearless soldier, whereas during festivities he was an agreeable companion, speaking eloquently, pouring wine and singing poetry. Several traits of the beloved in this early Persian love poetry became the basis of the Persian *ghazal* ("lyrical love poetry") of later centuries, in which the beloved is usually a male individual, in which references are made to beard growth, and the beloved is called a boy (*pisar* or *pūr*).[4] Depictions of such a beloved abound in Persian court poetry. One excellent example is Amīr Muʿizzī's (d. about 519/1125) panegyric (*qaṣīda*) of 39 couplets, composed for the Saljuq ruler Malikshāh (r. 465–85/1072–92), in which the poet elaborates on the qualities of the beloved. I quote only a few couplets:

این شوخ سواران که دل خلق ستانند
گویی ز که زادند و بخوبی به که مانند
ترکند به اصل اندرو شک نیست ولیکن
از خوبی و زیبایی خورشید زمانند
میران سپاهند و عروسان وثاقند
گردان جهانند و هژبران دمانند
مشکین خط و شیرین سخن و غالیه زلفند
سیمین بر و زرین‌کمر و موی میانند
شیرند به زور و به هنر گرچه غزالند
پیرند به عقل و به خرد گرچه جوانند
(...)

چون راحت روحند چو با ساغر راحند
چون حِصن حَصینند چو بر پشت حِصانند
(...)
مانند تذروند چو با جام شرابند
مانند هژبرند چو با تیغ و سِنانند
(...)
شیرند به بیشه در چون تیغ‌گذارند
ماهند به‌گردون بر چون اسب دوانند
(...)
در رزم به جز تیغ زدن رای نبینند
در بزم به جز دل سِتَدَن کار ندانند
(...)
هرگاه کز ایشان صنمی بینم با خویش
گویم خُنک آنراکه چنین نوش لبانند[5]

These spirited riders who seize people's hearts,
You would say, who has given birth to them? Whose beauty they have inherited?
They are Turks in origin, no doubt about it but
They are the sun of the world due to their beauty and loveliness
They are the army commanders, the brides of promise
They are the world champions, the lions of power
Their words are sweet, their locks curled, their down musky;
their breasts bright silver, their girdle of gold, their waist slender
they are lions in strength, although in virtue like a gazelle
they look old and wise in reasoning, although they are young
...
they are the peace of the heart, as they carry the goblets
they are an inaccessible fortress, as they ride on the camel's back.
...
when serving wine, they walk like a partridge;
when they are with swords and lances, they resemble lions.
...
They are lions in the thicket when they draw their blades
They are moons in the sky when they gallop on their horses
...
In battle, no thinking except striking the swords
In feast, no thoughts except seizing the hearts
...
Whenever I see any of such idols, I say
to myself: 'Happy is he who owns such lovely lips!'

Such depictions set out the ideal traits of a beloved for a Persian ruler. This panegyric ode is dedicated to Malikshāh, apparently showing that his retinue and army consisted of such idealized individuals. Also, the notion of love is often idealized. Love as depicted in this courtly poetry is commonly the profane erotic infatuation of a courtly figure in a high position who has fallen for an enslaved soldier, cupbearer or musician. The relationship is far from equal. The courtier is usually the active partner, often the owner of the person, whereas the soldier, the enslaved beloved, is the passive partner.[6] It often happened that one enslaved person would desire another master and vice versa, a situation that would usually lead to conflicts, which were ideally avoided.

The homoeroticism in medieval Persian culture does not limit itself to the realm of poetry. In the genre of "mirror for princes" (*Fürstenspiegel*), which imparts pieces of advice to princes, preparing them for proper conduct in their future function as a king, homoerotic relations are discussed. One well-known mirror for princes is *Qābūs-nāma* by ʿUnṣur al-Maʿālī Key-Kāvūs (b.ca. 412/1021-date of death unknown), a prince of the Caspian Sea area (Ṭabaristān), who wrote this book for his son Gīlānshāh.[7] The author approves of homoerotic love relationships, delineating the best ways to deal with loving emotions in a courtly context. In one instance he states, "From the slaves and women do not withhold your desire from one sex so that you enjoy both sexes and that one sex does not become your enemy."[8] After expounding the theory of temperaments, Key-Kāvūs advises his son to share his bed with male slaves in summer and women in winter.[9]

Characters of *mukhannath* and *khunthā*

In addition to a plethora of examples of homoerotic relationships in classical Persian poetry, we also have specifical references to the stock characters of *mukhannath* and *khunthā*. In this chapter, I will pose the question how intersex (*khunthā*) and effeminate persons (*mukhannath*) are identified in classical Persian poetry.[10] I will examine whether these two are defined as two distinct gender identities or one, and why Persian poets introduce these gender identities to explain religious and ethical norms and behaviors. In addition, I shall briefly allude to the way in which the utilization of such gender identities shifts our understanding of homoeroticism in Persian poetry, a central theme in Persian literary tradition. The terms *mukhannath* and *khunthā* refer to distinct concepts related to gender and sexual identity.[11] The noun *mukhannath* derives from the Arabic root *kh-n-th*, the passive particle of the second (causative) "form," indicating literally to make someone or something into a *khunthā*. In Persian texts, *mukhannath* refers to an effeminate and *khunthā* to intersex persons. Poets refer to their behavior, words and manners which are sometimes associated with women. Outwardly they often distinguish themselves from men by wearing female clothing and behaving like women. They blur the male-female gender orientations. Occasionally, the term *mukhannath* is translated into English as a "pederast," which signifies sexual interest in young boys and the active role in intercourse, making it an incorrect translation. Although the translation of "pederast" might be correct in a specific context, it does not show how fluid sexual identity was.[12] The term *mukhannath* may also refer to intersex individuals in a specific context, but a distinction is sometimes made between the two sexual identities. In many cases, the *mukhannath*'s behavior is considered feminine and is associated with weakness and fickleness, and someone who easily allows himself to be sexually penetrated.

The other term that I shall treat in this chapter is *khunthā*, which is usually translated as "intersex," alluding to a person who possesses both male and female genitals and/or whose sexual traits do not fit typical binary distinctions of male and female bodies. To my knowledge, there is no study of this particular stock character in Persian poetry, who appears in the writings of several Persian poets, showing not only that poets were aware of their existence in society but that their biological characteristics were used as a metaphor to define specific religious and ethical concepts. For the treatment of *mukhannath*, I limit myself to a few instances in the works of the Persian mystical poet, Farīd al-Dīn ʿAṭṭār (d. 618/1221). As regards the term *khunthā*, I shall limit myself mainly to one example from Jalāl al-Dīn Rūmī (604–672 /1207–1273) while also making passing reference to a few other poets' use of this stock character.

Farīd al-Dīn ʿAṭṭār and effeminates (*mukhannasān*)

Mukhannaths appear several times in the writing of ʿAṭṭār to explicate a mystical and pious subject. In his masterpiece, *Tazkirat al-owliyā*, ("Memoirs of the Saints"), we come across one anecdote about the ascetic saint, Ḥasan of Baṣra (21–110/642–728). "It is reported that Ḥasan said: 'I was astonished by the speech of four people: a child, a drunk, an effeminate, and a woman.' People asked why? He replied: 'One day I was passing an effeminate and I pulled my robe round me to avoid touching him. The effeminate responded: 'Sir, our true condition (*ḥāl*) is not yet apparent. Do not pull your robe away from me, for only the Lord knows how things will turn out in the future.'"[13] In this particular anecdote, Ḥasan shows his outward piety by humiliating a *mukhannath* while the latter teaches him a moral lesson, indicating that God and nobody else is the judge of our condition, even if that other person is a great ascetic saint. Another anecdote about the *mukhannath* appears in the chapter on the first Islamic mystic, Rābiʿa al-ʿAdaviyya (d. about 185/801). Here a group of ascetics goes to Rābiʿa to tease her, boasting of their own manly achievements and belittling women's spiritual ranking. ʿAṭṭār's own words are:

> It is related that a group went to see Rābiʿa to put her to the test. They said, "All the virtues have been dispersed among men. The crown of nobility has been placed upon the heads of men, and the belt of magnanimity has been tied around their waists. Prophecy has never descended upon any woman. What do you have to boast of?" Rābiʿa said, "Everything you said is true. But egoism, egotism, self-worship, and *I am your highest lord* have not welled up in any woman. And no woman has ever been a *mukhannath*."[14]

Another anecdote is told in the chapter on Sarī al-Saqaṭī (772–867), an ascetic from Baghdad who was the maternal uncle of the great mystic, Junayd (d. 297/910).[15] Here Junayd says that one day he was walking with Sarī when they passed a group of effeminates. Junayd said, "It occurred to my heart: 'what would be the conditions of these people [in the hereafter]?' Sarī said, 'I have no excellence over any created being in the entire creation.' Junayd then said, 'even you do not think you have excellence over *mukhannathān*?' he said, 'no.'" The message of this anecdote is that no mystic, however elevated his spiritual position is, can claim to be better than a *mukhannath*. Also, in this anecdote we see that ʿAṭṭār commands his reader to treat everyone, including effeminate persons, fairly.

Another anecdote derives from another chapter of ʿAṭṭār's *Memoirs* on the ascetic, Abū ʿAlī Thaqafī (d. 194/810).[16] Here it is recounted that Abū ʿAlī sees people who are taking the corpse of a *mukhannath* to be buried and he joins them. It is a touching story:

> Abū ʿAlī recounts: I saw a corpse carried by three men and a woman and they were bringing it [to the cemetery]. I took the side that the woman had in her hand and joined them to the cemetery. We performed a prayer and buried him. I said to them, "Did not you have other neighbours to help you?" They answered: "we have, but they have contempt for him." I asked: "has this person done something [wrong]?" They said: "He was a *mukhannath*." I had compassion for this man. When I slept at night, I dreamed that someone came to me. His face was beautiful like the full moon, he was dressed in distinguishing apparel. He was constantly smiling. I said, "who are you?" I am the same *mukhannath* that you performed a burial prayer for, and that you entrusted to the grave. The Elevated God showed compassion for me about those matters over which people showed contempt.[17]

The character of *mukhannath* also appears in ʿAṭṭār's masterpiece, *Manṭiq al-ṭayr* ("The Conference of the Birds"). In this allegorical story, the birds of the world come together to search for their king, Sīmurgh. They choose the hoopoe as their guide and start the journey, but it is not long before many birds start to complain. Each adds another pretext for not continuing on the journey. In the end, only 30 birds (*sī murgh*) reach their destination at the end of the world on Mount Qāf. Here they realize that they themselves were the Sīmurgh and that the goal of the journey was them. In this narrative, the birds stand for mystic travelers, the hoopoe for the spiritual guide and Sīmurgh for the Soul.

During the narrative, the hoopoe tries to convince the birds to continue on the journey, but each bird comes to the hoopoe, complaining that it is not fit for such an arduous journey. One of these birds identifies itself as *mukhannath* ("effeminate"). The bird does not say that it has become effeminate but that it was born effeminate, emphasizing that its effeminacy is its essence (*gowhar*). The word *gowhar* also connotes "nature," and "constitution." ʿAṭṭār is not using the term *mukhannath* simply for someone who is associated with sexuality and offering sexual services, which was a common connotation in this period,[18] but as an intersex individual. The non-binary character of this *mukhannath* is emphasized, also when it concerns ethical and religious matters:

دیگری گفتش مخنث گوهرم
هر زمانی مرغ شاخ دیگرم
گاه رندم، گاه زاهد، گاه مست
گاه هست و نیست و گاهی نیست و هست
گاه نفسم در خرابات افکند
گاه جانم در مناجات افکند
من میان هر دو حیران مانده
چون کنم در چاه و زندان مانده[19]

Another bird said, "My essence is effeminate.
Each time I am the bird of another branch.
Sometimes I'm a libertine, at times an ascetic, and then a drunk;
Sometimes He exists, at times He exists not, and sometimes He exists not, but He exists.
Sometimes my baser self throws me into taverns.
Sometimes my soul throws me into supplicating prayers.
I am perplexed between the two;
What should I do? I am stuck in the pit and the prison."

The hoopoe's answer is most respectful, trying to convince the *mukhannath* that individuals have diverse forms and natures. The only thing that matters is God's obedience and piety:

گفت باری این بود در هر کسی
زانک مرد یک صفت نبود بسی
گر همه کس پاک بودی از نخست
انبیا را کی شدی بعثت درست
چون بود در طاعتت دلبستگی
با صلاح آیی به صد آهستگی
(...)
چون تو دایم نفس سگ را پروری
کم نه آید از مخنث گوهری[20]

The Hoopoe replied, "Sure this is in everybody,
Because a man does not have one set of qualities.
If everyone were pure from the start,
How could the prophets' mission be rightful?
As your heart is attached to worship,
You will come to righteousness, but slowly.
...
Since you continually foster the dog of the baser self,
it turns out no less than of an effeminate disposition.[21]

Through this answer, the hoopoe invites the *mukhannath* to join the journey. To corroborate this invitation, the next anecdote is also about the *mukhannaths*.

Here the poet tells the story of the great mystic Shiblī from Baghdad (247–334/861–945), who was lost for some time and no one knew where he was until people searched for him again and found him unexpectedly in a *mukhannath-khāna*, ("house of effeminates"). It is not easy to describe precisely what such houses were; they are sometimes defined as brothels.[22] Here the inhabitants of such houses are characterized as *bī-adab* or "without decorum," "impolite" and, by expansion, it may even connote sexual transgression. Shiblī is depicted with his eyes full of tears and dry lips. When a person asks him why he, as a "seeker of secrets," has come to such a place, Shiblī characterizes himself as a *mukhannath* and replies:

گفت این قومند چون تردامنی
در ره دنیا نه مرد و نه زنی
من چو ایشانم، ولی در راه دین

نه زنی در دین نه مردی چند ازین
گم شدم در ناجوانمردی خویش
شرم می‌دارم من از مردی خویش[23]

This folk, because they are sullied,
In the way of the world are neither a man nor a woman.
I am like them, but in the way of religion,
neither a woman in religion nor a man. What's the point of this?
I am lost in my own unmanliness;
Ashamed am I of this 'manliness' of mine.

At this point, the narrator intervenes and supports Shiblī's argument by stating that whoever is aware in his soul of the mysteries of the world are all outward signs. Then, the narrator adds that the people of the heart choose wisdom, which is characterized as seeing no difference between praise and blame, otherwise the person is busy with sham piety. In ʿAṭṭār's view, a person should serve God and divest him/herself (themselves) of any pretentions. At the end of the anecdote, ʿAṭṭār comes back to the term *mukhannath*. Here it becomes clear that Shiblī took refuge in the *mukhannath* house in order to emancipate himself and even to protect himself from any sign of reverence which would lead to self-praise and ultimately hypocrisy:

چون ترا صد بت بود در زیر دلق
چون نمایی خویش را صوفی به خلق
ای مخنث، جامهٔ مردان مدار
خویش را زین بیش سرگردان مدار[24]

Since you have a hundred idols under the dervish cloak,
How can you parade yourself as a Sufi in front of people?
O effeminate! Do not dress yourself in the men's clothes;
Keep yourself no more flitting between this and that.

Here, ʿAṭṭār is emphasizing that people dress themselves to cover their traits and qualities, which probably do not correspond with their moral and religious virtues. So donning a mystical frock like a Sufi to show one's piety and devotion to people means that the frock is actually covering a hundred vices, which are symbolized here by idols. In addition, a man's dress covers effeminate people, but they do not become men.

ʿAṭṭār is deploying an antinomian motif in this story. For his audience, a *mukhannath* house was a sign of scandal which, paradoxically, was used as a shield to protect one's piety. During ʿAṭṭār's time, blasphemy had become an integral part of Khurasanian Sufism, which helped a mystic (and the audience) to find out about his own shortcomings on the mystical path. A heretical and blasphemous experience offered a space for Islamic mystics to scrutinize their own beliefs and piety critically.[25] In several cases, these mystics find out that they are so much occupied with the outward injunctions of the Sharia that they have forgotten the inner dimensions of their belief, which is love of God and salvation through love. After recognizing their shortcomings in behavior, they usually return to their old identity.

The subject of gender offers ʿAṭṭār a space to introduce a new topic which transcends gender distinctions. ʿAṭṭār introduces the notion of manliness and why virility is essential for spiritual growth. It is in the house of effeminates that Shiblī ponders on his manliness, both in a mundane physical sense and in spiritual terms. Shiblī's anecdote also appears in a very brief form in ʿAṭṭār's *Memoir* in which this mystic emphasizes that he wishes to transcend gender identities, "as for me, this is my place, for these [effeminate] people are neither men nor women in this world; me too, I am neither a man nor a woman in religion, so this place is my place."[26] In addition, as Shiblī is usually regarded as the embodiment of spiritual manliness, ʿAṭṭār is also saying that true faith is little to do with gender. In the same way that a dress covers a man and reveals specific social and religious ranks and hierarchies in society, so a person's gender covers his/her qualities and identities. In ʿAṭṭār's view, these are all mundane predicates which a pious man should ignore. In this anecdote, ʿAṭṭār also alludes to the beard, which is commonly a symbol of piety, but here the beard is depicted as "a napkin on the path," an obvious criticism of outward piety. In this particular couplet, the poet states:

هرکه جان خویش را آگاه کرد
ریش خود دستارخوان راه کرد[27]

Whoever has made his soul (*jān*) aware
s/he has made his beard the napkin for banquets on the road.

The message of this anecdote is to transcend binary gender identities as male or female.[28] In fact, the crux of the anecdote is to avoid any praiseworthy or blameworthy predicates. If not transcending such predicates, the person will remain entrapped in people's praise or condemnation, forgetting the main task, which is devotion to the love of God. One of the qualities of manliness (*javānmardī*) is the ability to negate all the qualities that create manliness and to arrive at unmanliness, which should also be negated. Shiblī literally says that "I am lost in his own unmanliness." The following couplet corroborates this interpretation:

مدح و ذمت گر تفاوت می‌کند
بتگری باشی که او بت می‌کند

If praise and blame make any difference to you,
Watch out! You might be he who fashions idols.[29]

Through these anecdotes about a group of people in society, ʿAṭṭār wishes to teach his audience moderation and tolerance, removing the binary gender identification on the spiritual path. The poet is inviting people to behave differently towards *mukhannath* persons, reflecting on their own behavior instead of condemning others. When the great ascetics with high spiritual ranks such as Sarī al-Saqatī, Abū ʿAlī Thaqafī and Shiblī refrain from judging the *mukhannath*, the ordinary people should certainly learn from them and avoid any judgementalism. We may cautiously conclude that ʿAṭṭār is offering these people, who were treated differently in society, a place in Sufi spirituality. We should also be careful to avoid positive interpretation because ʿAṭṭār himself sees *mukhannath*s as inferior in society. In the introduction to his *Tazkira*, he praises the effects of his book on his audience. In his view, his book is the best in creation and it is a commentary on the Qurʾān and the Traditions. He says: "it is a book that turns *mukhannath*s into men, men into lions, lions into archetypal beings, archetypal beings into the essence of pain (*dard*). For whoever reads this book the way it is conditioned to be read, he will become of the kind of pain it was in the souls of God's friends, who were able to perform such deeds and such words from their hearts to the desert."[30]

Ḥakīm Sanāʾī's allusions to the *mukhannath*

Ḥakīm Sanāʾī (d. 525/1131) alludes to the figure of *mukhannath* several times to criticize the piety and steadfastness of the representatives of religion in society. In one anecdote, the poet introduces a descendant of the first Shiite and the fourth Caliph, ʿAlī, an Islamic jurist (*faqīh*), and a *mukhannath*. The three men are fighting along the borders of Byzantium against the Christians when they are taken prisoner. The Christians, who are depicted as pagans in the story, arrest them and take them before an idol (a symbol for crucifix), giving them the choice of prostrating themselves or being burned alive. Hearing this, the prisoners deliberate on what to do. The *faqīh* says that he will prostrate himself before the idol and praise it as he will be saved in the Hereafter. ʿAlī's descendant (*ʿalavī*) says: "I also do because my noble descendants will intercede for me in the Hereafter on my behalf." The *mukhannath* says:

حیز گفتا به مرد دانشمند
که ز کار شما شدم خرسند
مر ترا علم تو دلیل بسست
علوی را پدر خلیل بسست
من که باشم مخنّث دو جهان
کز بد من شود جهان ویران
هرچه خواهید با تنم بکنید
گو بگیرید و گردنم بزنید
نیک و بد هست پیش من یکسان
نام نیکو گزیده‌ام ز جهان
سر فدی کرده‌ام پی دین را
چکنم جان و عار سجّین را
کُشته بهتر مرا به نام نکو
که بُوم زنده با هزار آهو
جان بداد و یکی سجود نکرد
بر درِ عار و شک قعود نکرد[31]

The catamite said to the learned man:
"I am glad of your decision.
As for you, your knowledge is enough for you;
As for the Shiite, his father as a friend is enough.
Who am I? The *mukhannath* of the two worlds.
Because of my bad actions, the world will be destroyed.
Do whatever you want with my body;
Say they can take me and sever my head.
Good and bad are the same to me;
I have chosen a good name from this world.
I offer my head for the pursuit of religion;
What should I do with this life, shamefully imprisoned?
It is better for me to be killed but have a good name,
Otherwise I have to live with a thousand sins.
He submitted his soul and did not prostrate himself;
He did not kneel at the door of shame and doubt.

In this story, Sanāʾī criticizes two powerful religious hierarchies of society: the jurists and the descendants of ʿAlī.[32] One is heir to religion through the Sharia laws and is the protector of those laws for the Muslim community, while the other is the descendant of the Caliph and the most holy saint of the Shiites. When danger comes, they both find a pretext to renounce their religion, while the *mukhannath*, who is commonly condemned in society, is the one who is the guardian of religion and offers his life to save the honor of Muslims.

The stock character, khunthā

This character appears in a wide range of genres in Persian literary tradition. One reference is made to it by the poet Masʿūd Saʿd-i Salmān in one of his ingeniously composed literary riddles. These riddles are often hard to guess as the poet does not indicate what he is describing. Also, modern editors of the collected poetry do not give any indication of the riddles' subject. Such riddles are a game between the poet and his connoisseur audience. The poet challenges them to guess what the object referred to is. In such riddles, the poem often starts with far-fetched metaphors and similes to misguide the audience and, the further one reads through it, the more clues to the answer are offered. If no one can answer the riddle, its whole purpose is lost, as the audience, who are courtly literary connoisseurs, is vexed. Having said this, there are Persian literary riddles that have puzzled the most seasoned scholars such as Edward G. Browne, the historian of Persian literature. Browne translated one of these riddles but admits that "[t]hese riddles are generally very obscure, and I regret to say that of the one here given I do not know the answer."[33] This musical instrument is played by both men and women. Masʿūd Saʿd-i Salmān does not define what type of musical instrument he is depicting, but it is interesting that he refers to the intersex person in couplet five. I have translated and analyzed the riddle elsewhere; here I give the translation of only the first ten couplets:[34]

ناجانور بدیع یکی شخص پر هنر
گه خامش است گاهی گویا چو جانور
ناجانور چراست هستش چهار طبع
ناکرده هیچ علت در طبع او اثر
ناله چرا کند چو به دل درش هیچ نیست
ور ناله می کند ز چه آرد همی بطر
افغان چگونه کرد تواند از آنکه هست
پیچیده در گلوگه او رشته سر به سر
خنثی اگر نبود ز بهر چرا بود
گه در کنار ماده و گه در کنار نر
از بهر چیست ویحک کوتاه قامتش
گر هست اصل و نسبتش از سرو غاتفر
فربیست او ز بهر چه معنی همی بود
رگهای او شده همه پیدا به پوست بر

رگهای او به ساعت گردد سریع نبض
گر دست بر رگانش تو برنهی ببر
چون گل به طبع و گردد ازو باغ چون بهار
چون نی به رنگ و آید ازو عیش چون شکر
پشتش چو خنچه خنچه و آن خنچه ها همه
دربسته همچو پهلوی مردم به یکدگر

1. A wondrous being, it has no soul, but is a person rich in talents:
Like an animate being, it is sometimes silent, sometimes eloquent.
2. No soul? How can it be, when it has the four humors?
No deficiency has marred its nature.
3. If it has no pain in its heart, why does it lament?
And if it does lament, why is it lost in amazement?
4. How is it able to lament, while cords
are twisted back and forth around its throat?
5. If it is not an intersex, why is it embraced
sometimes by the female, and sometimes by the male?
6. Well! Why is it so short of stature,
when it descends from the cypress from Ghātfar?[35]
7. It is fat, so what can it mean
that all its veins are showing through the skin?
8. If you put your hand upon those veins,
its pulse immediately increases.
9. By nature, it is like a rose, it turns the feast into a garden;
it has the color of the cane, pleasure flows from it like sugar.
10. Its back is like a spoon, or spoons bound together
side by side, like people lying front to back.[36]

Another allusion to *khunthā* appears in a panegyric (*qaṣīda*) by the poet Ḥakīm Sanāʾī in which he depicts his enemies, likening them to *khunthā*s and *mukhannath*s:

این ابلهان که بی‌سببی دشمن منند
بس بوالفضول و یافه‌درای و زنخ زنند
اندر مصاف مردی و در شرط شرع و دین
چون خنثی و مخنث نه مرد و نه زنند
مانند نقش رسمی بی‌اصل و معنیند
گر چه به نزد عامه و خطی مبینند
چون گور کافران ز درون پر عفونتند
گر چه برون به رنگ و نگاری مزینند

در قعر و دوزخند نه جنی نه انسیند
در چاه وحشتند نه یوسف نه بیژنند

These fools who are my enemies without reasons,
are so much inquisitive, prating babblers, braggarts,
In the battle to be a man and on the conditions of the Sharia and religion,
They are like *khunthā* and *mukhannath*; neither men nor women.
They are like drawn images without origin, without meaning.
Although they are evident to commoners and learned,
they are fully rotten inside, like unbeliever' graves.
Although they are adorned with colors and graphics outwardly,
they are in the depth of hell, they are neither jinn nor man.
They are in the pit of terror, they are neither Joseph nor Bijan.[37]

The value of Sanā'ī's allusion lies in his distinction between the *khunthā* and *mukhannath*, showing that these identities existed in society and that a poet would allude to them in his poetry when disparaging his adversaries. Needless to say, such allusions reiterate the patriarchal character of Persian society, in which such gender identities occupied a lower level in the hierarchy. Such a reference also raises the question of the nature of homoeroticism: although homoerotic love was the norm among the aristocracy, the *khunthā* and *mukhannath* were excluded from such sexual preferences. Apparently, a fully masculine identity was preferred over those of effeminate and intersex persons. This argument can be supported by references to beloveds who were soldiers, commanders and generals in the army.

Jalāl al-Dīn Rūmī and the intersex (*khunthā*)

I would like to finish this chapter with a story from Rūmī's *Spiritual Couplets* (*Mathnavī-yi ma'navī*). In book six, Rūmī compares an ignorant person to a *khunthā*. The context he creates in which to depict this individual is the avoidance of companionship with an untrustworthy person whom he identifies as a traitor, a two-faced person. This particular chapter is relatively long, amounting to 66 couplets, and it takes some 40 couplets before he comes to his treatment of the *khunthā*.[38] Rūmī's message to us is to associate with a good companion even if this companion might seem oppressive. Between the couplets Rūmī adds supplications to God such as "O Giver of understandings, come to my help!" (line 1444). Afterwards he refers to the concept of *jabr* which has a wide range of meanings, such as "compulsion, coercion; force, power, strength; predestination, and irreversible decree."[39] Nicholson translates *jabr* as "necessitarianism", and by this he wishes to explain that the same word has two contrasting implications but man must decide for himself the right implication of the word. Here Rūmī says, "necessitarianism is the wing and pinion of the perfect man; / necessitarianism is also the prison and chains of the slothful."[40]

Like many other anecdotes of the *Mathnavī*, this story has a homiletic application. The structure of the entire chapter is such as to enable Rūmī to give pieces of advice to his audience. The chapter starts with an anecdote about how the mighty Ghaznavid Sultan Maḥmūd takes an Indian boy as booty from India. Maḥmūd brings the boy to his court and places him near him on his throne. The boy cries continuously. When Maḥmūd asks him the reason for his weeping, the boy replies that his mother always made him scared of Sultan Maḥmūd. The boy's father used to intervene, quarrelling with the mother for her manipulative way of educating their son. The boy tells Maḥmūd that he was so confused and so scared of his parents, wondering why they always thought of Maḥmūd in terms of punishment, afflicting hellish pain and disaster. The boy emphasizes how scared he has always been of Maḥmūd. Any thought of Maḥmūd used to make him tremble in fear. The boy says that he is crying because he wishes his mother were present at court to see the elevated position Maḥmūd conferred upon her son.

In the immediate couplets, Rūmī explains that all the characters in this story are allegorical, and he elaborates on their symbolism. Maḥmūd stands for spiritual poverty and man's nature (*ṭabʿ*), making people afraid of living in poverty. But as one comes to know the mercifulness of the noble Maḥmūd, one will praise him. The boy's mother represents nature. Rūmī equates the mother a few lines later with the "baser self" (*nafs*), advising the reader not to listen to this "misguided nature" (*ṭabʿ-i mużil*). Here we see a clear misogyny, unfortunately typical of many medieval authors. The father stands for the noble intellect (*ʿaql-i rād*). Rūmī adds, "When you become a prey to poverty, you will certainly shed tears (of delight), like the Hindú boy, on the Day of Judgement."[41] After this couplet, Rūmī compares the boy to a mother who fosters the spirit, but this mother is "more inimical to you than a hundred enemies." In the next lines, Rūmī criticizes the body, which is an impediment to the emancipation of the soul. The care of the body occupies man. If the body falls ill, it makes man seek medicine, and if it grows strong, it makes man seek the devil. The body is full of sins. Rūmī compares it to a coat of mail, serving for neither winter nor summer. Rūmī says that the body is a bad associate (*yār-i bad*), which is paradoxically good because it teaches man how to be patient and how, in fortitude, one must overcome worldly desires. Rūmī surmises that the exercise of patience expands the heart (*ki gushāyad ṣabr ṣadr rā*).[42] At this point, Rūmī elaborates on the virtues of patience and then connects it to the theme of *khū*, "habit," and "nature," which is in turn connected to association with good company and avoiding ignorant people.

Rūmī deploys this story to demonstrate the damage an ignorant (*jāhil*) person, who is identified as being an intersex, can inflict upon people. Rūmī admonishes his audience to turn to God who has allotted nature and behavior to each created being. An ignorant person, however sweet his words might be, will at some point injure people and, therefore, man should avoid any association with him.

In the first lines of the following excerpt, Rūmī advises his reader to avoid giving one's trust (*amānat*) to a traitor (*khā'in*). The contrast is not between two types of individuals but more between God as the friend and human beings. In a few lines, Rūmī emphasizes that one should consort with Him who created human nature (*khū*) and the constitutions of the prophets. According to Rūmī, if a person gives a lamb to God, he will receive a whole flock. Having said this, Rūmī wonders why a person should then give trust (*amānat*) to a wolfish person. Even if a wolf appears to change its behavior by playing some fox-like tricks, it wants to fool others for its own benefit. Rūmī connects the metaphor of a wolf behaving like a fox to an ignorant person, a churl (*jāhil*), who, due to his churlishness, will hurt people. The way Rūmī depicts this person is as if this churl cannot act otherwise and that his actions are based on his innate nature. Rūmī introduces the churl as a *khunthā* ("intersex"), who in Rūmī's view possesses both male and female genitals. It is interesting to note here that the English translator, Reynold A. Nicholson, has decided to translate the description of the genitalia into Latin, a language less accessible for the general English public. Rūmī says:

تا که خود را خواهر ایشان کند   او ذکر را از زنان پنهان کند
تا که خود را جنس آن مردان کند   شله از مردان به کف پنهان کند
شله‌ای سازیم بر خرطوم او   گفت یزدان زان کس مکتوم او
در نیایند از فن او در جوال   تا که بینایان ما زان ذو دلال
هین ز جاهل ترس اگر دانش‌وری   حاصل آنک از هر ذکر ناید نری
کم شنو کان هست چون سم کهن   دوستی جاهل شیرین‌سخن

He will hide the penis from women
in order to make himself their sister.
She covers her vulva with her hand so that men may not see it
in order to make herself the same genus as men.
God said, "We will make from his hidden cunt
a vulva on his nose,
In order that Our seers may not be entrapped
by the artfulness of that ogler."[43]
The gist of the matter is that not every penis can show virility
beware of the ignorant man if you practice wisdom.
Do not listen to the sweet words of the friendship of an ignorant man,
for it is like virulent poison.

Apart from alluding to the genitals of this intersex character, whom Rūmī associates with an ignorant person, the allusion to "making from his hidden cunt a vulva on his nose" is unclear. It is probably a reference to the Sura Qalam ("Pen") of the Qur'ān (68:16) in which God says, "Anon We shall brand him on snout."[44] One meaning of Rūmī's verse is that their character will be visible on their faces. In medieval times, people believed that physical form revealed psychological traits and the personality of an individual. This was a field known as the "Science of Physiognomy" (*'ilm-i firāsat*), prominently present in Islamic intellectual tradition.[45] In Rūmī's example, there is an incongruity between physical appearance and mental qualities. Rūmī says that "not every penis can show virility," warning the reader that outward appearance could belie inward values.

Conclusion

This chapter started with the question of how the stock characters of *khunthā* and *mukhannath* are identified in classical Persian poetry and whether these two characters, which are usually taken as one category, are two distinct gender identities. As we have seen, Persian poets evidently distinguish between an effeminate (*mukhannath*) and an intersex (*khunthā*) person. While the former is sometimes associated with brothels and scandalous places, their manners and values form a reversed set of norms that teach the audience specific lessons. In the story of Shiblī, recounted by ʿAṭṭār, we see the emphasis on the complex concept of *javānmardī* and how, by hiding himself in the house of the *mukhannath*s, this reverent mystic sheykh critically scrutinizes his own personality as a *javānmard*, a fearless, chivalrous, altruistic traveler on the path of love. The story also teaches the audience that transcending gender norms (femininity and masculinity) is a prerequisite to spiritual growth. A true traveler is advised to divest himself of the outward, whether it is the dress or the body. Through such stories, ʿAṭṭār teaches his audience to avoid judging people and to leave this to the Creator.

Another conclusion to be drawn from this brief analysis is that Persian poets refer to *mukhannath* in pejorative terms, often as a prostitute.[46] For many poets, homoerotic sexuality required two males with masculine behavior rather than a man with a feminine manner.[47] As soon as a man exhibited a feminine character, he was stigmatized as a *mukhannath*. In the early Persian court poetry in which homoeroticism is the rule, the sexual partners are commonly courtly individuals who are active sexual partners. Passive sexual partners were also generally expected to exhibit masculine behavior, often being praised for their courage, gallantry and manliness on the battlefield.

The appearance of the intersex person in Rūmī's *Spiritual Couplet* is a mere metaphor for condemning the duality of worldly existence, which is based on the relationship between body and soul. The genitals of an intersex person apparently inspired Rūmī to blame them for duplicity. The intersex character in Rūmī's anecdote, like the other characters, is a mere metaphor, helping the audience to understand how to tread the path and how to travel to the spiritual goal, i.e., the annihilation of body and union of the soul with God. Having said this, it remains extremely uncomfortably misogynistic to represent the mother in this story as the "baser self" and the father as the "noble reason." Reading such medieval texts, we should be very much aware that these medieval poets and intellectuals possessed a completely different worldview from ours. Rūmī's use of the mother and the father as metaphors refers to the widespread notions of *abā-yi ʿulvā*), the "elevated fathers" or the nine heavens, and *ummahāt-i suflā*, the "lower mothers," or *ummahāt-i arbaʿa*, the four elements (water, fire, wind and earth), that foster creativity and growth.[48]

Notes

1 This chapter is part of the ERC-Advanced Grant project entitled *Beyond Sharia: The Role of Sufism in Shaping Islam*, which has received funding from the European Research Council (ERC) under the European Union's Horizon 2020 research and innovation programme (Grant agreement No. 101020403). I would like to thank Mehrdad Alipour and Indira Falk Gesink for their constructive comments and suggestions.

2 It should also be mentioned that certain ethnic denominations received specific connotation. As Zipoli states, the term "Ghur, a region in Afghanistan, was considered to be a land of infidels. Moreover, *ghur* also means a depraved, effeminate man, thus alluding to a possible offence which creates an even more disparaging picture." See Zipoli, *Irreverent Persia: Invective, Satirical and Burlesque Poetry from the Origins to the Timurid Period (10th to 15th Centuries)*, Leiden: Leiden University Press, 2015, 198, footnote 132.

3 J.T.P. de Bruijn, *Encyclopœdia Iranica*, s.v. Beloved; E. Yarshater, "The Theme of Wine-Drinking and the Concept of the Beloved in Early Persian Poetry," *Studia Islamica* 13, (1960), 43–53; Seyed-Gohrab, *Laylī and Majnūn: Love, Madness and Mystic Longing in Niẓāmī's Epic Romance* (Leiden / Boston: Brill, 2003), 219–24; idem, "Sufi Treatment of Same-Sex Poetry and Prose," in *Global Encyclopedia of Gay, Lesbian, Bisexual, Transgender, and Queer History*, ed. Howard Chiang, Charles Scribner's Sons, 2019, 1556–1562; EIr, in *Encyclopœdia Iranica*, s.v. "Homosexuality iii. In Persian Literature"; Lutz Richter-Bernburg, "Plato of Mind and Joseph of Countenance: The Notion of Love and the Ideal Beloved in Kay Kâ'ûs b. Iskandar's Andarznâme," *Oriens* 36, (2001): 276–87; S.O Murray, "Corporealizing Medieval Persian and Turkish Tropes," in *Islamic Homosexualities*, ed. S. Murray and W. Roscoe (New York: NYU Press, 1997): 132–41. W.M. Floor, "The Lūṭīs: A Social Phenomenon in Qājār Persia: A Reappraisal," in *Die Welt des Islams* 13, nos. 1-2 (1971), 103–20.

4 On the beard of the beloved see Seyed-Gohrab, "Insects in Classical Persian Literature: the Case of the Ant," *Persica: Annual of the Dutch-Iranian Society*, No. 16, Leuven: Peeters, 2000, 77–112; R.

Zipoli, "Poetic Imagery," in *History of Persian Literature*, ed. J.T.P. de Bruijn (London: I.B. Tauris, 2009), 204; on homoeroticism of the Persian ghazals see J.T.P. de Bruijn, "The Ghazal in Medieval Persian Poetry," in *A History of Persian Literature: Persian Lyric Poetry in the Classical Era, 800-1500 (Ghazals, Panegyrics and Quatrains)*, ed. Ehsan Yarshater (London: Bloomsbury, 2019): 315–487.

5 Amīr Muʿizzī, *Dīvān*, ed. N. Yayyirī, Tehran: Marzbān, 1362sh/1983, 178–9. For an alternative translation of this passage see EIr, in *Encyclopædia Iranica*, s.v. "Homosexuality iii. In Persian Literature"; on the poet see Hormoz Davarpanah, *Encyclopædia Iranica*, s.v. Moʿezzi Nišāburi.

6 For an elaborate study in Persian see S. Shamīsā, *Shāhid-bāzī dar adabiyyāt-i fārsī* (Tehran: Firdaws, 2002).

7 See J.T.P. de Bruijn, *Encyclopædia Iranica*, s.v. Kaykāvus (also Kaykāʾus) b. Eskandar.

8 *Qābūs-nāma*, ed. Gh.-Ḥ. Yūsufī, Tehran, 1371sh/1992, 86.

9 Ibid., 86–7; translation R. Levy, *A Mirror for Princes*, London, 1951, p. 78. Levy's translation on this topic runs as follows: "During the summer let your desires incline towards youths and during the winter towards women." Also see *Qābūs-nāma*, 86–7; Levy, *A Mirror, 77:* "As between women and youths do not confine your inclinations to either sex; thus, you may find enjoyment from both kinds without either of the two becoming inimical to you."

10 The term is defined differently. Ritter describe such a person as "a young man who sells sexual favors" (see *The Ocean of the Soul*, 269), while Losensky describe him as a 'pederast', which appears to be inaccurate.

11 For an examination of various gender and sexual categories in Persian literary tradition see Mehrdad Alipour, "Beyond Anachronism: Questioning Modern Gender and Sexuality Language in Classical Persian Literature," in *Gender and Sexuality in Persian Literary and Religious Traditions: Embodied Encounters*, ed. A.A. Seyed-Gohrab (Leiden: Leiden University Press, 2026): 181–206; idem., "Homosexuality in the Prospect of Before Revelation," in *Wege zu einer Ethik: Neue Ansätze aus Theologie und Recht zwischen modernen Herausforderungen und islamischer Tradition, eds., R.* Alsoufi, S. Kurnaz, & M. Sievers (Baden Baden: Nomos Publishing House, 2023): 201–35.

12 There are many examples to be given. Later in this chapter I refer to Paul Losensky's translation who has translated *mukhannath* as pederast: *Farid ad-Din 'Attar's Memorial of God's Friends: Lives and Sayings of Sufis*, translated and introduced by Paul Losensky (New York: Paulist Press, 2009), 75–6. For a definition of pederasty see Alipour, "Homosexuality in the Prospect of Before Revelation," 208.

13 See Farīd ad-Dīn ʿAṭṭār, *Taẕkirat al-owliyā'*, ed. H. Khalīlī, Tehran: Manūchihrī, 1370sh/1991, 39. My translation is based on Paul Losensky's rendition with a few changes. Losensky translates *mukhannath* as pederast, I prefer to use the term effeminate. See *Farid ad-Din 'Attar's Memorial of God's Friends: Lives and Sayings of Sufis*, translated and introduced by Paul Losensky (New York: Paulist Press, 2009), 75–6.

14 Farīd ad-Dīn ʿAṭṭār, *Taẕkirat al-owliyā'*, 75; *Farid ad-Din 'Attar's Memorial of God's Friends*, 109. Also in this case, Losensky uses pederast for *mukhannath* which I have changed in this translation. Her original answer runs as follows in Persian:
رابعه گفت: این همه هست ولکن منی و خود پرستی و انا ربکم الاعلی، از گریبان هیچ زن بر نیامده است
و هیچ زن هرگز مخنث نبوده است. اینها در مردان وادید آمده است.

15 Farīd ad-Dīn ʿAṭṭār, *Taẕkirat al-owliyā'*, 287; On Sarī al-Saqaṭī see Christian Lange, *Justice, Punishment, and the Medieval: Muslim Imagination* (Cambridge: Cambridge University Press, 2008), 114, in which Sarī al-Saqaṭī's famous remark is cited in the context of the fear of punishment, "I look at my nose twice every day, because I am afraid that my face may have turned black." For a comprehensive study on Junayd see Farīd al-Dīn Rād-Mihr, *Junayd-i Baghdādī (tāj al-ʿārifīn): taḥqīqī dar zindigī va afkār va āthār-i ū*, Tehran: Rowzana, 1380sh/2001.

16 Ritter, *The Ocean of the Soul*, 269

17 Farīd ad-Dīn ʿAṭṭār, *Taẕkirat al-owliyā*ʾ, 651–2.

18 Ritter, *The Ocean of the Soul*, 269, 305, 316.

19 Farīd ad-Dīn ʿAṭṭār, *Manṭiq aṭ-ṭayr*, ed. Sayyid Ṣādiq Gowharīn, Tehran: Shirkat-i Intishārāt-i ʿIlmī va Farhangī, 1368sh/1989, 106, lines 1911–14.

20 ʿAṭṭār, *Manṭiq aṭ-ṭayr*, 106, lines 1915–17 and 1921.

21 The translation of *The Conference of the Birds* is by Peter Avery while I have made a few changes, 171–2.

22 See Dick Davis, and A. Darbandi, *Farid ud-din Attar: The Conference of the Birds* (London: Penguin Classics, 1984), the introduction page 20 and translation 93; Austin O'Malley, *The Poetics of Spiritual Instruction: Farid al-Din ʿAttar and Persian Sufi Didacticism* (Edinburgh: Edinburgh University Press, 2023), 232.

23 ʿAṭṭār, *Manṭiq aṭ-ṭayr*, 107, lines 1926–28.

24 ʿAṭṭār, *Manṭiq aṭ-ṭayr*, 107, lines 1936–37.

25 For an analysis of the antinomian groups and the reaction of religious intellectuals see A.A. Seyed-Gohrab, *Of Piety and Heresy: Abū Ḥāmid Muḥammad Ghazzālī's Persian Treatises on Antinomians* (Berlin: De Gruyter, 2024).

26 See Farīd ad-Dīn ʿAṭṭār, *Taẕkirat al-owliyā*ʾ, 546.

27 ʿAṭṭār, *Manṭiq aṭ-ṭayr*, 107, line 1929. My translation is based on Avery's rendering with a few changes. See 173, line 1929.

28 For a different interpretation of this anecdote see Austin O'Malley, *The Poetics of Spiritual Instruction*, 233. O'Malley believes that ʿAṭṭār depicts Shiblī as being "so ashamed of his 'lack of manly chivalry' and undeserved reputation for 'manliness' that he took up residence in a *mokhannas-khana*, placing himself among those who were 'neither men nor women in the way of the world'. The narrative thus implies a drastic recalibration of the scale of spiritual achievement—if Shebli belongs in the *mokhannas-khana*, how about the rest of us?"

29 ʿAṭṭār, *Manṭiq aṭ-ṭayr*, 107, line 1932. This is Avery's translation, *The Speech of Birds*, Suffolk, 1998, 173, line 1932.

30 Farīd ad-Dīn 'Aṭṭār, *Taẕkirat al-owliyā*ʾ, 7; Losensky, 45.

31 Ḥakīm Majdūd ibn Ādam Sanāʾī, *Ḥadīqat al-ḥaqīqa va-sharīʿat aṭ-ṭarīqa*, ed. M.T. Mudarris Rażavī (Tehran: Intishārāt-i Dānishgāh-i Tehran, 1368sh/1989), 461–2; for a treatment of this anecdote see Ritter, *The Ocean of the Soul*, 305–6.

32 For stories in this influential poem see J.T.P. de Bruijn, "The Stories of Sanāʾī's Fakhrī-nāma," in *Pearls of Meanings: Studies on Persian Art, Poetry, Sufism and History of Iranian Studies in Europe by J.T.P. de Bruijn*, ed. A.A. Seyed-Gohrab (Leiden: Leiden University Press, 2020): 67–83.

33 Browne, *A Literary History of Persia*, vol. ii, p. 65. On the obscurity of Persian literary riddles see Seyed-Gohrab, *Courtly Riddles*, 16–18.

34 See Seyed-Gohrab, *Courtly Riddles*, 103–4.

35 Persian poets refer to Ghātfar as a city in Turkistān, celebrated for its handsome people and for its graceful cypress trees.

36 See Masʿūd Saʿd-i Salmān, *Dīvān*, ed. R. Yāsamī (Tehran: Amīr Kabīr, 1362sh/1983), 177–8.

37 Ḥakīm Majdūd ibn Ādam Sanāʾī, *Dīvān*, ed. M.T. Mudarris Rażavī (Tehran: Sanāʾī, 1362sh/1983), qaṣīda 46.

38 See Jalāl al-Dīn Muḥammad Rūmī, *Mathnavī-yi maʿnavī*, ed. M. Istiʿlāmī (Tehran: Zavvār, second print, 1372sh/1993), volume six, 70–73, couplets 1389–1455.

39 Francis Joseph Steingass, *A Comprehensive Persian–English Dictionary* (London: Kegan Paul, Trench, Trubner & Co, first published 1892, several reprints, s.v. *jabr*).

40 Nicholson's translation as adjusted, line 1442.

41 Nicholson's translation.

42 Nicholson's translation.

43 Nicholson's Latin translation runs as follows: "Ille duo instrumenta habet et androgynus est: amborum effectus sine dubio apparet. Penem oculis feminarum subtrahit ut sese earum sororem faciat. Vulvam ne viri videant manu obtegit, ut sese de genere virorum faciat. Dixit Deus, "Ex ejus cunno occulto scissuram in naso ejus faciemus."

44 Translation is by John A. Arberry. The Qur'ānic verses are not clear to me: "(68/16) We shall brand him upon the muzzle!. (68/17) Now We have tried them, even as We tried the owners of the garden when they swore they would pluck in the morning."

45 See more on this in the article by Christine van Ruymbeke who states that this science is attributed to "Aristotle (*Kitāb fī al-firāsa* and also the spurious *Kitāb Sirr al asrār*, both translated into Arabic in the ninth century) and were further developed by Polemon of Laodicea (d.c. AD 144), who was held in Arabic sources as the highest authority on physiognomy (*aflīmūn sāhib al-firāsa*)." Van Ruymbeke, "Dimna's Trial and 'Apologia' in Kashifī's 'Anvār-i Suhaylī'. Morality's Place in the Corrupt Trial of a Rhetorical and Dialectical Genius," *Journal of the Royal Asiatic Society* 26, no. 4 (2016): 549–83. See also M. van Zutphen, "The science of Physiognomy in the Safina," in *The Treasury of Tabriz: The Great Il-Khanid Compendium*, ed. A.A. Seyed-Gohrab and S. McGlinn (Leiden: Leiden University Press, 2007): 221–42.

46 On a history of prostitution in Iran see W. Floor, *A Social History of Sexual Relations in Iran*, Washington D.C., Mage Publishers, 2008, chapter three.

47 See many references to masculinity of the beloved in early Persian panegyrics in which they are portrayed as warlike, army leaders, and fully armed to break any army. See J. Scott Meisami, *Medieval Persian Court Poetry* (Princeton: Princeton University Press, 1987), 237–98.

48 See Seyed-Gohrab, *Laylī and Majnūn*, 285; De Bruijn, *Of Piety and Poetry: The Interaction of Religion and Literature in the Life and Works of Ḥakīm Sanā'ī of Ghazna*, Leiden: E.J. Brill, Publication of the "De Goeje Fund," No. 25 (1983), 276; F. Meier, *Die Fawā'iḥ al-Ǧamāl wa-Fawātiḥ al-Ǧalāl des Naǧm ad-Dīn al-Kubrā, eine Darstellung mystischer Erfahrungen im Islam aus der Zeit um 1200 n. Chr.*, Wiesbaden: Franz Steiner Verlag, 1957, 67–75; Jamal Elias, *The Throne Carrier of God: The Life and Thought of 'Alā' al-dawla as-Simnānī*, 74.

Bibliography

Alipour, M. "Homosexuality in the Prospect of Before Revelation." in *Wege zu einer Ethik: Neue Ansätze aus Theologie und Recht zwischen modernen Herausforderungen und islamischer Tradition*. edited by R. Alsoufi, S. Kurnaz, and M. Sievers. Baden Baden: Nomos Publishing House, 2023: 201–35.

Alipour, M. "Beyond Anachronism: Questioning Modern Gender and Sexuality Language in Classical Persian Literature," in *Gender and Sexuality in Persian Literary and Religious Traditions: Embodied Encounters*, ed. A.A. Seyed-Gohrab. Leiden: Leiden University Press, 2026: 181–206

Amīr Mu'izzī, *Dīvān*. edited by N. Yayyirī. Tehran: Marzbān, 1362sh/1983.

'Aṭṭār, Farīd ad-Dīn. *Manṭiq aṭ-ṭayr*. edited by Sayyid Ṣādiq Gowharīn. Tehran: Shirkat-i Intishārāt-i 'Ilmī va Farhangī, 1368sh/1989.

'Aṭṭār, Farīd al-Dīn. *Taẕkirat al-owliyā'*, edited by H. Khalīlī. Tehran: Manūchihrī, 1370sh/1991.

Avery, P. *The Speech of the Birds, Concerning Migration to the Real: The Mantiqu't-Tair*. Cambridge: The Islamic Texts Society, 1998.

Browne, E.G. *A Literary History of Persia*. 4 vols. Cambridge: Cambridge University Press, 1902–24 (several reprints).

Bruijn, J.T.P. de. "The Ghazal in Medieval Persian Poetry." in *A History of Persian Literature: Persian Lyric Poetry in the Classical Era, 800–1500 (Ghazals, Panegyrics and Quatrains)*. edited by Ehsan Yarshater. London: Bloomsbury, 2019: 315–487.

Bruijn, J.T.P. de. *Encyclopædia Iranica*, s.v. Beloved.

Bruijn, J.T.P. de. *Encyclopædia Iranica*, s.v. Kaykāvus (also Kaykā'us) b. Eskandar.

Bruijn, J.T.P. de. *Of Piety and Poetry: The Interaction of Religion and Literature in the Life and Works of Ḥakīm Sanā'ī of Ghazna*. Leiden: E.J. Brill, Publication of the "De Goeje Fund," No. 25, 1983.

Bruijn, J.T.P. de. "The Stories of Sanā'ī's Fakhrī-nāma." in *Pearls of Meanings: Studies on Persian Art, Poetry, Sufism and History of Iranian Studies in Europe by J.T.P. de Bruijn*. edited by A.A. Seyed-Gohrab. Leiden: Leiden University Press, 2020: 67–83.

Davarpanah, H. *Encyclopædia Iranica*, s.v. Moʿezzi Nišāburi.

Davis, D. and A. Darbandi, *Farid ud-din Attar: The Conference of the Birds*. London: Penguin Classics, 1984.

Editors of EIr, in *Encyclopædia Iranica*, s.v. Homosexuality iii. in Persian Literature.

Elias, J. *The Throne Carrier of God: The Life and Thought of 'Alā' al-dawla as-Simnānī*. Albany: State University of New York Press, 1995.

Floor, W.M. "The Lūṭīs: A Social Phenomenon in Qājār Persia: A Reappraisal." in *Die Welt des Islams* 13, nos. 1–2 (1971): 103–20.

Floor, W.M. *A Social History of Sexual Relations in Iran*. Washington D.C.: Mage Publishers, 2008.

Kay Kāwūs, ʿUnṣur al-Maʿālī, *Qābūs-nāma*. edited by G. Yūsufī. Tehran: ʿIlmī wa Farhangī, 1371sh/1992.

Lange, C. *Justice, Punishment, and the Medieval: Muslim Imagination*. Cambridge: Cambridge University Press, 2008.

Levy, R. *A Mirror for Princes*. London: Cresset Press, 1951.

Losensky, P. *Farid ad-Din 'Attar's Memorial of God's Friends: Lives and Sayings of Sufis*. translated and introduced by Paul Losensky. New York: Paulist Press, 2009.

Meier, F. *Die Fawā'iḥ al-Ğamāl wa-Fawātiḥ al-Ğalāl des Nağm ad-Dīn al-Kubrā, eine Darstellung mystischer Erfahrungen im Islam aus der Zeit um 1200 n. Chr.* Wiesbaden: Franz Steiner Verlag, 1957.

Meisami, J.S. *Medieval Persian Court Poetry*. Princeton: Princeton University Press, 1987.

Murray, S.O. "Corporealizing Medieval Persian and Turkish Tropes." in *Islamic Homosexualities*. edited by S. Murray and W. Roscoe. New York: NYU Press, 1997: 132–41.

Nicholson, R.A. ed. *The Mathnawi of Jalalu'ddin Rūmī*. 8 vols. London: Gibb Memorial Trust 1925–40.

O'Malley, A. *The Poetics of Spiritual Instruction: Farid al-Din ʿAttar and Persian Sufi Didacticism*. Edinburgh: Edinburgh University Press, 2023.

Rād-Mihr, Farīd al-Dīn. *Junayd-i Baghdādī (tāj al-ʿārifīn): taḥqīqī dar zindigī va afkār va āthār-i ū*. Tehran: Rowzana, 1380sh/2001.

Richter-Bernburg, L. "Plato of Mind and Joseph of Countenance: The Notion of Love and the Ideal Beloved in Kay Kâ'ûs b. Iskandar's Andarznâme." in *Oriens* 36, (2001): 276–87.

Ritter, H. *The Ocean of the Soul: Man, the World and God in the Stones of Farīd al-Dīn ʿAṭṭār*. translated by John O'Kane with Editorial Assistance of Bernd Radtke, Leiden 2003 (translation of *Das Meer der Seele: Mensch, Welt und Gott in den Geschichten des Fariduddin ʿAṭṭār*, Leiden: Brill, 1955).

Rūmī, Jalāl al-Dīn Muḥammad. *Mathnavī-yi maʿnavī*, edited by M. Istiʿlāmī, Tehran: Zavvār (second print) 1372sh/1993, six vols.

Ruymbeke, C. van. "Dimna's Trial and 'Apologia' in Kashifī's 'Anvār-i Suhaylī'. Morality's Place in the Corrupt Trial of a Rhetorical and Dialectical Genius." *Journal of the Royal Asiatic Society* 26, no. 4 (2016): 549–83.

Sa'd-i Salmān, Mas'ūd. *Dīvān*. edited by R. Yāsamī. Tehran: Amīr Kabīr, 1362sh/1983.

Sanā'ī, Ḥakīm Majdūd Ibn Ādam. *Dīvān*. edited by M.T. Mudarris Rażavī. Tehran: Sanā'ī, 1362sh/1983.

Sanā'ī, Ḥakīm Majdūd Ibn Ādam. *Ḥadīqat al-ḥaqīqa va-sharī'at aṭ-ṭarīqa*. Edited by M.T. Mudarris Rażavī. Tehran: Intishārāt-i Dānishgāh-i Tehran, 1368sh/1989.

Seyed-Gohrab, A.A. "Insects in Classical Persian Literature: The Case of the Ant." *Persica: Annual of the Dutch-Iranian Society*, No. 16, Leuven: Peeters, 2000: 77–112.

Seyed-Gohrab, A.A. *Laylī and Majnūn: Love, Madness and Mystic Longing in Niẓāmī's Epic Romance*. Leiden / Boston: Brill, 2003.

Seyed-Gohrab, A.A. *Courtly Riddles: Enigmatic Embellishments in Early Persian Poetry*. Leiden: Leiden University Press, 2010.

Seyed-Gohrab, A.A. "Sufi Treatment of Same-Sex Poetry and Prose." in *Global Encyclopedia of Gay, Lesbian, Bisexual, Transgender, and Queer History*. edited by Howard Chiang, Charles Scribner's Sons, 2019: 1556–62.

Seyed-Gohrab, A.A. *Of Piety and Heresy: Abū Ḥāmid Muḥammad Ghazzālī's Persian Treatises on Antinomians*. Berlin: De Gruyter, 2024.

Shamīsā, S. *Shāhid-bāzī dar adabiyyāt-i fārsī*. Tehran: Firdaws, 2002.

Steingass, F.J. *A Comprehensive Persian–English Dictionary*. London: Kegan Paul, Trench, Trubner & Co, first published 1892, several reprints.

Yarshater, E. "The Theme of Wine-Drinking and the Concept of the Beloved in Early Persian Poetry." *Studia Islamica*13, (1960): 43–53.

Zipoli, R. "Poetic Imagery." in *History of Persian Literature*. edited by J.T.P. de Bruijn. London: I.B. Tauris, 2009: 172–232.

Zipoli, R. *Irreverent Persia: Invective, Satirical and Burlesque Poetry from the Origins to the Timurid Period (10th to 15th Centuries)*. Leiden: Leiden University Press, 2015.

Zutphen, M. van. "The Science of Physiognomy in the Safina." in *The Treasury of Tabriz: The Great Il-Khanid Compendium*. edited by A.A. Seyed-Gohrab and S. McGlinn, Leiden: Leiden University Press, 2007: 221–42.

CHAPTER FOUR

'Al-khunthā laysa bi-naw': The Absence of the *Khunthā* in the Qur'ānic Narrative of the Creation of the Humans

Saqer Almarri

Abstract

The Qur'ānic narrative of the creation of the humans is a narrative about the creation of humans as gendered beings. Yet the *khunthā* is neither explicitly mentioned nor alluded to in the Qur'ān, despite being a recognized category in medieval Islamic discourse. This chapter examines the Qur'ānic commentaries written between the 5/11–11/18 centuries that developed an exegetical hermeneutic on the nature of sexual difference within the Qur'ān and incorporated the *khunthā* into that hermeneutic through a discussion of the creation of Adam and his mate, and the creation of beings with souls (*dhawī al-arwāḥ*). This exegetical hermeneutic appears in the commentaries in Qur'ān 4:1 and 92:3 such that the commentators conclude that the *khunthā* was a matter of human perception, but not of any underlying reality. This chapter examines this exegetical hermeneutic with an attention to how it addressed the complications posed by the *khunthā* as a living subject in their work to restore an idealized conception of the gender system as consisting of a male/female sexual dimorphism.

Keywords: Qur'ānic creation narratives, ontological status of intersex people, medieval tafsīr on gender, legal-theological hermeneutics of gender, gender binary in the Qur'ān

Introduction

The Qur'ānic narrative of the creation of the humans are also narratives about the creation of the gender system. Yet, as Karen Bauer tells us, the creation of the woman is not described in the Qur'ān.[1] The first woman, or Eve, remains unnamed by the Qur'ān, and her creation remains ambiguously described.[2] This elided story of the first woman has caused commentators on the Qur'ān, both medieval and modern, to find answers elsewhere. An impetus for meaning-making about Eve's creation was produced by the ambiguously brief creation narrative, leading the commentators to produce their own narratives about Eve that go beyond the Qur'ān's text.[3]

Karen Bauer's inquiry on the gender system of the Qur'ān provides us a solid foundation to expand the question of these elisions and ambiguities into gender ambiguity itself. This chapter explores how meaning was made through the Qur'ān commentaries as the commentators investigate an absence, not of a *figure* but of a social phenomenon. More specifically, I ask how the absence of the social phenomenon factors into the elaboration of the creation narratives of the human by these commentators. We may see in these commentaries how the gender system (and its hierarchy) in the Qur'ān is itself distinct from the gender system in the social environment of those who are engaging with it as religious scripture.

The social phenomenon examined here is the *khunthā* (commonly understood as intersex) as it appears in the Qur'ān commentary genre. In much of the discourses, the *khunthā* represents the intersex human that is identified as such through their body's genital structures. Yet the *khunthā* is also popularly connected to terms that share its etymological root such as *mukhannath*, and the modern *khanīth* in ways that go beyond linguistic ties.[4] Therefore, while it may be useful to use the term *khunthā* as a shorthand equivalent term to "intersex," we must consider both its specific legal context and its broader cultural implications. In Islamic legal discourse, as Indira Gesink demonstrates, the term specifically referred to individuals with ambiguous or mixed physical sexual characteristics, with legal recognition tied to genital structures. At the same time, we should also heed Leah DeVun's insights about such pre-modern terms: they often encompassed forms of gender variance that cannot be fully captured by modern categories like "intersex" or "nonbinary."[5] Thus, I leave the term untranslated (despite Lena Salaymeh's warning of the consequences of non-translations)[6] to preserve both its specific legal meaning within Islamic traditions and to acknowledge the complexity of how such categories functioned in different historical and social contexts.

The Qur'ān and its extant exegetical sources are separated by a significant stretch of historical time. Indeed, this temporal difference has led Feras Hamza to question whether there is any connection between the Qur'ān and its associated exegetical tradition.[7] While the traditional history of Qur'ānic exegesis relies on the earliest commentaries as transferring Ibn ʿAbbās's commentary to us, it is far more likely that the contents of these commentaries were separated by a century, or two, after the Qur'ān.[8] In this way, the Qur'ān's original milieu is not the same as the various milieus of the commentators. The question arises once again when we ask about the gender system, gender crossings, and gender variance in the Qur'ān. The absence of such a matter may seem like a glaring divine omission for a reader who exists in a world where such gender crossings and gender variance exist as part of everyday life.

Gender system(s) in the Qur'ān and its commentaries

Each of the sources, both the Qur'ān and each individual commentary, have their own gender systems which are a reflection of the gender systems that were dominant in the lives of their authors and milieu. For the purposes of this chapter, I do not begin with the assumption that the gender systems reflected in these sources are *binary* gender systems (*i.e.* with a rigid male/female gender dichotomy), rather I read closely into the text to provide a contingent, rather than a static, conception of the gender system at play within each text.

I work with a conception of gender that is necessarily open-ended in what it could mean. The usual definitions of gender are taken as working definitions as we go along. More importantly, I understand gender as a social system of meanings that Muslim scholars actively constructed and reconstructed over time. As a system of meanings, it is dynamic, ever-changing, dissipative and potentially open to much chaotic disruption that breaks symmetries.[9] This approach allows us to see how medieval Muslim scholars were not simply interpreting a predetermined gender system but were actively engaged in constructing and negotiating gender categories through their exegetical work. These symmetry-breaking events are caused by variations in the gender system that break these symmetrical norms, such as *khunūtha*. Douglas Robinson maps out the epistemic process that surrounds these normative gender systems. He argues that the gender systems tend toward symmetrical binaries but are constantly challenged by the emergence of gender variations that disrupt this symmetry. These disruptions, Robinson suggests, often provoke attempts to restore the binary symmetry through forms of epistemological violence.[10] His epistemological framework on gender systems is a useful tool in understanding the processes through which these sources' authors work. I am not here charging that these authors were engaged in transphobic or genderphobic epistemicide (for that would be a form of unproductive anachronism).[11] Rather, Robinson's model helps us understand how the presence of the *khunthā* in the commentators' own social milieus clashed with the Qur'ān's silence about the *khunthā*. I argue, and demonstrate here, that this clash itself is the precise locus for this disruption that causes symmetry-breaking and the restabilization that pushes the gender system to return to symmetry. While previous scholarship has examined how legal and medical discourses shaped the understanding of the *khunthā*, this study reveals how Qur'ānic exegetes played a crucial role in reinforcing the gender binaries through their interpretive work. These commentators' efforts to reconcile the presence of the *khunthā* in their societies with its absence in the Qur'ān represent a significant, yet previously unexamined, force in the development of Islamic gender systems. To make this argument, I engage in close readings of these authors' interventions into the Qur'ānic creation narrative to address the *khunthā* as a social phenomenon present in their lives but absent in the Qurʾān itself that in some cases attempts to erase it in order to return to the Qurʾānic binary gender system. I will also show in this chapter that the returns to symmetry are not all the same route of return to a binary gender system. In this way, I allow the gender systems at play in each of the textual sources to come into interrelation so that we may uncover how the *khunthā*, as a social phenomenon and as real beings, is a form of symmetry-breaking of gender systems.

It is no exaggeration to say that the Qurʾān speaks of gender, and that its gender system is often understood as a patriarchal binary gender system especially by the prominent commentators.[12] It is not in the scope of this chapter to argue otherwise, or that reading the Qurʾān's gender system in validly alternative ways is possible. Rather, I focus on how commentators reconciled the social reality with what they saw in the Qurʾān when it came to the *khunthā*.

Gender system(s) of the wider Islamic tradition

The Islamic legal tradition, across its many schools, is often the locus of much of the discourse about the *khunthā*. We often find the *khunthā* in discussions about complicated inheritance formulas that require all inheritors to be gendered according to patriarchal divisions. However, we also see within these legal traditions approaches that developed frameworks for the *khunthā*'s participation in religious and social life. These frameworks operated within a larger social organization and hierarchy that was produced by the jurists, who had to balance practical needs with legal and cosmological considerations. While these provisions enabled participation in community life, they remained embedded within the period's patriarchal structures and epistemological frameworks.[13] The Islamic legal tradition's approach to the *khunthā* has been subject to evolving scholarly interpretation. While earlier studies by Sanders suggests that jurists actively policed gender boundaries and enforced binary categories, more recent scholarship offers a more nuanced understanding.[14] Gesink's work, for instance, demonstrates that while jurists did develop detailed theoretical frameworks for identifying the *khunthā*, there is limited historical evidence that courts actually enforced these rigid gender assignments. Indeed, what Gesink reveals is not a system of strict enforcement, but rather a body of legal literature that theorized the *khunthā*'s defining features while allowing for practical flexibility.[15] Even seemingly definitive cases, such as the Fatimid example analyzed by Almarri may represent legal fiction designed to demonstrate ideal adjudication rather than actual judicial practice. The legal discourse on the matter appears more theoretical than prescriptive, suggesting that medieval Islamic courts may have been more accepting of gender ambiguity than previously understood, though more research into actual court cases across different regions is needed.[16]

The failure of these gendering processes resulting in a judicially declared gender leads to a series of legal hedging to avoid putting the entire society's status at risk of transgression, thus placing the *khunthā* (declared *mushkil* for their uncertainty and problematic ambiguity) into in-between spaces. Their embodiment becomes the embodiment of the boundaries within the patriarchal gender binary, *i.e.* a social space is carved out between men and women to accommodate, but not integrate, the *khunthā*.[17] This embodiment becomes a series of legal accommodations that leads Gesink to correctly describe the *khunthā* as a "medial sex."[18]

The *khunthā* is a topic that is not restricted to legal discourses; rather medical writers have described and explained why the *khunthā* is a possible form of the human in much of the major classical treatises on medicine and surgery.[19] The *khunthā* figure appears in other forms of writings, such as zoological and travel writings that describe the dangers of monstrosities such as the seemingly hermaphroditic hyena and crocodile.[20] The *khunthā* also features in historiographical and biographical sources along with popular literature, such as Muhammad b. Salama, Aliyya, and Budur and Qamar al-Zaman.[21] The *khunthā* featured in all these discourses is to show that the notion of the *khunthā* never really disappeared from the cultural imaginaries, even as social and religious pressures tended toward binary gender categories.[22] This pressure toward binarization appears to have stemmed less from systematic legal enforcement than from broader social expectations and theological understanding that most people were either male or female, and that the discourse in the Qur'ān itself was directed to males and females.

Silences and absences

If the Qur'ān was silent about the *khunthā*, and *khunūtha*, why were the Qur'ān commentators at all concerned with it? We will explore what the different commentators make out of the Qur'ān's silence on the matter of the *khunthā*. We find that the Qur'ān silence, or the *khunthā*'s absence, to be as relevant for the commentaries as the Qur'ān's explicit description of these matters. Indeed, the Qur'ān's silence on a matter need not be *meaningless*. Literary theorists have made much theoretical and methodological discussion about the silences of a text, a matter that must be considered when examining how Qur'ān commentaries engaged with the silences of the Qur'ān itself.[23] The Qur'ān makes no reference to the *khunthā*, and indeed makes no use of its root in any word in the whole text itself, and yet the *khunthā* was a known (a)gendered subject in the early Islamic milieu. The silences of the Qur'ānic text have been made meaningful in the discussion about the gender system within the Qur'ānic text itself, but also in relation to the milieus of its commentators.

I turn to the question of silences and its effects in light of what Terrence Deacon calls the "absential," a phenomenon that relies on something that is necessarily absent in order to make something possible. This is a significantly important notion underlying thinking around the evolution of life, meaning, and semiotics.[24] The absential can be extended to thinking about the necessary absences that constrain potential meanings that are made from a text.[25] That is to say: the absence of the *khunthā* in the Qur'ān is itself a constraint (in the form of "why is there no *khunthā* in this text?") upon the commentators' meaning-making processes as they construct their commentaries. Indeed, the Qur'ān's silence on the *khunthā* became a factor in understanding the Qur'ān, its creation narrative of the humans, and the potential meanings of gender variance among humans.

The first human

The creation of the first human is a crucial aspect of the creation narratives in the Abrahamic tradition, in its many variations, and yet contrary to popular conception, the specific narrative of the first human varies from Jewish and Christian narratives. In fact, the Qur'ānic narrative is quite different from the Jewish and Christian creation narratives. Daniel Boyarin writes of two distinct early Jewish interpretations of the creation of Adam: the first was from the *Genesis Rabbah* and the second from Philo of Alexandria.[26] In the *Genesis Rabbah*, a commentary work written in Late Antiquity on the Book of Genesis, Adam appears as a primordial being whose body encompassed two faces and two sexes such that to make the dyadic humans, God had "sawed it" in half and made a back for each of the two halves.[27] The Rabbi Samuel ben Naḥman, to whom this interpretation is attributed, further elaborated that the term צלע (*ṣela'*, the Hebrew cognate to Arabic ضلع *ḍil'*) refers not only to "rib" but also to "side."[28] Boyarin goes on to elaborate that the Rabbinic movement understood humanity as being created *with* sex, rather than developed as an aspect of their fallen nature. This second view of associating the fallen nature of humanity with their sex was the interpretation of Philo of Alexandria. Philo posed an interpretation of Adam as an androgynous figure, who despite the primal androgyny remained male.[29] Leah DeVun writes that interpretation of Philo of Alexandria influenced early Christian theologians like Origen of Alexandria and Gregory of Nyssa who argued that the first human was a spiritual androgynous being who only became sexed upon becoming corporeal, a position that was denounced by Augustine of Hippo.[30] This variety of interpretations among Jewish and Christian groups does not match well with the interpretations of the Qur'ānic creation narrative which I will present here. The Qur'ānic creation narrative does not offer a detailed account as Genesis does, but rather the narrative remains sparse and focused on the divine creation of a gender-differentiated humanity.

There are exceptions to this interpretation of the Qur'ānic creation narrative. However, those interpretations tend to be contemporary interpretations, rather than early Islamic interpretations. One such important example is the Muslim theology of Celene Ibrahim. Celene Ibrahim pays close attention to the Qur'ān's conception of the woman.[31] She argues that the gender system conceived in the Qur'ān is one of a bifurcation of humanity that reflects other bifurcations in worldly creation.[32] The creation of a primordial human is then bifurcated into dualities that "mutually interpose and interpenetrate".[33] Ibrahim's theology posits a Qur'ānic creation narrative that need not be read as the creation of Adam *before* Eve, but it may also be read as the creation of a primordial human, who was not gendered until the bifurcation into a sexed dyad. In this case, the primal androgyny of the first human, or the bifurcation into a sexed dyad does not feature any *khunthā* or a form of gender variance at a point after the bifurcation.

The absence

The absence of the *khunthā* in the Qur'ān itself may have been overlooked by some of the Qur'ān commentators; however for others, this very absence provided a cause in a significant amount of meaning-making as they sought to understand its significance. Cognition and the production of concepts in one's mind rely on the recognition and production of patterns in such a way that any breaking of the pattern has consequences on the reproduction of the concept in the mind.[34] Building on this insight and the insight on absentials, it could be argued that the absence of a cultural concept in a specific sphere where it is expected to be present creates its relevance, and its absence then becomes a constraint on thinking about matters which are expected to be associated with it. As scholars of religion and gender, we must take cognition-based explanations into account when discussing how the gender system was thought about by theologians. Pascal Boyer offers us an explanation of how religious concepts develop and take on a life of their own.[35] Boyer shows us that the mind is concerned with producing explanations through its multiple inference systems which attempt to define, redefine, imagine, and reimagine religious concepts.[36] These religious concepts become defined, imagined, developed in a cycle of loops that are not done in isolation, but in relation to other people's behaviors and utterances.[37]

The absence of the *khunthā* in the Qur'ān created a constraint for the commentators who knew of the *khunthā* as a concept and found its absence in the Qur'ān peculiar enough to warrant its investigation and discussion. This absence broke the pattern where the commentators were involved in a social reality where the *khunthā* was understood to exist, and where the Qurʾān is reflective of the created world, and therefore an absence of such a component of social reality needs to be explained. The commentators make use of the reality of the *khunthā* from their own social reality, and place it into juxtaposition with the Qurʾānic text in order to produce an explanation for why the Qurʾān itself is silent on the matter. The commentators' engagement with the absence shaped their interpretations of the Qurʾānic gender system and their theoretical approaches to gender variance. As we will see in the following analysis of specific commentaries, their attempts to reconcile the *khunthā*'s absence in the Qurʾān with its presence in scholarly discourses led to complex theological and interpretive strategies.

Two passages and their commentaries

In the following, I will cover the commentaries to two verses, Q4:1 and Q92:3. Each verse inspires a series of responses, some of which interrelate with the writings of others. I cover them here in chronological order based on their death dates derived from Khayr al-Dīn Ziriklī's *Aʿlām*. While many of these commentaries tend to be brief, they offer us glimpses into how the commentators thought about this glaring absence.[38]

Qurʾān 4:1

Qurʾān 4:1 is a significant verse from a Medinan chapter that contains many verses about inheritance, property. Yet the chapter itself begins by describing the creation of humanity from a single creature from which a second creature was created. Below I quote the passage with divisions of each of the six clauses, with a parallel translation taken from M.A.S. Abdel Haleem's translation.[39]

People, be mindful of your Lord,	يَٰٓأَيُّهَا ٱلنَّاسُ ٱتَّقُوا۟ رَبَّكُمْ	4:1-a
Who created you from a single soul,	ٱلَّذِى خَلَقَكُم مِّن نَّفْسٍ وَٰحِدَةٍ	4:1-b
And from it created its mate	وَخَلَقَ مِنْهَا زَوْجَهَا	4:1-c
And from the pair of them spread countless men and women far and wide;	وَبَثَّ مِنْهُمَا رِجَالًا كَثِيرًا وَنِسَآءً	4:1-d
Be mindful of God, in whose name you make requests of one another.	وَٱتَّقُوا۟ ٱللَّهَ ٱلَّذِى تَسَآءَلُونَ بِهِۦ	4:1-e
Beware of severing the ties of kinship: God is always watching over you.	وَٱلْأَرْحَامَ إِنَّ ٱللَّهَ كَانَ عَلَيْكُمْ رَقِيبًا	4:1-f

The clauses *b*, *c*, and *d* in the verse speak of the creation of the humans ("you") from a primordial "single soul," that becomes two. While the grammatical gender of *nafs*, *min-hā*, and *zawja-hā* are feminine, the soul itself is commonly understood by the commentators as referring to Adam, though the grammatical construction lends itself to other possible readings. Gender begins to appear in the verse in clause *d* where "countless men and women" come into being from this first couple.

The commentators that have connected this verse to the notion of the *khunthā* are four commentators: Makkī b. Abī Ṭālib (d. 437/1045), Ibn ʿAṭiyya (d. 542/1148), al-Qurṭubī (d. 671/1273), and Abū Ḥayyān al-Andalusī (d. 745/1344).

Makkī b. Abī Ṭālib (d. 437/1045) turns his attention to the *khunthā* as he discusses clause *d*. To him, the reference to "men and women" is a drawing of exclusive boundaries, such that these two forms of humanity are all that exist. Therefore, the *khunthā* may only be one of these two forms because those were the only two forms created from Adam, with no third form being created from him (*i.e.* a divinely described gender that is neither "man" nor "woman"). For him, the creation of the *khunthā* did not happen, rather the *khunthā* can only be either "man" or "woman" because there was nothing created from Adam's back (rather than his rib)[40] other than men and women.[41]

Ibn ʿAṭiyya (d. 542/1148) focuses on clause *c* and *d*, citing Ibn ʿAbbās, Mujāhid, al-Suddī, and Qatāda to argue that Eve was created out of Adam's rib because he was a solitary beast needing companionship. This couple goes on to produce only two forms of humans: men and women. Ibn ʿAṭiyya follows that limitation that there is no other "kind" that was created, and effectively erases the *khunthā* from the status of being a form equal to man and woman. Instead, Ibn ʿAṭiyya declares that the *khunthā* is not a "kind" [*al-khunthā laysa bi-nawʿ*], and that the ambiguous form of the *khunthā* has an underlying truth [*ḥaqīqah*] that points to one of the two kinds. We see in Ibn ʿAṭiyya's commentary an investigation into why the *khunthā* was absent from the Qur'ān, and the answer for him was that the *khunthā* was not a category within the gender system at all.[42] Shams al-Dīn al-Qurṭubī (d. 671/1273) argues similarly to Ibn ʿAṭiyya, but centers his discussion around clause *d*. In a similar language to Ibn ʿAṭiyya, al-Qurṭubī argues that the progeny of Adam and Eve are limited to two kinds, and therefore states the same conclusion of Ibn ʿAṭiyya verbatim: *al-khunthā laysa bi-nawʿ* and has an underlying truth that points to them. He elaborates that it is their "*adamic*-ness" [*al-ādamiyyah*] which points to their "true sex."[43]

Abū Ḥayyān al-Andalusī (d. 745/1344) bases a forceful argument on clause *d*, while similar to Ibn ʿAṭiyya and al-Qurṭubī in the argument about the restriction of the progeny of Adam and Eve to two forms of humans: men and women. He argues that the restriction of the progeny to men and women is evidence for the absence [*intifāʾ*] of the *khunthā*. Therefore, the ambiguous form of the *khunthā* (the *khunthā mushkil*) is only ambiguous to humans, where sufficient examinations can attribute it to the two forms of humans.[44]

Qur'ān 92:3

The verse in Qur'ān 92:3 is embedded within a Meccan chapter that begins with complementary dualities, with the prior verses (92:1–2) referring to the night and the day. Below I quote the passage with divisions of each of the six clauses, with a parallel translation taken from M.A.S. Abdel Haleem's translation.[45]

By the covering night,	وَٱلَّيۡلِ إِذَا يَغۡشَىٰ	92:1
By the radiant day,	وَٱلنَّهَارِ إِذَا تَجَلَّىٰ	92:2
By the male and female He created,	وَمَا خَلَقَ ٱلذَّكَرَ وَٱلۡأُنثَىٰ	92:3
The ways you take differ greatly.	إِنَّ سَعۡيَكُمۡ لَشَتَّىٰ	92:4

In this verse, presented above within its context, we see no mention of the first human, but rather the creation of the two forms, the two genders: the male and the female, following a mention of the duality of the night and day. What follows is a discussion of the Qur'ān commentators, once again, ordered chronologically: al-Zamakhsharī (d. 538/1144), Fakhr al-Dīn al-Rāzī (d. 606/1210), Niẓām al-Dīn al-Qummī al-Nīsābūrī (d. ca. 850/1446), the Jalālayn (d. 864/1459 and 911/1505), İsmail Hakkı Bursevî (d. 1127/1715).

Zamakhsharī (d. 538/1144) reads the verse as describing the creation of the male and female forms, and that the creation of souls was conditioned on the presence of masculinity and femininity such that there was no being with a soul that was not one of the two types. These gendered souls then, writes al-Zamakhsharī, are always either male or female, such that the *khunthā* remains ambiguous (i.e. *ambiguously male or female*) only among humans, but not ambiguous in God's knowledge. Rather their underlying truth is known to God.[46] The notion of gendered souls (*dhawī al-arwāḥ*) is a notion that becomes echoed throughout the commentaries on 92:3.

Fakhr al-Dīn al-Rāzī (d. 606/1210) echoes in his commentary the insights of al-Zamakhsharī in reference to the creation of Adam and Eve, and alternatively, the creation of male and female forms. al-Rāzī describes that the beings with souls are the highest forms of creation [*ashraf al-makhlūqāt*], such that all such creatures must be either male or female. The *khunthā*, once again, must be either one or the other, and never a gender form unto itself.[47] Niẓām al-Dīn al-Qummi al-Nīsābūrī (d. ca. 850/1446) follows the earlier authors mentioned here who argue that all creation that has a soul exists in one of two possible forms: masculine or feminine. It follows then that the *khunthā*, even in ambiguity to humans, remains determined and clear in God's knowledge [*mu'ayyan fī 'ilm allāh*].[48]

The Jalālayn unlike other commentators offer an extremely brief semantic and legalistic explanation of the text without delving into theological speculations. This explanation argues that the verse refers to Adam and Eve, and by extension all males and females. The text follows by stating simply that the *khunthā* when it remains ambiguous in human perception [*'indanā*] is ultimately known to God as being one of the two forms.[49]

İsmail Hakkı Bursevî follows the insights of his predecessors, citing specifically al-Zamakhsharī's commentary, and states that the creation of beings with souls also required the binary forms, such that there is not a soul that is not gendered. We find in each of the commentators that have discussed Qur'ān 92:3 an attempt to enforce a gender system that is rigidly binary in its form, where any gender variance must be attributed back into the two *created* forms of humans.

In sum

We find in the commentaries of Qur'ān 4:1 and 92:3 similar lines of reasoning in terms of the *khunthā*. The common thread among these writers in these 5/11–11/18 centuries is the attempt to reconcile the social reality of gender variance, commonly called the *khunthā*, with the Qur'ān's silence on the matter. The approach many of these commentators have taken is to consider the ambiguity of the *khunthā* a matter of human perception, rather than a matter of divine ordinance. In fact, following the discussion of *what* was created out of the first human, they conclude that the *khunthā* was at best not a real creation. However, this attempt to deny the ontological reality of the *khunthā* paradoxically resulted in further institutionalizing it within Islamic discourses. Rather than successfully abolishing the concept through their binary interpretation of the Qur'ānic gender system, the commentators actually produced a more complex framework: the *khunthā* became firmly established as a liminal subject positioned between masculinity and femininity, a form of gender ambiguity that required specialist interpretation but was understood to have a "true" gender in divine knowledge.

The exegetical hermeneutics involved in concluding that the *khunthā* was not a created being, but rather an ambiguity that humans experience through their fallible perceptions, sets the groundwork for the already existing legal doctrines that treat the *khunthā* as an exceptional ambiguity within the gender system. The Qur'ān commentators, by addressing the absence of the *khunthā* in the Qur'ān, are addressing a symmetry-breaking event (*i.e.* the *khunthā* as existing in social reality) through an attempt to restore the gender system into a binary gender system through argumentation about *what* precisely was created by God when he created the first human. In fact, among the crucial distinctions separating humans (and perhaps other higher beings) from non-humans is the distinction that humans have souls, and therefore are sexually dimorphic beings.

We also see a trajectory of the exegetical hermeneutics that is maintained across the time period examined. While this chapter has stopped at the threshold of modernity, it remains to be seen if modern and contemporary commentators on the Qurʾān follow similar forced binarization approaches to the *khunthā* and whether they extend these arguments in order to apply them to nonbinary, trans, and intersex subjects. I would not argue whether the pre-modern exegetical traditions surrounding the Qurʾān were engaged in genderphobic erasures through this forced binarization, however it is possible that their exegetical hermeneutic strategies may be extended to do precisely that in the modern commentaries.

Notes

1 Karen Bauer, *Gender Hierarchy in the Qur'ān: Medieval Interpretations, Modern Responses* (Cambridge: Cambridge University Press, 2015), 101.

2 Roberto Tottoli, "Eve," in *Encyclopaedia of Islam, THREE* (Brill, November 1, 2017).

3 Bauer, *Gender Hierarchy in the Qur'ān*, 135.

4 Saqer A. Almarri, "Identities of a Single Root: The Triad of the Khunthā, Mukhannath, and Khanīth," *Women & Language* 41, no. 1 (2018): 97–109; Everett K. Rowson, "The Effeminates of Early Medina," *Journal of the American Oriental Society* 111, no. 4 (1991): 671–93, at 671.

5 Leah DeVun, *The Shape of Sex: Nonbinary Gender from Genesis to the Renaissance* (New York: Columbia University Press, 2021).

6 Lena Salaymeh, "Decolonial Translation: Destabilizing Coloniality in Secular Translations of Islamic Law," *Journal of Islamic Ethics* 1 (March 5, 2021): 1–28.

7 Feras Hamza, "Tafsīr and Unlocking the Historical Qurʾan: Back to Basics?," in *Aims, Methods and Contexts of Qur'anic Exegesis (2nd/8th-9th/15th Centuries)*, ed. Karen Bauer, Qur'anic Studies Series 9 (Oxford: Oxford University Press, 2013), 19–39.

8 Claude Gilliot, "Exegesis of the Qurʾān: Classical and Medieval," in *Encyclopaedia of the Qurʾān* (Brill), accessed September 30, 2022.

9 Douglas Robinson, *Transgender, Translation, Translingual Address* (New York: Bloomsbury Academic, 2019), 19–20; Niklas Luhmann, "Complexity and Meaning," in *The Science and Praxis of Complexity: Contributions to the Symposium Held at Montpellier, France, 9–11 May, 1984*, ed. Shūhei Aida et al. (Tokyo: United Nations University, 1985).

10 Robinson, *Transgender, Translation, Translingual Address*, 20.

11 Charges of transphobic and genderphobic violence and epistemicide would be better used against modern authors and authorities who are engaged in recognizably exclusionary and exterminationist practices and rhetoric towards people who do not fit their ideal gender norms. This chapter, and this footnote, is not a venue for this.

12 Bauer, *Gender Hierarchy in the Qur'ān*; Kecia Ali, *Sexual Ethics and Islam: Feminist Reflections on Qur'an, Ḥadīth, and Jurisprudence*, Reprint (Oxford: Oneworld, 2012); Amina Wadud, *Qur'an and Woman: Rereading the Sacred Text from a Woman's Perspective*, 2nd ed. (New York: Oxford University Press, 1999); Asma Barlas, *"Believing Women" in Islam: Unreading Patriarchal Interpretations of the Qur'ān*, 1st ed (Austin: University of Texas Press, 2002); Amanullah De Sondy, *Crisis of Islamic Masculinities* (London: Bloomsbury, 2015).

13 Paula Sanders, "Gendering the Ungendered Body: Hermaphrodites in Medieval Islamic Law," in *Women in Middle Eastern History*, ed. Nikki R. Keddie and Beth Baron (New Haven: Yale University Press, 1991), 74–95; Saqer A. Almarri, "Non-Binary Sexual and Gender Identities in the Community: The Khunthā as an Isolated Being in the Mosque," *Body and Religion* 3, no. 2 (2020): 166–187.

14 Sanders, "Gendering the Ungendered Body: Hermaphrodites in Medieval Islamic Law"; Saqer A. Almarri, "The Khunthā and The Community" (Ph.D. Dissertation, Binghamton University, 2019); Indira Falk Gesink, "Intersex Bodies in Premodern Islamic Discourse: Complicating the Binary," *Journal of Middle East Women's Studies* 14, no. 2 (2018): 152–73.

15 Gesink argues against the interpretation of the sources that leads to using the term 'true sex' because it may be seen as anachronistic and forecloses the alternative reading that the determined sex was just one of many possibilities. I prefer to use the term 'true,' not of course because I believe in such truth in any gender system, but rather I am reflecting the discourses that reflect such notions: for example, al-Ramlī's own statement in response to the Mufti of Gaza uses the term '*mawqūf ḥattā yatabayyan*,' *i.e.* all legal obligations falling upon the *khunthā* are suspended until the truth is uncovered; similarly al-Ḥalabī in the discussion of manumission statements involving the *khunthā* writes '*lā yuʿtaq mā lam yastabin*', *i.e.* they are not manumitted unless their truth is made clear. We will see below more examples of the 'true sex' paradigms among the Qurʾān commentators.

16 Saqer A. Almarri, "'You Have Made Her a Man among Men': Translating the *Khuntha*' s Anatomy in Fatimid Jurisprudence," *TSQ: Transgender Studies Quarterly* 3, no. 3–4 (2016): 578–86; Almarri, "The Khunthā and The Community."

17 Almarri, "Non-Binary Sexual and Gender Identities in the Community."

18 Gesink, "Intersex Bodies in Premodern Islamic Discourse"; Indira Falk Gesink, "Intersex in Islamic Medicine, Law, and Activism," in *The Routledge Handbook of Islam and Gender* (London: Routledge, 2020): 116–29.

19 Sherry Sayed Gadelrab, "Discourses on Sex Differences in Medieval Scholarly Islamic Thought," *Journal of the History of Medicine and Allied Sciences* 66, no. 1 (2011): 40–81; Emily Selove and Rosalind Batten, "Making Men and Women: Arabic Commentaries on the Gynaecological Hippocratic Aphorisms in Context," *Annales Islamologiques*, no. 48.1 (August 25, 2014): 239–62; Ahmed Ragab, "One, Two, or Many Sexes: Sex Differentiation in Medieval Islamicate Medical Thought," *Journal of the History of Sexuality* 24, no. 3 (September 2015): 428–54.

20 Kathryn M. Kueny, *Conceiving Identities: Maternity in Medieval Muslim Discourse and Practice* (Albany: State University of New York Press, 2013), 173–74.

21 Gesink, "Intersex Bodies in Premodern Islamic Discourse"; Shireen Hamza, "Islamic History and Medicine in Trans Muslim Lives," JHI Blog, July 1, 2020; Zayde Antrim, "Qamarayn: The Erotics of Sameness in the 1001 Nights," *Al-ʿUṣūr al-Wusṭā* 28 (2020): 1–44.

22 I take the notion of "forced binarization" from a discussion with my friend Gabriel Varlant.

23 Gayatri Spivak, "The Politics of Translation," in *The Translation Studies Reader*, ed. Lawrence Venuti, Third Edition (London: Routledge, 2012), 311–30; Saidiya Hartman, "Venus in Two Acts," *Small Axe: A Caribbean Journal of Criticism* 12, no. 2 (2008): 1–14; George Steiner, *Language and Silence: Essays on Language, Literature, and the Inhuman* (New Haven: Yale University Press, 1998).

24 Terrence William Deacon, *Incomplete Nature: How Mind Emerged from Matter*, 1st ed (New York City: W.W. Norton & Co, 2012), 3.

25 Kobus Marais, *A (Bio)Semiotic Theory of Translation: The Emergency of Social-Cultural Reality*, (London: Routledge, 2018), 135.

26 Daniel Boyarin, "On the History of the Early Phallus," in *Gender and Difference in the Middle Ages*, ed. Sharon Farmer and Carol Braun Pasternack, NED-New edition, vol. 32 (Minneapolis: University of Minnesota Press, 2003), 3–44.

27 Ibid., 27.

28 Ibid.; Sefaria, "Bereishit Rabbah 8:1," Sefaria.org, accessed November 1, 2022, https://www.sefaria.org/Bereishit_Rabbah.8.1?lang=bi.

29 Boyarin, "On the History of the Early Phallus," 5–6.

30 DeVun, *The Shape of Sex*, 19–22.

31 Celene Ibrahim, *Women and Gender in the Qur'ān* (Oxford: Oxford University Press, 2020).

32 Ibid., 22–23.

33 Ibid

34 Marlie Tandoc and Robert K. Logan, "Human Cognition, Patterning and Deacon's Absentials: The Value of Absent-Mindedness in the Sense of Minding What Is Absent," *Philosophies* 3, no. 4 (2018): 26.

35 Pascal Boyer, *Religion Explained: The Evolutionary Origins of Religious Thought* (New York city: Basic Books, 2001).

36 Boyer, *Religion Explained*, 16–18.

37 Ibid., 32.

38 A note on citations: The commentaries were sourced from Altafsir.com, a resource of Qur'ān commentaries published by the Amman-based Royal Aal al-Bayt Institute for Islamic Thought; wherever possible I have cross-checked the passages with printed editions.

39 M.A.S. Abdel Haleem, *The Qur'ān*, 2nd ed. (Oxford: University Press USA – OSO, 2004), 50.

40 Makkī b. Abī Tālib's commentary relates the creative substance of men and women as appearing from Adam's back, but later relates the traditions taken from other commentators such as Mujāhid, Al-Suddī, Ibn Isḥāq, and Ibn ʿAbbās and others, all which describe the creation as occurring from Adam's rib.

41 Makkī b. Abī Tālib, *al-Hidāya ilā bulūgh al-nihāya fī ʿilm maʿānī al-Qur'ān wa-tafsīrihi wa-aḥkāmihi wa-jumal min funūn ʿulūmihi*, ed. al-Shāhid al-Būshīkhī (Sharjah: Jāmiʿat al-Shāriqah, 2008), 2: 211.

42 Ibn ʿAṭīyah, *al-Muḥarrar al-wajīz fī tafsīr al-kitāb al-ʿazīz*, ed. ʿAbd al-Salām ʿAbd al-Shāfī Muḥammad, 6 vols. (Beirut: Dār al-Kutub al-ʿIlmiyya, 1422/2001), 2:4.

43 Al-Qurṭubī, *al-Jāmiʿ li-aḥkām al-Qur'ān*, ed. Aḥmad al-Bardūnī and Ibrāhīm Aṭfīsh, 20 vols. (Cairo: Dār al-Kutub al-Miṣrīyah, 1964), 5:2.

44 Abū Ḥayyān Muḥammad b. Yūsuf al-Andalusī, *al-Baḥr al-muḥīṭ fī al-tafsīr*, ed. Ṣidqī Muḥammad Jamīl (Beirut: Dār al-Fikr, 1999), 3: 496.

45 Abdel Haleem, *The Qur'ān*, 424.

46 Al-Zamakhsharī, *al-Kashshāf ʿan ḥaqā'iq ghawāmiḍ al-tanzīl*, 4 vols. (Beirut: Dār al-Kitāb al-ʿArabī, 1986), 4: 762.

47 Al-Rāzī, *al-Tafsīr al-kabīr/mafātīḥ al-ghayb* (Beirut: Dār Iḥyā' al-Turāth al-ʿArabī, 1999), 31: 182.

48 Al-Qummī al-Naysābūrī, *Gharā'ib al-Qur'ān wa-raghā'ib al-furqān*, ed. Zakarīyā ʿUmayrāt (Beirut: Dār al-Kutub al-ʿIlmīyah, 1995) 6: 510–1.

49 Al-Maḥallī and al-Suyūṭī, *Tafsīr al-jalālayn*, 810.

Bibliography

Abdel Haleem, M.A.S. *The Qur'ān*. 2nd edition. Oxford: University Press USA – OSO, 2004.

Ali, Kecia. *Sexual Ethics and Islam: Feminist Reflections on Qur'an, Ḥadīth, and Jurisprudence*. Reprint. Oxford: Oneworld, 2012.

Almarri, Saqer A. "Identities of a Single Root: The Triad of the Khunthā, Mukhannath, and Khanīth." *Women & Language* 41, no. 1 (2018): 97–109.

Almarri, Saqer A. "Non-Binary Sexual and Gender Identities in the Community: The Khunthā as an Isolated Being in the Mosque." *Body and Religion* 3, no. 2 (2020): 166–87. https://doi.org/10.1558/bar.15722.

Almarri, Saqer A. "The Khunthā and the Community: A Study in the Medieval Islamic Understanding of the Body and a Critical Edition of 'Abd Al-Raḥīm al-Isnawī's Īḍāḥ al-Mushkil fī aḥkām al-khunthā al-mushkil." Ph.D. Dissertation, Binghamton University, State University of New York, 2019.

Almarri, Saqer. "'You Have Made Her a Man among Men': Translating the *Khuntha*'s Anatomy in Fatimid Jurisprudence." *TSQ: Transgender Studies Quarterly* 3, nos. 3–4 (2016): 578–86. https://doi.org/10.1215/23289252-3545251.

Al-Andalusī, Abū Ḥayyān Muḥammad b. Yūsuf. *al-Baḥr al-Muḥīṭ fī al-Tafsīr*. edited by Ṣidqī Muḥammad Jamīl. Beirut: Dār al-Fikr, 1999. https://shamela.ws/index.php/book/23591.

Antrim, Zayde. "Qamarayn: The Erotics of Sameness in the 1001 Nights." *al-'Uṣūr al-Wusṭā* 28, (2020): 1–44.

Barlas, Asma. *"Believing Women" in Islam: Unreading Patriarchal Interpretations of the Qur'ān*. 1st edition. Austin: University of Texas Press, 2002.

Bauer, Karen. *Gender Hierarchy in the Qur'ān: Medieval Interpretations, Modern Responses*. Cambridge: Cambridge University Press, 2015.

Boyarin, Daniel. "On the History of the Early Phallus." in *Gender and Difference in the Middle Ages*, edited by Sharon Farmer and Carol Braun Pasternack, NED-New edition 32. Minneapolis: University of Minnesota Press, 2003: 3–44. https://www.jstor.org/stable/10.5749/j.cttttsps.5.

Boyer, Pascal. *Religion Explained: The Evolutionary Origins of Religious Thought. Fulcrum.Org*. New York City: Basic Books, 2001.

De Sondy, Amanullah. *Crisis of Islamic Masculinities*. London: Bloomsbury, 2015.

Deacon, Terrence William. *Incomplete Nature: How Mind Emerged from Matter*. 1st edition. New York City: W.W. Norton & Co, 2012.

DeVun, Leah. *The Shape of Sex: Nonbinary Gender from Genesis to the Renaissance*. New York: Columbia University Press, 2021.

Gadelrab, Sherry Sayed. "Discourses on Sex Differences in Medieval Scholarly Islamic Thought." *Journal of the History of Medicine and Allied Sciences* 66, no. 1 (2011): 40–81.

Gesink, Indira Falk. "Intersex Bodies in Premodern Islamic Discourse: Complicating the Binary." *Journal of Middle East Women's Studies* 14, no. 2 (2018): 152–73. https://doi.org/10.1215/15525864-6680205.

Gesink, Indira Falk. "Intersex in Islamic Medicine, Law, and Activism." In *The Routledge Handbook of Islam and Gender*. London: Routledge, 2020: 116–29.

Gilliot, Claude. "Exegesis of the Qur'ān: Classical and Medieval," in *Encyclopaedia of the Qur'ān* (Brill), accessed September 30, 2022, https://referenceworks.brillonline.com/entries/encyclopaedia-of-the-quran/exegesis-of-the-quran-classical-and-medieval-EQCOM_00058.

Hamza, Feras. "Tafsīr and Unlocking the Historical Qur'an: Back to Basics?" in *Aims, Methods and Contexts of Qur'anic Exegesis (2nd/8th–9th/15th Centuries)*, edited by Karen Bauer, 19–39. Qur'anic Studies Series 9. Oxford: Oxford University Press, 2013.

Hamza, Shireen. "Islamic History and Medicine in Trans Muslim Lives." JHI Blog, July 1, 2020. http://jhiblog.org/2020/07/01/islamic-history-and-medicine-in-trans-muslim-lives/.

Hartman, Saidiya. "Venus in Two Acts." *Small Axe: A Caribbean Journal of Criticism* 12, no. 2 (2008): 1–14. https://doi.org/10.1215/-12-2-1.

Ibn 'Aṭīyah, 'Abd al-Ḥaqq. *al-Muḥarrar al-wajīz fī tafsīr al-kitāb al-'azīz*. edited by 'Abd al-Salām 'Abd al-Shāfī Muḥammad. 6 vols. Beirut: Dār al-Kutub al-'Ilmīyah, 1422/2001. https://shamela.ws/book/23632.

Kueny, Kathryn M. *Conceiving Identities: Maternity in Medieval Muslim Discourse and Practice*. Albany: State University of New York Press, 2013. https://muse.jhu.edu/book/27400.

Luhmann, Niklas. "Complexity and Meaning." in *The Science and Praxis of Complexity: Contributions to the Symposium Held at Montpellier, France, 9–11 May, 1984*. edited by Shūhei Aida, I. Prigogine, M. Zeleny, and E. Morin. Tokyo: United Nations University, 1985.

Al-Maḥallī, Jalāl al-Dīn, and Jalāl al-Dīn al-Suyūṭī. *Tafsīr al-Jalālayn*. Cairo: Dār al-Ḥadīth, n.d. https://shamela.ws/book/12876.

Makkī b. Abī Ṭālib. *al-Hidāya ilā bulūgh al-nihāya fī 'ilm ma'ānī al-Qur'ān wa-tafsīrihi wa-aḥkāmihi wa-jumal min funūn 'ulūmihi*. edited by al-Shāhid al-Būshaykhī. 13 vols. Sharjah: Jāmi'at al-Shāriqah, 1429/2008. https://shamela.ws/book/22593.

Marais, Kobus. *A (Bio)Semiotic Theory of Translation: The Emergency of Social-Cultural Reality*. Routledge Advances in Translation and Interpreting Studies 36. London: Routledge, 2018.

Al-Qummī al-Naysābūrī, Niẓām al-Dīn. *Gharā'ib al-Qur'ān wa-Raghā'ib al-Furqān*. edited by Zakarīyā 'Umayrāt. Beirut: Dār al-Kutub al-'Ilmīyah, 1995. https://shamela.ws/book/23613.

Al-Qurṭubī, Abū 'Abd Allāh Shams al-Dīn Muḥammad b. Aḥmad. *al-Jāmi' li-aḥkām al-Qur'ān*. edited by Aḥmad al-Bardūnī and Ibrāhīm Aṭfīsh. 20 vols. Cairo: Dār al-Kutub al-Miṣrīyah, 1964. https://shamela.ws/book/20855.

Ragab, Ahmed. "One, Two, or Many Sexes: Sex Differentiation in Medieval Islamicate Medical Thought." *Journal of the History of Sexuality* 24, no. 3 (2015): 428–54. https://doi.org/10.7560/JHS24304.

Al-Rāzī, Fakhr al-Dīn. *al-Tafsīr al-kabīr/mafātīḥ al-ghayb*. Beirut: Dār Iḥyā' al-Turāth al-'Arabī, 1999. https://shamela.ws/book/23635.

Robinson, Douglas. *Transgender, Translation, Translingual Address*. London: Bloomsbury Academic, 2019.

Rowson, Everett K. "The Effeminates of Early Medina." *Journal of the American Oriental Society* 111, no. 4 (1991): 671–93. https://doi.org/10.2307/603399.

Salaymeh, Lena. "Decolonial Translation: Destabilizing Coloniality in Secular Translations of Islamic Law." *Journal of Islamic Ethics* 1, (March 5, 2021): 1–28. https://doi.org/10.1163/24685542-12340054.

Sanders, Paula. "Gendering the Ungendered Body: Hermaphrodites in Medieval Islamic Law." in *Women in Middle Eastern History*. edited by Nikki R. Keddie and Beth Baron. New Haven: Yale University Press, 1991: 74–95.

Sefaria. "Bereishit Rabbah 8:1." Digital Library. Sefaria.org. Accessed November 1, 2022. https://www.sefaria.org/Bereishit_Rabbah.8.1?lang=bi.

Selove, Emily, and Rosalind Batten. "Making Men and Women: Arabic Commentaries on the Gynaecological Hippocratic Aphorisms in Context." *Annales Islamologiques*. no. 48.1 (August 25, 2014): 239–62. https://doi.org/10.4000/anisl.2670.

Spivak, Gayatri. "The Politics of Translation." in *The Translation Studies Reader*. edited by Lawrence Venuti, Third Edition. London: Routledge, 2012: 311–30.

Steiner, George. *Language and Silence: Essays on Language, Literature, and the Inhuman*. New Haven: Yale University Press, 1998.

Tandoc, Marlie, and Robert K. Logan. "Human Cognition, Patterning and Deacon's Absentials: The Value of Absent-Mindedness in the Sense of Minding What Is Absent." *Philosophies* 3, no. 4 (2018): 26. https://doi.org/10.3390/philosophies3040026.

Tottoli, Roberto. "Eve." In *Encyclopaedia of Islam Three*. Brill, November 1, 2017. https://referenceworks.brillonline.com/entries/encyclopaedia-of-islam-3/eve-COM_26256?s.num=0.

Wadud, Amina. *Qur'an and Woman: Rereading the Sacred Text from a Woman's Perspective*. 2nd edition. New York: Oxford University Press, 1999.

Al-Zamakhsharī, Jār Allāh. *al-Kashshāf 'an ḥaqā'iq ghawāmiḍ al-tanzīl*. 4 vols. Beirut: Dār al-Kitāb al-'Arabī, 1986. https://shamela.ws/book/23627.

CHAPTER FIVE

Of Camel-Drivers and Glass Vessels: Gender (In)stability in a Ḥadīth's Interpretive History

Ash Geissinger

Abstract

Studying references to *mukhannath*s in *ḥadīth*s and *ḥadīth* commentaries extends our knowledge of classical Muslim conceptions of gender and how these have developed over time. A case in point is a widely circulated *ḥadīth* ("the glass vessels tradition") that mentions a camel-driver, Anjasha. The complex interpretive history of this *ḥadīth* includes some textual instability in the gender attributed to this figure. The various versions of the glass vessels tradition as well as most of the interpretations of it in classical *ḥadīth* commentaries typically imply that Anjasha was male. Nevertheless, Ibn Ḥajar al-ʿAsqalānī (d. 852 AH/1449 CE) in his famed commentary on the Ṣāḥīḥ al-Bukhārī asserts that according to a *ḥadīth* related by al-Ṭabarānī (d. 360/971), Anjasha was a *mukhannath*. Several other *ḥadīth* commentators in Cairo from the 8th-10th/14th-16th centuries also recount or allude to this latter assertion. None of them reject it, and all seem to accord it some degree of probability. This article begins with an overview of gender in the Sunni *ḥadīth* corpus, including its representations of mukhannaths. Then, it traces the evolution of Anjasha's shadowy persona in biographical entries over time. Finally, it examines Anjasha's shifting roles within the glass vessels tradition's multifaceted history of interpretation.

Keywords: *ḥadīth*s, *ḥadīth* commentary, gender instability, *mukhannath*, Anjasha

The following discussion focuses on *mukhannath*s in the Sunni *ḥadīth* corpus. Several *ḥadīth*s portray *mukhannath*s as a class of persons living in Medina during the time of the prophet Muḥammad. While they had been born with a penis, they spoke, moved, and adorned themselves in ways that were regarded as more akin to what was deemed appropriate for females.[1] While the terms "*khunthā*" and "*mukhannath*" are both derived from the same Arabic root, these are different categories of persons. A *khunthā* is categorized as such due to the appearance of their genitals. *Mukhannath*s, however, were known by their distinctively gendered comportment. Muslim religious scholars typically have conceptualized, discussed, and legislated about persons belonging to these two categories in significantly different ways. Nevertheless, as Saqer Almarri observes, both *khunthā*s and *mukhannath*s "inhabit[ed] their bodies in the in-betweens and margins of gender, sex, and sexuality."[2] Studying representations of *mukhannath*s in *ḥadīth*s and *ḥadīth* commentaries expands our knowledge of classical Muslim understandings of gender and aspects of their development over time.

Introducing the glass vessels tradition

> ...Thābit al-Banānī—Anas b. Mālik said: The Prophet was on one of his journeys, and the camel-driver urged on (the camel) by singing. So the Prophet said, "Be gentle, O Anjasha—woe to you!—with the glass vessels (al-qawārīr)!"[3]

> ...Anas b. Mālik said: The Prophet came to some of his wives—and Umm Sulaym was with them. Then he said, "Woe to you, O Anjasha! Drive slowly with the glass vessels!"[4]

This rather cryptically worded *ḥadīth* (henceforth, "the glass vessels tradition") has come down to us in multiple variant versions. Its long and complex history of interpretation includes shifts in the gender attributed to the camel driver. Works of *ḥadīth* commentary (*sharḥ*) usually imply that the camel driver, who was called Anjasha according to most versions of the glass vessels tradition, was male. However, as G.H.A. Juynboll notes, Ibn Ḥajar al-ʿAsqalānī (d. 852/1449) in his *Fatḥ al-bārī*, a well-known commentary on the *Ṣaḥīḥ al-Bukhārī*, states that according to a *ḥadīth* related by al-Ṭabarānī (d. 360/971), Anjasha was a *mukhannath*.[5]

To anyone whose knowledge of the glass vessels tradition is mediated by contemporary Sunni Muslim confessional discourses, this claim related by Ibn Ḥajar is likely unexpected, as well as baffling. Such discourses about this *ḥadīth* typically present gender as self-evidently binary, meaning that all human beings are either "male" or "female." As a result, they do not usually acknowledge the existence of any persons who do not fit (whether consistently, or at all) within one or the other of these two categories. As we will see, this can be the case even when Ibn Ḥajar's *Fatḥ al-bārī* is among the sources used.

The claim that Anjasha was a *mukhannath* which Ibn Ḥajar recounts—as do several other *ḥadīth* commentators in 8th–10th/14th–16th century Mamluk Cairo—presents readers/audiences with a marginal figure in early Muslim sacred history whose implied or attributed gender seems to shift within and across texts. This raises several historical questions, one of which will be the focus here: What can this example tell us about how gender categories are envisaged in the Sunni *ḥadīth* corpus, as it is read through its premodern interpretive tradition?

As will become evident, Anjasha's textually unstable gender is produced by several factors. These include the ways that the Sunni *ḥadīth* corpus constructs gender, characteristics of the genre of *ḥadīth* commentary, and developments in the glass vessels tradition's interpretive history. This discussion begins with an overview of gender in the Ḥadīth literature, with particular attention to its portrayal of *mukhannath*s. Then, it charts the development of Anjasha's shadowy persona in biographical entries over time. Finally, Anjasha's evolving roles within the glass vessels tradition's complex history of interpretation will be examined.

Juynboll concludes that the glass vessels tradition does not go back to Anas, nor to his "direct 'pupils'," though it may have been put into circulation by a *mawlā* from Basra, Ḥammād b. Zayd (d. 179/795).[6] As the following analysis focuses on gendered meanings attributed to traditions, issues of dating will not be addressed in detail. As will become apparent, the significance of the glass vessels tradition over time is much less about its historical origins or its "original" meaning than its capacity to serve as an "imperial translation" of Muḥammad. While the ostensible setting of this tradition is 1st/7th century northwestern Arabia (the Ḥijāz), it has long been heard and read by Muslims as though it transcends time and space. This enables the prophet's reported words to the camel-driver to address various issues faced by later generations living in markedly different social, economic, and political contexts.[7]

A note on method and mistakes

Ḥadīth collections most often focus on the perspectives, experiences, and words of Muslim adult males who were free, sane and able-bodied, and were reportedly participants in or observers of the events described, or transmitters of others' recollections. Generally, they tend to present these men's standpoints as normative. All other persons, whether freeborn women, freeborn children, *mukhannath*s, enslaved persons of any gender, or other "not-men" (as Everett Rowson terms them)[8] are typically represented in *ḥadīth* compilations in relation to this adult free male norm, and as exceptions to it. Therefore, reading with a focus on any of these "not-men" typically involves reading against the grain of these texts, which usually position such types of persons as comparatively marginal, though to widely varying extents. Categories of persons associated with stigmatized kinds of gender non-normative behavior, such as *mukhannath*s, most often are relegated to the utmost margins of the *ḥadīth* corpus and its commentarial traditions. One result of such marginality is that representations of these types of persons are disproportionately affected by mistakes in transmission, scribes' attempts at "correction," scribal or printing errors, and the like.[9]

Given this broader dynamic, textual uncertainties can arise at times about the gender of a markedly obscure person of low social status (if in fact they existed historically). In such cases, it might never be possible to establish what the "original" gender attributed to them was, much less how they would have identified themselves. This study argues that rather than dismiss such uncertainties merely as errors, the recognition that mistakes do not arise in a vacuum should be the starting point for further analysis. Therefore, they should also be studied for what they can tell us about the ways that gender is constructed in the Ḥadīth literature, as well as the interpretive histories of individual *ḥadīth*s.

Gender in the Ḥadīth corpus

The Sunni *ḥadīth* corpus does not construct a unitary gender system. However, at the level of ideals it generally presents gendered categories of persons in ways that are comparable to a hierarchically arranged spectrum. Free Muslim adult males who are sane and able-bodied are placed at the top, and all other types of persons—including free women, free children, *mukhannath*s, enslaved persons of any gender—are positioned at varying removes below. In general, this textual genre presents such free Muslim adult males as the most fully realized type of human being. As a group, they are presumed to have been endowed with the greatest intellectual, spiritual and physical potential; therefore, they should also have the most power, authority, and ability to act autonomously.[10]

This idealized conception of cosmic and social order was shaped by multiple sources. These include established practices of the early Muslim community (the *sunna*), myths derived from biblical traditions (such as the story of Eve's creation from Adam's rib),[11] and Greek medical theories about conception and pregnancy. Such theories attempted to explain why a fetus develops as male, or as female, or has intersex characteristics, as well as why some people have gender nonnormative mannerisms.[12] In the first few centuries of Muslim history, what would become the *ḥadīth* corpus functioned somewhat like a living body, incorporating prestigious types of knowledge and bringing them under the aegis of Muḥammad's teachings. Concurrently, *ḥadīth* transmitters and compilers were also attempting to respond to complex social, economic and political realities, as well as human physical and psychological diversity.

Broadly speaking, the *ḥadīth* corpus constructs and portrays gender categories as relational, internally diverse, and intertwined in complex ways with various facets of human difference, including freeborn, freed, or enslaved status, lineage, ethnicity, occupation, and age, among others.[13] Given the role of legal and social status in gender categorization in these texts, it is perhaps not surprising that textual gender instability is particularly apt to affect figures with low social status such as servants or menial workers about whom barely anything is remembered.[14]

Notwithstanding such complexities, contemporary confessional Muslim discourses usually interpret the *ḥadīth* corpus through the lens of assumptions shaped by the impacts of major international political, economic, social and intellectual developments since the nineteenth century CE. Such assumptions include the notion that gender is binary, and that while males and females are in some sense equal before God, they have been created with different natures. Spouses are to play complementary roles, with the husband as head of the household and provider while the wife owes him obedience and is responsible for domestic affairs.[15] Features of the *ḥadīth* corpus as well as other premodern religious texts that do not fit harmoniously with such monolithically binary, complementarian and deterministic understandings of gender tend to be ignored or downplayed; this dynamic includes minority gender categories or expressions.[16]

An interesting illustration of how such contemporary confessional rereadings can shape interpretations of the glass vessels tradition is Muḥammad Muṣṭafā al-Jibāly's book, *The Fragile Vessels: Rights and Obligations Between the Spouses in Islam.*[17] It aims to steer Muslim audiences away from attitudes and practices that stem from the "misuse" of *ḥadīth*s or the influence of "non-Islāmic cultures,"[18] through a return to the sources—the Qurʾān and *sunna*. For him, the *sunna* is chiefly equated with *ḥadīth*s either found in the *Ṣaḥīḥ* collections of al-Bukhārī (d. 256/870) and/or Muslim (d.261/875), or their level of authenticity has been verified by his teacher Muḥammad Nāṣir al-Dīn al-Albānī (d. 1999 CE).[19]

According to al-Jibāly, as men are stronger, they need to protect and direct women, who are physically and emotionally weaker. Among the *ḥadīth*s he quotes as evidence of this view of gender is the glass vessels tradition. He states that according to a number of scholars, including al-Bukhārī, al-Qurṭubī,[20] and [Ibn Ḥajar] al-ʿAsqalānī," the prophet ordered Anjasha to drive the camels more slowly for two reasons: Their female passengers were at risk of injury or falling due to women's "delicate nature and build." Also, as women respond more emotionally to song and poetry, Anjasha's singing might "affect their hearts and bring *fitnah* [i.e. temptation] to them."[21]

While al-Jibāly here invokes multiple authorities for this explanation, he indicates that his source for their respective views is Ibn Ḥajar's *Fatḥ*.[22] The sub-chapter of the *Fatḥ* that al-Jibāly is evidently drawing upon refers to a *ḥadīth* credited to the Companion Wāthila b. al-Asqaʿ and related by al-Ṭabarānī which includes Anjasha among the *mukhannath*s who were banished by the prophet.[23] Nevertheless, it passes unmentioned in al-Jibāly's summary of this discussion by Ibn Ḥajar of the glass vessels tradition. This omission is in keeping with the book's overall tendency to harmonize differing views, and to sanitize or ignore elements of the past that might complicate its prescriptive message. The teachings it seeks to convey are based on the presumption that a gender binary and gender complementarity are self-evidently "natural" and timeless—though also in need of defense from "Western ideologies."[24] Such assumptions and political dynamics leave little to no room to acknowledge figures such as *mukhannath*s. They are however a contemporary example of ways that material and intellectual contexts can shape and foster shifts in confessional understandings of how the *ḥadīth* corpus presents gender.

Mukhannaths

As Everett Rowson's pioneering research demonstrates, available sources seem to indicate that at least as it was used in texts, the category of "*mukhannath*" underwent some significant changes from the 1st/7th century Ḥijāz to 3rd/9th century Baghdad. Linguistically speaking, "*mukhannath*" originally referred to a person born with a penis whose "languid" manner of moving as well as "soft" way of speaking was deemed similar to the movements and speech typically expected of women.[25] In other words, what set them apart from others seems to have been some aspects of their bodily comportment—at least in the eyes of their contemporaries.

Some sixty years after Muḥammad's death (i.e. during the early Umayyad period) available sources imply that the category of "*mukhannath*" had also come to be linked to an occupation, as well as a particular outlook on life. *Mukhannath*s in Mecca and Medina are presented as skilled and influential singers and musicians, who had a reputation for pleasure-seeking and an irreverent approach to authority. Their attire seems to have been distinctive, sometimes including items of clothing regarded as appropriate for women, hennaed hands, and hairstyles deemed non-masculine. They were typically assumed to lack sexual interest in females and often were permitted to visit with elite secluded women, but what (if any) sexual activities they engaged in seems to have varied. Some married women and fathered children, some had sex with males, and in the case of others nothing is reported about this aspect of their lives.[26]

In sources about the ʿAbbāsid caliph's court in 3rd/9th century Baghdad, *mukhannath*s are presented as paid entertainers. While some were musicians, they were particularly known and appreciated for their comedic talents. As their social status had by this point become even lower than previously, they could jest about sensitive topics without powerful persons feeling obliged to take offence. At this time, *mukhannath*s became associated with a specific and highly stigmatized sexual activity: playing the receptive role in anal intercourse. Rowson observes that this latter development may have played a part in the further deterioration of their status.[27]

Various *ḥadīth*s present *mukhannath*s in Medina during the prophet's lifetime as persons with a marginal yet ambiguous social status, who were distinctive in their patterns of socialization and possibly also adornment. Their ties to tribal networks in the Ḥijāz seem to have been through clientage rather than birth. As Rowson notes, the individual *mukhannath*s mentioned in *ḥadīth*s were *mawlā*s ("clients," or freedpersons) and their names were very atypical.[28] It is related that they visited with elite secluded women who did not mingle with free men not closely related to them, including the prophet's wives, because it was usually presumed that they were not sexually attracted to females—nor to anyone else, for that matter. Some *mukhannath*s reportedly adorned their hands and feet with henna, a practice deemed woman-like.

A few *ḥadīth*s specify the punishment (twenty lashes) for falsely accusing a man of being a *mukhannath*, and the notion that *mukhannath*s are to be rhetorically and/or spatially relegated to the communal margins is a recurrent theme in traditions mentioning them.[29] Such *ḥadīth*s construct and affirm their status as disreputable at best. Nevertheless, some biographical works on the prophet's Companions do include short entries for several *mukhannath*s,[30] recognizing their presence (however ambivalently) within the ranks of this storied generation.

A widely circulated *ḥadīth* (henceforth, "the Ghaylān's daughter tradition") depicts a *mukhannath* visiting Muḥammad's household:

> ...on the authority of Umm Salama, that the Prophet was with her while a *mukhannath* was in the house. The *mukhannath* said to Umm Salama's brother, "O ʿAbdallāh b. Abī Umayya, if tomorrow God grants you victory over al-Ṭāʾif, I direct you to the daughter of Ghaylān, as she comes with four and leaves with eight." He [the transmitter] said: The Messenger of God heard it, and said, "Do not allow this person to visit you."[31]

Ḥadīth commentators explain the *mukhannath*'s words—"she comes with four and leaves with eight"—as referring to the rolls of fat on Ghaylān's daughter's torso. They interpreted this description of her as demonstrating the *mukhannath*'s awareness of which features of women's bodies men typically find alluring.[32] It is unclear whether the *mukhannath* was no longer allowed to visit with the prophet's wives because his words were thought to imply that he found women sexually desirable, or because he had violated social and moral norms by providing ʿAbdallāh with an explicit description of an elite secluded woman's body.[33] Whatever the case, this *ḥadīth* constructs the prophet's wives' abode as an idealized space within which a legal debate about the allowability of *mukhannath*s' access to the women's quarters within a household can be authoritatively resolved.[34]

Another *ḥadīth* (henceforth, "the cursing tradition") recounts that "The Messenger of God cursed the *mukhannath*s among the men, and the *mutarajjila*s among the women."[35] Some versions add that he said, "Expel them from your homes!" Some forms of this tradition further state that certain persons—usually left unnamed—were indeed expelled, e.g.:

> "...then the Prophet expelled so-and-so (*fulān*), and ʿUmar expelled so-and-so (*fulān*)."[36]

> "...then the Prophet expelled so-and-so, and ʿUmar expelled such-and-such a female (*fulāna*)."[37]

> "...that the Prophet expelled a *mukhannath*, and that ʿUmar expelled so-and-so, and so-and-so."[38]

The "*fulāna*" version also appears in some printed editions of the *Ṣaḥīḥ al-Bukhārī* in the Chapter on Clothing.[39] The "*fulāna*" wording (rather than "*fulān*") here is reportedly in accordance with the transmission of the *Ṣaḥīḥ al-Bukhārī* by the famed *ḥadīth* scholar Abū Dharr al-Harawī (d. 434/1042–3).[40] This proliferation of variant endings of the cursing tradition eventually had an impact on the gender attributed to Anjasha in some *ḥadīth* commentaries.

In Juynboll's view, the Ghaylān's daughter tradition (at least as we now have it) was likely put into circulation by Hishām b. ʿUrwa (d. 146/763), an Arab *ḥadīth* transmitter who moved to Baghdad and died there,[41] while the person who played this role with regard to the cursing tradition was a Basran *mawlā* and *ḥadīth* transmitter Shuʿba b. al-Ḥajjāj (d. 160/776).[42] Both traditions would then owe their present form to early ʿAbbāsid Iraq. Johannes Thomann's analysis of the chains of transmitters and wordings of several variant forms of the cursing tradition also concludes that these "came into circulation in the first two decades of the Abbasid era (c. 750–770 CE) in Basra," and may have been a condemnatory response to caliphal court culture of the time.[43] Therefore, it is difficult to say to what extent these *ḥadīth*s might reflect conditions in the 1st/7th century Ḥijāz. It is quite probable that their present forms were shaped by later concerns—as is the case for their respective framings within *ḥadīth* collections.

Such concerns apparently included forms of socialization and recreation in elite households, and how these ought to relate to cosmic, social and familial gendered order. In contradistinction to elite men's enjoyment of frivolity at the ʿAbbāsid court,[44] the Ghaylān's daughter tradition as well as the versions of the cursing tradition commanding that *mukhannath*s be put out of believers' homes construct and enjoin a soberly pious and commanding ideal of elite masculine behavior.

Who was Anjasha?

Though not all versions of the glass vessels tradition name the camel-driver,[45] most state that he was called Anjasha. In premodern biographical sources which discuss the lives of the prophet Muḥammad's Companions, Anjasha is a shadowy figure at best. There is no biographical entry for Anjasha in Ibn Saʿd's (d. 230/845) famous *Ṭabaqāt*—which however does recount several versions of the glass vessels tradition in its entry for Umm Sulaym.[46] In this instance, the glass vessels tradition serves to underline her meritorious proximity to the prophet. However, a student of Ibn Saʿd's, al-Balādhurī (d. 279/892), does elect to incorporate a very brief entry for Anjasha in his *Ansāb*, in the section on the prophet Muḥammad's freedpersons (*mawālī*). It simply states: "Anjasha was Abyssinian; his *kunya* is Abū Māriya. He is the one to whom the Messenger of God said while he was driving the camels for the women, 'O Anjasha, treat the glass vessels gently!'"[47]

For al-Balādhurī as well as others who provide Anjasha with a biographical entry, the chief if not sole reason for doing so seems to be the glass vessels tradition's mention of this figure. Aside from that *ḥadīth* and the few details that can be extracted from various versions of it, they found little to recount about Anjasha.[48] It is unclear when he came to be reckoned among the prophet's followers. While one version of the tradition has Anjasha driving camels for the wives of the prophet in the year that Muḥammad performed the Farewell Pilgrimage (i.e. 10/632), others present him driving camels for the prophet on an unspecified journey.[49]

Ibn Ḥibbān's (d. 354/965) dictionary of reliable *ḥadīth* transmitters includes a very brief entry for Anjasha, which reads: "Anjasha, *mawlā* of the Messenger of God: The Prophet would joke with him and say to him, 'Slow down as you drive with the glass vessels!'"[50] His inclusion of this entry implies that Anjasha was remembered as a source of at least one *ḥadīth*. In Ibn Manda's (d. 395/1050) *Maʿrifat al-ṣaḥāba*, the entry for Anjasha asserts that "Abū Ṭalḥa and Anas b. Mālik narrated from him."[51] Nevertheless, Anjasha does not appear to have been credited with transmitting even one *ḥadīth* in any of the well-known Sunni compilations.[52]

Al-Balādhurī asserts that Anjasha had a *kunya*, Abū Māriya; a few late classical authors also recount this.[53] Nevertheless, it is unclear whether one can infer that Anjasha fathered a child[54] or relatedly if he ever married or took a concubine. Biographical entries often describe Anjasha as Abyssinian and/or Black (*aswad*),[55] calling attention to his physiognomy.[56] Several state that Anjasha had a good voice, or a good voice "for camel driving."[57] This point appears to have been derived from some versions of the glass vessels tradition,[58] and it would go on to play an important role in this tradition's interpretive history.

Biographical entries for Anjasha do not have anything to say about his lineage, nor his parents. To the extent that Anjasha is granted any link to Ḥijāzi tribal networks it seems to be through his relation to Muḥammad, though his precise status *vis à vis* the prophet is unclear: Was Anjasha one of his freedpersons? A free (or freed) camel-driver who occasionally or often worked for Muḥammad and/or his wives? Or was Anjasha enslaved—and if so, to Muḥammad, or perhaps to someone else who loaned or hired him out? As we have seen, Ibn Ḥibbān describes Anjasha as a "*mawlā* of God's Messenger." For his part, Ibn Manda simply calls him "Anjasha the camel-driver" and recounts a version of the glass vessels tradition which states that "the Messenger of God had a camel-driver who was called Anjasha."[59] Ibn Manda's entry gives no indication as to whether Anjasha was free, freed, or enslaved, though it seems to imply that he had worked for the prophet for a period of time. However, Ibn ʿAbd al-Barr (d. 463/1070) characterizes Anjasha as "the Black slave who used to drive camels for the wives of the Prophet." Also, one of the versions of the glass vessels tradition that Ibn ʿAbd al-Barr recounts in his entry for Anjasha begins with Anas stating: "Anjasha used to drive for the women, and al-Barāʾ b. Mālik used to drive for the men…."[60] These variations and uncertainties reflect differing versions of the glass vessels tradition.

Overall, this is a figure who is presented as deracinated[61] and of low social status, about whom almost nothing is remembered save his performance of a menial task. While tedious work such as camel driving kept daily life going in the Ḥijāz, labor like this is mostly taken for granted in biographical sources and usually passes unmentioned. Typically, Anjasha is granted a marginal place in communal memory by these authors because he drove camels for the prophet, or his wives and/or Umm Sulaym when she traveled with Muḥammad. Occasionally, it is because the glass vessels tradition forms part of a later *ḥadīth* transmitter's resume.[62]

It is unclear when the assertion that Anjasha was a *mukhannath* first began to appear in biographical writings. In his *Iṣāba*, Ibn Ḥajar concludes his entry for Anjasha with the statement that according to a *ḥadīth* which is related by Wāthila, "Anjasha was among the *mukhannath*s during the Messenger of God's time." Ibn Ḥajar then goes on to relate this *ḥadīth*—a variant version of the cursing tradition discussed above (henceforth, "the Wāthila variant")—which he says is quoted by al-Ṭabarānī with a *layyin* (lit. "soft," i.e. unreliable) chain of transmitters. It reads: "…The Messenger of God cursed the *mukhannath*s, and he said, 'Expel them from your houses!' The Prophet expelled Anjasha, and ʿUmar expelled so-and-so."[63] None of the biographical sources used in this study which predate Ibn Ḥajar's time recount or refer to this claim that Anjasha was a *mukhannath* in their respective entries for this figure.[64]

Ibn Ḥajar's decision to quote the Wāthila variant of the expulsion tradition in his entry for Anjasha in his *Iṣāba* appears to stem from several factors. Among these is a tendency for some later compilers of biographical writings about the Companions to attempt to flesh out marginal figures by combing through the *ḥadīth* corpus for clues. Variant endings of the cursing tradition had proliferated, through different transmissions and likely also individual mistakes; it is possible that the name Anjasha "originally" became affixed to it through scribal error or an attempt at "correction."[65] Also, the thematic similarities between some of the interpretive foci of the glass vessels tradition and the Ghaylān's daughter tradition—both of which came to be read as featuring an obscure subaltern figure whose problematic proximity to the prophet's secluded wives required Muḥammad's intervention—may have fostered the assimilation of Anjasha with the *mukhannath*. That *mukhannath*s were associated with the controversial topics of singing and music might have been a contributing factor. Nevertheless, whatever its origins, once the Wāthila variant was in circulation it became available for eventual incorporation into biographical works—as well as *ḥadīth* commentaries.

The glass vessels tradition: Shifting interpretations, layering meanings

It is apparent from 3rd/9th century sources that by that time, a plethora of versions of the glass vessels tradition were in circulation. Most bear the marks of interpretive efforts which include the addition of various details, as well as brief comments credited to transmitters.

As the first example of the glass vessels tradition quoted at the beginning of this study illustrates, some versions make no reference to the presence of any wives or women at all. Another similar example reads: "...Anas b. Mālik related that the Messenger of God said, 'O Anjasha, *that* is the way you treat glass vessels?!'"[66] The most straightforward reading of such versions would be that Muḥammad is simply telling someone driving a camel (or camels) laden with glassware to slow down, or reproving him for not being careful enough. Here, the prophet embodies a religious ideal: an elite masculinity that combines the authoritative supervision of a subordinate with calm restraint as he directs or reproves the latter.

Nevertheless, the glass vessels tradition has typically been interpreted in less literal and more figurative ways, which likewise have served to construct gender categories and hierarchically arranged gender roles. Questions were posed (early on, it seems) about the prophet's intent. If his comment is to be understood non-literally, was it intended as a joking remark about Anjasha's driving skills? If not, was "glass vessels" an allusion to the camels (which Anjasha was driving too forcefully),[67] or to the women riding upon them? If the latter, why would the prophet use this word to refer to the women in question? The comments attributed to transmitters of some versions of the glass vessels tradition attempt to steer the audience/reader toward certain interpretive possibilities while foreclosing others. The Successor Abū Qilāba for example reportedly recounted a version of the tradition and then commented, "The Prophet uttered an expression that you would have criticized if one of you had uttered it—'your driving of glass vessels'."[68] By this, Abū Qilāba seems to have meant that this expression of Muḥammad's was figurative in some way. Other transmitters' comments address the intended referent of "glass vessels." One such comment, also credited to Abū Qilāba, relates that after he recounted a version of this tradition which ends with the word "*qawārīr*" (glass vessels) he added, "Meaning, the women."[69] A transmitter's comment attributed to the Successor Qatāda asserts that this word means "the women's weakness."[70] One version of the glass vessels tradition attributes this latter comment to Anas himself,[71] which as al-Qurṭubī notes grants it more interpretive weight.[72]

In the form that they have come down to us, the *ḥadīth* collections organized according to topic provide further layers of interpretation of the glass vessels tradition. They do so through the decisions made (whether by the compiler, a subsequent transmitter of the work, or a later commentator)[73] to quote this tradition in chapters or sub-chapters devoted to certain matters rather than others. Through such acts of categorization, the glass vessels tradition is made to address broader ongoing debates on a variety of questions.

For example, in al-Bukhārī's *Adab al-mufrad* and the *Sunan* of al-Dārimī (d. 255/869) the glass vessels tradition is recounted in sub-chapters on the topic of joking.[74] This frames the prophet's words to Anjasha as a remark made in jest, which in turn brings this tradition to bear on debates as to whether the prophet laughed aloud with his Companions.[75] In al-Bukhārī's *Ṣaḥīḥ*, the glass vessels tradition is quoted in several different sub-chapters, including one addressing the permissibility of using equivocal or ambiguous expressions.[76] This question is linked to debates about the acceptability of poetry—a controversy to which the glass vessels tradition was also judged by al-Bukhārī to pertain.[77] Al-Bayhaqī's (d. 458/1066) *Sunan* recounts several versions of the glass vessels tradition in a sub-chapter which asserts that listening to songs used for urging on camels is permitted; therefore, doing so will not undermine a man's status as an upright witness in a court of law.[78]

The question of how to distinguish between types of relaxation or amusement that are deemed religiously acceptable and those that are dismissed as blameworthy frivolity is a gendered one, which is intertwined with legal and social status. Indulgence in recreational tastes associated with court life was a way to embody an elite masculinity associated with wealth, high status, and proximity to power. Attempting to counter this construction of masculinity, a number of classical texts polemically associate singing, music and the like with *mukhannath*s and women, as well as with men losing their manliness.[79] Of all people, freeborn adult elite men who were sane and able-bodied were legally granted the greatest level of bodily autonomy and control over their voices, labour power, time, and resources. Therefore, in theory at least, they—unlike the enslaved, the poor, the socially marginal—were the ones most able to embody the austerely pious ideal of the believer who avoids time-wasting worldly amusements. By shunning these, they would exhibit the masculine intellectual superiority and moral fortitude that elevated them above the likes of *mukhannath*s, women, and children.[80]

When taken together, *ḥadīth* compilations present multiple and at times contending interpretations of the glass vessels tradition. *Ḥadīth* commentaries further elaborate upon these layers of meaning, often attempting to adjudicate disagreements about these.

Traces of the debate about whether "glass vessels" refers to the camels or the women riding on them continued to appear in some *ḥadīth* commentaries. For example, in his commentary on the *Ṣaḥīḥ al-Bukhārī*, the Central Asian scholar al-Khaṭṭābī (d. 388/998) recounts that according to one view, Anjasha had a rough way of driving camels, so the prophet commanded him to treat them gently, driving them as one would an animal carrying a load of glassware.[81] Some subsequent commentators also mention this interpretation.[82] But as the view that "glass vessels" alludes to the women had largely prevailed, the focus was on the type(s) of female fragility—physical, emotional, and/or moral?—that it signifies.

A number of commentators mention the opinion that the prophet intervened in Anjasha's driving to make the women's travel more comfortable, or to protect them from possible physical injury, as women are less physically strong than men, and less able to hold on firmly or brace themselves when camels travel too fast. Like glassware, they are particularly prone to breakage if they fall.[83]

However, most of the *ḥadīth* commentators consulted for this study affirm the plausibility of opinions that deem "glass vessels" an allusion to female emotional suggestibility and/or moral weakness or prefer such views. Al-Khaṭṭābī calls attention to a version of the glass vessels tradition which states that Anjasha had a good voice and furthermore has a transmitter's comment (credited to Qatāda) that glosses "glass vessels" as "the women's weakness." In al-Khaṭṭābī's view, the prophet abhorred that the women hear Anjasha's singing as he urged on the camels, lest his pleasant voice stir their emotions. So, women are likened here to glass vessels due to their weak resolve (i.e. to steadfastly obey God's commands) and impressionability.[84] In his commentary on the *Ṣaḥīḥ Muslim*, the North African scholar al-Māzarī (d. 536/1141) elected to problematize the content of the poetry that Anjasha presumably had sung and chanted in order to urge on the camels. In al-Māzarī's view, not only might Anjasha's singing affect the women's hearts, but as the poetry would have contained amatory language, they were not safe from temptation. Therefore, the prophet commanded him to cease.[85]

That these interpretive developments had such an impact even on late classical Sunni *ḥadīth* commentary is noteworthy given that they do not seem to accord well with the theological axiom that no prophet's wife could ever be sexually unfaithful.[86] There evidently was some opposition in Ibn al-Jawzī's (d. 597/1201) time to assertions that the prophet had told Anjasha to cease because his nice voice was akin to the type of singing that can stir up desire, and women are particularly apt to be moved by it. Attempting to counter such objections, Ibn al-Jawzī argues that in fact, interpretations in this vein do not insinuate anything scandalous about the prophet's wives. After all, the hearers of song can be tempted by worldly desires or distracted from the remembrance of God—and the wives of the prophet were not immune from such things.[87]

But *ḥadīth* commentators seem to have been less concerned with what the glass vessels tradition might imply about the theological status of the prophet's wives (or for that matter, of Umm Sulaym[88]) than with the model it provides for elite men's oversight of their womenfolk as well as of male subordinates within the household, even in the liminal situation of travel. The claim that women's resolve is weak, which becomes a fairly predictable component of *ḥadīth* commentators' discussion of the glass vessels tradition,[89] constructs and affirms the centrality of male supervision and guidance to the maintenance of cosmic, social, and familial order.

The concern voiced by al-Māzarī about the possible impact of poetic male expressions of desire on female hearers partly reflects medieval ideals of male jealousy (*ghayra*)[90] and female seclusion. The Damascene scholar al-Nawawī (d. 676/1277) writes that among the meanings derived from the glass vessels tradition is that women ought to be kept distant from men who are not close relatives and should not hear them speak—except for men's preaching or the like.[91] Adhering to such an exacting standard of female seclusion—auditory as well as visual and spatial—would have been far beyond the ability of most non-elite households. However, the focus here was not most people's lived realities, but on constructing and upholding elite gender and status hierarchies. The attention to the content of what was chanted or sung by Anjasha is also part of a longstanding—and gendered—discourse on what types of singing can be religiously permitted,[92] as well as the dangers posed by music and song. In their discussions of the glass vessels tradition, some commentators quote the saying that song entices people to commit *zinā* (fornication or adultery).[93] Al-Qurṭubī adds that therefore, men ought to be wary of singing and should also keep women away from it.[94]

Most of the interpretations discussed so far construct elite masculinity and elite femininity through the prophet and his wives (and also at times Umm Sulaym), while paying little overt attention to Anjasha as a gendered figure. Nevertheless, some aspects of these constructions not only take for granted that Anjasha was male but seem to imply that therefore his singing or chanting posed a particular problem. It appears that the Wāthila variant of the expulsion tradition—and with it, the claim that Anjasha was a *mukhannath*—may first have entered *ḥadīth* commentators' discussions of the glass vessels tradition in late 8th/14th century Cairo.

The groundwork for this development may have been laid by Ibn al-Mulaqqin (d. 804/1401), a scholar in Cairo whose commentary on the *Ṣaḥīḥ al-Bukhārī* quotes the Wāthila variant in a passage discussing the Ghaylān's daughter tradition, in which he recounts various *ḥadīth*s and authorities' opinions about the *mukhannath*s of Muḥammad's time.[95] By incorporating the Wāthila variant into his *ḥadīth* commentary, it is possible that he drew the attention of other scholars in the city to the interpretive potential of this very obscure and quite dubious variant ending of the cursing tradition. Yet it is difficult to know which *ḥadīth* commentator might first have quoted it interpretively, partly because in Mamluk Cairo *ḥadīth* commentary was carried out orally in classes with students as well as in writing.[96]

For his part, Ibn Ḥajar does not quote the Wāthila variant at any of the points at which he comments on the Ghaylān's daughter tradition in his *Fatḥ*.[97] However, he elects to do so when discussing the cursing tradition and also the glass vessels tradition.[98] Two other Cairene scholars, al-Birmāwī (d. 831/1428) and al-ʿAynī (d. 855/1451) authored commentaries on the *Ṣaḥīḥ al-Bukhārī* which also quote the Wāthila variant. It is unclear whether or to what extent these men's decisions to do so stemmed from their familiarity with Ibn Ḥajar's interpretations.[99] Like Ibn Ḥajar, al-ʿAynī elects to quote the Wāthila variant when discussing the cursing tradition, as well as the glass vessels tradition.[100] (Interestingly, al-ʿAynī also quotes what might be yet another version of this variant—if it is not a subsequent scribal or printer's error—when discussing the Ghaylān's daughter tradition.)[101] Al-Birmāwī however only mentions the Wāthila variant in the course of his discussion of the cursing tradition, while recounting different opinions as to the names of the *mukhannaths* who were expelled:

> It is said that the Prophet expelled Mātiʿ—and it is said Mānniʿ, while the one who ʿUmar expelled was Mātiʿ—and it is said (that it was) Hidm. The transmission of Abū Dharr al-Harawī has "…then the Prophet expelled such-and-such female (*fulāna*)." Among Wāthila's *ḥadīth*s in al-Ṭabarānī is a similar one to Ibn ʿAbbās' *ḥadīth* [i.e. the cursing tradition], and it says that he expelled Anjasha. And it is also in *Fawāʾid Tammām*.[102]

Here al-Birmāwī further extends earlier commentators' efforts to identify the unnamed persons referred to in the cursing tradition by including additional evidence. His reference to another source for the Wāthila variant, Tammām b. Muḥammad al-Rāzī's (d. 414/1023) *Fawāʾid*, implies that this variant might deserve somewhat more credence.

A couple of later *ḥadīth* commentaries from Cairo on the *Ṣaḥīḥ al-Bukhārī* also refer to the Wāthila variant, though not in relation to the glass vessels tradition. In his discussion of the cursing tradition, al-Suyūṭī (d. 911/1505) comments: "'such-and-such female (*fulāna*)'—according to Abū Dharr; according to others [i.e. transmitters] 'so-and-so (*fulān*)', and he was named Anjasha."[103] Likewise, al-Qasṭallānī (d. 923/1517) states that "Ibn ʿAbbās said, '…and the Prophet expelled so-and-so': he is Anjasha the Black slave who sought to resemble women." The sources al-Qasṭallānī cites for this are not only al-Ṭabarānī and Tammām, but also Aḥmad b. Ḥanbal (d. 241/855).[104] Evidently, efforts to lend weight to the Wāthila variant continued—though due to interpretive interest in the ways that Muḥammad reportedly had dealt with *mukhannaths*, rather than in Anjasha as the camel-driver in the glass vessels tradition.

As noted above, the Wāthila variant may have originated in a mistake, and it was only one (and not the best attested) of several reported endings of the cursing tradition. Also, Ibn Ḥajar did not regard the chain of transmitters associated with the Wāthila variant as reliable. In addition, these texts attach significant stigma to the category of *mukhannath*. Yet, classical Sunni theological beliefs about the peerless status of the prophet's Companions tended to encourage a focus on aspects of their lives that typically were regarded as praiseworthy. This raises the question of why multiple Cairene scholars from the 8th–10th/14th–16th centuries would nevertheless elect to quote or allude to the Wāthila variant in their *ḥadīth* commentaries on al-Bukhārī's *Ṣaḥīḥ* and in so doing perpetuate the claim that Anjasha was a *mukhannath*.

In general, the *ḥadīth* commentaries of Ibn al-Mulaqqin, Ibn Ḥajar, al-Birmāwī, and al-ʿAynī reflect the expectations of their time and place that such works be comprehensive and display advanced knowledge of matters deemed relevant to interpretive debates, including different transmissions, textual uncertainties, and lesser-known versions of *ḥadīths*.[105] Ḥadīth commentators also typically built upon and otherwise engaged with the work of their peers, both those who had lived centuries ago as well as more recently. Therefore, once the Wāthila variant had entered the commentarial discourse, it would not be surprising if some others in turn quoted or alluded to it—especially once a particularly influential *ḥadīth* commentary such as Ibn Ḥajar's *Fatḥ* had done so. Ibn Ḥajar's *Fatḥ* quotes the Wāthila variant in several different subchapters, and by so doing made it more difficult for other contemporary and subsequent commentators on the *Ṣaḥīḥ al-Bukhārī* to ignore.

It is evident that those scholars discussed above who relate or refer to the Wāthila variant in their *ḥadīth* commentaries are more likely to do so in a sub-chapter that discusses *mukhannath*s—and most often, in relation to the cursing tradition. The genre of *ḥadīth* commentary had already accumulated some five centuries' worth of deliberation about the small number of *ḥadīth*s that mention *mukhannath*s, considering questions of definition and legal issues,[106] as well as reported examples from Muḥammad's lifetime and the era of the first few caliphs. As these examples were few, and little had been related about them, the Wāthila variant augmented this latter aspect of the discourse, adding the name of Anjasha to the scant number of early *mukhannath*s. It also provides an additional example of the prophet establishing "correct" household and communal order by banishing a *mukhannath*. Through such discussions, commentators attempted to map and reaffirm the boundaries and hierarchical arrangements of gender categories by differentiating the mannerisms, speech, attire, adornment, pastimes, and sexual proclivities of *mukhannath*s from those of others—particularly, of free and elite men.

Ibn Ḥajar's and al-ʿAynī's respective quotations of the Wāthila variant when discussing the glass vessels tradition provides an additional though dubious fragment of information about Anjasha, who as we have seen is a markedly obscure figure about whom very little is remembered. The notion that Anjasha was a *mukhannath* who furthermore came to be expelled from the prophet's home by Muḥammad himself also has the effect of further emphasizing the themes of gender hierarchy, elite male authority, and the need for strict controls on song that *ḥadīth* commentators had already derived from the glass vessels tradition.

Conclusion

The shifts in the gender category to which Anjasha is assigned in the texts discussed above are the outcome of several interrelated factors. These include the ways that gender is constructed in the Sunni *ḥadīth* corpus, the vagaries of transmission, and the nature of the genre of late classical *ḥadīth* commentary, as well as the ways that interpretive history of the glass vessels tradition unfolded over time.

The Sunni *ḥadīth* corpus constructs and acknowledges the existence of some minority gender categories and possibilities, however ambivalently. That several *ḥadīth*s—a couple of which were included in the *Ṣaḥīḥ*s of al-Bukhārī and Muslim—assert that the prophet's community contained a few *mukhannath*s granted this category of persons a very marginal presence in the *ḥadīth* corpus, and in turn in the genre of *ḥadīth* commentary.

It is probable that the Wāthila variant originated with transmission or scribal errors as well as attempts to "correct" these. But several other factors may also have been involved. The gender attributed to a low-status figure about whom very little was remembered such as Anjasha could be susceptible to undergoing textual shifts. The thematic similarities between interpretations of the Ghaylān's daughter tradition and the glass vessels tradition may have played a role in the textual assimilation of Anjasha into the category of *mukhannath*. Also, Anjasha's singing as well as the versions of the glass vessels tradition which specify that he drove camels for the prophet's wives or for the women may have lent the Wāthila variant further plausibility in the eyes of some. Regardless, this variant came to be incorporated into a few lesser-known *ḥadīth* collections.

Over the course of the interpretive history of the glass vessels tradition, the delineation of religiously ideal elite masculine characteristics and behavior has been a major theme. The prophet Muḥammad is presented as embodying such traits, whether in relation to male subordinates working for him, or persons within his household including his wives, female visitors, or various subaltern figures such as enslaved males or servants. Additionally, he does so even under anomalous and presumably stressful circumstances such as travel. He intervenes—perhaps to protect his wives from physical injury, though more likely (in the views of most *ḥadīth* commentators) to put a stop to a situation that might present an emotional or moral risk for the women. The underlying assumption of the commentators is that elite women—unlike their male counterparts—cannot be relied upon to determine what their own physical or moral safety requires, nor to act accordingly. Therefore, elite adult male authority and ongoing oversight is indispensable to establish and preserve order, whether in the household or in society more broadly.

Anjasha is presented as a subaltern (enslaved, freed, or perhaps free) who performed a menial job. Ḥadīth commentators show very little interest in his life and make no attempt to delve into his perspectives or motivations. What concerns them is Anjasha's actions, whether driving too energetically, singing, or (presumably) chanting poetry with amorous content. But even then, the focus is not primarily on Anjasha but on the prophet. By overseeing Anjasha at work, directing him, and intervening when needed to correct Anjasha's poor judgment, Muḥammad models religiously ideal elite male behavior as he authoritatively acts with calm restraint throughout.

In 8th–10th/14th–16th century Cairo, with the entrance of the Wāthila variant into commentarial discourses on the *Ṣaḥīḥ al-Bukhārī*, *ḥadīth* commentators consider the matter of Anjasha's gender. With al-ʿAynī and most consequentially Ibn Ḥajar, the Wāthila variant is linked to the glass vessels tradition itself. Nevertheless, the focus is not on the figure of Anjasha as an individual, but on what he was presumed to represent as a *mukhannath*. For these commentators, Anjasha as a *mukhannath* was a member of a disreputable class of persons with a nonnormative gender presentation, whose presence within Muḥammad's community and the storied generation of the Companions could be granted momentary recognition. In the same sentence, however, they relate that the prophet banished Anjasha from Medina along with some other *mukhannath*s. In this way, not only is Anjasha's proximity to the prophet's household reportedly brought to an unambiguous end, but he is textually relegated to the community's utmost margins.

The focus of the commentators' concern is far less about Anjasha or *mukhannaths* in general, than their ongoing discursive efforts to construct and uphold cosmic, social and familial order. Through their textual reiteration of free, elite men's powers of oversight and corrective intervention which ultimately enforces and maintains the communal marginality of a category of persons they deem properly marginal, these commentators reinforce the hierarchical nature of gender categories—yet also imply the fragility of their arrangement as well as their boundaries.

Notes

1 The classic study of *mukhannath*s in early Muslim history is Everett Rowson's "The Effeminates of Early Medina," *Journal of the American Oriental Society* 111. no. 4 (1991): 671–93. For more on "*mukhannath*" as a category, see below.

2 Saqer A. Almarri, "Identities of a Single Root: The Triad of the *Khunthā*, *Mukhannath*, and *Khanīth*," *Women & Language* 41. no. 1 (2018): 97–109, at 99.

3 Muḥammad b. Ismāʿīl al-Bukhārī, *The Translation of the Meanings of Ṣaḥīḥ al-Bukhārī* (Arabic-English), trans. Muḥammad Muḥsin Khān (Medina: Dār al-Fikr, 1979), 8: 148 (*K. al-Adab, Bāb al-maʿārīḍ mandūḥa ʿan al-kadhib*).

4 Al-Bukhārī, *Ṣaḥīḥ*, 8: 110–11 (*K. al-Adab, Bāb mā yajūz min al-shiʿr wa l-rajaz wa l-ḥudāʾ wa mā yukrah minhu*). Umm Sulaym was the mother of Anas b. Mālik, and both are well-known Medinese Companions; see Aḥmad b. ʿAlī Ibn Ḥajar al-ʿAsqalānī, *al-Iṣāba fī tamyīz al-ṣaḥāba*, eds. ʿĀdil Aḥmad ʿAbd al-Mawjūd et. al (Beirut: Dār al-Kutub al-ʿIlmiyya, 1995), 8: 408–10; 1: 275–8.

5 G.H.A. Juynboll, *Encyclopedia of Canonical Ḥadīth* (Leiden and Boston: Brill, 2007), 167, n.1. For an overview of the history of the genre of Sunni *ḥadīth* commentary, see Joel Blecher, *Said the Prophet of God: Ḥadīth Commentary Across a Millennium* (Oakland: University of California Press, 2018).

6 Juynboll, *Encyclopedia of Canonical Ḥadīth*, 165–6, 167.

7 For this function of *ḥadīth*s, see Ash Geissinger, "'Will You Not Teach *ruqyat al-namla* to This (Woman) …?': Notes on a Ḥadīth's Historical Uncertainties and Its Role in Translations of Muḥammad," in *Islam at 250: Studies in Memory of G.H.A. Juynboll*, eds. Petra M. Sijpesteijn and Camilla Adang (Leiden and Boston: Brill, 2020), 208–9.

8 Everett Rowson, "Gender Irregularity as Entertainment: Institutionalized Transvestism at the Caliphal Court in Medieval Baghdad," in *Gender and Difference in the Middle Ages*, eds. Sharon Farmer and Carol Braun Pasternack (Minneapolis: University of Minnesota Press, 2003): 45–72, at 55.

9 For an example of this dynamic in a *ḥadīth*'s chain of transmitters, see Ash Geissinger, *Gender and Muslim Constructions of Exegetical Authority: A Rereading of the Classical Genre of Qurʾān Commentary* (Leiden and Boston: Brill, 2015), 2–4, 14–15.

10 Ash Geissinger, "Applying Gender and Queer Theory to Premodern Sources," in *The Routledge Handbook of Islam and Gender*, ed. Justine Howe (London and New York: Routledge, 2021), 104–5.

11 This story is not found in the Qurʾān, but it is retold and alluded to in *ḥadīth*s and traditional stories of the prophets quoted in most premodern Qurʾān commentaries; see: Barbara Stowasser, *Women in the Qur'an, Traditions, and Interpretation* (New York and Oxford: Oxford University Press, 1994), 25–34.

12 Kathryn Kueny, *Conceiving Identities: Maternity in Medieval Muslim Discourse and Practice* (Albany: State University of New York Press, 2013), 54–61. Greek medical theories also are a key component of the historical background of early Christian texts' conceptualizations of gender and sexuality, as Bernadette Brooten's groundbreaking research shows; see her *Love Between Women: Early Christian Responses to Female Homoeroticism* (Chicago and London: The University of Chicago Press, 1996).

13 Marion Holmes Katz, "Textual Study of Gender," in *Islamic Studies in the Twenty-First Century: Transformations and Continuities*, ed. Léon Buskens and Annemarie van Sandwijk (Amsterdam: Amsterdam University Press, 2016): 87–107.

14 For a few examples of such textual uncertainties, see: Muslim b. al-Ḥajjāj, *Ṣaḥīḥ Muslim li l-imām Abī l-Ḥusayn Muslim b. al-Ḥajjāj al-Qushayrī al-Nīsābūrī* (Beirut: Dār Iḥyāʾ al-Turāth al-ʿArabī, 2000),

407 (*K. al-Janā'iz*); Aḥmad Ibn Ḥanbal, *Musnad al-Imām Aḥmad b. Ḥanbal*, ed. Muḥammad ʿAbd al-Salām ʿAbd al-Shāfī (Beirut: Dār al-Kutub al-ʿIlmiyya, 1993), 3: 606, #16082.

15 How these teachings ought to be manifested in practice continues to be debated by believers. For some recent examples of confessional arguments in favor of more egalitarian reinterpretations, see: Dina El Omari, Juliane Hammer, and Mouhanad Khorchide (eds.), *Muslim Women and Gender Justice: Concepts, Sources, and Histories* (Abingdon and New York: Routledge, 2020).

16 E.g. Geissinger, "Applying Gender," 102–4. For examples of authors downplaying or ignoring slavery, see: Kecia Ali, *Sexual Ethics and Islam: Feminist Reflections on Qur'an, Ḥadīth, and Jurisprudence* (Oxford: Oneworld, 2016).

17 This book's title is a reference to the glass vessels tradition (Muhammad Mustafa al-Jibaly, *The Fragile Vessels: Rights and Obligations Between the Spouses in Islam*, revised ed. (Arlington TX, Beirut and Medina: Al-Kitab & as-Sunnah Publishing, 2005), 40, n.3).

18 Al-Jibāly, *The Fragile Vessels*, xxiii–xxv.

19 Ibid., xx.

20 Abū l-ʿAbbās al-Qurṭubī (d. 656/1258) wrote a well-known commentary on the *Ṣaḥīḥ Muslim*.

21 Al-Jibāly, *The Fragile Vessels*, 40–1. Neither of these interpretations are given in the text of al-Bukhārī's *Ṣaḥīḥ*. However, Ibn Ḥajar infers that al-Bukhārī regarded the second interpretation—though not the first—as correct, because he included the glass vessels tradition in the sub-chapter discussing ambiguous speech (*taʿrīḍ*); see: Abū l-Faḍl Aḥmad b. ʿAlī Ibn Ḥajar al-ʿAsqalānī, *Fatḥ al-bārī bi-sharḥ Ṣaḥīḥ al-Bukhārī*, eds. ʿAbd al-ʿAzīz b. Bāz and Muḥammad Fu'ād ʿAbd al-Bāqī (al-Fajjāla: Maktabat Miṣr, 2001), 10: 770 (*K. al-Adab, Bāb mā yajūz min al-shiʿr wa l-rajaz wa l-ḥudā' wa mā yukrih minhu*).

22 Al-Jibāly, *The Fragile Vessels*, 40, n.5.

23 See Ibn Ḥajar, *Fatḥ al-bārī*, 10: 768, 770 (*K. al-Adab, Bāb mā yajūz min al-shiʿr wa-l-rajaz wa-l-ḥudā' wa-mā yukrih minhu*).

24 Al-Jibāly, *The Fragile Vessels*, 1.

25 Rowson, "The Effeminates," 672–3.

26 Ibid., 677–81.

27 Rowson, "Gender Irregularity as Entertainment," 57–63.

28 Rowson, "The Effeminates," 78. Later biographical works present the names of *mukhannath*s such as Anna, Mātiʿ, and Hīt as unique to these individuals among Muḥammad's followers; see n.30 below.

29 Rowson, "The Effeminates," 673–6.

30 E.g. ʿIzz al-Dīn Ibn al-Athīr Abū l-Ḥusayn ʿAlī b. Muḥammad al-Jazarī, *Usd al-ghāba fī maʿrifat al-ṣaḥāba*, eds. ʿAlī Muḥammad Muʿawwiḍ et.al (Beirut: Dār al-Kutub al-ʿIlmiyya, 1996), 5: 3–4, 395–6; Ibn Ḥajar, *Iṣāba*, 1: 284, 5: 519, 6: 440–2.

31 Muslim, *Ṣaḥīḥ*, 964 (*K. al-Salām*). Another version of this *ḥadīth* which is credited to ʿĀ'isha immediately follows (Ibid.) Versions of this *ḥadīth* also appear in al-Bukhārī's *Ṣaḥīḥ* and several other *ḥadīth* compilations; for an overview, see Rowson, "The Effeminates," 674.

32 E.g. Abū ʿAbdallāh Muḥammad b. ʿAlī b. ʿUmar al-Māzarī, *al-Muʿlim bi-fawā'id Muslim*, ed. Muḥammad al-Shādhilī al-Nayfar (Beirut: Dār al-Gharb al-Islāmī, 1992), 3: 89–90 (*K. al-Adab*); Abū l-Ḥasan ʿAlī b. Khalaf b. ʿAbd al-Malik Ibn Baṭṭāl, *Sharḥ Ibn Baṭṭāl ʿalā Ṣaḥīḥ al-Bukhārī*, ed. Muṣṭafā ʿAbd al-Qādir ʿAṭā (Beirut: Dār al-Kutub al-ʿIlmiyya, 2003), 7: 294 (*K. al-Riḍāʿa*).

33 Rowson, "The Effeminates," 676.

34 For Qur'ān commentaries' constructions of Muḥammad's wives' living space in order to perform similar legal and pietistic functions, see Geissinger, *Gender and Muslim Constructions*, 211.

35 E.g. ʿAbd al-Razzāq b. Hammām al-Ḥimyarī, *al-Muṣannaf*, ed. Ḥabīburraḥmān Aʿẓamī (Beirut: Al-Maktab al-Islāmī, 1970-2), 11: 242 (*K. al-Jāmiʿ*), #20433; Ibn Ḥanbal, *Musnad*, 1: 475, #3457; 2:

90, #5327, 124, #5651. *Mutarajjilas* are women who intentionally behave like men; see Johannes Thomann, "Illusions of Androgyny: Cross-dressing Women (*ghulāmiyyāt*) in Abbasid Society," in *Sex and Desire in Muslim Cultures: Beyond Norms and Transgression from the Abbasids to the Present Day*, eds. Aymon Kreil et.al (London: I.B. Tauris, 2022): 47–65, at 51.

36 E.g. Al-Bukhārī, *Saḥīḥ*, 8: 545–6 (*K. al-Muḥāribīn min ahl al-kufr wa l-ridda*); Ibn Ḥanbal, *Musnad*, 1: 296–7, #1987, 299, #2011.

37 Abū Muḥammad ʿAbdallāh b. ʿAbd al-Raḥmān b. al-Faḍl b. Bahrām al-Dārimī, *Musnad al-Dārimī al-maʿrūf bi-Sunan al-Dārimī*, ed. Ḥusayn Salīm Asad al-Dārānī (Riyadh: Dār al-Mughnī; Beirut: Dār Ibn Ḥazm, 2000), 3: 1733 (*K. al-Istiʾdhān*), #2691.

38 Jamāl al-Dīn Abū l-Ḥajjāj Yūsuf b. ʿAbd al-Raḥmān al-Mizzī, *Tuḥfat al-ashrāf bi-maʿrifat al-aṭrāf*, ed. ʿAbd al-Ṣamad Sharaf al-Dīn (Beirut: Dār al-Kutub al-ʿIlmiyya, 1999), 5: 173.

39 Al-Bukhārī, *Ṣaḥīḥ*, 7: 513–4 (*K. al-Libās*).

40 E.g. Shams al-Dīn al-Birmāwī, *al-Lāmiʿ al-Ṣabīḥ bi-sharḥ al-Jāmiʿ al-Ṣaḥīḥ* (Damascus, Beirut and Kuwait: Dār al-Nawādir, 2012), 14: 477 (*K. al-Libās*); Ibn Ḥajar, *Fatḥ*, 10: 472 (*K. al-Libās*). For the impact of al-Ḥarawī's transmission of the *Ṣaḥīḥ al-Bukhārī* on the history of *ḥadīth* commentary see Blecher, *Said the Prophet of God*, 26, 100–1.

41 Juynboll, *Encyclopedia of Canonical Ḥadīth*, 184, 204.

42 Ibid., 471, 521.

43 Thomann, "Illusions of Androgyny," 54.

44 Rowson, "Gender Irregularity."

45 Muḥammad Nāṣir al-Dīn al-Albānī, *al-Taʿlīqāt al-ḥisān ʿalā Ṣaḥīḥ Ibn Ḥibbān wa-tamyīz saqīmihi min ṣaḥīḥihi wa-shādhdhihi min maḥfūẓihi* (Jeddah: Dār Abāwazīr, 2003), 8: 273–4, #5772.

46 *Kitāb al-Ṭabaqāt al-kabīr*, ed. ʿAlī Muḥammad ʿUmar (Cairo: Maktabat al-Khānjī, 2001), 10: 400–1.

47 *Ansāb al-ashrāf*, ed. Muḥammad Bāqūr al-Maḥmūdī (Beirut: Dār al-Taʿārif li l-Maṭbūʿāt, 1977), 1: 482.

48 E.g.: Abū Ḥātim Muḥammad Ibn Ḥibbān, *Kitāb al-Thiqāt*, eds. Ibrāhīm Shams al-Dīn and Turkī Farḥān al-Muṣṭafā (Beirut: Dār al-Kutub al-ʿIlmiyya, 1998), 1: 258; Abū ʿAbdallāh Muḥammad b. Isḥāq b. Yaḥyā Ibn Manda al-Aṣbahānī, *Maʿrifat al-ṣaḥāba*, ed. ʿĀmir Ḥasan Ṣabrī (UAE: Maṭbūʿāt Jāmiʿat al-Imārāt al-ʿArabiyya al-Muttaḥida, 2005), 1: 206–7; Abū ʿUmar Yūsuf b. ʿAbdallāh b. Muḥammad Ibn ʿAbd al-Barr, *al-Istīʿāb fī maʿrifat al-aṣḥāb*, eds. ʿAlī Muḥammad Muʿawwiḍ et.al (Beirut: Dār al-Kutub al-ʿIlmiyya, 1995), 1: 226; Ṣalāḥ al-Dīn Khalīl b. Aybak al-Ṣafadī, *Kitāb al-Wāfī bi-l-wafayāt*, eds. Aḥmad al-Arnāʾūṭ and Turkī Muṣṭafā. (Beirut: Dār Iḥyāʾ al-Turāth al-ʿArabī, 2000), 9: 234.

49 E.g. Ibn ʿAbd al-Barr, *al-Istīʿāb*, 1: 226; al-Ṣafadī, *Kitāb al-Wāfī*, 9: 234. ʿIzz al-Dīn Ibn al-Athīr's entry for Anjasha states that he drove camels for the prophet's wives during the Farewell Pilgrimage (*Usd*, 1: 284).

50 Ibn Ḥibbān, *Kitāb al-Thiqāt*, 1: 258.

51 Ibn Manda, *Maʿrifat al-ṣaḥāba*, 1: 206. Abū Ṭalḥa was Anas' stepfather (Ibn Ḥajar, *Iṣāba*, 2: 502–4).

52 There is no entry for Anjasha in al-Mizzī's (d. 742/1341) *Tahdhīb al-kamāl*, his encyclopedia of *ḥadīth* transmitters. Nor is Anjasha listed in a contemporary dictionary of the *ḥadīth* transmitters found in nine well-known Sunni compilations; see ʿAbd al-Ghaffār Sulaymān al-Bandarī and Sayyid Kasrawī Ḥasan, *Mawsūʿat rijāl al-kutub al-tisʿa*, 4 vols (Beirut: Dār al-Kutub al-ʿIlmiyya, 1993).

53 Ibn Ḥajar, *Iṣāba*, 1: 269; Shams al-Dīn al-Sakhāwī, *al-Tuḥfat al-laṭīfa fī tārīkh al-Madīna al-Sharīfa* ([Cairo]: Asʿad Ṭarābazūnī al-Ḥusaynī, 1979–80), 1: 339.

54 I have not so far been able to find any trace of any "Māriya" likely to be Anjasha's daughter.

55 However, neither Ibn Manda nor Ibn Ḥibbān make this assertion, reflecting the absence of this information in some versions of the glass vessels tradition.

56 For physiognomy in *ḥadīths*, see Michael Muhammad Knight, *Muḥammad's Body: Baraka Networks and the Prophetic Assemblage* (Chapel Hill: The University of North Carolina Press, 2020), 35ff.

[57] Ibn ʿAbd al-Barr, *al-Istīʿāb*, 1: 226; ʿIzz al-Dīn Ibn al-Athīr, *Usd*, 1: 284; al-Ṣafadī, *Kitāb al-Wāfī*, 9: 234; Ibn Ḥajar, *Iṣāba*, 1: 269.

[58] E.g. Muslim, *Ṣaḥīḥ*, 1013 (*K. al-Faḍāʾil*).

[59] Ibn Manda, *Maʿrifat al-ṣaḥāba*, 1: 206.

[60] Ibn ʿAbd al-Barr, *al-Istīʿāb*, 1: 226. Al-Barāʾ was Anas' brother or half-brother (Ibn Ḥajar, *Iṣāba*, 1: 412–14).

[61] For enslavement and deracination, see Matthew Gordon, "Slavery in the Islamic Middle East (c. 600–1000 CE)," in *The Cambridge World History of Slavery, Volume 2: AD 500-AD 1420*, eds. Craig Perry et.al (Cambridge: Cambridge University Press, 2021): 337–61, at 341.

[62] E.g. Abū Nuʿaym Aḥmad b. ʿAbdallāh al-Aṣfahānī, *Ḥilyat al-awliyāʾ wa-Ṭabaqāt al-aṣfiyāʾ* (Beirut: Dār al-Kutub al-ʿIlmiyya, n.d.), 3: 106.

[63] Ibn Ḥajar, *Iṣāba*, 8: 270.

[64] Though it does at times appear in later works, e.g. al-Sakhāwī, *al-Tuḥfat al-laṭīfa*, 1: 340.

[65] In a recent printed edition of al-Ṭabarānī's *Muʿjam*, the cursing tradition credited to Wāthila has the following ending: "…So the Prophet expelled the Abyssinians (*al-Ḥabasha*) and ʿUmar expelled so-and-so" (Abū l-Qāsim Sulaymān b. Aḥmad al-Ṭabarānī, *al-Muʿjam al-kabīr*, ed. Abū Muḥammad al-Asyūṭī (Beirut: Dār al-Kutub al-ʿIlmiyya, 2007), 9: 182, #12666. While it is unclear where and when this ending originated, the similar shapes among some of the relevant consonants (m-kh-n-th, ʾn-j-sh-(t), ʾl-ḥ-b-sh-(t)) suggest scribal error and attempts at correction, and/or possibly printer's errors.

[66] "*Yā Anjasha ka-dhāka sayruka bi l-qawārīr*" (Ibn Ḥanbal, 3: 253, #13148; Abū Nuʿaym, 3: 106).

[67] E.g. "…Anas said, "A man used to drive for the Mothers of the Believers; he was called Anjasha. He was harsh with regard to driving (*ishtadd fī l-siyāqa*) [i.e. the camels]. So, the Messenger of God said to him, 'O Anjasha, slowly in your driving with the glass vessels!'" (Ibn Ḥanbal, 3: 131, #12047).

[68] Muḥammad b. Ismāʿīl al-Bukhārī, *al-Adab al-mufrad* (Jubayl: Dār al-Ṣādiq, 2000), 98 (*Bāb al-muzāḥ*). Similarly: al-Bukhārī, *Ṣaḥīḥ*, 8: 110–11 (*K. al-Adab, Bāb mā yajūz min al-shiʿr wa-l-rajaz wa-l-ḥudāʾ*); Muslim, 1013, (*K. al-Faḍāʾil*); Ibn Ḥanbal, 3: 228, #12940.

[69] Al-Bukhārī, *Ṣaḥīḥ*, 8: 148–9 (*K. al-Adab, Bāb al-maʿārīḍ mandūḥat ʿan al-kadhib*).

[70] Al-Bukhārī, *Ṣaḥīḥ*, 8: 149 (*K. al-Adab, Bāb al-maʿārīḍ mandūḥat ʿan al-kadhib*); Muslim, *Ṣaḥīḥ*, 1013 (*K. al-Faḍāʾil*); Ibn Ḥanbal, 3: 308, #13649.

[71] Muslim, *Ṣaḥīḥ*, 1013 (*K. al-Faḍāʾil*).

[72] Abū l-ʿAbbās Aḥmad b. ʿUmar b. Ibrāhīm al-Qurṭubī, *al-Mufhim li-mā ashkala min talkhīṣ Kitāb Muslim*, eds. Muḥyī al-Dīn Dīb Mattū et.al (Damascus and Beirut: Dār Ibn Kathīr, 2010), 6: 114 (*K. al-Nabawāt*).

[73] The chapter headings presently found in the *Ṣaḥīḥ Muslim* were added by al-Nawawī (Blecher, *Said the Prophet of God*, 115). The question of when the *ḥadīth* collections used here acquired the chapter and sub-chapter headings they now have is beyond the scope of this study.

[74] Al-Bukhārī, *Adab al-mufrad*, 98 (*Bāb al-muzāḥ*); al-Dārimī, 3: 1770 (*K. al-Istiʾdhān*).

[75] For these debates as reflected in the Sunni *ḥadīth* corpus, see Ze'ev Maghen, "The Merry Men of Medina: Comedy and Humanity in the Early Days of Islam," *Der Islam* 83 (2008): 277–340.

[76] Al-Bukhārī, *Ṣaḥīḥ*, 8: 148–9 (*K. al-Adab, Bāb al-maʿārīḍ mandūḥat ʿan al-kadhib*).

[77] Al-Bukhārī, *Ṣaḥīḥ*, 8: 110–11 (*K. al-Adab, Bāb mā yajūz min al-shiʿr wa l-rajaz wa l-ḥudāʾ*); Abū l-Ḥasan ʿAlī b. Khalaf b. ʿAbd al-Malik Ibn Baṭṭāl, *Sharḥ Ibn Baṭṭāl ʿalā Ṣaḥīḥ al-Bukhārī*, ed. Muṣṭafā ʿAbd al-Qādir ʿAṭā (Beirut: Dār al-Kutub al-ʿIlmiyya, 2003), 9: 333 (*K. al-Adab*).

[78] Abū Bakr Aḥmad b. al-Ḥusayn b. ʿAlī al-Bayhaqī, *al-Sunan al-kubrā*, ed. Muḥammad ʿAbd al-Qādir ʿAṭā (Beirut: Dār al-Kutub al-ʿIlmiyya, 2010), 10: 383–4 (*K. al-Shahādāt*).

[79] Fitzroy Morrissey, "The Status of Music in Islamic Law: Ibn Ḥajar al-Haytamī's (d. 974/1567) Treatise Against Recreation in its Polemical Context," *Islamic Law and Society* 31, no. 3 (2024): 194–234, at

230–1. For a detailed discussion of how gender was intertwined with debates over music and singing, see Lisa Nielson, "Gender and the Politics of Music in the Early Islamic Courts," *Early Music History* 31 (2012): 235–61.

80 Morrissey, "The Status of Music," 231.

81 Ḥamd b. Muḥammad al-Khaṭṭābī, *Aʿlām al-ḥadīth fī sharḥ Ṣaḥīḥ al-Bukhārī*, ed. Muḥammad b. Saʿīd b. ʿAbd al-Raḥmān Āl Suʿūd (Mecca: Markaz Iḥyāʾ al-Turāth al-Islāmī, 1988), 3: 2203 (*K. al-Adab, Bāb mā yajūz min al-shiʿr wa-l-rajaz wa-l-ḥudāʾ, wa-mā yukrah minhu*).

82 Al-Qurṭubī, *al-Mufhim*, 6: 114 (*K. al-Nabawāt*); Shams al-Dīn Muḥammad b. Yūsuf b. ʿAlī al-Kirmānī, *al-Kawākib al-darārī sharḥ Ṣaḥīḥ al-Bukhārī* (Beirut: Dār Iḥyāʾ al-Turāth al-ʿArabī, 1981), 22: 22 (*K. al-Adab, Bāb mā yajūz min al-shiʿr wa-l-rajaz wa-l-ḥudāʾ wa-mā yukrah minhu*); Sirāj al-Dīn Abū Ḥafṣ ʿUmar b. ʿAlī b. Aḥmad al-Anṣārī al-Shāfiʿī al-maʿrūf bi-Ibn Mulaqqin, *al-Tawḍīḥ li-sharḥ al-Jāmiʿ al-Ṣaḥīḥ*, eds. Khālid al-Ribāṭ et. al (Damascus and Beirut: Dār al-Nawādir, 2008), 28: 553 (*K. al-Birr wa l-ṣila; Bāb mā yajūz min al-shiʿr wa-l-rajaz wa-l-ḥudāʾ wa-mā yukrah minhu*).

83 E.g. Ibn Baṭṭāl, 9: 336 (*K. al-Adab, Bāb mā yajūz min al-shiʿr wa-l-rajaz wa-l-ḥudāʾ wa-mā yukrah minhu*); Abū l-Faraj ʿAbd al-Raḥmān b. ʿAlī Ibn al-Jawzī, *Kashf al-mushkil li-Ibn al-Jawzī ʿalā Ṣaḥīḥ al-Bukhārī wa-maʿahu al-Tanqīḥ li-alfāẓ al-Jāmiʿ al-Ṣaḥīḥ li-Badr al-Dīn Muḥammad b. Bahādur al-Zarkashī wa-maʿahu ḥawāshī al-Ḥāfiẓ Ibn Ḥajar al-ʿAsqalānī ʿalā Tanqīḥ al-Zarkashī*, ed. Muḥammad Ḥasan Muḥammad Ḥasan Ismāʿīl (Beirut: Dār al-Kutub al-ʿIlmiyya, 2004), 7: 326 (*K. al-Adab, Bāb mā yajūz min al-shiʿr wa-l-rajaz wa-l-ḥudāʾ wa-mā yukrah minhu*); al-Qurṭubī, *al-Mufhim*, 6: 114 (*K. al-Nabawāt*).

84 Al-Khaṭṭābī, *Aʿlām al-ḥadīth*, 3: 2203 (*K. al-Adab, Bāb mā yajūz min al-shiʿr wa-l-rajaz wa-l-ḥudāʾ wa-mā yukrah minhu*).

85 al-Māzarī, *al-Muʿlim*, 3: 127 (*K. al-Manāqib*); see also Abū l-Faḍl ʿIyāḍ b. Mūsā b. ʿIyāḍ al-Yaḥṣabī, *Ikmāl al-Muʿlim bi-fawāʾid Muslim*, ed. Yaḥyā Ismāʿīl (Manṣūra: Dār al-Wafāʾ li l-Ṭibāʿa wa-l-Nashr wa-l-Tawzīʿ, 1998), 7: 287 (*K. al-Faḍāʾil*).

86 For the impact of this belief on Sunni Qurʾān commentary, see Geissinger, *Gender and Muslim Constructions*, 134–5.

87 Ibn al-Jawzī, *Kashf al-mushkil*, 7: 327 (*K. al-Adab, Bāb mā yajūz min al-shiʿr wa-l-rajaz wa-l-ḥudāʾ wa-mā yukrah minhu*).

88 This is rather ironic given her overall image in biographical entries as a strongminded woman of unswerving faith (e.g. Ibn Saʿd, *Kitāb al-Ṭabaqāt al-kabīr* 10: 395–404; Ibn Ḥajar, *Iṣāba*, 8: 408–10).

89 E.g. al-Māzarī, *al-Muʿlim*, 3: 127 (*K. al-Manāqib*); al-Yaḥṣabī, *Ikmāl al-Muʿlim*, 7: 287 (*K. al-Faḍāʾil*); Muḥyī al-Dīn Abī Zakariyā b. Sharaf al-Nawawī, *al-Minhāj fī sharḥ Ṣaḥīḥ Muslim b. al-Ḥajjāj al-musammā ikhtiṣāran Sharḥ Ṣaḥīḥ Muslim*, ed. Wahba al-Zuḥaylī (Sidon and Beirut: al-Maktabat al-ʿAṣriyya, 2007), 15: 474 (*K. al-Faḍāʾil*); Jalāl al-Dīn ʿAbd al-Raḥmān al-Suyūṭī, *al-Tawshīḥ sharḥ al-Jāmiʿ al-Ṣaḥīḥ*, ed. Riḍwān Jāmiʿ Riḍwān (Riyadh: Maktabat al-Rushd, 1998), 8: 3702 (*K. al-Adab, Bāb mā yajūz min al-shiʿr wa-l-rajaz wa-l-ḥudāʾ wa-mā yukrah minhu*).

90 See Marion Holmes Katz, "Beyond *Ḥalāl* and *Ḥarām*: *Ghayra* ('Jealousy') as a Masculine Virtue in the World of Ibn Qayyim al-Jawziyya," *Cultural History* 8, no. 2 (2019): 202–25.

91 Al-Nawawī, *al-Minhāj*, 15: 475 (*K. al-Faḍāʾil*).

92 E.g. al-Yaḥṣabī, *Ikmāl al-Muʿlim*, 7: 288 (*K. al-Faḍāʾil*).

93 "*Al-ghināʾ ruqyat al-zinā*" (lit. singing is the incantation of fornication or adultery); al-Yaḥṣabī, *Ikmāl al-Muʿlim*, 7: 288 (*K. al-Faḍāʾil*); al-Qurṭubī, *al-Mufhim*, 6: 114 (*K. al-Nabawāt*); al-Nawawī, *al-Minhāj*, 15:474 (*K. al-Faḍāʾil*). This saying appears in Ibn Abī l-Dunyā's (d. 281/894) *Dhamm al-malāhī*; see James Robson (trans.), *Tracts on Listening to Music* (London: The Royal Asiatic Society, 1938), 27, 49.

94 Al-Qurṭubī, *al-Mufhim*, 6: 114 (*K. al-Nabawāt*).

95 Ibn Mulaqqin, *al-Tawḍīḥ*, 21: 480 (*K. al-Maghāzī*).

[96] For the roles played by Ibn Ḥajar's oral and written commentary in his composition of *Fatḥ al-bārī*, see Blecher, *Said the Prophet of God*, 52–3.

[97] i.e. in *K. al-Maghāzī*, *K. al-Nikāḥ*, and *K. al-Libās*.

[98] Ibn Ḥajar, *Fatḥ al-bārī*, 10: 472 (*K. al-Libās*), 768 (*K. al-Adab, Bāb mā yajūz min al-shiʿr wa-l-rajaz wa-l-ḥudāʾ wa-mā yukrah minhu*).

[99] Mustafa Macit Karagözoğlu, "Commentaries," in *The Wiley Blackwell Concise Companion to the Ḥadīth*, ed. Daniel Brown (Hoboken: Wiley Blackwell, 2020), 159–85, at 167; Blecher, *Said the Prophet of God*, 58–62.

[100] *ʿUmdat al-qārī sharḥ Ṣaḥīḥ al-Bukhārī* (Beirut: Dār al-Kutub al-ʿIlmiyya, 2001), 22: 65 (*K. al-Libās*), 289 (*K. al-Adab, Bāb mā yajūz min al-shiʿr wa-l-rajaz wa-l-ḥudāʾ wa-mā yukrah minhu*).

[101] "...and in al-Ṭabarānī from the *ḥadīth*s of Wāthila b. al-Asqaʿ: that he (may God bless him and grant him peace) expelled al-Ḥurr, and ʿUmar expelled so-and-so, and so-and-so" (*ʿUmdat*, 17: 405 (*K. al-Maghāzī*). This may be yet another example of the proliferation of variant endings of the cursing tradition.

[102] Al-Birmāwī, *al-Lāmiʿ*, 14: 477 (*K. al-Libās, Bāb Ikhrāj al-mutashabbihīn bi l-nisāʾ min al-buyūt*).

[103] Al-Suyūṭī, *al-Tawshīḥ*, 8: 3602 (*K. al-Libās, Bāb Ikhrāj al-mutashabbihīn bi l-nisāʾ min al-buyūt*). For al-Suyūṭī's approach to *ḥadīth* commentary see Blecher, *Said the Prophet of God*, 129–36. Tellingly, al-Suyūṭī does not cite or refer to the Wāthila variant in his *Dībāj*, his *ḥadīth* commentary in Muslim's *Ṣaḥīḥ*.

[104] Abū l-ʿAbbās Aḥmad b. Muḥammad al-Qasṭallānī, *Irshād al-sārī li-sharḥ Ṣaḥīḥ al-Bukhārī* (Beirut: Dār Ibn Ḥazm, 2021) 17: 319–20 (*K. al-Libās, Bāb Ikhrāj al-mutashabbihīn bi l-nisāʾ min al-buyūt*).

[105] For such expectations, see Blecher, *Said the Prophet of God*, 80ff.

[106] For a brief overview of this discourse, see Rowson, "The Effeminates," 675–6.

Bibliography

ʿAbd al-Razzāq b. Hammām al-Ḥimyarī. *al-Muṣannaf.* edited by Ḥabīburraḥmān Aʿẓamī. 11 vols. Beirut: al-Maktab al-Islāmī, 1970-2.

Abū Nuʿaym Aḥmad b. ʿAbdallāh al-Aṣfahānī, *Ḥilyat al-awliyāʾ wa-ṭabaqāt al-aṣfiyāʾ*. 10 vols. Beirut: Dār al-Kutub al-ʿIlmiyya, n.d.

Al-Albānī, Muḥammad Nāṣir al-Dīn. *al-Taʿlīqāt al-ḥisān ʿalā Ṣaḥīḥ Ibn Ḥibbān wa-tamyīz saqīmihi min ṣaḥīḥihi wa-shādhdhihi min maḥfūẓihi.* Jeddah: Dār Abāwazīr, 2003.

Ali, Kecia. *Sexual Ethics and Islam: Feminist Reflections on Qurʾān, Ḥadīth, and Jurisprudence.* Oxford: Oneworld, 2016.

Almarri, Saqer A. "Identities of a Single Root: The Triad of the *Khunthā*, *Mukhannath*, and *Khanīth*," *Women & Language* 41, no. 1 (2018): 97–109.

Al-ʿAynī, Badr al-Dīn Abī Muḥammad Maḥmūd b. Aḥmad. *ʿUmdat al-qārī sharḥ Ṣaḥīḥ al-Bukhārī.* 25 vols. Beirut: Dār al-Kutub al-ʿIlmiyya, 2001.

Al-Balādhurī, Aḥmad b. Yaḥyā. *Ansāb al-ashrāf.* edited by Muḥammad Bāqūr al-Maḥmūdī. 5 vols. Beirut: Dār al-Taʿārif li l-Maṭbūʿāt, 1977.

Al-Bandarī, ʿAbd al-Ghaffār Sulaymān, and Sayyid Kasrawī Ḥasan. *Mawsūʿat rijāl al-kutub al-tisʿa.* 4 vols. Beirut: Dār al-Kutub al-ʿIlmiyya, 1993.

Al-Bayhaqī, Abū Bakr Aḥmad b. al-Ḥusayn b. ʿAlī. *al-Sunan al-kubrā.* edited by Muḥammad ʿAbd al-Qādir ʿAṭā. 11 vols. Beirut: Dār al-Kutub al-ʿIlmiyya, 2010.

Al-Birmāwī, Shams al-Dīn. *al-Lāmi' al-Ṣabīḥ bi-sharḥ al-Jāmi' al-Ṣaḥīḥ*. 18 vols. Damascus, Beirut and Kuwait: Dār al-Nawādir, 2012.

Blecher, Joel. *Said the Prophet of God: Ḥadīth Commentary Across a Millennium*. Oakland: University of California Press, 2018.

Brooten, Bernadette. *Love Between Women: Early Christian Responses to Female Homoeroticism*. Chicago and London: The University of Chicago Press, 1996.

Al-Bukhārī, Muḥammad b. Ismā'īl. *al-Adab al-mufrad*. Jubayl: Dār al-Ṣādiq, 2000.

Al-Bukhārī, Muḥammad b. Ismā'īl. *The Translation of the Meanings of Ṣaḥīḥ al-Bukhārī* (Arabic-English). translated by Muḥammad Muḥsin Khān. 9 vols. Medina: Dār al-Fikr, 1979.

Al-Dārimī, Abū Muḥammad 'Abdallāh b. 'Abd al-Raḥmān b. al-Faḍl b. Bahrām. *Musnad al-Dārimī al-ma'rūf bi-Sunan al-Dārimī*. edited by Ḥusayn Salīm Asad al-Dārānī. 4 vols. Riyadh: Dār al-Mughnī; Dār Ibn Ḥazm, 2000.

El Omari, Dina, Juliane Hammer, and Mouhanad Khorchide, eds. *Muslim Women and Gender Justice: Concepts, Sources, and Histories*. Abingdon and New York: Routledge, 2020.

Geissinger, Ash. Gender and Muslim Constructions of Exegetical *Authority: A Rereading of the Classical Genre of Qur'ān Commentary*. Leiden and Boston: Brill, 2015.

Geissinger, Ash. "Applying Gender and Queer Theory to Premodern Sources." in *The Routledge Handbook of Islam and Gender*. edited by Justine Howe. London and New York: Routledge, 2021: 101–15.

Geissinger, Ash. "'Will You Not Teach *ruqyat al-namla* to This (Woman) …?': Notes on a Ḥadīth's Historical Uncertainties and Its Role in Translations of Muḥammad." in *Islam at 250: Studies in Memory of G.H.A. Juynboll*. edited by Petra M. Sijpesteijn and Camilla Adang. Leiden and Boston: Brill, 2020: 207–34.

Gordon, Matthew. "Slavery in the Islamic Middle East (c. 600–1000 CE)." in *The Cambridge World History of Slavery, Volume 2: AD 500–AD 1420*. edited by Craig Perry et.al. Cambridge: Cambridge University Press, 2021: 337–61.

Ibn 'Abd al-Barr, Abū 'Umar Yūsuf b. 'Abdallāh b. Muḥammad. *al-Istī'āb fī ma'rifat al-aṣḥāb*. edited by 'Alī Muḥammad Mu'awwiḍ et.al. 4 vols. Beirut: Dār al-Kutub al-'Ilmiyya, 1995.

Ibn Baṭṭāl, Abū l-Ḥasan 'Alī b. Khalaf b. 'Abd al-Malik. *Sharḥ Ibn Baṭṭāl 'alā Ṣaḥīḥ al-Bukhārī*. edited by Muṣṭafā 'Abd al-Qādir 'Aṭā. 10 vols. Beirut: Dār al-Kutub al-'Ilmiyya, 2003.

Ibn al-Ḥajjāj, Muslim. *Ṣaḥīḥ Muslim li l-imām Abī l-Ḥusayn Muslim b. al-Ḥajjāj al-Qushayrī al-Nīsābūrī*. Beirut: Dār Iḥyā' al-Turāth al-'Arabī, 2000.

Ibn Ḥajar al-'Asqalānī, Aḥmad b. 'Alī. *al-Iṣāba fī tamyīz al-ṣaḥāba*. edited by 'Ādil Aḥmad 'Abd al-Mawjūd et.al. 8 vols. Beirut: Dār al-Kutub al-'Ilmiyya, 1995.

Ibn Ḥajar al-'Asqalānī, Abū l-Faḍl Aḥmad b. 'Alī. *Fatḥ al-bārī bi-sharḥ Ṣaḥīḥ al-Bukhārī*. edited by 'Abd al-'Azīz b. Bāz and Muḥammad Fu'ād 'Abd al-Bāqī. 15 vols. Al-Fajjāla: Maktabat Miṣr, 2001.

Ibn Ḥanbal, Aḥmad. *Musnad al-Imām Aḥmad b. Ḥanbal*. edited by Muḥammad 'Abd al-Salām 'Abd al-Shāfī. 6 vols. Beirut: Dār al-Kutub al-'Ilmiyya, 1993.

Ibn Ḥibbān, Abū Ḥātim Muḥammad. *Kitāb al-Thiqāt*. edited by Ibrāhīm Shams al-Dīn and Turkī Farḥān al-Muṣṭafā. 5 vols. Beirut: Dār al-Kutub al-'Ilmiyya, 1998.

Ibn al-Jawzī, Abu l-Faraj 'Abd al-Raḥmān b. 'Alī. *Kashf al-mushkil li-Ibn al-Jawzī 'alā Ṣaḥīḥ al-Bukhārī wa-ma'ahu al-Tanqīḥ li-alfāẓ al-Jāmi' al-Ṣaḥīḥ li-Badr al-Dīn Muḥammad b. Bahādur al-Zarkashī wa-ma'ahu ḥawāshī al-Ḥāfiẓ Ibn Ḥajar al-'Asqalānī 'alā Tanqīḥ al-Zarkashī*. edited by Muḥammad Ḥasan Muḥammad Ḥasan Ismā'īl. 9 vols. Beirut: Dār al-Kutub al-'Ilmiyya, 2004.

Ibn Manda al-Aṣbahānī, Abū 'Abdallāh Muḥammad b. Isḥāq b. Yaḥyā. *Ma'rifat al-ṣaḥāba*. edited by 'Āmir Ḥasan Ṣabrī. United Arab Emirates: Maṭbū'āt Jāmi'at al-Imārāt al-'Arabiyya al-Muttaḥida, 2005.

Ibn al-Mulaqqin, Sirāj al-Dīn Abū Ḥafṣ ʿUmar b. ʿAlī b. Aḥmad al-Anṣārī al-Shāfiʿī. *al-Tawḍīḥ li-sharḥ al-Jāmiʿ al-Ṣaḥīḥ*. edited by Khālid al-Ribāṭ et.al. 36 vols. Damascus and Beirut: Dār al-Nawādir, 2008.

Ibn Saʿd, Muḥammad. *Kitāb al-Ṭabaqāt al-kabīr*. edited by ʿAlī Muḥammad ʿUmar. 11 vols. Cairo: Maktabat al-Khānjī, 2001.

ʿIzz al-Dīn Ibn al-Athīr, Abū l-Ḥusayn ʿAlī b. Muḥammad al-Jazarī. *Usd al-ghāba fī maʿrifat al-ṣaḥāba*. edited by ʿAlī Muḥammad Muʿawwiḍ et.al. 8 vols. Beirut: Dār al-Kutub al-ʿIlmiyya, 1996.

Al-Jibaly, Muhammad Mustafa. *The Fragile Vessels: Rights and Obligations Between the Spouses in Islam*, rev. edited by Arlington TX. Beirut and Medina: al-Kitab & as-Sunnah Publishing, 2005.

Juynboll, G.H.A. *Encyclopedia of Canonical Ḥadīth*. Leiden and Boston: Brill, 2007.

Karagözoğlu, Mustafa Macit. "Commentaries." in *The Wiley Blackwell Concise Companion to the Ḥadīth*. edited by Daniel Brown. Hoboken: Wiley Blackwell, 2020: 159–85.

Katz, Marion Holmes. "Beyond *Ḥalāl* and *Ḥarām*: *Ghayra* ('Jealousy') as a Masculine Virtue in the World of Ibn Qayyim al-Jawziyya." *Cultural History* 8, no. 2 (2019): 202–25.

Katz, Marion Holmes. "Textual Study of Gender." in *Islamic Studies in the Twenty-First Century: Transformations and Continuities*. edited by Léon Buskens and Annemarie van Sandwijk. Amsterdam: Amsterdam University Press, 2016: 87–107.

Al-Khaṭṭābī, Ḥamd b. Muḥammad. *Aʿlām al-ḥadīth fī sharḥ Ṣaḥīḥ al-Bukhārī*. edited by Muḥammad b. Saʿīd b. ʿAbd al-Raḥmān Āl Suʿūd. 4 vols. in 2. Mecca: Markaz Iḥyāʾ al-Turāth al-Islāmī, 1988.

Al-Kirmānī, Shams al-Dīn Muḥammad b. Yūsuf b. ʿAlī. *al-Kawākib al-darārī sharḥ Ṣaḥīḥ al-Bukhārī*. 25 vols. Beirut: Dār Iḥyāʾ al-Turāth al-ʿArabī, 1981.

Knight, Michael Muhammad. *Muḥammad's Body: Baraka Networks and the Prophetic Assemblage*. Chapel Hill: The University of North Carolina Press, 2020.

Kueny, Kathryn. *Conceiving Identities: Maternity in Medieval Muslim Discourse and Practice*. Albany: State University of New York Press, 2013.

Maghen, Ze'ev. "The Merry Men of Medina: Comedy and Humanity in the Early Days of Islam." *Der Islam* 83 (2008): 277–340.

Al-Māzarī, Abū ʿAbdallāh Muḥammad b. ʿAlī b. ʿUmar. *al-Muʿlim bi-fawāʾid Muslim*. edited by Muhammad al-Shādhilī al-Nayfar. 3 vols. Beirut: Dār al-Gharb al-Islāmī, 1992.

Al-Mizzī, Jamāl al-Dīn Abū l-Ḥajjāj Yūsuf b. ʿAbd al-Raḥmān. *Tuḥfat al-ashrāf bi-maʿrifat al-aṭrāf*. edited by ʿAbd al-Ṣamad Sharaf al-Dīn. 16 vols. Beirut: Dār al-Kutub al-ʿIlmiyya, 1999.

Morrissey, Fitzroy. "The Status of Music in Islamic Law: Ibn Ḥajar al-Haytamī's (d. 974/1567) Treatise Against Recreation in its Polemical Context." *Islamic Law and Society* 31, no. 3 (2024): 194–234.

Al-Nawawī, Muḥyī al-Dīn Abī Zakariyā b. Sharaf. *al-Minhāj fī sharḥ Ṣaḥīḥ Muslim b. al-Ḥajjāj al-musammā ikhtiṣāran Sharḥ Ṣaḥīḥ Muslim*. edited by Wahba al-Zuḥaylī. 18 vols. in 2. Sidon and Beirut: al-Maktabat al-ʿAṣriyya, 2007.

Nielson, Lisa. "Gender and the Politics of Music in the Early Islamic Courts." *Early Music History* 31 (2012): 235–61.

Al-Qasṭallānī, Abū l-ʿAbbās Aḥmad b. Muḥammad. *Irshād al-sārī li-sharḥ Ṣaḥīḥ al-Bukhārī*. 20 vols. Beirut: Dār Ibn Ḥazm, 2021.

Al-Qurṭubī, Abū l-ʿAbbās Aḥmad b. ʿUmar b. Ibrāhīm. *al-Mufhim li-mā ashkala min talkhīṣ Kitāb Muslim*. edited by Muḥyī al-Dīn Dīb Mattū et.al. 7 vols. Damascus and Beirut: Dār Ibn Kathīr, 2010.

Robson, James, trans. *Tracts on Listening to Music*. London: The Royal Asiatic Society, 1938.

Rowson, Everett. "Gender Irregularity as Entertainment: Institutionalized Transvestism at the Caliphal Court in Medieval Baghdad." in *Gender and Difference in the Middle Ages*. edited by Sharon Farmer and Carol Braun Pasternack. Minneapolis: University of Minnesota Press, 2003: 45–72.

Rowson, Everett. "The Effeminates of Early Medina." *Journal of the American Oriental Society* 111, no. 4 (1991): 671–93.

Al-Ṣafadī, Ṣalāh al-Dīn Khalīl b. Aybak. *Kitāb al-Wāfī bi l-wafayāt*. edited by Aḥmad al-Arnā'ūṭ and Turkī Muṣṭafā. 29 vols. Beirut: Dār Iḥyā' al-Turāth al-'Arabī, 2000.

Al-Sakhāwī, Shams al-Dīn. *al-Tuḥfat al-laṭīfa fī tārīkh al-Madīna al-Sharīfa*. 3 vols. [Cairo]: As'ad Ṭarābazūnī al-Ḥusaynī, 1979-80.

Stowasser, Barbara. *Women in the Qur'an, Traditions, and Interpretation*. New York and Oxford: Oxford University Press, 1994.

Al-Suyūṭī, Jalāl al-Dīn 'Abd al-Raḥmān. *al-Tawshīḥ sharḥ al-Jāmi' al-Ṣaḥīḥ*. edited by Riḍwān Jāmi' Riḍwān. 9 vols. Riyadh: Maktabat al-Rushd, 1998.

Al-Ṭabarānī, Abū l-Qāsim Sulaymān b. Aḥmad. *al-Mu'jam al-Kabīr*. edited by Abū Muḥammad al-Asyūṭī. 11 vols. Beirut: Dār al-Kutub al-'Ilmiyya, 2007.

Thomann, Johannes. "Illusions of Androgyny: Cross-dressing Women (*ghulāmiyyāt*) in Abbasid Society." in *Sex and Desire in Muslim Cultures: Beyond Norms and Transgression from the Abbasids to the Present Day*. edited by Aymon Kreil et.al. London: I.B. Tauris, 2022: 47–65.

Al-Yaḥṣabī, Abū l-Faḍl 'Iyāḍ b. Mūsā b. 'Iyāḍ. *Ikmāl al-Mu'lim bi-fawā'id Muslim*. edited by Yaḥyā Ismā'īl. 9 vols. Manṣūra: Dār al-Wafā' li-l-Ṭibā'a wa-l-Nashr wa-l-Tawzī', 1998.

CHAPTER SIX

Shurayḥ, ʿAlī, and the *Khunthā*: Gender and Narrative Fluidity

Saqer Almarri

Abstract

I return to a case I have described from a Fatimid legal code,[1] in which a *khunthā* presents at court claiming to have fathered a child. While my work at the time suggested the uniqueness of the narrative, I have since found more material narrating the court event involving Shuraiḥ, ʿAlī, and the *khunthā*. We are faced with limited and fragmented information about the case, and through an application of digital humanities methods to search through digital corpora, *scholars* may be able to piece together such fragmentation and produce a fluid narrative that provides insight to the case where Shurayḥ was confounded by a *khunthā* who fathered a child, and where ʿAlī voided the *khunthā*'s marriage to declare them a man. I explore this intriguing case of gender testing in early Islamic law from the perspective of digital philology and provide insights on different perspectives of this case from different authors that portrayed it for different reasons. Through this digital philological approach, I use these fragmented parts to construct a synoptic reading that demonstrates how different aspects of the narrative were emphasized for different purposes. This digital philological method offers a model for working with fragmentary historical sources to produce richer contextual understanding of the matter.

Keywords: Shurayḥ al-Qāḍī, ʿAlī b. Abī Ṭālib, digital philology, synoptic reconstruction, gender testing in jurisprudence

Introduction

A Fatimid legal code written by the Ismaili jurist al-Qāḍī al-Nuʿmān narrated a court case involving a *khunthā* spouse who fathered a child with their husband's servant.[2] The case was translated and published in 2016.[3] The case itself narrativized a court case that involved a *khunthā* who appeared before the judge Shurayḥ. The *khunthā* explained that they had both male and female genitalia, had been married to a man, and had fathered a child with their husband's servant. Unable to resolve the case, Shurayḥ consulted the Caliph ʿAlī to determine the gender of the *khunthā*.

I had argued at the time that the judge was making the unfamiliar familiar by placing a misunderstood body morphology within a gender binary system that is familiar within wider society. In earlier stages of analyzing the narrative, in the audience of academics in transgender studies, I found that there are questions that I was unable to answer: who were the different characters in this scene? How do we know this story? Why was the husband berated for daring to have intercourse with his *khunthā* wife? Why was the *khunthā* wife not berated for having intercourse with their enslaved servant? Further to that, I found myself in awe of the resolutions and responses by the judges. Shurayḥ knew a basic resolution but was confounded by the slightly more complex case. ʿAlī was straightforward in his questioning, and cites Adam's rib, as he resolves that the *khunthā* must be gendered through their rib count. What was going on in the room as the *khunthā*'s ribs were counted by the two women?

When I first resolved to re-read this text, which I had first read many years earlier, I sat there in my library carrel in Binghamton counting out my ribs, recounting one side then recounting the other, over and over, trying to see if there was a way to miscount the ribs. What I was trying to ask was whether the ribs can be miscounted, but what I was actually trying to ask was: could a pact have been made in that room as the ribs were being counted for the *khunthā*?

The questions proliferated: Was there any other narrative about this case involving Shurayḥ and others? What is the reliability of such a text considering that it was written many generations later than the generation that experienced it? Could we trace out a lineage for this narrative? Was it following some sort of genre-specific pattern? Where else could I find similar court narratives? And could we infer from the narrative some underlying discourses?

At the time, I figured the form of the text meant that it was a fairly unique narrative. It was a text constructed out of memories and oral tradition to argue a point about how to gender a person whose gender remained ambiguous, and placed within a chapter of inheritance-related cases. But discussions of gender and ambiguity in gender was nothing unique in the Arabic and Islamic corpora. There is a long lineage to these texts, for example in Islamic legal discourses, Indira Gesink, and Paula Sanders have shown that this was a discussion that concerned many jurists across the variety of legal schools, whereas Ahmed Ragab, Emily Selove, and Rosalind Batten have pointed out that there is a long lineage to these discourses in medical writings.

To trace out the long lineage to these texts, I chose an alternative to manuscript studies. I have begun engaging with digital humanities corpora that I could find. Initially, I used disorganized corpora that I had found online, such as Al-Warraq, and linguistic corpora, such as Arabicorpus at Brigham Young University. Others were informally crowd-sourced online corpora like Wikisource and al-Maktaba al-Shamela. Most of these corpora proved to be difficult to work with. Working with undergraduate assistants to index and manually tag texts led to an index of approximately 300 texts discussing the *khunthā* at varying lengths and themes. In informal discussions with colleagues working on the Islamic Digital Humanities, colleagues convinced me to take a look at the Open Islamicate Text Initiative corpus developed by Maxim Romanov and colleagues.[4] I sat down to dig around. The index, now outputted digitally through corpus analysis software called AntConc,[5] reached multiple thousands. Now not all citations of *khunthā* were actually about the *khunthā* as an ambiguous gender category, at times they are merely a subject of discussion for other reasons. There are obvious biases in the text that are inherited from their source corpora.[6]

As I explored the OpenITI corpus, I understood that it is a corpus designed for scholarly use, and therefore is fairly reliable and citeable. Yet, what we end up with is largely fragmented information. In what follows, I will demonstrate how we can make use of fragmented information that arises through corpus analysis.

The core narrative

The Arabic-Islamic writing tradition often resists simple genre classifications, as authors regularly combined different types of writing within single works. For al-Qāḍī al-Nuʿmān's text demonstrates this practice by weaving narrative storytelling into what is primarily a legal manual. Perhaps we can understand al-Qāḍī al-Nuʿmān's work as such a genre-mixing text, it is written with an authorial intent to present a legal code for judges but inserts within it *adab* literary forms and narratives. The narrative of the *khunthā* in the court of Shurayḥ and ʿAlī is one such genre-bending text that has some form of narrative fluidity.

I understand narrative fluidity as a literary analogue of gender fluidity. Much like the gender specifics of gender fluid individuals, and the *khunthā* as well, is hard to pin down for observers, something similar is at play for literary works that offer narratives where many specifics remain dynamic and difficult to pin down for literary observers.

Let me explain, the narrative as depicted by al-Qāḍī al-Nuʿmān gives us just the court event. With no mention of what occurred prior to it, and nothing after it. We know next to nothing about the life of the *khunthā*, nor the marriage specifics, nor the life of the enslaved servant that the *khunthā* sired a child with, nor the life of the husband whose marriage was voided. What are we to do with a narrative that tells us very little about the lives of the people the court changed so significantly?

To attempt to address this, I find myself working through the OpenITI corpus to find varieties of this narrative. The corpus analysis would allow us to construct fabula to the narrative, while maintaining the narrative fluidity.

The main way I explore the OpenITI corpus is to use AntConc alongside primarily basic "search" functions, and when things get a bit too big, a set of topic models to categorize them into groups based on similarity. (To explain what I mean, I've used the topic model as a finding aid approach in cases where the results were 500+ rows of cited materials.) Doing this resulted in 50 instances of the material that are found through searching for the regular expression string [**khunthā*] with the added context of the name [*Shurayḥ*] with 25 words around the string itself. Fifty instances is a sufficient sample size for us to begin constructing a comprehensive synoptic version, involving a syuzhet and the fabula.

Allow me to explain my logic for bringing Russian Formalism into this analysis. Russian Formalism emerged as a school of literary criticism in the early 20th century, providing us with essential theoretical tools for understanding how narratives are constructed and transmitted. The Formalists, such as Boris Ejxenbaum, Viktor Shklovsky, and Yuri Tynyanov, were concerned with examining the constituent parts of literary works (Erlich 2012, 171). Of particular relevance to our analysis is the systematic distinction between the fabula and the syuzhet. Shklovsky established a connection between the literary narrative's plot (the syuzhet), and the events in the literary narrative (the fabula). The fabula represents the basic story and its series of events ordered in accordance with their temporal succession and causality and their semantic relationships. The syuzhet represents how these events are transformed away from their chronological and causal logic into a redistributed narrative.[7]

This framework is relevant for our analysis of the *khunthā* as our fabula represents the basic chronological sequence involving Shurayḥ, the Khunthā, and ʿAlī, while the syuzhet represents how the different authors and scholars arranged and emphasized these events. In effect, the influence of the scholars and authors in creating a "labyrinth of linkages" (to quote Victor Erlich).[8] This distinction allows us to separate the underlying historical events from their various presentations across different texts.

While some may validly argue that the Shurayḥ, the *Khunthā*, and ʿAlī court narrative is not a fragment, I think of it as such. We have no introduction nor conclusion to the narrative, simply a problem and a resolution, but no aftermath, and no preface. This is dissatisfying. We find this form of dissatisfaction in Saidiya Hartman's attempt to address the appearance of Black Venus in the archival materials she examines.[9] To address this dissatisfaction with the archive, she engages in what she calls a critical fabulation, a recombinant speculation of what could have been.

I am attempting to do something similar here. We have components of the fabula, but how did we get here and what is next is what I am attempting to deal with. This is how I come to the synoptic reading by examining how different authors and texts present varying aspects of this narrative to create a more complete understanding of the case and its significance.

I cite here the extended version of the translated text in Almarri 2016:

> From him [Jaʿfar ibn Muhammad], peace be upon him, that they have said, "The inheritance for and from the *khunthā* depends on his urethral orifice [*mabal*]. The case is the same for the jurisprudential rules applying to him. If he urinates from the penis [*dhakar*], then he is a man, to him what men have, and obliged of him what is obliged of men. If the urine exits from the vulva [*faraj*], then she is a woman, to her what women have, and obliged of her what is obliged of women. If he urinates from both orifices, then the orifice where the urine exits from first is what takes precedence. However if the urine exits from both orifices at the same moment, it was narrated to us about such a case from ʿAlī, peace be upon him, that a woman stood before Shurayḥ the Judge and said, "Judge, I have a case." To which the judge responded, "Who is challenged in this case?" "You are, so empty this court." The judge ordered everyone to leave the court and allowed her to speak. "I am a woman, I have a penis [*ihlil*] and a vulva [*faraj*]." The judge responded, "There was a similar case presented before Amir Al-Mu'minin [Caliph ʿAlī], and he gave the inheritance relying on where the urine exits." She responded, "It comes from both of them." The judge said, "He has also judged to which the urine precedes from." The woman responded that neither precedes the other: "They begin at the same time, and end at the same time." Shurayḥ the judge said, "You astonish me!" The woman explained her circumstances, "I will tell you more, my paternal uncle's son married me, and gifted me a servant-girl, whom I had coitus with, so she bore me a child. I have only come because of what was born of me so that you may judge in my situation. If I were a man, that you separate me from my husband." Shurayḥ stood up in the court and went to consult with Amir Al-Mu'minin ʿAlī, peace be upon him; he told him of the case of the woman. He summoned her, and asked, to which she responded as the judge had told him. He summoned her husband, and told the husband, "She is your wife, and the daughter of your uncle." The man said it was true. So he was asked by ʿAlī, "Did you gift her a servant-girl?" The man said it was true. So he was asked, "So she had intercourse with her, and impregnated her?" The man said it was true. So ʿAlī asked him, "And after that you had intercourse with your wife after that?" The man said, "Yes." ʿAlī responded, "You are certainly foolishly braver than a man who dares to castrate a lion." He summoned two women and a barber. He ordered the two women to enter a home and count the ribs on each side. They did so, and reported to him, "On the right, we counted twelve ribs, and on the left we counted eleven ribs." Amir Al-Mu'minin exclaimed, "God is indeed great, bring me the barber." He commanded the barber, "Cut this man's hair." Then he stripped off her robe-cloth and redressed her with it in the way men wrap it. Then he said, "Go, there is no need for this [women's robes] on you, marry and wed whomever you desire among the women." The man [the husband] then said, "Amir Al-Mu'minin, my wife, and paternal uncle's daughter, you have made her a man among men, wherefrom did

you bring such a judgment?" He responded, "From my ancestor Adam, peace be upon him, because Hawwa' [Eve] was created from his rib, therefore the ribs of men are less than the ribs of women."[10]

We can take this narrative and reconstruct it as the primary fabula and syuzhet:

Upper Syuzhet (abbreviated as us-1; us-2):
1. The Isnād: Introduction of the case by Ja'far ibn Muhammad.
2. The Fiqh: Explanation of inheritance rules for *khunthā* based on urination.

The Fabula (abbreviated as F-1, F-2, etc.):
1. A woman approaches Shurayḥ the Judge and requests a private audience to reveal her condition (having both penis and vulva).
2. Shurayḥ's response is to mention the standard solution to the condition (the urination rule), and attempts to apply it.
3. The woman's explanation that she urinates from both orifices simultaneously, discloses impregnating a servant-girl gifted by her husband.
4. An astonished Shurayḥ consults with Caliph ʿAlī.
5. ʿAlī's investigation involves confirming the story, summoning the husband and berating him.
6. ʿAlī's resolution of the case is by summoning two women and a barber, so orders the women to count the person's ribs.
7. ʿAlī passes judgment and declares the person to be a man, orders the barber to cut their hair, changes their clothing to men's style, instructs them to be a man among men.

Lower Syuzhet (abbreviated as ls-1):
1. Husband questions the judgement, invites ʿAlī's explanation as based on the creation of Eve from Adam's rib.

In what follows, I will explore what other versions of this narrative tell us, how they vary, and what alternative reconstructions of the fabula and syuzhet look like.

The alternative narratives in the corpus

In thinking about alternative narratives, I turned to the OpenITI corpus (specifically the 2023_1_8 version). In it, we can find variations, repetitions, and re-articulations of the narrative through running the corpus in a corpus analysis software. We find that these alternative narratives are varying through the perspective of the authors, rather than the perspective of the characters themselves.

In a Luhmannian sense, we are examining how the event was observed differently by different observers.[11] When we examine the observers and their activities, we are engaging in a second-order observation, rather than a first-order observation (participating in the activity of observing the event itself). In other words, I am in the business of observing what it is that the observers, or authors, are doing when they discuss the event itself. When we examine the observers and their activities through the digital philological methods, we are engaging in a second-order observation that reveals how different authors utilized this narrative. This methodological approach allows us to trace not only the event itself, but also its deployment within the texts.

In the 2016 article, I made an argument about the gender system and its framework by attempting to understand the definition of the *khunthā*. That was a first-order observation, in that I was engaging in making sense of the event itself. I have since started asking: who is speaking about this? Why are they speaking about this?

I have described the goal of this paper is to construct a synoptic reading of the narrative. To do this, we must engage in an observation of the observers, in order to determine what details may have been embellishments and what may have specifically motivated by the author's worldview and ideologies. What the second-order observation and its resulting synoptic reading is one that allows us to understand how the authors perceived the event, and how they fit it into their conceptual frameworks.

Through OpenITI I saw the following variations, which I cite using the URI-based filenames provided by the OpenITI itself:

1. The text of *Akhbār al-quḍāt* by Muhammad ibn Khalaf ibn Hayyan (d. 306) references the event but presents an alternative *isnād*, rather than the Fatimid imamate lineage like in al-Qāḍī al-Nuʿmān. The *isnād* that is provided in this text traces its lineage through the paternal line from ʿAlī b. Abdallah b. Mu'awiyah b. Maysirah b. Shurayḥ the judge himself.[12]
2. In the text of *Masālik al-afhām ilā tanqīḥ sharāʾiʿ al-Islām* by al-Shahīd al-Thānī (d. 966), the variation does not mention an isnād nor details. It simply offers "what was reported of Shurayḥ in the case of the *khunthā* that fathered and mothered [children] (*lit.* she gave birth and she made someone give birth)".[13]
3. The text of *Majmaʿ al-fāʾida wa-l-burhān fī sharḥ Irshād al-adhhān* of Muḥaqqiq al-Ardabīlī (d. 993) refers to an underlying logic for gendering a *khunthā* through their rib count and it cites the case of ʿAlī b. Abī Ṭālib presiding over the case that Shurayḥ adjudicated involving a *khunthā* that came to him with an "astonishing tale that is well-known" both among "our people and our rivals".[14]

4. The text of *Man lā yaḥḍuruhu l-faqīh* by Ibn Bābawayh al-Qummī (better known as al-Shaykh al-Ṣadūq) (d. 381) provides one of the more extensive narratives in existence besides al-Qāḍī al-Nuʿmān's. This gives us a slightly different set of events with a different *isnād*.[15] The *isnād* relates the narrative as being reported by ʿĀṣim b. Ḥumayd from Muḥammad ibn Qays from Abu Ja'far Muḥammad al-Baqir, reporting the narrative about Shurayḥ adjudicating the case. In this narrative, Shurayḥ exhibits astonishment before the *khunthā* adds that the husband has impregnated her and has given birth, and the *khunthā* had impregnated the servant as well. Following that, ʿAlī b. Abī Ṭālib gets involved. What is different in this narrative is the mentioning of the fathering and mothering of the *khunthā*, and the reference to the rib count by involving Qanbar to take the *khunthā* to a woman's home to count the ribs. Then involving Dinar the Eunuch to change the khunthā's clothes into the men's form. The rib count here was numbered as 17 ribs: 9 on the right and 8 on the left.
5. In *Tadhkirat al-khawāṣṣ* by Sibṭ ibn al-Jawzī (d. 654), we find that the text offers a singular broken isnād that only refers to the narrative as being reported from al-Ḥasan al-Baṣrī. This narrative gives us a curious detail about the rib count. The left ribs were 17 ribs, whereas the right were 18 ribs, and the rib count itself was not what was useful for gendering, but the asymmetry of the rib counts was.[16]

Weaving a narrative anew

By examining the variations, we can analyze how different authors transformed the basic narrative elements (fabula) through their distinct presentations (syuzhet). Each version reflects specific theological, legal, or social priorities through its narrative choices. The following table constructs a synoptic version of the narrative, and highlights elements that may appear to be missing, in order to reveal the distinct narrative strategies and priorities of the authors:

Table 6.1: Synoptic version of the narrative

	Core Narrative of Al-Qadi al-Nu'man 4th/10th centuries (Syuzhet/Fabula)	**Variation 1 (Akhbar al-Qudat, ca. 3rd/9th)****	**Variation 2 (Masalik al-Afham, ca. 10th/16th)****	**Variation 3 (Majma' al-Fa'ida, ca. 10th/16th)****	**Variation 4 (Man la Yahduruhu al-Faqih, ca. 4th/10th)****	**Variation 5 (Tadhkirat al-Khawas, ca. 7th/13th)****
Upper Syuzhet (us-1)	Isnād via Ja'far ibn Muhammad	Isnād via paternal line from Shurayḥ	No isnād, mentions khuntha fathered and mothered children	No isnād, references well-known tale by ʿAlī	Isnād via 'Asim ibn Humayd, Muhammad ibn Qays, Abu Ja'far Muhammad al-Baqir	Isnād broken, via Al-Hassan Al-Basri
Upper Syuzhet (us-2)	Urination rule for khuntha	Same as default	Same as default	Gender determined by rib count	Rib count (17 total) used for gendering, with involvement of Qanbar and Dinar the Eunuch	Focus on rib asymmetry (17 ribs left, 18 right) for gendering
Fabula (F-1)	Woman approaches Shurayḥ with condition (penis and vulva)	Same as default	Implied, no details	Khuntha presents "astonishing tale"	Khuntha mentions both fathering and giving birth	Implied, focused on rib count
Fabula (F-2)	Shurayḥ applies urination rule	Same as default	Implied	Implied, focus on ʿAlī's decision	Shurayḥ astonished, consults ʿAlī	Implied, no specific details

	Core Narrative of Al-Qadi al-Nu'man 4th/10th centuries (Syuzhet/Fabula)	**Variation 1 (Akhbar al-Qudat, ca. 3rd/9th)****	**Variation 2 (Masalik al-Afham, ca. 10th/16th)****	**Variation 3 (Majma' al-Fa'ida, ca. 10th/16th)****	**Variation 4 (Man la Yahduruhu al-Faqih, ca. 4th/10th)****	**Variation 5 (Tadhkirat al-Khawas, ca. 7th/13th)****
Fabula (F-3)	Woman urinates from both orifices, impregnated by husband and impregnated servant	Same as default	Khuntha both fathered and mothered children	Same as default, fewer details	Khuntha explains both roles (impregnated and impregnating)	Implied, focus on rib asymmetry
Fabula (F-4)	Shurayḥ consults ʿAlī	Same as default	No mention of ʿAlī	ʿAlī presides over case	Ali gets involved after Shurayḥ consults him	Implied, ʿAlī's involvement less central
Fabula (F-5)	ʿAlī investigates, summons husband, berates him	Same as default	No details	Implied, no details	Ali confirms story, involves Qanbar (rib count) and Dinar (clothing change)	Focus on rib asymmetry (17 left, 18 right) as key to gendering
Fabula (F-6)	ʿAlī uses rib count for gendering	Same as default	No details	Rib count used for gender determination	Rib count (17 total), 9 right, 8 left	Rib asymmetry (17 left, 18 right) determines gender, not count itself

	Core Narrative of Al-Qadi al-Nu'man 4th/10th centuries (Syuzhet/Fabula)	**Variation 1 (Akhbar al-Qudat, ca. 3rd/9th)****	**Variation 2 (Masalik al-Afham, ca. 10th/16th)****	**Variation 3 (Majma' al-Fa'ida, ca. 10th/16th)****	**Variation 4 (Man la Yahduruhu al-Faqih, ca. 4th/10th)****	**Variation 5 (Tadhkirat al-Khawas, ca. 7th/13th)****
Fabula (F-7)	ʿAlī declares person a man, cuts hair, changes clothes, orders manly behavior	Same as default	No details	Implied	Dinar changes khuntha into men's attire after ʿAlī's ruling	No mention of clothing change or transformation
Lower Syuzhet (ls-1)	Husband questions ʿAlī's judgment, ʿAlī justifies with creation of Eve from Adam's rib	Same as default	No mention	Same as default	No mention	No theological justification, focus on rib asymmetry

As we see demonstrated in the table above, the narratives vary in their treatment of the isnād, the method of gender determination, and the role of ʿAlī b. Abī Ṭālib. This gives us an interpretative flexibility in reading the story. The isnād can be traced primarily through Shurayḥ's descendants, or through the imamate. The approach to gender determination varies significantly particularly in emphasis on the rib count, either by the total number of ribs or the asymmetry between the left and right sides of the rib cage. The involvement of ʿAlī b. Abī Ṭālib is central across most variations, but his role and the process of adjudication differ, with some texts offering detailed procedural steps, while other variations implying his intervention without detail or elaboration. Moreover, the resolution of the case, particularly the legal determination of the *khunthā* as a man, is explicitly described in certain narratives, including actions such as changing clothes and haircut; whereas in others, it is implied or entirely absent. These variations underscore the narrative's fluidity in allowing a range of interpretative emphases depending on the text.

In constructing this synoptic narrative, we can uncover under-reported details. This would allow us to think through the narrative and engage in a critical fabulation.[17] The *khunthā* remains unnamed, but let us construct a dramatis personae for the courtroom:

1. Shurayḥ the Judge: The central legal authority who initially hears the case of the *khunthā*. In most variations, Shurayḥ is approached with the problem and, after hearing the case, he consults with ʿAlī for resolution.
2. The *khunthā*: The intersex individual at the heart of the narrative. The *khunthā*'s biological condition and dual roles as both a father and a mother are key elements in many versions. The *khunthā*'s gender is determined based on various criteria, including urination, rib count, or rib asymmetry.
3. ʿAlī b. Abī Ṭālib: The Caliph and final adjudicator of the case in most variations. ʿAlī is often the figure who resolves the legal matter by ordering the rib count. His judgment and involvement in transforming the *khunthā* into a man play a pivotal role in the narrative.
4. The *khunthā*'s husband: The *khunthā*'s spouse appears in many versions as part of their complicated relationship. The husband is summoned by ʿAlī and is in some narratives, berated for his role in the case.
5. The servant: In some versions, the *khunthā* has impregnated a servant, further complicating the case. The servant is mentioned as a key figure in revealing the *khunthā*'s dual reproductive capabilities.
6. Qanbar: A character introduced in the version of the narrative in *Man la Yahduruhu al-Faqih* who assists in taking the *khunthā* to a woman's home for rib counting. His role supports ʿAlī's adjudication process. In traditional biographical narratives about ʿAlī b. Abī Ṭālib, Qanbar was his servant and a member of his inner circle.[18]

7. Dīnar the Eunuch: Another figure from the version of the narrative in *Man la Yahduruhu al-Faqih*. Dīnar is tasked with changing the *khunthā*'s clothes into men's attire after ʿAlī's judgment, symbolizing the transformation following the legal resolution. It is likely that this is another of ʿAlī b. Abī Ṭālib's confidantes.
8. Two Women: Summoned by ʿAlī in the default version and *Man la Yahduruhu al-Faqih* to assist in the rib counting process. They represent part of the procedural approach to determining the *khunthā*'s gender.

Narrative arrangements and their purposes

The variations in how these narratives are arranged reveal distinct authorial purposes and priorities. We can identify two primary narrative strategies: the juridical arrangement and the wisdom arrangement.

The texts like *Akhbār al-quḍāt* and *Masalik al-afhām* structure the narrative to emphasize legal procedure and precedent. These versions begin with the established urination rule for determining the *khunthā*'s status. Then they present Shurayḥ's initial handling as a procedural model, and frame the intervention of ʿAlī as an extension of the legal methodology. The emphasis in the narrative attempts to focus on the systematic nature of the juridical process, by questioning witnesses and examining the subject, and conclude this procedure with a clear legal ruling that can be replicated in future cases. This arrangement serves to establish legal precedent and methodology by using the narrative as a guide for future jurists and judges facing similar cases.

In contrast, the texts like *Tadhkirat al-khawāṣṣ* and *Man La...* arrange the narrative to highlight ʿAlī's divinely inspired wisdom. These versions foreground the extraordinary nature of the case, and emphasize Shurayḥ's inability to resolve it independently. ʿAlī intervenes as a demonstration of inspired knowledge that is connected to sacred history (the knowledge of Adam's rib and its connection to gendering). It therefore presents the narrative as a revelation of truth. This arrangement demonstrates the wisdom of ʿAliī's unique authority.

There are alternative arrangements that combine the juridical and the wisdom arrangements. These hybrid arrangements maintain the legal framework alongside the relationship that ʿAlī has with divine wisdom. The text by al-Qāḍī al-Nuʿmān demonstrates this balanced arrangement to establish both legal precedent and religious authority in order to integrate the legal methodologies with theological symbolism.

These varying arrangements demonstrate for us how the same core elements could be redeployed to serve different ideological purposes in the Islamic discourses.

Marginalized and queer strata

The variations uncovered through the methodologies described above have helped us uncover narrative variations that exist in the written tradition. The fluidity it exhibits not only reflected the complexities of gender and law in early Islamic law, but also how malleable narratives are themselves.

Through this reconstructed synoptic narrative and the dramatis personae, the detailed and richer narrative context allowed us to find underreported details. I find the presence of Qanbar and Dīnar to be critically relevant and interesting. Qanbar the Servant, a *mawla*, and Dīnar the Eunuch suggests the intermingling of marginalized strata of society into the matters that affect the queer stratum of early Islamic society. They were not present in the Fatimid version of the narrative.

The presence of Qanbar and Dīnar in variations of the narratives brings to the fore the possibility of a queer stratum of the early Islamic society and their engagements with other marginalized strata. The *khunthā*, the *servant*, and the *eunuch* being present in the same courtroom suggests that this is not an isolated engagement. They may perhaps be engaging in other social interactions beyond the courtroom.

Methodological insights and narrative significance

This digital philological approach to analyzing the narrative has demonstrated how corpus analysis tools can be deployed to help scholars piece together fragmentary historical sources and constructing richer understandings of the contexts. By examining multiple versions across the OpenITI corpus, we were able to identify the key variations in the narrative's transmission and construct a comprehensive synoptic reading that reveals both consistent elements and meaningful divergences.

The differences between the narrative versions were significant in a variety of ways: the juridical arrangements emphasize the legal procedure and precedent, while the wisdom arrangements highlight ʿAlī's divine authority. These varying emphases reflect different priorities among the authors. Moreover, the variations reveal an intriguing social dimension to the narratives: the presence of multiple marginalized figures (the *khunthā*, the servant, and the eunuch) suggest interactions and interconnections between different marginalized strata in the early Islamic society. Their appearance together in some versions of the narrative hints at broader social networks that merit further investigation.

This digital philological method of constructing synoptic readings offers us a model for future scholarship of fragmentary sources. It allows us to move beyond isolated readings of individual texts to understand how the narratives evolved and were used for different ideological and rhetorical purposes across the Islamic intellectual tradition.

Notes

1 Saqer A. Almarri, "'You Have Made Her a Man among Men': Translating the *Khuntha*'s Anatomy in Fatimid Jurisprudence," *TSQ: Transgender Studies Quarterly* 3, no. 3–4 (2016): 578–86.
2 Al-Qāḍī al-Nuʿmān, *Daʿāʾim al-Islām*, edited by A.A.A. Fyzee, vol. 2 (Cairo: Dāʾirat al-Maʿārif, 1961).
3 Almarri, "You Have Made Her a Man among Men," 584–86.
4 Lorenz Nigst et al., "OpenITI: A Machine-Readable Corpus of Islamicate Texts," *Zenodo* (2023). Based on guidance from Sarah Bowen Savant on citing specific files in the OpenITI, I include the Uniform Resource Identifier (URI), which also identifies the source in open digital libraries (https://kitab-project.org/A-New-Application-that-Helps-You-Find-Texts-in-the-OpenITI-Corpus/).
5 Laurence Anthony, "AntConc" (Tokyo: Waseda University, 2023).
6 Peter Verkinderen, "Al-Maktaba Al-Shāmila: A Short History," *KITAB*, December 3, 2020.
7 Ḥāfiẓ Ṣabrī, *The Genesis of Arabic Narrative Discourse* (London: Saqi Books, 1993); Peter Steiner, *Russian Formalism* (Ithaca: Cornell University Press, 2016).
8 Victor Erlich, *Russian Formalism: History – Doctrine* (Berlin: De Gruyter Mouton, 2012), 241.
9 Saidiya Hartman, "Venus in Two Acts," *Small Axe: A Caribbean Journal of Criticism* 12, no. 2 (2008): 1–14.
10 Almarri, "'You Have Made Her a Man among Men'," 585–6.
11 Niels Åkerstrøm Andersen, *Discursive Analytical Strategies: Understanding Foucault, Koselleck, Laclau, Luhmann* (Bristol: Policy Press, 2003); Niklas Luhmann, *Theories of Distinction: Redescribing the Descriptions of Modernity*, edited by William Rasch (Stanford: Stanford University Press, 2022).
12 Ibn Ḥayyān, *akhbār al-quḍāt*, 2: 196.
13 Al-Shahīd al-Thānī, *Masālik al-afhām ilā tanqīḥ Sharāʾiʿ al-islām*, 13: 254.
14 Al-Muḥaqqiq al-Ardabīlī, *Majmaʿ al-fāʾida wa-l-burhān fī sharḥ Irshād al-adhhān*, 11: 578.
15 Ibn Bābawayh, *Man lā yaḥḍuruhu l-faqīh*, 4: 326–7.
16 Sibṭ Ibn al-Jawzī, *Tadhkirat al-khawāṣṣ*, 1: 411.
17 Saidiya Hartman, "Venus in Two Acts," *Small Axe: A Caribbean Journal of Criticism* 12, no. 2 (2008): 1–14.
18 Yadollah Gholami, Matthew Melvin-Koushki, Faramarz Haj Manouchehri, et al. "ʿAlī b. Abī Ṭālib," in *Encyclopaedia Islamica Online* (Leiden: Brill, 2024).

Bibliography

Almarri, Saqer A. "'You Have Made Her a Man among Men': Translating the *Khuntha*' s Anatomy in Fatimid Jurisprudence." *TSQ: Transgender Studies Quarterly* 3, nos. 3–4 (2016): 578–86. https://doi.org/10.1215/23289252-3545251.

Andersen, Niels Åkerstrøm. *Discursive Analytical Strategies: Understanding Foucault, Koselleck, Laclau, Luhmann*. Policy Press, 2003.

Anthony, Laurence. "AntConc." Tokyo, Japan: Waseda University, 2023. https://www.laurenceanthony.net/software.

Erlich, Victor. *Russian Formalism: History – Doctrine*. De Gruyter Mouton, 2012. https://www.degruyterbrill.com/document/doi/10.1515/9783110873375/html.

Gesink, Indira Falk. "Intersex Bodies in Premodern Islamic Discourse: Complicating the Binary." *Journal of Middle East Women's Studies* 14, no. 2 (2018): 152–73. https://doi.org/10.1215/15525864-6680205.

Gesink, Indira Falk. "Intersex in Islamic Medicine, Law, and Activism." In *The Routledge Handbook of Islam and Gender*. London: Routledge, 2020: 116–29.

Gholami, Yadollah, Matthew Melvin-Koushki, and Faramarz Haj Manouchehri. "ʿAlī b. Abī Ṭālib." Translated by Matthew Melvin-Koushki, Reza Shah-Kazemi, Ali Bahramian, Ahmad Pakatchi, et al. In *Encyclopaedia Islamica Online*, 2024. Brill. https://doi.org/10.1163/1875-9831_isla_COM_0252.

Ḥāfiẓ, Ṣabrī. *The Genesis of Arabic Narrative Discourse: A Study in the Sociology of Modern Arabic Literature*. London: Saqi Books,1993.

Hartman, Saidiya. "Venus in Two Acts." *Small Axe: A Caribbean Journal of Criticism* 12, no. 2 (2008.): 1–14. https://doi.org/10.1215/-12-2-1.

Ibn Ḥayyān, Muḥammad ibn Khalaf. *Akhbār al-quḍāt*. URI: 0306WAKIC.AKHBARQUDAT.SHIA-003426VOLS-ARA1. In *OpenITI: A Machine-Readable Corpus of Islamicate Texts* (Version 2022.2.7), Zenodo, 2023. https://doi.org/10.5281/zenodo.7687795. Also accessible via https://archive.org/details/bensaoud_gmail_20170312_1857 and https://shamela.ws/book/150.

Ibn al-Jawzī, Sibt. *Tadhkirat al-khawāṣṣ*. URI: 0654SIBTIBNJAWZI.TADHKIRATKHAWASS.SHAMAY0033599-ARA1. In *OpenITI: A Machine-Readable Corpus of Islamicate Texts* (Version 2022.2.7), Zenodo, 2023. https://doi.org/10.5281/zenodo.7687795. Also accessible via https://archive.org/details/TazkiratolKhavaas.

Luhmann, Niklas. 2022. *Theories of Distinction: Redescribing the Descriptions of Modernity*. Edited by William Rasch. Cultural Memory in the Present. Stanford, CA: Stanford University Press. http://proxy.library.nyu.edu/login?url=https://www.degruyter.com/openurl?genre=book&isbn=9781503619340.

Al-Muḥaqqiq al-Ardabīlī. *Majmaʿ al-fāʾida wa-al-burhān fī sharḥ Irshād al-adhhān*. URI: 0993MUHAQQIQARDABILI.MAJMACFAIDA.MASAHA001171VOLS-ARA1. In *OpenITI: A Machine-Readable Corpus of Islamicate Texts* (Version 2022.2.7), Zenodo, 2023. https://doi.org/10.5281/zenodo.7687795. Also accessible via https://lib.eshia.ir/10147/1/0.

Nigst, Lorenz, Maxim Romanov, Sarah Bowen Savant, Masoumeh Seydi, and Peter Verkinderen. "OpenITI: A Machine-Readable Corpus of Islamicate Texts." Zenodo, 2023. https://doi.org/10.5281/zenodo.7687795.

Ragab, Ahmed. "One, Two, or Many Sexes: Sex Differentiation in Medieval Islamicate Medical Thought." *Journal of the History of Sexuality* 24, no. 3 (2015): 428–54. https://doi.org/10.7560/JHS24304.

Al-Qāḍī al-Nuʿmān. *Daʿāʾim al-Islām*. Edited by A.A.A. Fyzee. Vol. 2. 2 vols. Cairo: Dāʾirat al-Maʿārif, 1961.

Al-Ṣadūq, Ibn Bābawayh al-Shaykh. *Man lā yaḥḍuruhu l-faqīh*. URI: 0381IBNBABAWAYHSADUQ.MANLAYAHDURUHUFAQIH.ZAYDIYYA0000239. In *OpenITI: A Machine-Readable Corpus of Islamicate Texts* (Version 2022.2.7), Zenodo, 2023. https://doi.org/10.5281/zenodo.7687795; Also accessible via https://lib.eshia.ir/11021/1/0.

Sanders, Paula. "Gendering the Ungendered Body: Hermaphrodites in Medieval Islamic Law." In *Women in Middle Eastern History*, edited by Nikki R. Keddie and Beth Baron. New Haven: Yale University Press, 1991: 74–95.

Savant, Sarah Bowen. "A New Application that Helps You Find Texts in the OpenITI Corpus." 2019: https://kitab-project.org/A-New-Application-that-Helps-You-Find-Texts-in-the-OpenITI-Corpus/.

Selove, Emily, and Rosalind Batten. "Making Men and Women: Arabic Commentaries on the Gynaecological Hippocratic Aphorisms in Context." *Annales Islamologiques*, no. 48.1 (August 2014.), 239–62. https://doi.org/10.4000/anisl.2670.

Al-Shahīd al-Thānī. *Masālik al-afhām ilā tanqīḥ Sharāʾiʿ al-islām*. URI: 0966SHAHIDTHANI.MASALIKAFHAM.MASAHA001193VOLS-ARA1. In *OpenITI: A Machine-Readable Corpus of Islamicate Texts* (Version 2022.2.7), Zenodo, 2023. https://doi.org/10.5281/zenodo.7687795. Also accessible via https://lib.eshia.ir/10151/1/2.

Steiner, Peter. *Russian Formalism*. Cornell University Press, 2016. https://doi.org/10.1353/book.47557.

Verkinderen, Peter. "Al-Maktaba Al-Shāmila: A Short History." KITAB. December 3, 2020. https://kitab-project.org/Al-Maktaba-al-Sh%C4%81mila-a-short-history/.

CHAPTER SEVEN

The Intersex Body in Classical Shiʿi Scriptural and Legal Traditions: Embodiment, Agency, and Beyond*

Mehrdad Alipour

Abstract

In this chapter, I examine intersex-related discourse in early Shiʿi *ḥadīth* literature and the classical Twelver Shiʿi legal tradition, tracing how *ḥadīth* and legal scholars conceptualized the intersex body and its juridical status.[1] I draw on both conventional methods of source-based historical research and digital humanities techniques, using the latter to facilitate the systematic identification and analysis of relevant material across major Shiʿi *ḥadīth* corpora. While inheritance emerges as the most thoroughly treated domain, due to the prominence of inheritance-related narrations, my analysis also reveals juristic engagement in areas such as marriage, (un)intentional homicide, congregational prayer, and funerary rites. Through close readings of *ḥadīth* and legal texts, I explore how intersex identity was constructed through anatomical indicators and, in certain contexts, through limited acknowledgements of self-identification. I further examine how jurists understood the legal personhood of intersex individuals in relation to their rights and responsibilities. The chapter concludes with an analysis of a novel question concerning the binary–non-binary conceptual framework introduced by the later classical jurist Ibn Idrīs al-Ḥillī (d. 1202), a development that proved pivotal in shaping Shiʿi legal discourse from the thirteenth to the early twentieth century.

Keywords: Islamic body politics, Shiʿi legal history, intersex individuals, *khunthā*, *mamsūḥ*, (non)binary ontological sex, (non)binary legal sex

Introduction

While matters concerning intersex people have been addressed in various areas of Islamic law, they have predominantly been discussed in relation to inheritance. This emphasis arises from the fact that the majority of *ḥadīth*s concerning intersex individuals address inheritance issues. Consequently, when Shiʿi jurists compiled legal texts, discussions of intersex individuals were primarily situated within the debates on inheritance, although they also raised the matter in other legal contexts, such as marriage, (un)intentional homicide, intersex participation in congregational prayers, and funeral prayer. These issues were addressed in accordance with the teachings found in the key *ḥadīth* compilations, where intersex-related matters were debated alongside other legal rulings.

Although the discussion of terminology concerning intersex related issues has been sufficiently covered in the introduction and first chapter of this book, I will briefly clarify the scope of my study and the terms used in this chapter. The modern term *intersex* refers to variations in congenital sexual anatomy that are considered atypical for males or females. The UN Office for the High Commissioner of Human Rights defines *intersex* as "an umbrella term used to describe a wide range of innate bodily variations in sex characteristics. 'Intersex' people are born with sex characteristics that do not fit typical definitions for male or female bodies, including sexual anatomy, reproductive organs, hormonal patterns, and/or chromosomal patterns."[2]

In classical Muslim discourse, a group of people whose biological appearance and (often) sexual anatomy do not fit the definition of male or female bodies—those who are currently classed as *intersex*—were commonly referred to as *khunthā* (pl. *khanāthā* or *khināth*), derived from the same root—*kh-n-th*—as *mukhannath* (effeminate, a different category of humankind in Muslim culture). They were sometimes defined as individuals who are neither male nor female,[3] which likely suggests that such persons occupy a third or indeterminate category, or perhaps a liminal state that resisted binary classification. Others defined *khunthā* as persons who possess both female and male sexual organs or genitalia.[4]

These definitions highlight the debates surrounding the conceptualization of *khunthā*: Does the term refer to a male, a female, a combination of both, or neither? While the latter definition was more widely accepted among lexicographers, the former prompted extensive discussion in Islamic medical and juristic literature.[5] Classical Muslim jurists often describe *khunthā*s as individuals who possess both male and female sexual organs or lack distinct male or female genitalia.[6] However, classical Shiʿi jurists articulated intersex identity somewhat differently. According to them, individuals lacking both male and female genitalia are categorized as *mamsūḥ* and those with both male and female genitalia as *khunthā*.[7] To the best of my knowledge, the earliest discussion of *mamsūḥ* is that of the jurist al-Qāḍī Ibn al-Barrāj (d. 481/1088).[8]

Studies have shown that the terms *sex* and *gender* did not exist in premodern Islamic discourse; therefore, applying them to classical debates would be anachronistic.[9] I make a concerted effort to avoid using these terms whenever possible. However, I may occasionally need to employ them to enhance the clarity of the debates for readers. In such cases, I will also use general terms such as *category*, *nature*, or *type* to indicate that the term does not fully correspond to the modern denotations of *sex* or *gender*.

A snapshot of scriptural texts

Although the Qurʾān contains little to no explicit reference to intersex individuals, the *sunna*—the second primary source of Islamic scripture, encompassing the *ḥadīths* narrated from the Prophet Muḥammad in the Sunni context, and from Muḥammad, the Twelve Imāms, and Fāṭima—Muḥammad's daughter—in the Twelver Shiʿi context—addresses intersex individuals in various instances. While the term *khunthā* appears in *ḥadīth* literature on several occasions, other descriptions are also employed to refer to intersex people: "an individual who has both male and female genitalia" (*man kāna lahu mā li-l-rijāl wa-mā li-l-nisāʾ*) and "an individual who has neither male nor female genitalia" (*man laysa lahu mā li-l-rijāl wa-mā li-l-nisāʾ*).

According to a widely accepted approach among Twelver Shiʿi *ḥadīth* scholars, the early Shiʿi community possessed several recorded *ḥadīths* from the fourteen infallible figures, primarily from the Twelve Imāms, particularly the fifth Imām, Muḥammad al-Bāqir (d. 114/732 or 117/735), and the sixth Imām, Jaʿfar al-Ṣādiq (d. 148/765). These recorded reports were famously known as *uṣūl* (treatises, sing. *aṣl*).[10] Consequently, it is reasonable to suggest that most of these *uṣūl* were written in the eighth century by the companions of the aforementioned two Imāms. However, some of them likely originated from later Imāms, ranging from the seventh to the twelfth, thereby dating to the ninth century as well. It was often believed that these *uṣūl* numbered up to 400 *aṣl*, though some even mentioned the number 700 as well.[11] While most such *uṣūl* have not survived, around sixteen have been saved. These extant *uṣūl* are recorded in two relatively late *ḥadīth* compilations: *Biḥār al-anwār* of Muḥammad Bāqir al-Majlisī (d. 1110/1699) and *Mustadrak wasāʾil al-shīʿa* of al-Mīrzā Ḥusayn al-Nūrī (d. 1320/1902).[12] It is commonly thought that the primary Shiʿi *ḥadīth* compilations were based on these *uṣūl*, which still existed at that time.

My examination of the extant *uṣūl* treatises demonstrates that they do not contain any *ḥadīth* addressing intersex people. However, as we will see, the Shiʿi *ḥadīth* compilations do include reports on matters concerning intersex people, and in some cases, even the term *khunthā* is used. Trusting the authenticity of these *ḥadīth* texts, one likely explanation is that matters concerning intersex people had been addressed in those treatises that have not survived but were still extant and accessible to the authors of the primary *ḥadīth* compilations at the time of their composition.

Around the second half of the ninth century, relatively expanded *ḥadīth* collections emerged. Unlike the earlier *uṣūl*, these texts often included a greater number of *ḥadīths*, encompassed a wider range of topics, and were sometimes arranged into thematic chapters based on the content of the reports. Some of these collections contain a few *ḥadīths* addressing intersex people.

By applying available digital philological methods to trace and connect fragmented references, I identified *Masāʾil ʿAlī ibn Jaʿfar*, compiled by ʿAlī b. Jaʿfar (d. between 210/825 and 250/864), as the earliest Twelver Shiʿi *ḥadīth* collection containing a *ḥadīth* that addresses *khunthā*. The *ḥadīth* concerns a *khunthā* who deceives his wife by claiming that he is a man:

> I [i.e, ʿAlī b. Jaʿfar] asked him [i.e, the seventh Imām Mūsā b. Jaʿfar] about a *khunthā* who deceived *his* wife—what is the legal decree here? He said: "The *khunthā* should be beaten in the back and subjected to a painful disciplinary punishment. The *khunthā* [also] must pay the full dowry (*mahr*) if the *khunthā* has consummated the marriage; if not, the *khunthā* must pay half the dowry."[13]

The term *khunthā* is employed in this report, which may be regarded as the first Shiʿi *ḥadīth* document to utilize this term, unless it is subsequently demonstrated that a similar *ḥadīth*, preserved in other, often later, compilations, instead pertains to a case of eunuch (*khaṣī*). For example, there is a *ḥadīth* attributed to the sixth Imām Jaʿfar al-Ṣādiq and collected by Abū l-ʿAbbās ʿAbd Allāh b. Jaʿfar b. Ḥusayn al-Ḥimyarī al-Qummī (alive in 297/909-10) in *Qurb al-isnād* (though the book is also attributed to his son Muḥammad b. ʿAbd Allāh), but instead of *khunthā*, the question concerns a eunuch (*khaṣī*).[14] A comparable *ḥadīth*, though to a lesser extent, is recorded from the sixth Imām by al-Kulaynī and al-Ṭūsī, also referring to a eunuch.[15] Furthermore, in *Daʿāʾim al-islām* by al-Qāḍī al-Nuʿmān, a similar *ḥadīth* is also recorded, likely from the sixth Imām, though it could be attributed to Imām ʿAlī, the first Imām (d. 40/661). This narration uses the term *majbūb* (a type of eunuch who is castrated by the removal of his penis while the testicles remain; occasionally referred to as *al-khāṣī al-majbūb*).[16] Therefore, it is far beyond definitive to claim that the term *khunthā* was originally used in the *ḥadīth* collected by ʿAlī b. Jaʿfar and not added by later scholars.

Another early collection which includes a *ḥadīth* referring to intersex people is *al-Maḥāsin* of Aḥmad b. Muḥammad Khālid al-Barqī (d. 274/887–8 or 280/893–4). The *ḥadīth*, which is recorded in a chapter on casting lots, suggests a way in which one can determine the inheritance share of intersex individuals who possess neither male nor female genitalia. Al-Barqī, however, does not use the term *khunthā* (or *mamsūḥ*, a term commonly applied to this group of intersex individuals in later Shiʿi legal tradition). Instead, he describes them as "individuals who have neither male nor female genitals". Let us consider the *ḥadīth*:

> Fuḍayl b. Yasār said: "I asked Abū ʿAbd Allāh [the sixth Imām] (peace be upon him) about a newborn who possesses neither the genitalia of men nor that of women. He replied: 'The Imām should draw lots for them, writing *ʿAbd Allāh* on one lot and *Amat Allāh* on another. Then, the Imām or the one conducting the lot-drawing says: "O God,

> You are Allāh; there is no god but You, the Knower of the unseen and the seen. You judge between Your servants on the Day of Resurrection concerning that in which they used to differ. Make clear to us the case of this newborn so that we may assign to them the inheritance You have ordained for them in Your Book." Then, the two lots are placed among other unidentified lots and shuffled. Whichever lot is drawn determines the inheritance the newborn shall receive.'"[17]

Ibrāhīm b. Muḥammad b. Saʿīd b. Hilāl al-Thaqafī (d. 283/896–7) in *al-Ghārāt* (The Raids)[18] also records two *ḥadīth*s concerning *khunthā*s, both of which address their inheritance. One of them narrates a series of questions sent to ʿAlī b. Abī Ṭālib by Muʿāwiya b. Abī Sufyān (d. 60/680). These questions, it is said, were originally posed by the ruler of Rome to Muʿāwiya, with the stipulation that if Muʿāwiya could provide satisfactory answers, he would be exempt from paying tribute (*kharāj*); otherwise, Muʿāwiya would be obliged to pay the tribute to the Roman king. Unable to respond to these queries, Muʿāwiya turned to ʿAlī, seeking his expertise in answering them.

Among the ten questions directed at ʿAlī, one specifically concerns the determination of inheritance shares for intersex individuals. In response, ʿAlī states that the inheritance should be determined by observing how the *khunthā* urinates: if urination occurs from the penis, the person should receive the inheritance of a male; otherwise, the person should receive the inheritance of a female:

> Aṣbagh b. Nubāta [one of ʿAlī's companion in Kūfa] said: "The ruler of Rome wrote to Muʿāwiya asking him about ten matters. Muʿāwiya was at a loss, like a donkey stuck in the mud. So, he sent a rider to ʿAlī (peace be upon him) while he was at the Raḥba. The rider greeted him, saying, 'Peace be upon you, O Commander of the Believers.' ʿAlī (peace be upon him) replied, 'Are you not one of my subjects?' The rider said, 'Yes [I am not], I am a man from Shām. Muʿāwiya sent me to ask you about ten matters that the ruler of Rome had written to him about. The ruler of Rome said, "If you answer me, I will send you the tribute; otherwise, you will send me your tribute." Since Muʿāwiya did not know how to answer, he sent me to you to ask for your response.'" ʿAlī (peace be upon him) said: "What are they?" The rider replied: "...how should the inheritance of a *khunthā* be divided?" ʿAlī (peace be upon him) said: ... As for *khunthā*, when the person urinates, if the urine exits from the penis, the person should be given the share of males; if it exits from other than the penis, the person should be given the share of females. Muʿāwiya wrote this down and sent it to the ruler of Rome, who, upon receiving the letter, sent him the tribute. He said, "This ruling could only have come from the writings of prophethood. It is what was revealed by God in the Gospel to ʿĪsā b. Maryam (peace be upon him)." According to a Shaykh from the Fazara [tribe], ʿAlī (peace be upon him) said: "Among the things that Allāh has done for you is that your enemy writes to you about the landmarks of their religion (*maʿālim dīnihim*)."[19]

The other report recorded in *al-Ghārāt* is more personal, addressing a petition brought to ʿAlī by a group of people from Shām, where Muʿāwiya had self-appointed himself as the governor. ʿAlī asks them why they did not bring the case to Muʿāwiya, to which they respond that they did, but he was unable to make a judgment on the matter. Thus, they came to ʿAlī. ʿAlī, while expressing his dissatisfaction with the people of Shām and Muʿāwiya—who accused him of deviating from Islam but accepted his legal decisions—responds in a manner similar to the previous *ḥadīth*, advising that they should examine how the *khunthā* urinates:

> Al-Ḥasan b. Bakr al-Bajalī from his father, who said: We were with ʿAlī (peace be upon him) in Raḥba, when a group approached and greeted. When ʿAlī (peace be upon him) saw them, he did not recognise them, so he asked: "Are you from the people of Shām or from the people of the Jazīra?" They replied, "Rather, we are from Shām. Our father passed away, leaving behind much wealth and children, both men and women. Among us was a *khunthā* with modesty (*ḥayāʾ*) [referring to female genitals] like that of a woman and a penis like that of a man, and our *khunthā* sibling wanted to inherit as a man among us, but we refused. Then, ʿAlī (peace be upon him) asked, 'Why did not you go to Muʿāwiya?' They replied, 'We went to him, but he did not know what to decide.'" Then ʿAlī (peace be upon him) looked to his right and left and said, 'May Allāh curse a people who accept our legal rulings and yet accuse us in our religion. Take your companion and look at the path of your sibling's urine. If it exits from the male organ, your sibling inherits as a man; if it exits from another place, then inherit your sibling with the women [share].' [They examined and saw that] the urine exited from their sibling's male genital; thus they inherited him as they would a man."[20]

A similar, though more detailed, *ḥadīth* is found in Zaydī Shiʿi sources. In the *Musnad* of Zayd, a collection of reports from Zayd b. ʿAlī (d. 122/740) compiled by Abū Khālid al-Wāsiṭī (d. after 145/762), the narration reads as follows:[21]

> Al-Imām Abū l-Ḥusayn Zayd b. ʿAlī narrated to me, from his father, from his grandfather, from Amīr al-Muʾminīn ʿAlī [b. Abī Ṭālib], peace be upon him, who said: "A newborn child was brought before Muʿāwiya in Shām, who had both male and female genitalia. Muʿāwiya did not know how to rule on the matter, so he sent a group of people to consult ʿAlī, peace be upon him, regarding the child's condition." ʿAlī, peace be upon him, said to them: "What is this matter that you are troubling me with? Inform me of the news!" He then remarked: "May Allah curse a people who seek our judgment, yet consider it permissible to fight us." He then continued: "Examine how this person urinates. If the person urinates from the male orifice, he is a male. If the person urinates from the female orifice, the person is a female." They responded: "O

> Amīr al-Muʾminīn, this child urinates from both orifices altogether?" He replied: "In that case, the child should inherit half of the male share and half of the female share."[22]

This report presents a case in which the intersex individual urinates from both male and female orifices, thereby subjecting them to an inheritance ruling commonly accepted in the Shiʿi legal context: receiving half of a male share and half of a female share. In fact, should it be established that this book indeed contains reports from Zayd, compiled by al-Wāsiṭī, one could further conclude that it represents the earliest extant report within the Shiʿi context concerning the inheritance share of a *khunthā* who urinates from both male and female orifices.

From the tenth century onwards, references to intersex individuals in Shiʿi *ḥadīth* texts became more frequent, and the number of reports addressing various matters related to intersex people increased. Notably, between the tenth and eleventh centuries, the major Twelver Shiʿi *ḥadīth* compilations, known as *al-Kutub al-arbaʿa* (the Four Books), were produced: *al-Kāfī fī ʿilm al-dīn* (henceforth, *al-Kāfī*), compiled by Muḥammad b. Yaʿqūb al-Kulaynī (d. 329/940–1); *Man lā yaḥḍuruhu al-faqīh* (henceforth, *al-Faqīh*), compiled by Muḥammad b. ʿAlī b. Bābawayh al-Qummī, known as al-Ṣadūq (d. 381/991–2); *Tahdhīb al-aḥkām* (henceforth, *Tahdhīb*); and *al-Istibṣār fī-mā ukhtulifa min al-akhbār* (henceforth, *al-Istibṣār*), both compiled by Muḥammad b. Ḥasan al-Ṭūsī (d. 460/1067). As for the Ismāʿīlī *madhhab*, by this time, the most prominent collection of *ḥadīth*s, titled *Daʿāʾim al-islām*, was compiled by Abū Ḥanīfa al-Nuʿmān b. Muḥammad, better known as al-Qāḍī al-Nuʿmān (d. 363/974). The Zaydī *madhhab*, however, follows a different trajectory, as *ḥadīth* and legal opinions were often composed together.

In these collections, discussions regarding intersex individuals emerge across various legal topics, such as inheritance, prayers, marriage, and funeral rites. These discussions serve as the foundation for later, more expansive debates on intersexuality within Islamic juristic discourse. For example, regarding the inheritance shares of intersex individuals, al-Kulaynī compiles nine *ḥadīth*s, al-Ṣadūq gathers five *ḥadīth*s, and al-Ṭūsī records eleven *ḥadīths*.[23] Additionally, al-Ṭūsī, in *Tahdhīb*, includes one *ḥadīth* detailing the punishment for using derogatory language, such as calling someone a *khunthā* or *khanzīr* (pig).[24] Al-Qāḍī al-Nuʿmān, in *Daʿāʾim al-Islām*, records five *ḥadīth*s on the inheritance of intersex individuals,[25] one concerning their inclusion in funeral prayers,[26] and another referring to the *lot* in which the sixth Imām refers to ʿAlī's judgment on the *khunthā*.[27] Furthermore, he includes a *ḥadīth* addressing the eligibility of individuals to lead prayer, in which *khunthā* is also mentioned.[28]

Also, among the *ḥadīth*s on the inheritance of intersex people, there is a *ḥadīth* recorded by al-Qāḍī al-Nuʿmān, al-Ṣadūq, and al-Ṭūsī which addresses a petition from an intersex woman who went to Shurayḥ, the *qāḍī* (judge) of ʿAlī in Kūfa.

He was unable to make a decision in her case and, therefore, brought her to ʿAlī to resolve the matter. In this report, the intersex person in question was married to a man, and in some versions of the story, she claims to have borne a child for her husband and even made a woman pregnant. Thus, the *ḥadīth* concerns the marriage, sexual intercourse, and pregnancy of *khunthā*s.[29]

It should be noted that Shiʿi *ḥadīth*s outline three signs to determine whether a *khunthā* should be classified as male or female, and thus whether inheritance should be allocated in the manner appropriate for either category/sex. These signs are the mode of urination, drawing lots, and counting the ribs. It seems that these *ḥadīth*s, by introducing such markers, primarily aim to establish a legal status for *khunthā*s to address and resolve their legal matters. There is no indication that the texts were concerned with the actual nature or sex of these individuals. However, the language used in a few *ḥadīth*s implicitly suggests that if a person urinates from the male organ, the person is a male, and if the person urinates from the female orifice, the person is a female.[30] Also, in some accounts of the aforementioned story of the *khunthā* brought before Shurayḥ and ʿAlī in Kūfa, it is stated that after discovering that the person's ribs on both sides were unequal, ʿAlī ruled that the *khunthā* was a man. This means if the ribs on both sides had been equal, the person would have been considered a woman.[31] Does this imply that the urination or counting the ribs not only determines the legal allocation of inheritance but also provides insight into the true nature of intersex individuals? One might be inclined to affirmatively answer this question, but this is insufficient to draw reliable conclusions about the categorization of intersex people. Generally speaking, the issue of the true nature of intersex people does not appear to have been a primary concern in the Shiʿi *ḥadīth* sources. As such, the question of whether intersex people are in reality male, female, a blend of both, or neither remains open and hardly can be concluded at this stage.

The evolution of *ḥadīth* literature, particularly in relation to its expansion within the cultural and societal contexts of the periods in which the *Imām*s, their companions, and the *ḥadīth* collectors lived, remains an area in need of further research. Such an analysis would require a thorough investigation into the historical contexts of these texts and their subsequent development. However, this discussion falls beyond the scope of this chapter and necessitates further inquiry to comprehensively examine the development of *ḥadīth* literature, its transmission, and its contextual dynamics.[32]

Nevertheless, a quick examination of the *ḥadīth* literature demonstrates that by the tenth century, the time the major *ḥadīth* compilations were being assembled, Muslim society had already begun grappling with various dilemmas related to individuals who did not conform to the traditional male-female dichotomy, such as intersex people.[33] The cultural and economic stability within the relatively settled

Islamic world of the ninth and tenth centuries provided a unique opportunity for intellectual inquiry into matters that, under more chaotic circumstances, would likely have been avoided. Although this chapter does not aim to examine all *ḥadīth*s on intersexuality, where relevant, some of them will be addressed and analysed later in greater detail.

Examining classical legal texts

> If a man leaves behind an intersex child (*khunthā*), [to determine the inheritance of the *khunthā*,] one should observe the orifice from which the *khunthā* urinates. If the urine exits from the orifice associated with men, the *khunthā* inherits as a male; if it exits from the orifice associated with women, the *khunthā* inherits as a female. If urine exits from both orifices, inheritance is determined based on which exits first. If the urine exits from both simultaneously, the *khunthā* receives half the inheritance of a male and half that of a female.
>
> If the individual has neither the [sexual] characteristics of males nor those of females, two lots are prepared—one labelled *ʿAbd Allāh* (male servant of God) and the other *Amat Allāh* (female servant of God). These are placed among other unspecified lots, and then the *imām* or the person conducting the draw recites: "O Allah, You judge among Your servants in matters of dispute. Make clear to us the status of this newborn so that we may allocate to them the inheritance You have ordained in Your Book." The lots are then drawn, and the inheritance is determined according to the outcome (*Fiqh al-Riḍā*).[34]

By the early tenth century, Shiʿi jurists, drawing upon the *ḥadīth* literature, began to extensively discuss the legal rights of intersex individuals across various domains of Islamic jurisprudence. This will be explored in the remainder of this chapter. I will first offer a brief analysis of Shiʿi debates on intersex-related topics, tracing their development from the formative period of Shiʿi law to the 14th century.

The excerpt above is from a book currently known as *Fiqh al-Riḍā* (also referred to as *Fiqh al-Raḍawī*). The authorship of this work remains a subject of ongoing debate among Shiʿi scholars. Some attribute it to the work titled *al-Taklīf* by Muḥammad b. ʿAlī al-Shalmaghānī (d. 322/934), while others suggest it was authored by ʿAlī b. Bābawayh al-Qummī (d. 329/940–1). Some even contend that it was written by the eighth Imām, ʿAlī b. Mūsā al-Riḍā (d. 203/818).[35] Despite these differing views, there is general consensus that, irrespective of its true author, the text is a Shiʿi work, most likely compiled in the early tenth century. Although the book's style closely reflects the language of *ḥadīth* reports, it represents one of the earliest attempts within the Shiʿi tradition to structure a legal manual in a more systematic and organized manner, with distinct chapters and headings. This structured approach and language were subsequently adopted by scholars such as Muḥammad b. ʿAlī b. Bābawayh al-Qummī, known as al-Ṣadūq, in *al-Muqniʿ* and by al-Shaykh al-Mufīd (d. 413/1022) in *al-Muqniʿa*.

The quoted text addresses legal issues related to the inheritance rights of *khunthā*, encompassing individuals with both male and female genitalia, as well as those without any genitalia—a category later identified as *mamsūḥ* in the Shiʿi tradition. Al-Ṣadūq, in *al-Muqniʿ*, and al-Mufīd, in *al-Muqniʿa*, discuss this matter using almost identical wording.[36]

Although classical juristic discussions primarily centered on inheritance, it is important to recognize that they also addressed other legal matters concerning intersex individuals, including marriage, prayers, and the amount of financial compensation (*diya*) in cases of both intentional and unintentional homicide. While these references were not the focal point of their legal discourse, they reflect a broader consideration of intersex individuals within early Islamic legal thought beyond the specific context of inheritance. The legal opinions of classical jurists on these matters will be examined in detail later.

Legal identification of intersex individuals

Classical Muslim jurists developed a set of markers or signs to determine the nature or sex of intersex individuals. These signs were typically divided into two categories: primary signs, which were considered relevant before puberty—such as the mode of urination and the number of ribs of the *khunthā*—and secondary signs, which would emerge around or after puberty, including facial hair (for males), menstruation, and breast development (for females).[37] It is significant to note that, with the exception of Ibn Abī ʿAqīl al-ʿUmānī (late ninth/early tenth century), classical Shiʿi jurists did not address the secondary markers. However, since none of al-ʿUmānī's works have survived, it remains impossible to substantiate the extent to which he engaged with these secondary signs in his writings. Consequently, our understanding of his perspective is based on the interpretations of later scholars, notably al-ʿAllāma al-Ḥillī (d. 726/1325).[38]

Secondary signs or markers, in the Shiʿi context, began to appear more prominently in the works of fourteenth-century jurists, particularly al-ʿAllāma al-Ḥillī and his son, Fakhr al-Muḥaqqiqīn al-Ḥillī (d. 771/1369–70).[39] From this period onward, these indicators became a subject of discussion within Shiʿi legal discourse. However, their validity as determinants of a *khunthā*'s classification remained contested. While jurists such as al-ʿAllāma al-Ḥillī and Fakhr al-Muḥaqqiqīn al-Ḥillī appear to have accepted their use, others, such as Shams al-Dīn Muḥammad b. Makkī al-ʿĀmilī (d. 786/1384), referred to these signs but considered them unreliable for assessing a *khunthā's* status.[40] Meanwhile, some scholars, including Zayn al-Dīn b. ʿAlī al-Jubaʿī al-ʿĀmilī (d. 965/1557–8), following the precedent of early classical jurists, did not address secondary markers at all.[41]

Depending on the primary or secondary markers, Muslim jurists placed *khunthā*s into two categories:[42]

1. *al-khunthā ghayr al-mushkil* (uncomplicated intersex): those individuals whose sex may easily be assessed using primary markers during childhood or secondary markers after puberty.
2. *al-khunthā al-mushkil* (complicated intersex): those individuals whose sex cannot be ascertained through primary or secondary markers, making it impossible to assign them a sex.

Due to limitations on medical knowledge, classical Muslim legal (and medical) experts[43] were able to assign a sex only to those individuals whose visible sex characteristics, including sexual anatomy and reproductive organs, differed from the norm. Individuals with different hormonal or chromosomal patterns who had no physical manifestations were categorized as male or female based on their visible sex characteristics. For this reason, classical discussions of *khunthā* and *mamsūḥ* did not encompass every individual who at present would be classified as intersex.

Intersex individuals' agency for self-identification

The question of intersex agency or self-determination appears to have received little attention in classical Shiʿi legal discourse. In assessing the sex or legal classification of *khunthā*s, as outlined previously, Shiʿi jurists predominantly relied upon two physical indicators: the mode of urination and the number of ribs. Consequently, the expressed self-identification of such a *khunthā* was only occasionally acknowledged as a determining factor in legal deliberations.

Al-Qāḍī Ibn al-Barrāj, in addressing cases of intentional injury inflicted upon a *khunthā*, refers—so far as I can determine—for the first time in the Shiʿi legal tradition to the notion of self-determination in relation to *khunthā*s. He presents a case in which an individual severs the *khunthā*'s hand or foot or puts out the *khunthā*'s eye. In such instances, the legal ruling concerning the injury is to be suspended until the *khunthā*'s status becomes clear. Significantly, Ibn al-Barrāj adds that if the *khunthā* in question claims to be either male or female, such a claim is not to be taken into consideration. Instead, the individual's physical characteristics must be examined—presumably based on the two commonly cited indicators, namely the mode of urination and the number of ribs—and once the status is clarified, the appropriate legal course is to be followed. Ibn al-Barrāj's discussion illustrates that self-identification was not recognized as a valid legal marker by classical Shiʿi jurists, at least in cases involving financial liability.[44]

Nevertheless, al-Shaykh al-Ṭūsī, in *al-Mabsūṭ fī fiqh al-imāmiyya*, refers to sexual desire as a potential marker—suggesting a degree of agency and self-determination on the part of the *khunthā*s in relation to their sexed body. Let us begin by reading his rather lengthy statement, as it provides a useful basis for the analysis:

> A *khunthā* is one who possesses both the penis of a male and the vulva of a female. One who has this characteristic cannot be considered both a man and a woman; rather, such a person must be classified as one of the two. We uphold the assessment of this individual's nature/sex in accordance with the mode of urination: if the individual urinates from the penis, he is a man; if from the vulva, the individual is a woman. If urination occurs from both organs, then the one from which urine emerges first [is taken into account]; but if both begin simultaneously, then the one from which it ceases last determines the ruling. Should urination emerge from both at the same time and cease at the same time, then the matter is referred to drawing lots (*qurʿa*). Some have said that recourse should be made to whichever organ emits less or more urine, and there are two opinions on this.
>
> If none of these methods yield clarity, then one may consider the inclination of the *khunthā*'s innate [sexual] disposition (*yamīl ṭabʿuh*[u]) and acts accordingly. Others have said the number of ribs should be counted: if both sides are equal, the *khunthā* is a woman; if they differ, the *khunthā* is a man. This view has also been transmitted by our companions.
>
> As for the one who claims that innate [sexual] inclination should be the determining factor, if such an individual says, "I incline towards women," and performs the sexual act (with them), then he is a man. Conversely, if the individual inclines towards men and desires to be penetrated, then she is a woman.
>
> One should not consider what gives this individual pleasure, for it is possible that an effeminate man (*mukhannath*) might desire men, and a masculinized/mannish woman (*mudhakkara*) may desire women. Rather, one returns to the individual's innate disposition (*ṭabʿ*) as determined at the point of creation and acts accordingly.
>
> Any subsequent retraction of what the individual initially states is not accepted. If the individual is ruled to be a man, he may marry a woman; and if ruled to be a woman, she may be married to a man.[45]

Before proceeding further, it is worth noting that al-Ṭūsī attributes the view that sexual desire may serve as a valid indicator for determining sex to an unspecified group of scholars, without identifying them as Shiʿi, nor stating explicitly whether he agrees with their position. By contrast, he clearly attributes the view that the number of ribs may serve as an indicator to Shiʿi jurists. This contrast suggests that the former opinion was not upheld within the Shiʿi tradition but rather reflects a position advanced by some Sunni jurists (see Chapter Eight). This interpretation appears plausible, as there is no evidence in extant Shiʿi legal texts prior to al-Ṭūsī that sexual desire was employed as a legal sign in determining the sex or status of intersex individuals. It is therefore likely that the unnamed scholars referenced by al-Ṭūsī were Sunni jurists.

According to the aforementioned text, innate sexual desire is presented as a potential legal indicator for determining the sexed body of an intersex person. As this sign relies entirely on the individual's own admission—since only the intersex person can disclose the nature of their sexual inclination—it may be understood as a form of self-determinacy or agency by which the subject participates in defining their bodily status. Unlike the earlier case discussed by Ibn al-Barrāj, where the intersex individual makes a general self-identification as male or female, here sexual desire functions as a juridical sign. However, because the basis of this sign remains the individual's self-reported desire, it continues to reflect a form of self-determination and agency in the legal recognition of their sexed embodiment.

Crucially, this line of reasoning rests on the assumption that sexual desire is deemed "innate" or "natural" only when it is oriented towards the opposite sex. Accordingly, if the intersex individual expresses sexual desire towards a man, these jurists categorize them as female, and vice versa. This assumption, however, entirely overlooks the possibility that an intersex person might be homosexual and thus inclined towards individuals of the same sex. To his credit, al-Ṭūsī appears to recognize this complication and addresses it by distinguishing between innate sexual inclination and mere sexual pleasure. This distinction—regardless of its empirical accuracy—is conceptually significant. In al-Ṭūsī's view, individuals described as effeminate (in the case of males) or mannish (in the case of females) may indeed exhibit same-sex desire, but such inclinations are not regarded as expressions of a natural or innate disposition. Rather, they are characterized as deviations or defects from an original, divinely ordained state. As such, al-Ṭūsī contends that these individuals must return to their "natural" condition and primordial constitution.

Finally, al-Ṭūsī notes that those who accept sexual inclination or desire as a valid indicator for determining sex of intersex people also maintain that any subsequent retraction of the individual's initial statement is not admissible. In other words, if the intersex person declares sexual desire towards women and is therefore legally classified as male, this person may marry a woman; conversely, if the intersex person expresses desire for men and is thereby classified as female, this person may marry a man. Once this legal determination is made, it is considered final and binding; such an individual cannot later identify as belonging to the opposite sex.

Intersex regulations and rights

Intersex individuals are addressed in various juristic issues within classical Islamic law. These discussions intertwine their rights and responsibilities within a legal framework that primarily differentiates between men and women. However, these categories are not always adequate to capture the complexities of human sex and gender categories, leading to debates over how these individuals should be treated in legal matters. Consequently, discussions regarding intersex individuals span the entire Islamic legal framework, encompassing both private matters—such as purity, prayer, fasting, pilgrimage, marriage, and financial topics—and public issues, including participation in congregational prayers, dress codes, engagement in the public sphere, and holding roles such as judge or legal authority within society. In the following, I will address a number of such matters concerning intersex people and examine how, in classical Shiʿi juristic tradition, these issues related to intersex individuals are treated and debated.

Inheritance

Legal discussions of intersex-related topics primarily appeared in juristic texts on inheritance. Because inheritance shares are determined partly by the sex of the heirs, jurists had to classify them as male or female before calculating their share of the inheritance. In some cases, the heirs cannot be identified as either male or female because they have both a vulva and a penis, because their urinary exit cannot be categorized as either a penis or vulva, or because they have no identifiable sexual organs. With regard to people with neither a penis nor a vulva (*mamsūḥ*), Shiʿi jurists hold that "drawing lots" (*qurʿa*) is the appropriate method to determine their share of the inheritance.[46]

Shiʿi inheritance law on intersex people with both a vulva and penis (*khunthā*s) was based on *ḥadīth*s that addressed two primary sex indicators—urination and the number of ribs.[47] There was a strong consensus among classical Shiʿi jurists that urination is determinative. According to these Shiʿi jurists, a *khunthā* who urinates through the penis is a male, and one who urinates through the vulva is a female. If urination occurs from both the penis and vulva, but not simultaneously, sex is determined by the genitalia from which the urination issues first. However, if urination occurs from both orifices simultaneously, then one considers the orifice from which it ends.[48] In all these cases, the *khunthā* may be identified as male or female: these people were classified as *al-khunthā ghayr al-mushkil.*

However, if a *khunthā*'s urination begins and ends from both orifices simultaneously, then the individual's sex is a matter of dispute. According to the majority position, the person is a *khunthā mushkil:* such a person has the right to half of the male and half of the female inheritance share. According to a minority opinion, it is possible to establish the sex/nature of such persons by having a judge or a righteous person count their ribs. If the number of ribs on both sides are equal, then the person is a woman; if they are not equal, then he is a man.

Following the majority opinion, in the aforementioned condition the *khunthā* should be classified as *mushkil* and the inheritance should be determined differently from the inheritance of a male and a female. The question remains: What is the sex of these individuals? Do they belong to a third category of human being, neither male nor female, or are they both male and female? I will return to this point later in this chapter.

Retaliation and financial compensation

It is important to note that, similar to the discussion of inheritance, if the sex of a *khunthā* can be determined—whether through primary or secondary indicators—as either male or female, then the legal rulings concerning retaliation (*qiṣāṣ/qawad*) and financial compensation or blood money (*diya*) in cases involving such individuals are identical to those applied to men and women. In such instances, no legal distinction is made. The question arises when the *khunthā* in question—whether as perpetrator or victim—is a *khunthā mushkil*, whose sex cannot be conclusively identified. With this in mind, the following section elaborates on the classical Shiʿi legal view on the matter.[49]

As early as the tenth century, Shiʿi legal manuals gradually began to address *khunthā* in matters concerning homicide retaliation (*qiṣāṣ fī l-nafs*), retaliation for injury and amputation of a body part (*qiṣāṣ fī l-jarḥ wa-l-qaṭʿ*), and financial compensation/blood money (*diya*). For example, al-Ṣadūq in *al-Muqniʿ* briefly addresses *khunthā* in a case where someone amputates or injures the penis and two testicles of a *khunthā*: "*wa-fī dhakar*[i] *al-khunthā wa-unthayayh*[i] *thulth al-diya*." According to al-Ṣadūq, the perpetrator must pay one-third of the full *diya*, which amounts to ten thousand dirhams—⅓ of 10,000 *dirhams* = 3,333 (plus a fraction).[50] Al-Ṣadūq does not explain why he holds this position or on what criterion he calculated this amount—namely, one-third of full *diya*—for the injury or amputation of a *khunthā*'s penis and two testicles. Strikingly, the jurists who succeeded him did not engage with this case until the fourteenth century, when al-ʿAllāma al-Ḥillī, in *Mukhtalaf al-Shīʿa*, briefly refers to it by citing al-Ṣadūq. He does not, however, elaborate on the point, except to mention a distinct and more detailed position attributed to Ibn Junayd al-Iskāfī, a tenth-century Shiʿi scholar. The section he reports from Ibn Junayd reads as follows:

> This is the same for the penis of a child who has not reached puberty, the impotent man (*ʿinnīn*), and the *khunthā* who is ruled to be male. However, if the *khunthā* is ruled to be female, one-third of the *diya* applies.[51]

Since the original source of Ibn Junayd from which al-ʿAllāma al-Ḥillī cites has not survived, it is impossible to determine with certainty the precise meaning intended by Ibn Junayd in this statement. However, given that al-ʿAllāma al-Ḥillī elsewhere affirms that Ibn Junayd holds that the full *diya* applies in cases of injury to, or removal of, the penis of a child or an impotent man, this statement may be understood as expressing a disagreement with al-Ṣadūq's approach. Accordingly, Ibn Junayd perhaps suggests that in cases of the amputation of the penis or testicles of a *khunthā*, the full *diya* should likewise apply, similar to the case of a child's or an impotent man's penis.[52] This would mean that, in Ibn Junayd's view, the removal of a male's penis entails a full *diya* regardless of whether the individual is an adult male, a child prior to puberty, an impotent man, or a *khunthā* who has been determined to be male. However, based on the final segment of Ibn Junayd's statement, if the *khunthā* is ruled to be female, the removal of the penis would warrant one-third of a full *diya*, as in such a case the penis is regarded as an additional, non-functional part.

The distinction between the positions of al-Ṣadūq and Ibn Junayd—one that al-ʿAllāma al-Ḥillī does not interrogate in this context—may be outlined as follows. Al-Ṣadūq appears to adopt a general view whereby, in cases involving injury to or amputation of the penis or testicles of a *khunthā*, one-third of the *diya* is to be awarded. His formulation seems to apply indiscriminately to all intersex individuals, whether classified as *mushkil* or *ghayr mushkil*, and in the latter case, regardless of whether the *khunthā* has been legally designated male or female. Such a generalization, however, appears to stand in tension with broader principles of Shiʿi legal reasoning concerning gender determination and bodily injury. Ibn Junayd, by contrast, restricts the application of the one-third *diya* to cases in which the *khunthā* has been legally ruled as female. As will be examined below, this position, too, raises questions concerning its consistency with prevailing doctrines in Shiʿi legal tradition.

This is perhaps why al-ʿAllāma al-Ḥillī interprets Ibn Junayd's view in a manner that renders it compatible with Shiʿi legal doctrines. He clarifies that if the *khunthā* is legally determined to be male, he is entitled to full *diya* for each of his penis and testicles. Consequently, if both are injured or amputated, he would receive two full compensations, consistent with the entitlement of any other male. Conversely, if the *khunthā* is determined to be female, compensation for the removal of the penis or testicles is not awarded as *diya*, but rather as *arsh*—a fractional portion of the *diya* prescribed in Islamic law. The specific amount of *arsh* is determined through a judicial process known as evaluative judgment (*ḥukūma*), by which a judge assesses and legally establishes the appropriate compensation.[53] This is because, as al-ʿAllāma al-Ḥillī remarks, in such cases the penis or testicles are considered superfluous, non-functional flesh. Similarly, if the status of the *khunthā* remains complicated, the compensation likewise takes the form of *arsh*, to be determined by a judge through evaluative judgment.[54]

Although al-ʿAllāma al-Ḥillī appears to be offering a reading that brings Ibn Junayd's view into alignment with legal principles established by later Shiʿi jurists, the passage he cites—as discussed above—does not fully support this interpretation.[55] It is, however, quite likely that he had access to a more complete version of Ibn Junayd's work, which could account for his confidence in presenting the view in this manner.

There is yet another significant point concerning the views of these two early jurists in cases involving injury to, or removal of, the penis and testicles of a *khunthā*. Neither al-Ṣadūq's position—granting a third of the *diya* to the *khunthā* in general—nor Ibn Junayd's view—awarding the same amount to a *khunthā* who has been legally determined as female—appears to accord with the dominant legal principle of *arsh* based on *ḥukūma* in such cases. According to this principle, when the penis or testicles of a legally female *khunthā* or a *khunthā mushkil* are injured or removed, the compensation should not be a fixed portion of the *diya*, but rather an *arsh*—an amount assessed by a judge through *ḥukūma*. The rationale underlying the views of al-Ṣadūq and Ibn Junayd thus remains unclear. Notably, neither al-ʿAllāma al-Ḥillī nor later jurists who upheld the principle of *ḥukūma* in such cases addressed this discrepancy or offered any justification for why these earlier scholars specified one third of the *diya* as compensation.

Apart from the views of these two early jurists, classical Shiʿi legal texts often complicate the *khunthā*'s right to retaliation or financial compensation in cases involving genital injury or amputation in the following ways.[56] They illustrate four possible scenarios in this regard: the *khunthā* being determined as male, as female, as *mushkil*, or whose status is yet to be determined.

In the first possible scenario, namely when the *khunthā* is determined as male, if a man has inflicted injury to the penis and testicles of this *khunthā* or has amputated them, then retaliation (*qiṣāṣ/qawad*) applies. However, if the perpetrator is a woman, then *diya* applies, and, as al-Shaykh al-Ṭūsī further elaborates, if the injury occurred to both the penis and testicles of this *khunthā*, the female perpetrator must pay two full *diya*s for each penis and testicles entitled for a full *diya*. On the other hand, if the perpetrator—whether a man or a woman—has injured or amputated this *khunthā*'s vulva (*farj*) or labia (*shafrān*), an *arsh* through *ḥukūma* is due, as the vulva and labia in this case are not considered essential but rather an additional or non-functional part.

In the second scenario, where the *khunthā* is determined as female, if the infliction of injury upon or amputation of the vulva or labia is caused by a woman, it gives rise to three divergent juridical opinions. The first, endorsed by jurists such as al-Shaykh al-Ṭūsī and al-ʿAllāma al-Ḥillī, asserts that only a full diya is applicable, on the basis that retaliation (*qiṣāṣ*) is not prescribed for injuries to the vulva or labia. The second position, advanced by al-Muḥaqqiq al-Ḥillī (d. 676/1277), maintains that retaliation is indeed warranted in such cases. Finally, Ibn Ḥamza (d. after 566/1171) holds that the *khunthā* may exercise discretion in choosing between retaliation and financial compensation. However, if the perpetrator is a man, according to the classical jurists, the full *diya* is applicable for amputation or injury to the vulva or labia of such a *khunthā*. On the other hand, if the perpetrator—whether male or female—has caused amputation or injury to the penis or testicles of such a *khunthā*, then an *arsh* through *ḥukūma* applies, as the penis and testicles, in this case, are not considered essential but rather an additional or non-functional part.

In the third scenario, where the *khunthā* is considered *mushkil*, if a man or a woman has inflicted injury to either male or female genitalia of such a *khunthā*, then full *diya* is due, not retaliation. This is because, in this case, as these jurists note, there is no way to determine whether the *khunthā* is male or female, and thus, it is not possible to rule out retaliation accordingly.[57]

Finally, in the fourth possible scenario, where the status of a *khunthā* has yet to be determined, in the event of injury to such a *khunthā*, legal recourse must be postponed until the status of the *khunthā* can be established as falling under one of the three preceding categories, in order to determine whether *diya* or retaliation is applicable. Nevertheless, if postponement is not possible, or if—due to any reason—the ruling is not delayed until the determination of this person's status, retaliation is not granted, even if requested. This is due to the prevailing uncertainty regarding the sex of such a person, and in this respect, there is no distinction between whether the perpetrator is male or female. However, this person may request *diya*, which will be awarded based on what is certain. Specifically, in such a case, the person is certainly entitled to receive *diya* for the labia and vulva because it is the least amount of *diya* that this person is certainly entitled to simply because in the case of considering the person as a male then each of the penis and testicles are entitled for full *diya*s. If it is subsequently established that the person is female, then an *arsh* through *ḥukūma* is given for the remainder, i.e., the penis and testicles. Conversely, if it becomes clear that the person is male, the remainder is fulfilled by awarding the *diya* for the penis and testicles, alongside *arsh* through *ḥukūma* for the vulva and labia. These jurists further explain that if such a person claims *diya* for one sexual organ—whether male or female—while reserving the right to retaliation for the remaining organ(s), this is not permissible. However, if the person requests an *arsh* through *ḥukūma* while retaining the right to retaliation, this is permitted, and such a person will be awarded whichever of the two *arsh*s is lesser.[58]

The question remains as to how the classical law would address a situation in which one *khunthā* amputates the genitalia of another. In this case, as al-ʿAllāma al-Ḥillī notes, retaliation is applicable if both *khunthā*s—i.e., the perpetrator and the victim—are determined in the same category, namely that both are categorized as male or both as female. In such a case, for the original sexual organ, retaliation applies, and for the additional sexual organ, *arsh* applies. However, if their statuses are determined without concordance—such that the perpetrator is male and the victim female, or vice versa—then retaliation is not legally conceivable. In this case, *diya* is due for the original sexual organ and *arsh* for the additional one. Thus, in the first scenario, where the perpetrator is male and the victim female, *diya* applies for the penis and testicles, along with *arsh* for the vulva. In the second scenario, where the perpetrator is female and the victim male, *diya* is due for the vulva, and *arsh* is applied for the penis and testicles.[59]

With regard to the amputation of genitalia, intersex individuals who possess neither male nor female genitalia—referred to as *maṣmūḥ*—are generally not discussed in the legal literature, as the absence of genitalia, according to these jurists, renders considerations of retaliation or financial compensation inapplicable in this context.

Concerning homicide retaliation (*qiṣāṣ fī l-nafs*), al-Mufīd (d. 413/1022), in *al-Muqniʿa*, presents a case involving a *khunthā* as a perpetrator of intentional homicide.[60] He begins by outlining a scenario in which a man and a woman jointly and deliberately kill a free man. According to al-Mufīd, the heirs of the victim are entitled to seek retaliation and may, therefore, execute both perpetrators. However, the heirs of the perpetrators are in turn entitled to compensation amounting to 5,000 dirhams,[61] to be divided among them in accordance with the relevant Islamic legal principle, as follows:

- Two-thirds of 5,000 dirhams to the heirs of the man = 3,333 dirhams (plus ⅓ of a dirham)
- One-third of 5,000 dirhams to the heirs of the woman = 1,667 dirhams (plus ⅔ of a dirham).

Al-Mufīd then continues by considering a case in which a *khunthā* whose sex remains difficult to determine (*khunthā mushkil*) participates in the offence alongside the aforementioned man and woman. In such a scenario, the heirs of the victim retain the right to execute all three perpetrators. However, they must subsequently pay a total of 12,500 dirhams to the heirs of the executed parties, with the amount distributed according to the respective *diya* assigned to each. Al-Mufīd stipulates that the heirs of the *khunthā mushkil* are entitled to receive half of the male share and half of the female share, analogous to the rules governing inheritance. The method of calculation itself is particularly noteworthy. According to al-Mufīd, the sum of 12,500 *dirhams*[62] is to be apportioned among the parties as follows:

- The man is entitled to one-third plus one-ninth of the total amount, i.e., 12,500 *dirhams*. This equals 5,555 *dirhams*, ½ *dirham*, 2 grains (*ḥabbas*), and ⅔ of a grain (*ḥabba*).

- The *khunthā* receives one-third of the total amount, which equals 4,166 *dirhams* and ⅔ of a *dirham*.
- The woman's share is one-fifth plus one-ninth of one-fifth of the total amount. This equals 2,777 dirhams, 4 *dānīq*s, 5 grains, and ⅓ of a grain.

Together, these shares complete the full sum of 12,500 dirhams.

Similarly, according to al-Mufīd, if the third participant is an intersex person with neither male nor female genitalia, i.e., *mamsūḥ*, the heirs of the *mamsūḥ* should receive half of the male share and half of the female share, that is, 4,166 *dirhams* (plus a fraction).[63]

With regard to the *khunthā mushkil* as the victim of either intentional or unintentional homicide, classical Shiʿi jurists often hold that in cases of unintentional homicide, *diya* is applicable.[64] However, these jurists held differing views regarding the consequences of intentional homicide. One group maintained that intentional homicide gives rise to two possible outcomes: retaliation or financial compensation. Each of these, they argued, constitutes an independent and valid legal consequence. The victim's legal heirs (*awliyāʾ al-damm*), those who may legally demand retaliation or compensation, may choose either option, and once a choice is made, it becomes binding while the other lapses. Similarly, if one is waived, the alternative is also no longer applicable. By contrast, other jurists argued that intentional homicide entails only retaliation. According to this view, the victim's legal heirs may either demand retaliation or choose to pardon. If retaliation is carried out, the matter is concluded. However, if they pardon in exchange for compensation, retaliation is waived and compensation becomes established as a substitute—though in this framework, compensation is regarded as a contingent alternative, rather than an original entitlement.

As al-Shaykh al-Ṭūsī notes, the majority of Shiʿi jurists—including himself—adhere to the view that intentional homicide entails solely retaliation. The victim's legal heir may either pursue retaliation or grant pardon. If retaliation is implemented, no further claim remains. However, if pardon is granted, compensation is not established unless the perpetrator consents. Should the perpetrator insist on facing retaliation and refuse to offer compensation, the victim's legal heirs have no further legal recourse. Yet if the victim's legal heirs request compensation and the perpetrator is willing to pay, then compensation becomes due accordingly.[65]

If the victim's legal heirs ask for compensation and the perpetrator gave consent to it, then the compensation must be paid. The *diya* of a *khunthā mushkil*, according to these jurists, is calculated as half the *diya* of a male and half that of a female—that is, half of 10,000 *dirhams* and half of 5,000 *dirhams*, amounting to a total of 7,500 *dirhams*.[66]

Now, if the perpetrator is another *khunthā mushkil*, retaliation is applicable. It appears that retaliation also applies if the perpetrator is a female. In both of these cases, there is no financial burden placed on the legal heirs of the *khunthā mushkil* who demand retaliation. However, if the perpetrator is a free male, retaliation may still apply, but only if the legal heirs of the *khunthā mushkil* are willing to pay the difference between the compensation of a male and that of a *khunthā mushkil*—that is, an additional amount of 2,500 (assuming a standard male *diya* of 10,000 and a *khunthā mushkil*'s *diya* of 7,500).[67]

Interestingly, as seen, these jurists appear to apply the same legal ruling regarding retaliation and financial compensation for the *khunthā mushkil* to the *mamsūḥ*. Thus, unlike what they suggest in cases of inheritance—where they often recommend drawing lots to determine these individuals' share of inheritance—in the case of financial compensation, they do not suggest drawing lots. This implies that drawing lots in cases of inheritance, which is based on a sound *ḥadīth*, according to such jurists, should be limited to that context, without being extended to other matters involving *mamsūḥ*.

It is also worth noting that, as previously discussed, in the context of inheritance, a minority of jurists denied the existence of the *khunthā mushkil* and consequently rejected the ruling that allocates such a person half the share of a male and half that of a female. It would seem consistent, then, for this minority to adopt a similar position regarding *khunthā*s in cases of retaliation and compensation. In principle, this would be expected. However, I have not found any of these classical jurists who explicitly raise this point. Notably, Ibn Idrīs al-Ḥillī—who, as will be discussed later in this chapter, challenges the very notion of *khunthā mushkil* in the context of inheritance—does not address the category of *khunthā* at all in his treatment of retaliation or financial compensation.

This silence introduces a degree of ambiguity, making it difficult to determine with certainty the views of such jurists—including Ibn Idrīs—on this matter. However, the absence of any independent discussion of *khunthā*s in this context may suggest that, in line with his position on inheritance, Ibn Idrīs regarded *khunthā*s as always ultimately determinable—either male or female. As such, their legal treatment in cases of retaliation and compensation would follow the rulings already established for males and females, thereby rendering any separate mention unnecessary.

Testimony

The question of whether the testimony of a *khunthā* would be admissible in a court of law is also addressed in the classical juristic literature. In his *al-Nihāya*, al-Shaykh al-Ṭūsī affirms the admissibility of testimony offered by a deaf person (*aṣamm*), stipulating, however, that only the first statement made by such an individual should be accepted as valid, while subsequent remarks must be set aside to prevent confusion.[68] Al-Ṭūsī does not extend this discussion to other cases, including the *khunthā*. His pupil, Abū l-Ṣalāḥ al-Ḥalabī, however, includes the testimony of the *khunthā*, the blind person (*aʿmā*), and the eunuch (*khāṣī*) alongside that of the deaf person, thereby filling the lacuna left by his teacher. He contends that the testimonies of all such individuals are acceptable, provided that the essential criterion for valid testimony—namely, that the witness is just (*ʿadl*)—is fulfilled. Moreover, Abū l-Ṣalāḥ does not impose the limitation that only the first statement of such a witness is to be admissible.[69]

Al-ʿAllāma al-Ḥillī endorses Abū l-Ṣalāḥ al-Ḥalabī's view, maintaining that the testimonies of these individuals—including *khunthā*—are to be admissible without restricting them to the first statement. He buttresses this position with legal reasoning drawn from Qurʾānic exegesis. He cites the following verse: "… *And call two just persons among yourselves to witness and uphold the testimony for God…*"[70] (Qurʾān, 65: 2), emphasizing that this verse is articulated in absolute terms and imposes no additional restrictions beyond the general requirement that the witness be just (*ʿadl*).

Furthermore, al-ʿAllāma al-Ḥillī argues that the testimony of such individuals, whether it is the first testimony or any subsequent statement, yields the requisite presumption (*ẓann*) necessary for the acceptance of testimony in Islamic law.[71]

Manumission

The question of *khunthā*, owing to the ambiguous sex, also arises in classical juristic discussions on manumission (*kitāba*) of slaves. Al-Shaykh al-Ṭūsī raises the issue that when a slave owner concludes a contract of manumission with either a male or female slave, a question emerges: what is the ruling concerning an enslaved *khunthā* whose sex has been clarified as male or female? In other words, in cases where the *khunthā* is *ghayr mushkil*—that is, where the sex has been determined—is it permissible to grant manumission to such individuals under the aforementioned contract?

Al-Ṭūsī affirms that it is permissible, arguing that an enslaved *khunthā* classified as male falls under the term male slave (*ʿabd*), and thus is included in the relevant legal category. Similarly, an enslaved *khunthā* classified as female falls under the term female slave (*ama*), and so is encompassed within that legal framework. Therefore, manumitting an enslaved male or female *khunthā* would suffice to fulfil the slave owner's obligation under the contract.[72]

Al-Ṭūsī further raises this question that if the slave owner stipulates in the manumission contract that one of his slaves is to be freed without specifying the sex of the individual to be manumitted. Is it permissible to extend the manumission to a male, a female, or, crucially, to a *khunthā mushkil*? Al-Ṭūsī holds that, in such cases, it is permissible to grant manumission to any of these individuals, thereby fulfilling the owner's contractual obligation.[73]

With regard to this latter scenario, Ibn al-Barrāj contends that manumitting either a male or a female slave would suffice to discharge the slave owner's obligation under the manumission contract, since both fall under the general category of "slave" (*raqīq*). However, he maintains that manumitting a *khunthā mushkil* would not suffice until the sex of that individual is determined.[74]

It is noteworthy that the logic Ibn al-Barrāj employs—that both male and female slaves are encompassed within the category of "slave"—could, in principle, apply to a *khunthā mushkil* as well. This interpretive possibility underlies al-ʿAllāma al-Ḥillī's endorsement of al-Shaykh al-Ṭūsī's position. He observes that the term "slave" (*raqīq*) extends to a *khunthā mushkil* as long as the individual remains in a state of bondage, and thus the manumission obligation would apply.[75]

Although the jurists did not explicitly address the case of *mamsūḥ*, there is no reason to assume that such individuals would be excluded from this legal reasoning.

Prayers

With regard to prayers, classical Shiʿi jurists primarily addressed two issues concerning the *khunthā*: congregational prayers and funeral prayers. In the context of congregational prayers, the key questions were whether a *khunthā mushkil* could act as an *imām* to lead prayers, and where such a *khunthā* should be positioned among the followers (*maʾmūmīn*).

In response to the first question, the more accepted view among these jurists was that a *khunthā mushkil* could not lead prayers for males, as the *khunthā* might in fact be a woman, and Islamic law traditionally does not permit a woman to lead males in prayer. Similarly, a *khunthā mushkil* could not lead prayers for another *khunthā mushkil*, since the *imām* could in reality be a woman while the *maʾmūm* might be a man—once again rendering the situation impermissible under traditional norms. However, these jurists held that a *khunthā mushkil* may lead prayers for women, as women are permitted to follow either male or female *imāms*, and in case the *khunthā mushkil* is female it would still be permissible for her to lead the prayers for females.[76]

Ibn Ḥamza disagrees with the widely accepted position which holds that a *khunthā mushkil* cannot lead prayers for other *khunthā mushkils*. He contends that it is permissible, provided that the *khunthā* meets the necessary qualifications for leading congregational prayer—namely, being a believer, exhibiting justice, and having the most proficient recitation of the Qurʾān.[77] Al-ʿAllāma al-Ḥillī critiques Ibn Ḥamza's position by reiterating the previously mentioned concern: that the *khunthā mushkil* acting as *imām* may, in fact, be female, while the *khunthā mushkil* acting as *ma'mūm* might be male. He further asserts that, according to the consensus (*ijmāʿ*) of Muslim scholars, a female may not lead males in prayer.[78]

With regard to the second question, namely the position of order of standing in congregational prayers, jurists often hold that if a woman and a *khunthā mushkil* are present, the *khunthā* stands behind the *imām* and the woman behind the *khunthā*.[79] In case there are men, women, *khunthās*, and boys all present in congregational prayers, al-Ṭūsī holds that the men stand directly behind the *imām*, followed by the boys, then the *khunthās*, and then the women.[80] Ibn Ḥamza expresses the same view, but he adds two additional groups—slaves and naked individuals—among the worshippers, placing them ahead of the *khunthā mushkil* and women in their standing positions during prayer, though naked individuals must be in the sitting position in the row.[81]

However, other jurists—such as Ibn al-Junayd (as reported by al-ʿAllāma al-Ḥillī), Ibn Idrīs al-Ḥillī, and al-ʿAllāma al-Ḥillī himself—held a different position and maintained that the *khunthā mushkil* should precede the child, as the *khunthā* is legally accountable (*mukallaf*), bears a resemblance to maleness, and possesses a more complete intellect; thus, granting the *khunthā* precedence is more appropriate than granting it to boys.[82] Ibn Idrīs al-Ḥillī also remarks that if eunuchs are present among the congregation, the eunuchs would takes precedence over the *khunthā*. Accordingly, in such a configuration, the order of standing behind the *imām* would be as follows: first the males, followed by the eunuchs, then the *khunthā mushkil*, followed by the boys, and finally the females.

Regarding funeral prayers, the primary question that classical jurists sought to address was the following: if there are various groups of deceased—such as men, women, *khunthās*, and boys—and a single *imām* is to lead the funeral prayer for all of them at once, how should the corpses be arranged in front of the *imām*?

These jurists often maintained that the arrangement should be the reverse of the order observed in congregational prayers. Accordingly, as *Sallār al-Daylamī (*d. 463/1071*)* notes, the women's corpses are to be placed closest to the *qibla*, furthest from the *imām*, followed by the boys, then the *khunthās*, and finally the men, with the *imām* standing at the position aligned with the men.[83]

Al-Shaykh al-Ṭūsī, however, holds that after the women, the *khunthās* should be placed, followed by the boys and then the men, with the *imām* likewise standing at the position of the men. Furthermore, he adds that, with regard to burial, it is preferable that each individual be buried in a separate grave. Nonetheless, if necessity demands otherwise, it is permissible to bury two or three individuals in a single grave in the following manner: the men should be placed closest to the *qibla*, followed by the boys, then the *khunthā*, and finally the women.[84]

Ibn al-Barrāj, by contrast, maintains that the boys should be placed closest to the *qibla*, furthest from the *imām*, followed by the women, then the *khunthā mushkil*, then male slaves, and finally free men.[85] Ibn Idrīs al-Ḥillī slightly revises this position by introducing a distinction based on the age of the boys: if they are under six years of age, they are placed first, followed by the women and the rest as indicated. However, if they are over six years of age, they are to be placed between the male slaves and the freemen.[86]

Classical Shiʿi jurists do not explicitly address the case of the *mamsūḥ* in the context of ritual prayer. Nevertheless, in the absence of any scriptural texts specifically pertaining to the *mamsūḥ* in this regard, and in light of established legal principles, and given that earlier juristic discussions—particularly those concerning retaliation and financial compensation—often treated the *mamsūḥ* in parallel with the *khunthā mushkil*, one may reasonably infer that the legal provisions applied to the *khunthā mushkil* could also be extended to the *mamsūḥ* in matters of congregational and funeral prayers.

Marriage

The debates concerning the marriage of the *khunthā ghayr al-mushkil*—those who are legally identified as either male or female—do not, in general, raise significant concerns for jurists. Classical Shiʿi jurists commonly hold that it is permissible to marry such individuals, and, in principle, a *khunthā* legally identified as male may also marry a *khunthā* legally identified as female, though I have not encountered any classical Shiʿi sources that explicitly address this particular case. As a result, jurists do not typically discuss the permissibility of such a marriage per se; rather, the issue tends to arise in the context of defects (*ʿuyūb*) that may warrant the annulment of a marriage. The central question is whether the condition of being a *khunthā* constitutes a defect that would entitle the other party—whether male or female—to annul the marriage. Al-Shaykh al-Ṭūsī, in *al-Khilāf*, writes:

> Issue 125: If … a person is a *khunthā* who has been determined as male, this condition is not considered a defect warranting annulment of the marriage. Similarly, if a person is a *khunthā* who has been determined as female, the same ruling applies. [Imām] al-Shāfiʿī has two opinions on this matter:
>
> 1. The first opinion aligns with the aforementioned ruling—that is, the condition does not grant the right to annul the marriage.
> 2. The second opinion is that the spouse has the option to annul the marriage in such cases.
>
> Our evidence is that the marriage contract is valid by consensus, and establishing the option to annul the marriage due to this condition requires specific evidence.[87]

In *al-Mabsūṭ*, al-Ṭūsī further elaborates on the question of physical defects by distinguishing between two types of presumed deficiencies related to the sexual organs: those that prevent sexual intercourse and those that do not. If the defect prevents intercourse—such as in cases where the entire penis is removed, or only a small portion remains which is deemed insufficient for penetration—the wife has the right to annul the marriage. However, if enough of the organ remains to allow for intercourse, even if only the gland is present, then the wife does not have the right to annul the marriage. This is because the legal rulings concerning sexual relations in Islamic law, according to al-Ṭūsī, are based on the capacity to engage in intercourse rather than fertility. Al-Ṭūsī then turns to the case of the *khunthā* who is legally categorized as male and poses the following question: Does the wife of such a person have the right to annul the marriage? He again reports two opinions among jurists:

1. The wife does have the right to annul the marriage, as the condition of being a *khunthā* deviates from normative expectations.
2. The wife does not have the right to annul the marriage, because the individual in question is capable of sexual intercourse like other men. In this view, the intersex condition is considered merely an additional physical characteristic—analogous to possessing an extra finger—and does not constitute a defect. Al-Ṭūsī considers this second opinion stronger.

In response to a possible objection on *khunthā* being sterile—that is, incapable of biological paternity—he adds that if the husband is found to be sterile, this does not provide grounds for annulment, as the ability to engage in intercourse remains intact, and infertility is regarded as a matter determined by divine will.

Al-Ṭūsī then poses the converse scenario: if the wife is considered as a *khunthā*, does the husband have the right to annul the marriage? Here again, two opinions are reported, mirroring the same reasoning and legal considerations as in the previous case.[88]

Al-Ṭūsī, elsewhere in *al-Mabsūṭ*, further clarifies that the aforementioned legal position—namely, the two opinions regarding the (im)permissibility of annulment—applies specifically to cases in which a man or a woman contracts marriage without knowing that the prospective spouse is a *khunthā*, categorized as either female or male, and where the *khunthā* status is only discovered after the conclusion of the marriage. In contrast, in cases where the individual knowingly enters into marriage with a *khunthā*, classical jurists, as al-Ṭūsī notes, maintain that no right to annulment exists, as the contract was concluded with full awareness of the partner's condition.[89]

Al-ʿAllāma al-Ḥillī, however, disagrees with al-Ṭūsī regarding cases in which the status of the *khunthā* is unknown, asserting that even in such cases, the stronger opinion, in his view, is that annulment of marriage is not permitted.[90] But we should note, as he elaborates elsewhere, that this is when the sexual intercourse is possible, otherwise al-ʿAllāma al-Ḥillī also holds that annulment of marriage is permissible in this case.[91]

Regarding the marriage of the *khunthā mushkil*, the discussion proves to be more complex than often assumed in modern time. While contemporary Shiʿi jurists largely hold that a *khunthā mushkil* cannot enter into marriage, the classical legal tradition appears to have offered a more nuanced approach.[92] The discussion likely began with al-Shaykh al-Ṭūsī who explicitly refers to a case of inheritance in which a *khunthā mushkil* is considered married. His brief mention suggests that, under certain circumstances, such a *khunthā* could indeed be considered legally married.

With respect to inheritance, as previously noted, the majority of classical Shiʿi jurists held that a *khunthā mushkil* should receive a share equal to half that of a male and half that of a female. However, al-Ṭūsī introduces further distinctions, elaborating on various cases in which a *khunthā mushkil* might find themselves. Among these is the possible case of a *khunthā* who is identified as a father and mother which, according to al-Ṭūsī, is not conceivable because the *khunthā* is either a father which would be a male or a mother which would be a female. In fact, this is not particularly problematic, as it may be claimed that such a person is in fact a *khunthā ghayr al-mushkil*. The more intricate issue arises when an actual *khunthā mushkil* is involved in a marriage, whether in the role of a husband or a wife. According to him, in this case—if we assume the *khunthā* in question as a husband—this person receives half the inheritance share of a husband and half that of a wife. This is likely because the *khunthā* is *mushkil*, and we cannot assertively know whether this person is male or female. Thus, such a person's inheritance follows the same ruling mentioned earlier in the case of a *khunthā mushkil*: namely, half the share of a male and half that of a female. Let us review al-Ṭūsī's statement:

> It is not conceivable for a *khunthā* to be both father and mother because if he is a father then he is certainly a male and if she is a mother then she is certainly a female. [However,] it is conceivable for a *khunthā* to be either a husband or a wife, as reported in some traditions [attributed to Shurayḥ and Imām ʿAlī]. If the *khunthā* is a husband, he receives half the inheritance share of a husband and half that of a wife.[93]

Al-Muḥaqqiq al-Ḥillī refers to al-Ṭūsī's position on this matter; however, in the first part of his discussion, instead of presenting a *khunthā* as both father and mother, he introduces a different case in which *khunthā* can be fathers or grandfathers. Al-Muḥaqqiq al-Ḥillī considers this view to be far from accurate, arguing that if a person is capable of procreation as a father or grandfather, then he is not a *khunthā* but rather a man. He then refers to the *ḥadīth* attributed to Imām ʿAlī and Shurayḥ—discussed earlier in this chapter—and softens his earlier assertion by suggesting that, unless one bases their legal opinion on this *ḥadīth* and accepts that a *khunthā* may both conceive and be conceived, the position remains problematic[94] or, as al-ʿAllāma al-Ḥillī asserts, should impregnate.[95] However, this passage of the *ḥadīth* is important because it suggests that the *khunthā* in question would simultaneously occupy the roles of both father and mother: a mother to a child carried in their own womb, and a father to a child conceived by another through them.

Fakhr al-Muḥaqqiqīn al-Ḥillī further elaborates on the reason for considering the aforementioned case problematic or for rejecting it. According to him, the issue lies in the fact that the semen of a man alone is insufficient for the formation of a child, and neither is the semen of a woman sufficient; rather, a combination of both is required. Thus, if a *khunthā* possesses the generative capacity to function as a father or male, this person would not simultaneously possess the generative capacity to function as a mother or female.[96] However, al-Jubaʿī al-ʿĀmilī objects to this reasoning, arguing that it is possible for the semen of the *khunthā* to combine both of these qualities, just as the *khunthā* embodies both male and female aspects.[97]

With regard to the second point that al-Ṭūsī raised, that is a *khunthā mushkil* could be either a husband or a wife, al-Muḥaqqiq al-Ḥillī raises no objection. The only point of divergence, as noted, lies in the phrasing: the version of al-Ṭūsī's text I consulted states that if the *khunthā*'s role is to be the husband, he receives half of a husband's inheritance and half of a wife's inheritance.[98] By contrast, al-Muḥaqqiq al-Ḥillī presents this ruling in more general terms, which implies that if the *khunthā* acts as a wife, she too would receive half of a husband's and half of a wife's inheritance.[99]

Although al-ʿAllāma al-Ḥillī refers to the same point from al-Ṭūsī in some of his juristic works without offering any critical commentary,[100] in *Qawāʿid al-aḥkām* he critiques al-Ṭūsī's position. In doing so, he presents a case involving a *khunthā mushkil* who is simultaneously both a husband and a wife—unlike the depictions found in the works of al-Ṭūsī, al-Muḥaqqiq al-Ḥillī, and in his own earlier writings, where the *khunthā* is portrayed as either a husband or a wife. He then maintains that a marriage involving such a *khunthā*, who has both fathered and given birth to a child, would give rise to a legal problem. This is due to the ambiguity of the genealogical relationship between the two children: the *khunthā* is the mother of one and the father of the other, yet for a sibling relationship to be established in law, it is required that the children share at least one parent. This condition, however, is not fulfilled in this case.[101] Again, it is important to note that al-Ṭūsī does not raise such a scenario. In fact, the version of the *ḥadīth* he cites, as discussed earlier, refers only to a case in which the *khunthā* fathers a child, with no mention of giving birth to a child.

Al-Jubaʿī al-ʿĀmilī, however, offers an additional critique, arguing that al-Ṭūsī's assertion is entirely unjustified. For if the *khunthā* is a husband, his spouse would be a woman—so how could the *khunthā* be entitled to any share designated for a wife? And if the *khunthā* is a wife, her spouse would be a man—so how could the *khunthā* be entitled to any share designated for a husband?

He then attempts to justify al-Ṭūsī's view by noting that this ruling, in al-Tusi's view, was likely restricted to a case in which a *khunthā mushkil* is married to another *khunthā mushkil*. Given that both spouses are *khunthā mushkil*, and we cannot determine which is male and which is female, it is possible to assume that the deceased was a woman and the survivor a man, or vice versa; hence, due to this uncertainty, the survivor is given half of each of the two shares. However, if the spouse of the *khunthā* is a man, then—if the *khunthā* is a woman—she is entitled to the wife's share; but if the *khunthā* is a man, he receives nothing, as the basis for inheritance is absent due to the invalidity of the marriage in this case. The same applies if the *khunthā* is married to a woman.

He further argues that even on this basis, al-Shaykh al-Ṭūsī's position does not hold. This is because if the ambiguity regarding the *khunthā*'s sex existed prior to the marriage, the marriage would not have been valid. But if, at the time of the marriage, there was no such ambiguity, then the marriage is valid—regardless of whether the *khunthā* was a husband or a wife.[102]

Makkī al-ʿĀmilī, in extending the discussion to cases in which a *khunthā* serves as a mother or grandmother, argues that it is generally improbable for a *khunthā* to occupy roles such as father, grandfather, mother, or grandmother while their status remains ambiguous. This improbability, he notes, stems from the fact that assuming any of these familial roles would necessarily reveal the individual's sex, thereby resolving the ambiguity. An apparent exception to this principle is found in a narration transmitted by Maysara b. Shurayḥ from his father, Shurayḥ, from Imām ʿAlī, which recounts the case of a *khunthā* who both gave birth and impregnated another. This highly unusual case challenges the assumption that such roles inevitably clarify a *khunthā*'s legal sex. It is important to note that Makkī al-ʿĀmilī refers specifically to the version of the *ḥadīth* transmitted by al-Ṭūsī in *Tahdhīb al-aḥkām*, reported through Maysara. As previously discussed, this version only mentions the *khunthā* having impregnated someone, without reference to them being impregnated. In contrast, another version of the *ḥadīth*, recorded by al-Ṣadūq in *al-Faqīh*, includes both elements: the *khunthā* is said to have both impregnated another and been impregnated. It appears likely that Makkī al-ʿĀmilī, relying on memory, inadvertently conflated the two reports. Despite explicitly citing al-Ṭūsī's version, his discussion more closely reflects the version preserved by al-Ṣadūq.

Makkī al-ʿĀmilī then turns to the case of a *khunthā* assuming the role of a husband or wife. In his view, this is even less likely than the previously discussed familial case, given the invalidity of marriage as long as the *khunthā*'s sexual status remains unresolved—regardless of whether the *khunthā* were to marry a male, a female, or another *khunthā*. In explaining al-Shaykh al-Ṭūsī's ruling—namely, that such a *khunthā mushkil* is entitled to half the share of a husband and half the share of a wife—Makkī al-ʿĀmilī suggests that al-Ṭūsī may have been referring to a case in which a *khunthā* marries another *khunthā*, and the union is considered valid. However, Makkī al-ʿĀmilī ultimately rejects this reading, asserting that it lacks evidentiary basis and thus constitutes an unreliable opinion.[103]

In this discussion, I did not find any reference to *mamsūḥ*. A straightforward explanation might be that, in the case of a *mamsūḥ*—someone born without genitalia—marriage would not be plausible according to the classical Shiʿi legal scholars, since the capacity for sexual intercourse is considered a condition for the validity of marriage.

Conclusion and further discussion on the emergence of binary/non-binary debates in Twelver Shiʿi legal discourse

As demonstrated, the biological ambiguity of the intersex people posed significant challenges for classical Shiʿi jurists, particularly in areas such as inheritance, financial compensation, prayer, manumission, and marriage. These complexities led to the development of a diverse range of legal opinions and interpretive strategies.

According to some of these views—such as those concerning inheritance and financial compensation for *khunthā mushkil* and *mamsūḥ*, which differ from the shares and compensations assigned to males and females—one might conclude that a group of early Shiʿi legal scholars, albeit *implicitly*, conceptualized these individuals as occupying a liminal legal state that resisted binary classification as male or female. I stress "implicitly" since I have not found any classical Shiʿi, or for that matter Sunni, legal text that explicitly employs terms such as "third" or "liminal" legal category or sex with reference to *khunthā* and *mamsūḥ*. Yet, given that their rulings on various issues diverge from those governing males and females, one can infer that these jurists effectively recognized more than two sex categories in law by treating *khunthā mushkil* and *mamsūḥ* as legally neither male nor female—a status I describe as a liminal sex. Such nuanced legal reasoning reflects the early classical jurists' sophisticated engagement with the complexities of human embodiment within the framework of Islamic law.

However, what is significant in the early classical Shiʿi legal texts is that the question of the *khunthā mushkil*'s and *mamsūḥ*'s ontological status does not appear to have been raised. Perhaps it was simply taken at face value that *khunthā mushkil*s and *mamsūḥ*s were, ultimately, either male or female. Consequently, the possibility that such a *khunthā* or *mamsūḥ* might be neither male nor female, but constitute a third category of human being, was not considered. At least up to the twelfth century, I have found no evidence that Shiʿi jurists engaged with this question in any explicit or systematic way.

To the best of my knowledge, Ibn Idrīs al-Ḥillī (d. 598/1202), who held the minority position, was the first to raise the binary and non-binary problem regarding *khunthā mushkil*s in the Shiʿi context. Ibn Idrīs notes that the majority position, according to which the *khunthā mushkil* inherits an amount different from that of both males and females, that is, half of the male and half of the female inheritance share, implies that *khunthā*s are neither male nor female; otherwise, they would have received the share of either a male or a female. Ibn Idrīs argues that a *khunthā mushkil* cannot be both male and female because males and females are two different categories of humanity that cannot exist in one person. Therefore, scholars holding the majority position have no choice but to conclude that a *khunthā mushkil* belongs to a third category. If so, Ibn Idris remarks, this conclusion goes against Islamic scriptural teaching, particularly verses of the Qurʾān such as the following:

Q. 4:1
O mankind! Reverence your Lord, Who created you from a single soul and from it created its mate, and from the two has spread abroad a multitude of men and women.

Q. 42:49
Unto God belongs sovereignty over the heavens and the earth; He creates whatsoever He will, bestowing females upon whomsoever He will, and bestowing males upon whomsoever He will.

Q. 75:39
[A]nd made from him the two [pairs], male and female.

Q. 92:3
[B]y Him Who created the male and the female.

Drawing on these verses, Ibn Idris articulates a theological argument that may be summarized as follows:[104]

1. In these verses, God addresses the categories of humans in different ways: as a pair of males and females or simply as males and females.
2. These verses refer to various categories of humans.

3. However, in all the aforementioned verses, God mentions only two categories (*tathniya*), male and female; He does not mention a third category (*qism thālith*), such as intersex (*khunthā*).
4. If there were a third category of humankind, like intersex, He would have informed humans about this category out of His grace (*imtinān*).
5. Because He did not inform us about such a category, we may infer that males and females are the only categories of humans, and there is no other/third category.

Curiously, jurists who lived shortly after Ibn Idrīs, such as al-Muḥaqqiq al-Ḥillī (d. 676/1277), al-ʿAllāma al-Ḥillī (d. 726/1325), and Fakhr al-Muḥaqqiqīn al-Ḥillī (d. 771/1369–70), overlooked his binary argument.[105] However, al-ʿAllāma al-Ḥillī, in his *Mukhtalaf al-shīʿa*, did address it while reporting Ibn Idrīs's view on the inheritance of *khunthā*s, although he did not assess it either positively or negatively.[106] The first scholar to challenge Ibn Idrīs's theological argument was Makkī al-ʿĀmilī (d. 786/1384). He writes:

> Ibn Idris holds that *khunthā*s are either male or female, which implies that they cannot be categorized as a third nature (*ṭabīʿa thālitha*). His argument is based on the words of God [such as] Q. 42:49. However, such an understanding [of the Qurʾān] is inaccurate, as there are no signs in these verses to exclude a third category of human being. Moreover, it appears that God in these verses is only addressing the dominant categories of humans, namely male and female, but not all humans inclusively.[107]

Al-Shahīd al-Awwal challenges Ibn Idrīs's second point, namely, that the qurʾānic verses refer comprehensively to categories of humans. Instead, he suggests, these verses address only the majority of humankind or the members of those sexes who make up the vast majority of the human population—namely, males and females—but not the entirety of humanity. In fact, as he notes, there is no evidence in these verses or elsewhere in the Qurʾān that God did *not* create other categories of humans. Therefore, the existence of a third category/nature (*ṭabīʿa thālitha*) is plausible: al-Shahīd al-Awwal argues that no theological doctrine contradicts the idea that legal rulings on *khunthā mushkil* can differ from those on males and females.

Ever since al-Shahīd al-Awwal put forward his argument on the plausibility of a third category of humans, there have been two opposing camps in Shiʿi legal discourse: one group of jurists, including Ibn Fahd al-Ḥillī (d. 841/1437–8), rejects the notion of a third category and defends Ibn Idrīs's position and his theological argument;[108] a second group explores the plausibility and possibility of a third category of humanity. This latter group includes al-Suyūrī al-Ḥillī, known as al-Fāḍil al-Miqdād (d. 826/1422–3); Zayn al-Dīn b. ʿAlī al-Jubaʿī al-ʿĀmilī (d. 965/1557–8); Mullā

Aḥmad al-Narāqī (d. 1245/1829); Mīr Fattāḥ al-Marāghī (d. 1250/1834), Muḥammad Ibrāhīm al-Yazdī (d. 1321/1903); and Sayyid Kāẓim al-Ṭabāṭabāʾī al-Yazdī (d. 1337/1919).[109]

I would like to conclude this chapter by drawing attention to a critical point concerning the binary and non-binary dimensions of intersex-related discussions in Shiʿi legal discourse. At the heart of this matter lies a central juristic question: What are the legal ramifications of adopting a binary versus a non-binary framework when addressing the category of the *khunthā*? More precisely, how would legal rulings—whether concerning private or individual matters (such as ritual obligations, purity laws, inheritance rights, bodily integrity, legal retaliation, or financial compensation) or public and societal matters (such as eligibility for legal testimony, various forms of religious and communal leadership, including leading prayers, or holding positions such as being judges or *muftīs*)—differ under these two conceptual models? This is a question of substantial legal consequence, with far-reaching implications for both the theoretical coherence and practical implementation of Shiʿi law.

As demonstrated in this chapter, early classical Shiʿi jurists did not engage with the binary/non-binary question in their treatment of the *khunthā*. This conceptual distinction had not yet emerged as a juristic problem, and consequently, their discussions did not frame the issue in these terms. It was not until the time of Ibn Idrīs al-Ḥillī that the question began to be explicitly raised and juridically theorized. Since then, Shiʿi legal thought has increasingly grappled with whether the *khunthā* must ultimately be assigned to either the male or female category or may be recognized as occupying a sustained legal or ontological status outside the binary. This has led to the development of two different juridical approaches: one that seeks to integrate the *khunthā* into the existing binary framework by determining their sex as either male or female, and another that classifies *khunthā* as a third ontological category beyond male and female categories.

A comprehensive comparison of the specific legal rulings that emerge from these two approaches lies beyond the scope of the present chapter. However, I have examined these issues in greater depth elsewhere.[110] There, I argue that the adoption of either model results in markedly different outcomes concerning the rights, obligations, and legal recognition of intersex persons in Shiʿi law.

Notes

* This chapter is part of the project Beyond Binaries: Intersex in Islamic Legal Tradition (Project Number: vi.Veni.211F.093), funded by the Dutch Research Council (NWO) under the Veni Talent Programme.

1 Other branches of the Shiʿi legal tradition, such as the Ismāʿīlī and Zaydī schools, will not be addressed in this chapter. The Ismāʿīlī tradition—particularly the contributions of al-Qāḍī al-Nuʿmān on this subject—has been partially discussed in another chapter of this volume. The Zaydī legal tradition, which is as expansive as any of the major Islamic legal schools, has not yet been studied in this context and remains open to further research.

2 OHCHR, *Background Note on Human Rights* (United Nations: Human Rights Office of the High Commissioner, 2019), 2, Accessed March 2024: https://www.ohchr.org/en/documents/tools-and-resources/background-note-human-rights-violations-against-intersex-people; Monro and colleagues briefly address the UN Office for the Commissioner of Human Rights' definition of intersex (Surya Monro et al, "Intersex: Cultural and Social Perspectives," *Culture, Health and Sexuality* 23, no. 4 [2021]: 431–40, at 433). Also see Dan Christian Ghattas, "Protecting Intersex People in Europe: A Toolkit for Law and Policy Makers," *OII Europe*, (2023[2019]), 9, Accessed March 2024: https://www.oiieurope.org/wp-content/uploads/2019/05/Protecting_intersex_in_Europe_toolkit.pdf. According to the Intersex Society of North America (ISNA), "Intersex is a general term used for a variety of conditions in which a person is born with a reproductive or sexual anatomy that doesn't seem to fit the typical definitions of female or male" (Intersex Society of North America, "What Is Intersex?" Accessed March 2024: https://isna.org/faq/what_is_intersex/). Although ISNA dissolved itself in 2008, its website remains available and its two successor organisations also host the same content: Accord Alliance, www.accordalliance.org and InterACT: Advocates for Intersex Youth, https://interactadvocates.org, "What Is Intersex?"

3 See Abū ʿAbd al-Raḥmān al-Khalīl b. Aḥmad al-Farāhīdī (d. between 160/777–8 and 175/790–1), *Kitāb al-ʿayn*, ed. Mahdī al-Makhzūmī and Ibrāhīm al-Sāmarrāʾī, 8 vols. (Baghdad: Dār al-Rashād, 1980), 4: 248.

4 Abū Naṣr Ismāʿīl al-Jawharī (d. 393/1003), *al-Ṣiḥāḥ tāj al-lugha wa-ṣiḥāḥ al-ʿarabiyya*, ed. Aḥmad ʿAbd al-Ghafūr ʿAṭṭār, 6 vols. (Beirut: Dār al-ʿIlm li-l-Malāyin, 1407/1986–7), 1: 281.

5 For example, al-Azharī (d. 370/980) repeats al-Jawharī's definition of *khunthā* (Muḥammad b. Aḥmad al-Azharī, *Tahdhīb al-lugha*, 15 vols. [Beirut: Dār Iḥyāʾ al-Turāth al-ʿArabī, 2001], 7: 145). Al-Fayyūmī (d. 770/1368), however, describes a *khunthā* as a person who has both a vulva (*farj al-marʾa*) and a penis (*farj al-rajul*) (Aḥmad b. Muḥammad b. ʿAlī al-Fayyūmī, *al-Miṣbāḥ al-munīr fī gharīb al-sharḥ al-kabīr*, 2 vols. [Beirut: al-Maktaba al-ʿIlmiyya, 1994], 1: 183). Like al-Khalīl, Ibn Manẓūr (d. 711/1311–2) defines *khunthā* as a person who is not exclusively a female or a male, suggesting that *khunthā*s cannot always be categorized as male or female: in some cases, they belong to a distinct category separate from both male and female. Ibn Manẓūr explains that the term *khunthā* can be applied either as an adjective (and thus it makes sense to say a "*khunthā* man", which means a male individual who has both male and female sexual organs) or as a noun without qualification, namely, using *khunthā* alone, which implies a person who has biological signs of a male and female, such as a beard and breasts (Muḥammad b. Mukarram b. Manẓūr, *Lisān al-ʿarab*, 15 vols. [Beirut: Dār Ṣādir li-l-Ṭibāʿa wa-l-Nashr, 1414], 2: 145).

6 See, for example, Yaḥyā b. Sharaf al-Nawawī (d. 676/1277), *al-Majmūʿ sharḥ al-Muhadhdhab*, 20 vols. (Beirut: Dār al-Fikr, 1990), 2: 46–7; Muḥammad b. Aḥmad al-Sarakhsī, *al-Mabsūṭ*, 30 vols. (Beirut: Dār al-Maʿrifa, 1414/1993), 30: 91; Abū l-Ḥusayn ʿAlī b. al-Ḥusayn b. Muḥammad al-Sughdī, *al-Nutaf*

fī l-fatāwā, ed. Ṣalāḥ al-Dīn al-Nāhī, 2 vols. (Amman: Dār al-Furqān/Beirut: Muʾassasat al-Risāla, 1404/1984), 2: 857–8; Abū l-Ḥasan ʿAlī b. Muḥammad al-Māwardī al-Baṣrī (d. 450/1058), *al-Ḥāwī l-kabīr fī fiqh madhhab al-imām al-Shāfiʿī*, 18 vols. (Beirut: Dār al-Kutub al-ʿIlmiyya, 1419/1999), 8: 108. However, several Sunni legal experts refer to *khunthā* as people with both male and female genitalia: see, for example, Abū Muḥammad ʿAbd al-Wahhāb b. ʿAlī al-Thaʿlabī, *al-Maʿūna ʿalā madhhab ʿālim al-madīna "al-Imām Mālik b. Anas,"* ed. Ḥamīsh ʿAbd al-Ḥaqq, 3 vols. (Makka: al-Maktaba al-Tijāriyya, 1995), 3: 657; Abū l-Ḥusayn Aḥmad b. Muḥammad al-Qudūrī, *Mukhtaṣar al-Qudūrī fī l-fiqh al-Ḥanafī*, ed. Muḥammad Muḥammad ʿAwīḍa (Beirut: Dār al-Kutub al-ʿIlmiyya, 1418/1997), 137; ʿAlī b. Abī Bakr b. ʿAbd al-Jalīl al-Marghīnānī (d. 593/1196–7), *al-Hidāya fī sharḥ Bidāyat al-mubtadī*, ed. Ṭalāl Yūsuf, 4 vols. (Beirut: Dār Iḥyāʾ al-Turāth al-ʿArabī, 2010), 4: 546.

7 See, for example, Jaʿfar Kāshif al-Ghiṭāʾ, *Kashf al-ghiṭāʾ ʿan mubhamāt al-sharīʿa al-gharrāʾ*, 4 vols. (Mashhad: Maktab al-Iʿlām al-Islāmī, 1380sh), 1: 233–4; Muḥammad Jawād al-Ḥusaynī al-ʿĀmilī, *Miftāḥ al-karāma fī sharḥ Qawāʿid al-ʿAllāma*, 11 vols. (Beirut: Dār Iḥyāʾ al-Turāth al-ʿArabī, n.d.), 1: 113 and 3: 139; Muḥammad Ḥasan al-Najafī (d. 1266/1849), *Jawāhir al-kalām fī sharḥ Sharāʾiʿ al-islām*, ed. ʿAbbās al-Qūchānī, 43 vols. (Beirut: Dār Iḥyāʾ al-Turāth al-ʿArabī,1981), 2: 6 and 3: 8; Murtaḍā b. Muḥammad Amīn al-Anṣārī, *Kitāb al-ṭahāra*, 5 vols. (Qum: Majmaʿ al-Fikr al-Islāmī, 1415), 3: 326; Mīr ʿAbd al-Fattāḥ al-Ḥusaynī al-Marāghī, *al-ʿAnāwīn al-fiqhiyya*, 2 vols. (Qum: Muʾassasat al-Nashr al-Islāmī, 1417), 1: 38; Sayyid Kāẓim al-Yazdī, *Ḥāshiyat Farāʾid al-uṣūl*, compiled by Muḥammad Ibrāhīm al-Yazdī, 3 vols. (Qum: Dār al-Hudā, 1426), 1: 225. The term *mamsūḥ* signifies "effaced," "rubbed off," and "smoothed." According to Ibn Manẓūr, people who have no genitalia are called *mamsūḥ* because it was thought that due to the lack of genitals, the inner sides of their thighs would rub against each other and become smooth (Ibn Manẓūr, *Lisān al-ʿarab*, 2: 593–5). Although the term *mamsūḥ* for intersex people apparently is not used in Sunni legal schools, it has been applied to a group of castrated people—that is, eunuchs—in both the Sunni and Shiʿi legal traditions. To briefly explain, discussions of eunuchs were raised in relation to several juristic topics, including fasting, prayer, purity, pilgrimage, retaliation, and compensation. There are three types of eunuchs: (1) a male who is castrated by removing his testicles or causing them no longer to function is called *khāṣī*; (2) a male who is castrated by the removal of his penis while the testicles still remains is often called *majbūb* or, occasionally, *al-khāṣī al-majbūb*; and (3) a male who is castrated by the removal of both his penis and testicles is often named *mamsūḥ* or, occasionally, *al-khāṣī al-mamsūḥ*. Nevertheless, the definition and usage of these terms are highly contested among jurists. For definition of *khāṣī*, see multiple unknown authors, *al-Mawsūʿa al-fiqhiyya al-Kuwaytiyya*, 45 vols. (Kuwayt: Wazārat al-ʾAwqāf wa-l-Shuʾūn al-Islāmiyya, 1404–1427), 39: 51–2; Abū Ḥāmid Muḥammad al-Ghazalī, *al-Wasīṭ fī l-madhhab*, ed. Aḥmad Maḥmūd Ibrāhīm and Muḥammad Muḥammad Tāmir, 7 vols. (Cairo: Dār al-Salām, 1417), 6: 109; Shams al-Dīn Muḥammad b. Makkī al-ʿĀmilī, *al-Lumʿa al-dimashqiyya fī fiqh al-imāmiyya* (Qum: Dār al-Fikr, 1411), 50; ʿAlī b. Ḥusayn ʿAbd al-ʿĀlī al-Karakī, *Jāmiʿ al-maqāṣid fī sharḥ al-Qawāʿid*, 13 vols. (Qum: Muʾassasat Āl al-Bayt li-Iḥyāʾ al-Turāth,1414), 12: 36; Āqā Ḥusayn al-Khānsārī, *Takmīl mashāriq al-shumūs fī sharḥ al-Durūs* (Qum: Muʾassasat Āl al-Bayt li Iḥyāʾ al-Turāth, 1311), 417; Yusūf al-Baḥrānī, *al-Ḥadāʾiq al-nāḍira fī aḥkām al-ʿitra al-ṭāhira*, 25 vols. (Qum: Muʾassasat al-Nashr al-Islāmī, 1409), 13: 162; Aḥmad al-Narāqī, *al-Ḥāshiya ʿalā l-Rawḍa al-bahiyya fī sharḥ al-Lumʿa al-dimashqiyya fī fiqh al-imāmiyya* (Qum: Muʾassasat al-Nashr al-Islāmī, 1425), 442. On sources in English about eunuchs in Islamic law and society, see David Ayalon, *Eunuchs, Caliphs and Sultans: A Study of Power Relationships* (Jerusalem: Magnes Press, Hebrew University, 1999); idem, *Outsiders in the Lands of Islam: Mamluks, Mongols and Eunuchs* (London: Variorum Reprints, 1988), 67–124; Shaun Marmon, *Eunuchs and Sacred Boundaries in Islamic Society* (Oxford: Oxford University Press, 1995); Serena Tolino, "Eunuchs in the Sunni Legal Discourse: Reflections on the Gender of Castrated Men," *Studi Magrebini* 20, no. 2 (2022): 117–36; Glaire D. Anderson, "16

Concubines, Eunuchs, and Patronage in Early Islamic Córdoba," in *Reassessing the Roles of Women as 'Makers' of Medieval Art and Architecture*. ed. Therese Martin (Leiden: Brill, 2012): 650–64. It is striking that none of these works mentions the term *mamsūḥ* in this context, despite the fact that it was frequently discussed by classical Sunni and Shiʿi jurists.

8 ʿAbd al-ʿAzīz Ibn al-Barrāj, *al-Muhadhdhab*, 2 vols. (Qum: Muʾassasat al-Nashr al-Islāmī, 1406), 2: 171–2.

9 See, for example, Mehrdad Alipour, "Navigating Body Politics in Shiʿi Legal Tradition: Examining Sayyid Kāẓim al-Yazdī's Account of Non-Binary Intersex," *Islamic Law and Society* 32, no. 3 (2025): 262–315; Ash Geissinger, "Applying Gender and Queer Theory to Pre-modern Sources," in *The Routledge handbook of Islam and gender*, ed. Justine Howe (London: Routledge, 2021): 101–15.

10 See Etan Kohlberg, "Shīʿa Ḥadīth: Introduction," in *The Study of Shiʿi Islam: History, Theology and Law*, eds. Farhad Daftary and Gurdofarid Miskinzoda (London: I.B. Tauris Publishers and Co. Ltd and the Institute of Ismaili Studies, 2014): 165–79.

11 Muḥammad b. ʿAlī b. Shahr-āshūb al-Māzandarānī, *Manāqib āl Abī Ṭālib*, vols. 3 (Najaf: al-Maktaba al-Ḥaydariyya, 1376), 1: 218. To find detailed information on this issue, see Etan Kohlberg, "Al-Uṣūl al-Arbaʿumiʾa," in *Jerusalem Studies in Arabic and Islam: Jahiliyya and Islamic Studies in Honour of M. J. Kister: Septuagenarian (II)*. 10 (1987): 128–66.

12 They are also published independently. See *al-Uṣūl al-sitta ʿashar min al-uṣūl al-awwaliyya*, ed. Ḍiyāʾ al-Dīn al-Maḥmūdī (Qum: Dār al-Ḥadīth, 1423).

13 ʿAlī b. Jaʿfar, *Masāʾil ʿAlī ibn Jaʿfar* (Qum: Muʾassasat Āl al-Bayt li-Iḥyāʾ al-Turāth, 1409/1368sh), 104, Ḥ. 3. In both *ḥadīth* literature and classical Islamic legal texts, the male pronoun is often used to refer to a *khunthā*, even in cases where the *khunthā* has been legally determined to be female. I interpret this as a stylistic convention that allowed the use of male pronouns in cases of ambiguity. However, I am cautious not to read too much into this, even though some scholars have drawn conclusions from it. Therefore, when translating texts that use a male pronoun for a *khunthā* determined to be female, I will avoid using either a male or female pronoun, as doing so could be misleading or confusing. Instead, I will use the noun *khunthā* which the pronoun refers to.

14 ʿAbd Allāh b. Jaʿfar b. Ḥusayn al-Ḥimyarī al-Qummī, *Qurb al-isnād* (Qum: Muʾassasat Āl al-Bayt li-Iḥyāʾ al-Turāth, 1413), 247–48, Ḥ. 977.

15 Muḥammad b. Yaʿqūb al-Kulaynī, *al-Kāfī fī ʿilm al-dīn*, ed. ʿAlī Akbar Ghaffārī, 8 vols. (Tehran: Dār al-Kutub al-Islāmiyya, 1407/1367sh), 5: 411, Ḥ. 6; Muḥammad b. Ḥasan al-Ṭūsī, *Tahdhīb al-aḥkām*, ed. Ḥusayn Khirsān, ʿAlī Ākhūndī, and Muḥammad Ākhūndī, 10 vols. (Tehran: Dār al-Kutub al-ʿIlmiyya, 1365sh), 7: 432, Ḥ. 1721.

16 Al-Qāḍī al-Nuʿmān, *Daʿāʾim al-islām*, 2 vols. (Cairo: Dār al-Maʿārif, 1383/1963), 2: 230, Ḥ. 864.

17 Aḥmad b. Muḥammad Khālid al-Barqī, *al-Maḥāsin*, ed. Jalāl al-Dīn Muhaddith, 2 vols. (Qum: Dār al-Kutub al-Islāmiyya, 1371), 2: 603, Ḥ. 29. It is worth noting that I could not find further reports on intersex matters in other early collections, such as *Kitāb al-nawādir* of Aḥmad b. Muḥammad b. ʿĪsā al-Ashʿarī al-Qummī (alive in 274/887–8); *Baṣāʾir al-darajāt* of Muḥammad b. al-Ḥasan al-Ṣaffār al-Qummī (d. possibly 290/902–3); and *Qurb al-isnād* of Abū l-ʿAbbās ʿAbd Allāh b. Jaʿfar b. al-Ḥusayn al-Ḥimyarī al-Qummī (alive in 297/909–10).

18 This work is primarily a historical account narrating *ḥadīth*s about ʿAlī's life during his caliphate, with a particular focus on events related to Muʿāwiya's forces raiding ʿAlī's territories. However, it also includes *ḥadīth*s on other matters due to their connection to ʿAlī's legal rulings or judgments.

19 Ibrāhīm b. Muḥammad b. Saʿīd b. Hilāl al-Thaqafī, *al-Ghārāt*, 2 vols. (Qum: Dār al-Kitāb al-Islāmī, 1410), 1: 111–2.

20 Ibrāhīm b. Muḥammad b. Saʿīd b. Hilāl al-Thaqafī, *al-Ghārāt*, 1: 114–5.

21 This counts as the earliest book of Zaydī Shiʿis. It is more commonly known among Zaydīs as *al-Majmūʿ*, which is divided into two parts: *al-Majmūʿ al-ḥadīthī* and *al-Majmūʿ al-fiqhī*. Although the attribution of the book to Zayd, or even to al-Wāsiṭī as its compiler, cannot be confirmed with certainty, Zaydī Shiʿis almost unanimously regard this attribution as accurate. The book was first published in a modern edition in Milan, Italy, in 1919 by Griffini and was later republished in Beirut, Lebanon, in 1966 by ʿAbd al-Wāsiʿ b. Yaḥyā al-Wāsiʿī. More recently, the book was edited and published in Yemen. This version is used in this chapter.

22 Zayd b. ʿAlī, *al-Majmūʿ al-ḥadīthī wa-l-majmūʿ al-fiqhī* (*Musnad al-Imām Zayd b. ʿAlī*), ed. ʿAbdallāh b. Ḥamūd b. Dirham al-ʿAzzī (Saʿda: Dār al-Imām Zayd b. ʿAlī li-l-Ṭibāʿa wa-l-Nashr, 1435/2014), 296.

23 Al-Kulaynī, *al-Kāfī*, 7: 156–9; Muḥammad b. ʿAlī b. Bābawayh al-Qummī al-Ṣadūq, *Man lā yaḥḍuruhu l-faqīh*, ed. ʿAlī Akbar Ghaffārī, 4 vols. (Qum: Muʾassasat al-Nashr al-Islāmī, 1404), 4: 326–29; al-Ṭūsī, *Tahdhīb*, 9: 353–7.

24 Al-Ṭūsī, *Tahdhīb*, 10: 81. However, al-Kulaynī recorded this *ḥadīth* differently, using the term *khabīth* (vile) instead of *khunthā* (al-Kulaynī, *al-Kāfī*, 7: 241).

25 Al-Qāḍī al-Nuʿmān, *Daʿāʾim al-Islām*, 2: 387–90.

26 Ibid., 1: 235.

27 Ibid., 2: 522.

28 Ibid., 1: 151.

29 Al-Ṣadūq, *al-Faqīh*, 4: 327–8, Ḥ. 5704; al-Qāḍī al-Nuʿmān, *Daʿāʾim al-Islām*, 2: 387–8, Ḥ. 1377; al-Ṭūsī, *Tahdhīb*, 9: 354–5, Ḥ. 5.

30 See, for example, al-Qāḍī al-Nuʿmān, *Daʿāʾim al-Islām*, 2: 387, Ḥ. 1377.

31 For this account, see, for example, al-Ṣadūq, *al-Faqīh*, 4: 327–8, Ḥ. 5704; al-Qāḍī al-Nuʿmān, *Daʿāʾim al-Islām*, 2: 387–8, Ḥ. 1377.

32 This question, among others, raises a valid inquiry into how the expansion of *ḥadīth* literature on intersex topics in Islam, particularly within the Shiʿi context, occurred. It is crucial to understand why the surviving *uṣūl* treatises contain no *ḥadīth*s concerning intersex individuals. Moreover, why did earlier collections, unlike the Four Books, include so few of these reports? Did their compilers lack access to such *ḥadīth*s, despite being chronologically closer to the infallible Imāms? Shiʿi scholars generally believe that most early *uṣūl* treatises—whether 400 or 700 in number—were available during the lifetimes of those who compiled the Four Books and *Daʿāʾim al-Islām*, suggesting that these later authors had access to them. If this is accurate, then earlier *ḥadīth* scholars preceding the compilers of the Four Books—some of whom were mentioned previously—should also have had access to these *ḥadīth*s. Why, then, are such reports absent from their collections? Could this imply that *ḥadīth*s concerning intersex individuals were fabricated later, either during the time of the compilers of the Four Books or by them? While this is a possibility, it is certainly not the most convincing explanation. A less likely argument would be that earlier *ḥadīth* collectors were aware of these reports but judged them unreliable and, therefore, chose not to include them in their compilations. However, a more plausible explanation is that early *ḥadīth* collections—some of which were mentioned above—were typically subject-oriented and heavily dependent on the *ḥadīth* literature known in their respective geographical regions or transmitted by the compilers' own *shaykh*s, whom they considered trustworthy. Consequently, these collections were far from comprehensive. Their compilers did not necessarily travel extensively to collect *ḥadīth*s from all available scholars, nor did they seek out every existing *uṣūl* treatise to complete their works. Furthermore, they did not claim to have compiled exhaustive collections. By contrast, the authors of the Four Books intended to produce extensive compilations that would eliminate the need to rely on earlier *uṣūl* treatises. Nevertheless, they also exercised selectivity, including only those *ḥadīth*s they deemed authentic. These observations raise the need for further examination of the matter.

33 This supports my argument, as similar discussions and reports appear in Islamic scriptural, legal, and medical sources concerning eunuchs, effeminate men, mannish women, and individuals born with two heads and chests (now referred to as conjoined twins, specifically dicephalic parapagus and thoracopagus twins). For secondary literature on these topics, see, for example, Everett K. Rowson, "The Effeminates of Early Medina," *Journal of the American Oriental Society* 111, no. 4 (1991): 671–93; Mehrdad Alipour, *Negotiating Homosexuality in Islam: A Legal-Hermeneutical Examination of Modern Shi'i Discourse* (Leiden: Brill, 2024), 104–13; Marmon, *Eunuchs and Sacred Boundaries in Islamic Society*, particularly chaps. 1 and 2; Serena Tolino, "Eunuchs in the Sunni Legal Discourse: Reflections on the Gender of Castrated Men," *Studi Magrebini* 20, no. 2 (2022): 117–36; Anderson, "16 Concubines, Eunuchs, and Patronage in Early Islamic Córdoba," 650–64.

34 Uncertain author, *Fiqh al-Riḍā* (Qum: Mu'assasat Āl al-Bayt li-Iḥyā' al-Turāth, 1406), 290–1.

35 Sayyid Ḥasan al-Ṣadr provides an excellent examination of this book in *Faṣl al-qaḍā' fī l-kitāb al-mushtahar bi-Fiqh al-Riḍā*, ed. Riḍā Ustādī (Qum: Mu'assasat al-Nashr al-Islāmī, 1373sh).

36 Muḥammad b. ʿAlī b. Bābawayh al-Ṣadūq, *al-Muqniʿ* (Qum: Mu'assasat al-Imām al-Hādī, 1415), 503; Muḥammad b. Muḥammad b. Nuʿmān al-ʿUkbarī (al-Mufīd), *al-Muqniʿa* (Qum: al-Mu'tamar al-ʿĀlamī li-Alfiyyat al-Shaykh al-Mufīd,1413), 698.

37 For Sunni legal sources on primary and secondary markers, see al-Marghīnānī, *al-Hidāya*, 4: 546; Muwaffaq al-Dīn Abū Muḥammad Ibn Qudāma al-Maqdisī (d. 620/1223), *al-Mughnī*, 10 vols. (Cairo: Maktabat al-Qāhira, 1388/1968), 6: 336; al-Sughdī, *al-Nutaf fī l-fatāwā*, 2: 858; al-Sarakhsī, *al-Mabsūṭ*, 30: 92.

38 Ḥasan b. Yūsuf al-Ḥillī (ʿAllāma), *Mukhtalaf al-shīʿa fī aḥkām al-sharīʿa*, 9 vols. (Qum: Mu'assasat al-Nashr al-Islāmī, 1374sh), 9: 94.

39 See al-Ḥillī (ʿAllāma), *Mukhtalaf al-shīʿa*, 9: 95–6; idem, *Qawāʿid al-aḥkām*, 3 vols. (Qum: Mu'assasat al-Nashr al-Islāmī, 1419), 3: 383; Muḥammad b. Ḥasan b. Yūsuf al-Ḥillī (Fakhr al-Muḥaqqiqīn), *Iḍāḥ al-fawāʾid fī sharḥ mushkilāt al-Qawāʿid*, 4 vols. (Qum: Mu'assasa-yi Ismāʿīliyān, 1387), 4: 249.

40 Shams al-Dīn Muḥammad b. Makkī al-ʿĀmilī, *al-Durūs al-sharʿiyya fī fiqh al-imāmiyya*, 3 vols. (Qum: Mu'assasat al-Nashr al-Islāmī, 1417), 2: 378–9.

41 Zayn al-Dīn b. ʿAlī al-Jubaʿī al-ʿĀmilī, *al-Rawḍa al-bahiyya fī sharḥ al-Lumʿa al-dimashqiyya fī fiqh al-imāmiyya*, 2 vols. (Qum: Intishārāt-i Daftar-i Tablīghāt-i Islāmī, 1412/1373sh), 2: 331–4. For some later Shiʿi discussion of primary and secondary markers, see Niẓām al-Dīn Sāwujī, *Jāmiʿ ʿabbāsī (takmila)*, 2 vols. (Tehran: Farāhānī, 1350sh), 2: 412; Bahā' al-Dīn Muḥammad b. Ḥasan al-Fāḍil al-Hindī (d. 1137/1725), *Kashf al-lithām wa-l-ibhām ʿan Qawaʿid al-ahkām*, 11 vols. (Qum: Mu'assasat al-Nashr al-Islāmī, 1416), 9: 485; Ḥusaynī al-ʿĀmilī, *Miftāḥ al-karāma*, 8: 219; Aḥmad b. Muḥammad al-Narāqī, *Mustanad al-shīʿa*, 19 vols. (Qum: Mu'assasat Āl al-Bayt li-Iḥyā' al-Turāth, 1415), 19: 441; al-Najafī, *Jawāhir al-kalām*, 39: 281.

42 See, for example, al-Nawawī, *al-Majmūʿ*, 2: 47–50; al-Sarakhsī, *al-Mabsūṭ*, 30: 103–5; Maḥmūd b. Aḥmad Badr al-Dīn al-ʿAynī (d. 855/1451), *al-Bināya sharḥ al-Hidāya*, ed. Ayman Ṣāliḥ Shaʿbān, 13 vols. (Beirut: Dār al-Kutub al-ʿIlmiyya, 1420/2000), 13: 528–30; al-Ḥillī (ʿAllāma), *Mukhtalaf al-shīʿa*, 9: 95–6 and *Qawāʿid al-aḥkām*, 3: 382–83; al-Ḥillī (Fakhr al-Muḥaqqiqīn), *Iḍāḥ al-fawāʾid*, 4: 249–50.

43 For medical discourse, see Muḥammad b. Zakariyyā l-Rāzī, *al-Ḥāwī fī l-ṭibb*, 7 vols. (Beirut: Dār Iḥyā' al-Turāth al-ʿArabī, 1422/2002), 3: 192; Ibn Sīnā, *al-Qānūn fī l-ṭibb*, 4 vols. (Beirut: Dār Iḥyā' al-Turāth al-ʿArabī, 2005), 3: 449; Abū l-Qāsim al-Zahrāwī [Albucasis], *Kitāb al-taṣrīf li-man ʿajaza ʿan al-taʾlīf: al-maqāla al-thalāthūn: al-Jarāḥa* (Riyadh: Maktabat al-Malik Fahd al-Waṭaniyya, 1422/2001), 306.

44 Ibn al-Barrāj, *al-Muhadhdhab*, 2: 172.

45 Muḥammad Ḥasan al-Ṭūsī, *al-Mabsūṭ fī fiqh al-imāmiyya*, 8 vols. (Tehran: al-Maktabat al-Murtaḍawiyya li-Iḥyā' al-Āthār al-Jaʿfariyya, 1387), 4: 266. This discussion appears to have been absent from Shiʿi legal discourse prior to al-Ṭūsī. His treatment of the issue in *al-Mabsūṭ* constitutes the first

substantial engagement with the topic, and it remains, to my knowledge, unique within his corpus. Al-Ṭūsī does not refer to the innate sexual desire of the *khunthā* as a legal marker in any of his other works, nor in other sections of *al-Mabsūṭ* that I have consulted where he discusses *khunthā*-related rulings.

46 One *ḥadīth* refers to urination as a marker to determine the sex of a *mamsūḥ*: if a *mamsūḥ* releases urine suddenly and forcefully (*naḥḥā*), then he is a man, and if the *mamsūḥ* does not release it forcefully (*lā yunaḥḥī/lā yatanaḥḥī*) but rather dribbles it between the thighs, then she is a woman. This *ḥadīth* was collected by al-Kulaynī and al-Ṭūsī, although with slightly different *isnāds*. The chains of transmission are identical towards the end of the transmission line: both al-Kulaynī and al-Ṭūsī narrated it from Ḥasan b. ʿAlī b. Faḍḍāl from ʿAbdallāh b. Bukayr (a companion of the Sixth Imām, Jaʿfar b. Muḥammad al-Ṣādiq, although ʿAbdallāh b. Bukayr does not attribute this *ḥadīth* to this Imām), from a group of the companions of the Imāms, from the Imāms/one of the two Imāms. However, the chains of transmission are slightly different at the beginning of the lines: Al-Kulaynī transmits the *ḥadīth* from Muḥammad b. Yaḥyā [al-ʿAṭṭār al-Qummī], from Aḥmad b. Muḥammad [b. ʿIsā al-Ashʿarī al-Qummī], from Ḥasan b. ʿAlī b. Faḍḍāl, from ʿAbdallāh b. Bukayr, from a group of the companions, from one of the two Imāms (al-Kulaynī, *al-Kāfī*, 7: 157). Al-Ṭūsī, however, one time narrates the *ḥadīth* from ʿAlī b. al-Ḥasan b. ʿAlī b. Faḍḍāl, from [his brothers] Muḥammad and Aḥmad, from their father Ḥasan b. ʿAlī b. Faḍḍāl, from ʿAbdallāh b. Bukayr, from some of the companions, from the Imāms (Muḥammad Ḥasan al-Ṭūsī, *al-Istibṣār fī-mā ukhtulifa min al-akhbār*, ed. Ḥasan al-Khirsān, 4 vols. (Tehran: Dār al-Kutub al-Islāmiyya, 1363sh], 4: 187); and another time from Aḥmad b. Muḥammad [b. ʿĪsā al-Ashʿarī al-Qummī], from Muḥammad and Aḥmad, the sons of al-Ḥasan, from their father Ḥasan b. ʿAlī b. Faḍḍāl, from ʿAbdallāh b. Bukayr, from some of the companions, from the Imāms (al-Ṭūsī, *Tahdhīb*, 9: 357). In al-Kulaynī's chain, the *ḥadīth* is attributed to "one of the two Imāms", whereas al-Ṭūsī attributes it to "the Imāms". Although ʿAbdallāh b. Bukayr was a companion of the Sixth Imām, he does not transmit this *ḥadīth* directly from him or any other Imām. He narrates the *ḥadīth* from a group of Shiʿi *ḥadīth* transmitters without specifying their names. Hence, this group of transmitters might have been the companions of several Imāms, at least, from the Fourth to the Seventh Imāms, namely, Zayn al-ʿĀbidīn ʿAlī b. al-Ḥusayn, Muḥammad b. ʿAlī al-Bāqir, Jaʿfar b. Muḥammad al-Ṣādiq, Mūsā b. Jaʿfar al-Kāẓim. At first glance, it appears that al-Ṭūsī's attributions to "the Imāms" in a plural form is more accurate. Nevertheless, one might argue that because ʿAbdallāh b. Bukayr was a companion of the Sixth Imām, it is plausible that he narrated either from those who were also the companions of this Imām or from those who were not very far from his generation; that is, the companions of the Fifth Imām, Muḥammad b. ʿAlī al-Bāqir. However, it is less plausible that he met the companions of the Fourth and Third Imāms, Zayn al-ʿĀbidīn ʿAlī b. al-Ḥusayn and Ḥusayn b. ʿAlī. It is also not plausible that he heard the *ḥadīth* from later imāms because he was a follower of Faṭaḥī Madhhab, a Shiʿi group that does not recognise the Imāms after the Sixth Imām. Thus, al-Kulaynī's statement may be more precise, and the *ḥadīth* should be attributed to either the Fifth or Sixth Imām. However, as noted, all three chains are broken (*mursal*), that is, the chains of the *ḥadīth* are missing one or more narrators before the *ḥadīth* can be attributed to an Imām. This may be why Imāmī jurists have barely addressed this marker as a method to assess the sex of a *mamsūḥ*. Instead, they often hold that "drawing lots" (*qurʿa*) is a way to determine the inheritance of such a person, basing their position on those *ḥadīth*s that refer to drawing lots as a marker to determine the inheritance share of *mamsūḥ*s. Although al-Ṭūsī finds it more cautious to adopt a position that prefers the *ḥadīth*s addressing the use of drawing lots to determine the inheritance of *mamsūḥ*, he argues that there is also no contradiction between these *ḥadīth*s and the above-mentioned one. He explains that drawing lots, as suggested

by these *ḥadīths*, can be applied when there are no other markers to determine a *mamsūḥ*'s sex (al-Ṭūsī, *al-Istibṣār*, 4: 187).

47 Such *ḥadīths* can be found in al-Ṣadūq, *al-Faqīh*, 4: 326–8, Ḥ: 5701, 5702, 5704; al-Ṭūsī, *Tahdhīb*, 9: 353–5, Ḥ: 1267, 1268, 1269, 1270, 1271; al-Qāḍī al-Nu'mān, *Da'ā'im al-islām*, 2: 387–9, Ḥ: 1377, 1378, 1379, 1380. Al-Kulaynī collected only those *ḥadīths* that address urination as a marker and not those referring to the number of ribs (see al-Kulaynī, *al-Kāfī*, 7: 156–7, Ḥ: 1 to 5). He recorded the following *ḥadīth*: when urine exits from both orifices simultaneously, one should assess a *khunthā*'s condition based on the orifice from which the urine runs out with abundant quantity, and if urine exits from both abundantly, then the *ḥadīth* suggests the one from which urine exits farther (*fa-min ab'adihimā*) (al-Kulaynī, *al-Kāfī*, 7: 157, Ḥ: 5). According to the jurists, "*ab'ad*" signifies either "farther in time" or "farther in place". The former implies that one should consider the orifice from which urine ends or lasts longer; the latter implies the orifice from which the urine exits with more pressure and, thus, goes a greater distance (*al-Kāfī*, 7: 157). This *ḥadīth* is not found in other early Shi'i compilations or in *Da'ā'im al-islām* of al-Qāḍī al-Nu'mān.

48 Several jurists added the following sub-criterion to the aforementioned list: if a *khunthā*'s urination starts and ends from both orifices simultaneously, then one should examine the orifice from which a larger quantity of urine exits. When a *khunthā*'s urination starts and ends from both simultaneously and with the same quantity, this case becomes a matter of dispute. For this position, see, for example, Muḥammad b. Muḥammad b. Nu'mān al-'Ukbarī (al-Mufīd), *al-I'lām bi-mā ittafaqat 'alayhi l-imāmiyya min al-aḥkām*, ed. Muḥammad al-Ḥassūn, (Qum: al-Mu'tamar al-'Ālamī li-Alfiyyat al-Shaykh al-Mufīd, 1413), 62; Abū l-Qāsim 'Alī b. al-Ḥusayn al-Sharīf al-Murtaḍā, *Rasā'il* (Qum: Dār al-Qur'ān al-Karīm, 1405), 263; idem, *al-Intiṣār fī infirādāt al-imāmiyya* (Qum: Mu'assasat al-Nashr al-Islāmī, 1415), 594. There is no Shi'i *ḥadīth* that explicitly addresses the quantity of urine as a sub-marker, except for a *ḥadīth* collected by al-Kulaynī (*al-Kāfī*, 7: 157, Ḥ: 5), discussed in the previous footnote: this *ḥadīth* states that when urine exits from both orifices simultaneously, one should determine a *khunthā*'s condition based on the orifice from which the urine runs out with abundant quantity, and if urine exits from both abundantly, then the one from which urine exits farther (*fa-min ab'adihimā*). The orifice from which urine exits farther, whether in time or place, implies that there would be more quantity of urine from that orifice. Concerning this sub-criterion, there is also a dispute among classical Sunni legal experts about whether the quantity of urine should be considered as a valid marker. For example, al-Qudūrī (d. 428/1036–7) indicates that reliance on the quantity of urine emerging from each orifice is not a valid method of assessment according to Abū Ḥanīfa (d. 150/767, although his most prominent pupils, al-Qāḍī Abū Yūsuf (d. 182/798–9) and Muḥammad b. al-Ḥasan al-Shaybānī (d. 189/804–5), hold that the quantity of urine is a reliable sub-marker (al-Qudūrī, *Mukhtaṣar*, 137).

49 See, for example, Ḥamaz b. 'Abd al-'Azīz *Sallār* (Sālār*) al-Daylamī (*d. 463/1071*), al-Marāsim al-'alawiyya fī l-fiqh wa-aḥkām al-nabawiyya*, ed. Muḥsin al-Ḥusaynī al-Amīnī (Qum: al-Majma' al-'Ālamī li-Ahl al-Bayt, 1414), 239–40; al-Mufīd, *al-Muqni'a*, 752–3. Al-Mufīd, in *al-Muqni'a*, refers only to the case of the *khunthā mushkil* and the *mamsūḥ*, simply because, in his view, the case of *khunthā ghayr al-mushkil* is either a male or a female, with no ambiguity requiring separate treatment.

50 al-Ṣadūq, *al-Muqni'*, 512. Note that the amount of full compensation (*diya*) has been calculated in different forms, with 10,000 *dirhams* (silver coins) being only one example. Other forms include 1,000 *dīnār* (golden coins), 100 camels, 200 cows, 1,000 sheep, and 200 *ḥullas* (a type of clothing consisting of two pieces made from Yemeni woven fabric, *burd Yamānī*).

51 Al-Ḥillī ('Allāma), *Mukhtalaf al-Shī'a*, 9: 435.

52 It is worth noting that, according to al-Ṣadūq, the full *diya* applies in cases where the penis of a child or an impotent man (*'innīn*) is amputated (al-Ṣadūq, *al-Muqni'*, 522).

53 *Ḥukūma* is a process through which the portion of the *diya* to be paid to the victim is determined. In classical Islamic law, this estimation is made by assessing the victim as though they were a slave, considering the attributes they possess at the time of the injury. The victim is then re-evaluated once the wound has healed, alongside the injury itself. Any deficiency resulting from this comparison must be compensated proportionally from the *diya*, as the full *diya* guarantees the entire person, and thus parts of the person are guaranteed by parts of the *diya*. For instance, if the victim's value before the injury was 100 camels (used as the standard payment), the question is raised: What is their value after the injury? If it is assessed as 90 camels, then the difference is one-tenth. Consequently, one-tenth of the *diya* of the soul is obligatory, which equates to one-tenth of the number of camels. If the value is not precisely determined, it is stipulated that the injury must not amount to the full value of the *diya*. The process is referred to as *ḥukūma* because it is determined solely by the evaluation and decision of the judge, with no legal effect if any other individual attempts to exercise independent judgment in this matter (Muṣṭafā al-Khann, Muṣṭafā al-Bughā, ʿAlī al-Sharbjī, *al-Fiqh al-manhajī ʿalā madhhab al-imām al-Shafiʿī*, 8 vols [Damascus: Dār al-Qalam li-l-Ṭibāʿa wa-l-Nashar wa-l-Tawzīʿ], 8: 4).

54 Al-Ḥillī (ʿAllāma), *Mukhtalaf al-Shīʿa*, 9: 435.

55 See, for example, Bahāʾ al-Dīn Muḥammad b. Ḥasan al-Fāḍil al-Hindī, *Kashf al-lithām wa-l-ibhām ʿan Qawaʿid al-ahkām*, 11 vols. (Qum: Muʾassasat al-Nashr al-Islāmī, 1416), 11: 395; al-Najafī, *Jawāhir al-kalām*, 43: 269–70.

56 See, for example, al-Ṭūsī, *al-Mabsūṭ*, 7: 51–2; Muḥammad b. ʿAlī Ibn Ḥamza al-Ṭūsī (d. after 566/1171), *al-Wasīla ilā nayl al-faḍīla*, ed. Muḥammad al-Ḥssūn (Qum: Manshūrāt Maktabat Āyatallāh al-Marʿashī al-Najafī, 1408), 452. Najm al-Dīn Jaʿfar b. Ḥasan al-Ḥillī (Muḥaqqiq), *Sharāʾiʿ al-islām fī masāʾil al-ḥalāl wa-l-ḥarām*, 4 vols. (Qum: Nashr-i Istiqlāl, 1409/1367sh), 4: 222. al-Ḥillī (ʿAllāma), *Irshād al-adhhān ilā aḥkām al-īmān*, 2 vols. (Qum: Muʾassasat al-Nashr al-Islāmī, 1410), 2: 208. These texts do not often address offences involving injury or amputation of non-genital body parts of *khunthās* as distinct cases, which most likely implies that such individuals are entitled to the same rights as other individuals with regard to retaliation or financial compensation for harm to body parts other than their sexual organs.

57 This case has been explicitly addressed only by Ibn Ḥamza (*al-Wasīla*, 452).

58 Al-Ṭūsī, al-Mabsūṭ, 7: 51–2; al-Ḥillī (Muḥaqqiq), *Sharāʾiʿ al-islām*, 4: 222; al-Ḥillī (ʿAllāma), *Irshād al-adhhān*, 2: 208–9.

59 Al-Ḥillī (ʿAllāma), *Irshād al-adhhān*, 2: 209. Al-ʿAllāma al-Ḥillī's formulation is brief and ambiguous. To clarify his position on this point, one must refer to his commentators, particularly to al-Ardabīlī (d. 993/1585) in the following source: Aḥmad al-Muqaddas al-Ardabīlī, *Majmaʿ al-fāʾida wa-l-burhān fī sharḥ Irshād al-adhhān*. ed. Mujtabā al-ʿIrāqī, ʿAlīpanāh al-Ishtihārdī, and Ḥusayn al-Yazdī, 14 vols. (Qum, Iran: Muʾassasat al-Nashr al-Islāmī, 1422), 14:108–9.

60 Al-Mufīd, *al-Muqniʿa*, 752–3. It should be noted that in the case of unintentional homicide only *diya* applies according to Islamic law.

61 The calculation of the value of *dirham* and *dinār* coins is fascinating but highly disputed and complicated. To read on this topic in a primary source, see Sayyid Mūsā al-Ḥusaynī al-Māzandarānī, *al-ʿIqd al-munīr fī taḥqīq mā yataʿllaq bi-l-darāhim wa-l-danānīr* (Tehran: Maktabat al-Ṣadūq, 1382sh). For secondary sources, see Ahamed Kameel Mydin Meera, "Islamic Gold Dinar: The Historical Standard," *International Journal of Islamic Economics and Finance (IJIEF)* 1, no. 1 (2018): 109–22; Adam Abdullah, "The Islamic Monetary Standard: The Dinar and Dirham," *International Journal of Islamic Economics and Finance Studies* 6, no. 1 (2020): 1–29; Zarra M. Nezhad, "A Brief History of Money in Islam and Estimating the Value of Dirham and Dinar," *Review of Islamic Economics* 8, no. 2 (2004): 51–65. For more comprehensive information on coinage, see Stuart D. Sears, "An ʿAbbasid

Revolution Hoard from the Western Jazira (AL-RAQQA?)," *American Journal of Numismatics* (1989-) 12 (2000): 171–93; Tim Wilkes, "Islamic Coins and Their Values" *Volume 1: The Mediaeval Period* (London: Spink and Son, Ltd, 2015).

62 Although the discrepancy in compensation—from 5,000 to 12,500 dirhams—when a *khunthā mushkil* is added to the pair of perpetrators is not explicitly addressed in al-Mufīd's *al-Muqniʿa*, the (Shiʿi) Islamic legal principles governing *qiṣāṣ* and *diya* offer the necessary interpretive framework for understanding such a calculation. In the first instance, where a man and a woman jointly and intentionally kill a free man, the combined *diya* is 15,000 dirhams—10,000 for the male perpetrator and 5,000 for the female. As the victim is male, and thus entitled to a *diya* of 10,000 dirhams, the surplus of 5,000 dirhams must be paid to the heirs of the two perpetrators—but not in equal shares, as explained in the text. In the second instance, where a *khunthā mushkil*—a person whose sex remains difficult to determine—is added to the pair of perpetrators, and the *khunthā*'s *diya* is calculated as the mean between male and female rates (i.e., 7,500 dirhams), the total *diya* owed by the three perpetrators amounts to 22,500 dirhams. The resulting surplus, relative to the male victim's *diya* of 10,000 dirhams, is therefore 12,500 dirhams. This amount must be distributed among the heirs of all three perpetrators, though not in equal shares, as outlined in the text.

63 Al-Mufīd, *al-Muqniʿa*, 753. Also, see *Sallār al-Daylamī, al-Marāsim*, 239–40; Taqī l-Dīn b. Najm al-Dīn Abū l-Ṣalāḥ al-Ḥalabī (d.447/1055), *al-Kāfī fī l-fiqh*, ed. Riḍā Ustādī (Iṣfahān: Maktabat Imām Amīr al-Muʾminīn, 1403), 386.

64 See, for example, al-Ṭūsī, *al-Mabsūṭ*, 7: 53-54; al-Ḥillī (ʿAllāma), *Mukhtalaf al-shīʿa*, 9: 288.

65 Al-Ṭūsī, *al-Mabsūṭ*, 7: 52. Also, see al-Mufīd, *al-Muqniʿa*, 735; *Sallār al-Daylamī, al-Marāsim*, 237; Abū l-Ṣalāḥ al-Ḥalabī, *al-Kāfī fī l-fiqh*, 383; Ibn Ḥamza, *al-Wasīla*, 432; Muḥammad b. Aḥmad b. Idrīs al-Ḥillī, *al-Sarāʾir al-ḥāwī li-taḥrīr al-fatāwī*, 3 vols. (Qum: Muʾassasat al-Nashr al-Islāmī, 1410/1386sh), 3: 326; al-Ḥillī (Muḥaqqiq), *Sharāʾiʿ al-islām*, 4: 228; al-Ḥillī (ʿAllāma), *Mukhtalaf al-shīʿa*, 9: 286. As al-ʿAllāma al-Ḥillī observes, in contrast to the majority of classical Shiʿi jurists who stipulate that compensation in cases of pardon is contingent upon the perpetrator's consent, Ibn al-Junayd maintains that in cases of intentional homicide, the victim's legal heir has the right to choose between seeking retaliation, accepting financial compensation, or granting a pardon. If the heir opts for compensation but the perpetrator refuses and instead offers himself for retaliation, the decision nevertheless remains with the heir. Should the perpetrator flee and the heir subsequently decide to claim compensation from the perpetrator's estate, the court ought to uphold this claim. The same principle applies in cases of intentional bodily harm. Moreover, if the heir or the injured party waives the right to retaliation, this does not entail the forfeiture of the right to claim compensation. Al-ʿAllāma al-Ḥillī further notes that Ibn Abī ʿAqīl holds a comparable position, asserting that if the victim's legal heirs pardon the perpetrator from retaliation, the perpetrator is not to be executed but remains liable to pay compensation. For classical Sunni discussion on this matter, see al-Māwardī, *al-Ḥāwī*, 12: 96–7; Muḥammad b. Aḥmad b. Rushd (d. 595/1126), *Bidāyat al-mujtahid wa-nihāyat al-muqtaṣid*, 4 vols. (Cairo: Dār al-Ḥadīth), 4: 184.

66 Al-Mufīd, *al-Muqniʿa*, 753. We should note that al-Mufīd explicitly states that the compensation of a *mamsūḥ* is half that of a man and half that of a woman. However, as previously explained, he had just prior to this statement affirmed that both retaliation and compensation for a *mamsūḥ* are the same as those for a *khunthā mushkil*. This implies that if the victim is a *mamsūḥ* and compensation is sought, the amount would be half that of a male and half that of a female—and thus, the same would apply to a *khunthā mushkil*. Moreover, in the earlier case where a *khunthā mushkil*, along with others, was complicit in a homicide, al-Mufīd implicitly referred to the compensation of the *khunthā mushkil*, which likewise suggests the same amount: half of a male's and half of a female's compensation. Also, see Abū l-Ṣalāḥ al-Ḥalabī, *al-Kāfī fī l-fiqh*, 386; al-Ḥillī (ʿAllāma), *Taḥrīr al-aḥkām*

al-sharʿiyya ʿalā madhhab al-imāmiyya, ed. Ibrāhīm al-Bahādurī, 5 vols. (Qum: Muʾassat al-Imām al-Ṣādiq, 1420), 5: 623. As the editor of the latter source notes, one manuscript of this work records only this view as being attributed to al-ʿAllāma al-Ḥillī. Other manuscripts of the same work, however, include an additional—albeit non-assertive—position attributed to him, according to which the amount of compensation in this case could be considered equivalent to that given to a woman, since this is the amount upon which there is certainty.

67 See, for example, Abū l-Ṣalāḥ al-Ḥalabī, *al-Kāfī fī l-fiqh*, 386; al-Ḥillī (ʿAllāma), *Taḥrīr al-aḥkām*, 5: 623.

68 Al-Ṭūsī, *al-Nihāya fī mujarrad al-fiqh wa-l-fatāwā* (Beirut: Dār al-Kitāb al-ʿArabī, 1400), 327.

69 Abū l-Ṣalāḥ al-Ḥalabī, *al-Kāfī fī l-fiqh*, 436. It is worth noting that the published edition of *al-Kāfī* does not address the testimony of a deaf person (*aṣamm*) in this context. However, in al-ʿAllāma al-Ḥillī's transmission of Abū l-Ṣalāḥ al-Ḥalabī's view here, a deaf person is explicitly included among those whose testimony is considered permissible.

70 The translations of the qurʾānic verses in this chapter are by Nasr et al., *The Study Quran: A New Translation and Commentary* (San Francisco: HarperOne, 2015).

71 Al-Ḥillī (ʿAllāma), *Mukhtalf al-Shīʿa*, 8: 507.

72 Al-Ṭūsī, *al-Mabsūṭ*, 6: 153. Ibn al-Barrāj suggests the same position on this case (*al-Muhadhdhab*, 2: 395).

73 Al-Ṭūsī, *al-Mabsūṭ*, 6: 153.

74 Ibn al-Barrāj, *al-Muhadhdhab*, 2: 395

75 Al-Ḥillī (ʿAllāma), *Mukhtalf al-Shīʿa*, 8: 138.

76 Al-Ṭūsī, *al-Mabsūṭ*, 1: 153; al-Ḥillī (Muḥaqqiq), *al-Mukhtaṣar al-nāfiʿ fī fiqh al-imāmiyya* (Beirut: Dār al-Aḍwāʾ, 1985), 47. Al-Muḥaqqiq al-Ḥillī, in the latter source, in fact states that a woman may not lead prayers for males or for a *khunthā mushkil*, which implicitly suggests that a *khunthā mushkil* may lead prayers for women.

77 Ibn Ḥamza, *al-Wasīla*, 105.

78 Al-Ḥillī (ʿAllāma), *Mukhtalf al-Shīʿa*, 3: 63.

79 Al-Ṭūsī, *al-Mabsūṭ*, 1: 155. Al-Muḥaqqiq al-Ḥillī further explains that if one adopts the view that it is prohibited for those led in prayer to stand side by side with the *imām*, or for a woman and a *khunthā mushkil* to stand adjacent to one another, then it becomes obligatory for the *khunthā* to stand behind the *imām*, and for the woman to stand behind the *khunthā*. Otherwise, this arrangement is merely recommended and not legally binding (al-Ḥillī [Muḥaqqiq], *Sharāʾiʿ al-islām*, 1: 115–6).

80 Al-Ṭūsī, *al-Mabsūṭ*, 1: 155; Ibn Ḥamza, *al-Wasīla*, 108.

81 Ibn Ḥamza, *al-Wasīla*, 108.

82 Ibn Idrīs al-Ḥillī, *al-Sarāʾir*, 1: 282; al-Ḥillī (ʿAllāma), *Mukhtalf al-Shīʿa*, 3: 82.

83 *Sallār al-Daylamī, al-Marāsim, 79.*

84 Al-Ṭūsī, *al-Mabsūṭ*, 1: 155.

85 Ibn al-Barrāj, *al-Muhadhdhab*, 1: 130.

86 Ibn Idrīs al-Ḥillī, *al-Sarāʾir*, 1: 358–9.

87 Al-Ṭūsī, *al-Khilāf fī l-aḥkām*, 6 vols. (Qum: Muʾassat al-Nashr al-Islāmī, 1407), 4: 348. Al-ʿAllāma al-Ḥillī objects to al-Ṭūsī's claim that there is no evidence to support annulment in such cases, citing three *ḥadīth*s that classify impotence as a defect warranting annulment. Interestingly, however, all three reports refer specifically to the category of the eunuch (*khāṣī*), rather than the *khunthā* (al-Ḥillī [ʿAllāma], *Mukhtalaf al-shīʿa*, 7: 210). For al-Shāfiʿī's view, see al-Nawawī, *al-Majmūʿ*, 16: 286.

88 Al-Ṭūsī, *al-Mabsūṭ*, 4: 250–1, also 263 (in this latter page, al-Ṭūsī explains the procedure for establishing impotence—whether in a man or a *khunthā* legally identified as male—follows the legal framework involving confession, evidence, or oath-taking). Also, see Ibn al-Barrāj, al-*Muhadhdhab*,

2: 233; al-Ḥillī (ʿAllāma), *Mukhtalaf al-shīʿa*, 7: 219; idem, *Qawāʿid al-aḥkām*, 3: 66; al-Ḥillī (Fakhr al-Muḥaqqiqin), *Iḍāḥ al-fawāʾid*, 3: 176.

89 Al-Ṭūsī, *al-Mabsūṭ*, 4: 266.

90 Al-Ḥillī (ʿAllāma), *Mukhtalaf al-shīʿa*, 7: 219.

91 Ibid., *Qawāʿid al-aḥkām*, 3: 66.

92 See Alipour, "Navigating Body Politics," 312–4.

93 Al-Ṭūsī, *al-Mabsūṭ*, 4: 117. The only tradition that al-Ṭūsī includes in his *ḥadīth* compilation *Tahdhīb al-aḥkām* concerning the case of the *khunthā*'s marriage is the report attributed to Shurayḥ and ʿAlī (*Tahdhīb al-aḥkām*, 9: 354–5, Ḥ. 1271). Those who have commented on al-Ṭūsī's position have likewise identified this report as the tradition to which he is referring (see, for example, Fakhr al-Muḥaqqiqīn al-Ḥillī, *Iḍāḥ al-fawāʾid*, 4: 266; Zayn al-Dīn b. ʿAlī al-Jubaʿī al-ʿĀmilī, *Masālik al-afhām ilā tanqīḥ Sharāʾiʿ al-islām*, 15 vols. [Qum: Intishārāt-i Bunyād-i Maʿārif-i Islāmī, 1425], 13: 256; al-Ardabīlī, *Majmaʿ al-fāʾida*, 11: 587).

94 It is important to note that the version of the *ḥadīth* in which the *khunthā* is said to have both conceived and been conceived is based on a narration recorded by al-Ṣadūq (al-Faqīh, 4: 327–8, Ḥ. 5704). In contrast, the account of the *ḥadīth* collected by al-Ṭūsī records only that the *khunthā* had conceived someone.

95 Al-Ḥillī (ʿAllāma), *Qawāʿid al-aḥkām*, 3: 392.

96 Al-Ḥillī (Fakhr al-Muḥaqqiqin), *Iḍāḥ al-fawāʾid*, 4: 266.

97 Al-Jubaʿī al-ʿĀmilī, *Masālik al-afhām*, 13: 255.

98 Several classical scholars addressed this point in the same manner (see, for example, al-Ḥillī (Fakhr al-Muḥaqqiqin), *Iḍāḥ al-fawāʾid*, 4: 265; al-Jubaʿī al-ʿĀmilī, *Masālik al-afhām*, 13: 256).

99 Al-Ḥillī (Muḥaqqiq), *Sharāʾiʿ al-islām*, 4: 41. Also, see al-Ḥillī (ʿAllāma), *Qawāʿid al-aḥkām*, 3: 392; idem, *Irshād al-adhhān*, 2: 133; idem, *Taḥrīr al-aḥkām*, 5: 81.

100 See, for example, al-Ḥillī (ʿAllāma), *Taḥrīr al-aḥkām*, 5: 81; idem, *Irshād al-adhhān*, 2: 133.

101 Al-Ḥillī (ʿAllāma), *Qawāʿid al-aḥkām*, 3: 392. Also, see al-Ḥillī (Fakhr al-Muḥaqqiqin), *Iḍāḥ al-fawāʾid*, 4: 267.

102 Al-Jubaʿī al-ʿĀmilī, *Masālik al-afhām*, 13: 256. Also, see al-Ardabīlī, *Majmaʿ al-fāʾida*, 11: 587–8.

103 Makkī al-ʿĀmilī, al-Durūs, 2: 380.

104 For Sunni account of this matter, see Alipour, "Navigating Body Politics," 285–7, n64.

105 See al-Ḥillī (Muḥaqqiq), *Sharāʾiʿ al-islām*, 4: 38–41; idem, *al-Mukhtaṣar al-nāfiʿ*, 266–7; al-Ḥillī (ʿAllāma), *Qawāʿid al-aḥkām*, 3: 382–92; idem, *Tabṣirat al-mutaʿallimīnfī aḥkām al-dīn* (Tehran: Intishārāt-i Faqīh, 1368sh), 232–4; idem, *Irshād al-adhhān*, 2: 132–3; idem, *Taḥrīr al-aḥkām al-sharʿiyya*, 5: 73–81; al-Ḥillī (Fakhr al-Muḥaqqiqīn), *Iḍāḥ al-fawāʾid*, 4: 249–54.

106 Al-Ḥillī (ʿAllāma), *Mukhtalaf al-shīʿa*, 9: 100–1.

107 Makkī al-ʿĀmilī, *al-Durūs*, 2: 379.

108 See Jamāl al-Dīn Aḥmad b. Fahd al-Ḥillī, *al-Muhadhdhab al-Bāriʿ fī sharḥ al-Mukhtaṣar al-nāfiʿ*, 5 vols. (Qum: Muʾassasat al-Nashr al-Islāmī, 1407), 4: 423–4.

109 See Jamāl al-Dīn Miqdād b. ʿAbd Allāh al-Suyūrī al-Ḥillī (al-Fāḍil al-Miqdād), *al-Tanqīḥ al-rāʾiʿ li-Mukhtaṣar al-sharāʾiʿ*, 4 vols. (Qum: Maktabat Āyatallāh al-Marʿashī al-Najafī, 1404), 4: 212; al-Jubaʿī al-ʿĀmilī, *al-Rawḍa al-bahiyya*, 2: 332; al-Narāqī, *Mustanad al-shīʿa*, 2: 279–80, 6: 106, 19: 228; al-Marāghī, al-*ʿAnāwīn al-fiqhiyya*, 1: 38.

110 Alipour, "Navigating Body Politics," 299–314.

Bibliography

Abdullah, Adam. "The Islamic Monetary Standard: The Dinar and Dirham." *International Journal of Islamic Economics and Finance Studies* 6, no. 1 (2020): 1–29.

Abū l-Ṣalāḥ al-Ḥalabī, Taqī l-Dīn b. Najm al-Dīn. *al-Kāfī fī l-fiqh*. edited by Riḍā Ustādī. Iṣfahān: Maktabat Imām Amīr al-Muʾminīn, 1403.

Accord Alliance, www.accordalliance.org.

ʿAlī b. Jaʿfar. *Masāʾil ʿAlī ibn Jaʿfar*. Qum: Muʾassasat Āl al-Bayt li-Iḥyāʾ al-Turāth, 1409/1368sh.

Alipour, Mehrdad. "Navigating Body Politics in Shiʿi Legal Tradition: Examining Sayyid Kāẓim al-Yazdī's Account of Non-Binary Intersex." *Islamic Law and Society* 32, no. 3 (2025): 262–315.

Alipour, Mehrdad. "The Nexus between Gender-Confirming Surgery and Illness: Legal-Hermeneutical Examinations of Four Islamic Fatwas." *Journal of Middle East Women's Studies* 18, no. 3 (2022): 359–86.

Alipour, Mehrdad. "Transgender Identity, the Sex-Reassignment Surgery Fatwās and Islamic Theology of a Third Gender." *Religion and Gender* 7, no. 2 (2017): 164–79.

Alipour, Mehrdad. *Negotiating Homosexuality in Islam: A Legal-Hermeneutical Examination of Modern Shiʿi Discourse*. Leiden: Brill, 2024.

Anderson, Glaire D. "16 Concubines, Eunuchs, and Patronage in Early Islamic Córdoba." in *Reassessing the Roles of Women as 'Makers' of Medieval Art and Architecture*. edited by Therese Martin. Leiden: Brill, 2012: 650–64.

Al-Anṣārī, Murtaḍā b. Muḥammad Amīn. *Kitāb al-ṭahāra*. 5 vols. Qum: Majmaʿ al-Fikr al-Islāmī, 1415.

Ayalon, David. *Eunuchs, Caliphs and Sultans: A Study of Power Relationships*. Jerusalem: Magnes Press, Hebrew University, 1999.

Ayalon, David. *Outsiders in the Lands of Islam: Mamluks, Mongols and Eunuchs*. London: Variorum Reprints, 1988.

Al-ʿAynī, Maḥmūd b. Aḥmad Badr al-Dīn. *al-Bināya sharḥ al-Hidāya*. edited by Ayman Ṣāliḥ Shaʿbān. 13 vols. Beirut: Dār al-Kutub al-ʿIlmiyya, 1420/2000.

Al-Azharī, Muḥammad b. Aḥmad. *Tahdhīb al-lugha*. 15 vols. Beirut: Dār Iḥyāʾ al-Turāth al-ʿArabī, 2001.

Al-Baḥrānī, Yusūf. *al-Ḥadāʾiq al-nāḍira fī aḥkām al-ʿitra al-ṭāhira*. 25 vols. Qum: Muʾassasat al-Nashr al-Islāmī, 1409.

Al-Barqī, Aḥmad b. Muḥammad Khālid. *al-Maḥāsin*. edited by Jalāl al-Dīn Muhaddith. 2 vols. Qum: Dār al-Kutub al-Islāmiyya, 1371.

Al-Fāḍil al-Hindī, Bahāʾ al-Dīn Muḥammad b. Ḥasan. *Kashf al-lithām wa-l-ibhām ʿan Qawaʿid al-ahkām*. 11 vols. Qum: Muʾassasat al-Nashr al-Islāmī, 1416.

Al-Farāhīdī, Abū ʿAbd al-Raḥmān al-Khalīl b. Aḥmad al-Farāhīdī. *Kitāb al-ʿayn*. edited by Mahdī al-Makhzūmī and Ibrāhīm al-Sāmarrāʾī. 8 vols. Baghdad: Dār al-Rashād, 1980.

Al-Fayyūmī, Aḥmad b. Muḥammad b. ʿAlī. *al-Miṣbāḥ al-munīr fī gharīb al-sharḥ al-kabīr*. 2 vols. Beirut: al-Maktaba al-ʿIlmiyya, 1994.

Geissinger, Ash. "Applying Gender and Queer Theory to Pre-modern Sources." in *The Routledge Handbook of Islam and Gender*. edited by Justine Howe. London: Routledge, 2021: 101–15.

Ghattas, Dan Christian. "Protecting Intersex People in Europe: A Toolkit for Law and Policy Makers." *OII Europe*, (2023[2019]), 9, Accessed March 2024: https://www.oiieurope.org/wp-content/uploads/2019/05/Protecting_intersex_in_Europe_toolkit.pdf.

Al-Ghazalī, Abū Ḥāmid Muḥammad. *al-Wasīṭ fī l-madhhab*. edited by Aḥmad Maḥmūd Ibrāhīm and Muḥammad Muḥammad Tāmir. 7 vols. Cairo: Dār al-Salām, 1417.

Al-Ḥillī (Fakhr al-Muḥaqqiqīn), Muḥammad b. Ḥasan b. Yūsuf. *Iḍāḥ al-fawā'id fī sharḥ mushkilāt al-Qawā'id*. 4 vols. Qum: Mu'assasa-yi Ismā'īliyān, 1387.

Al-Ḥillī (Muḥaqqiq), Najm al-Dīn Ja'far b. Ḥasan. *al-Mukhtaṣar al-nāfi' fī fiqh al-imāmiyya*. Beirut: Dār al-Aḍwā', 1985.

Al-Ḥillī (Muḥaqqiq), Najm al-Dīn Ja'far b. Ḥasan. *Sharā'i' al-islām fī masā'il al-ḥalāl wa-l-ḥarām*. 4 vols. Qum: Nashr-i Istiqlāl, 1409/1367sh.

Al-Ḥillī ('Allāma), Ḥasan b. Yūsuf. *Irshād al-adhhān ilā aḥkām al-īmān*. 2 vols. Qum: Mu'assasat al-Nashr al-Islāmī, 1410.

Al-Ḥillī ('Allāma), Ḥasan b. Yūsuf. *Qawā'id al-aḥkām*. 3 vols. Qum: Mu'assasat al-Nashr al-Islāmī, 1419.

Al-Ḥillī ('Allāma), Ḥasan b. Yūsuf. *Tabṣirat al-muta'allimīn fī aḥkām al-dīn*. Tehran: Intishārāt-i Faqīh, 1368sh.

Al-Ḥillī ('Allāma), Ḥasan b. Yūsuf. *Taḥrīr al-aḥkām al-shar'iyya 'alā madhhab al-imāmiyya*. edited by Ibrāhīm al-Bahādurī. 5 vols. Qum: Mu'assat al-Imām al-Ṣādiq, 1420.

Al-Ḥillī ('Allāma), Ḥasan b. Yūsuf. *Mukhtalaf al-shī'a fī aḥkām al-sharī'a*. 9 vols. Qum: Mu'assasat al-Nashr al-Islāmī, 1374sh.

Al-Ḥimyarī al-Qummī, 'Abd Allāh b. Ja'far b. Ḥusayn. *Qurb al-isnād*. Qum: Mu'assasat Āl al-Bayt li-Iḥyā' al-Turāth, 1413.

Al-Ḥusaynī al-Māzandarānī, Sayyid Mūsā. *al-'Iqd al-munīr fī taḥqīq mā yata'llaq bi-l-darāhim wa-l-danānīr*. Tehran: Maktabat al-Ṣadūq, 1382sh.

Al-Ḥusaynī al-'Āmilī, Muḥammad Jawād. *Miftāḥ al-karāma fī sharḥ Qawā'id al-'Allāma*. 11 vols. Beirut: Dār Iḥyā' al-Turāth al-'Arabī, n.d.

Ibn al-Barrāj, 'Abd al-'Azīz. *al-Muhadhdhab*. 2 vols. Qum: Mu'assasat al-Nashr al-Islāmī, 1406.

Ibn Fahd al-Ḥillī, Jamāl al-Dīn Aḥmad. *al-Muhadhdhab al-Bāri' fī sharḥ al-Mukhtaṣar al-nāfi'*. 5 vols. Qum: Mu'assasat al-Nashr al-Islāmī, 1407.

Ibn Ḥamza, Muḥammad b. 'Alī. *al-Wasīla ilā nayl al-faḍīla*. edited by Muḥammad al-Ḥssūn. Qum: Manshūrāt Maktabat Āyatallāh al-Mar'ashī al-Najafī, 1408.

Ibn Idrīs al-Ḥillī, Muḥammad b. Aḥmad. *al-Sarā'ir al-ḥāwī li-taḥrīr al-fatāwī*. 3 vols. Qum: Mu'assasat al-Nashr al-Islāmī, 1410/1386sh.

Ibn Manẓūr, Muḥammad b. Mukarram. *Lisān al-'arab*. 15 vols. Beirut: Dār Ṣādir li-l-Ṭibā'a wa-l-Nashr, 1414.

Ibn Qudāma al-Maqdisī, Muwaffaq al-Dīn Abū Muḥammad. *al-Mughnī*. 10 vols. Cairo: Maktabat al-Qāhira, 1388/1968.

Ibn Rushd, Muḥammad b. Aḥmad. *Bidāyat al-mujtahid wa-nihāyat al-muqtaṣid*. 4 vols. Cairo: Dār al-Ḥadīth.

Ibn Shahr-āshūb al-Māzandarānī, Muḥammad b. 'Alī. *Manāqib āl Abī Ṭālib*. 3 vols. Najaf: al-Maktaba al-Ḥaydariyya, 1376.

Ibn Sīnā, *al-Qānūn fī l-ṭibb*. 4 vols. Beirut: Dār Iḥyā' al-Turāth al-'Arabī, 2005.

InterACT: Advocates for Intersex Youth. "What Is Intersex?" Accessed March 2024 https://interactadvocates.org.

Intersex Society of North America. "What Is Intersex?" Accessed March 2024: https://isna.org/faq/what_is_intersex/.

Al-Jawharī, Abū Naṣr Ismā'īl. *al-Ṣiḥāḥ tāj al-lugha wa-ṣiḥāḥ al-'arabiyya*. edited by Aḥmad 'Abd al-Ghafūr 'Aṭṭār. 6 vols. Beirut: Dār al-'Ilm li-l-Malāyin, 1407/1986–7.

Al-Juba'ī al-'Āmilī, Zayn al-Dīn b. 'Alī. *al-Rawḍa al-bahiyya fī sharḥ al-Lum'a al-dimashqiyya fī fiqh al-imāmiyya*. 2 vols. Qum: Intishārāt-i Daftar-i Tablīghāt-i Islāmī, 1412/1373sh.

Al-Juba'ī al-'Āmilī, Zayn al-Dīn b. 'Alī. *Masālik al-afhām ilā tanqīḥ Sharā'i' al-islām*. 15 vols. Qum: Intishārāt-i Bunyād-i Ma'ārif-i Islāmī, 1425.

Al-Karakī, ʿAlī b. Ḥusayn ʿAbd al-ʿĀlī. *Jāmiʿ al-maqāṣid fī sharḥ al-Qawāʿid*. 13 vols. Qum: Muʾassasat Āl al-Bayt li-Iḥyāʾ al-Turāth, 1414.

Al-Kāshif al-Ghiṭāʾ, Jaʿfar. *Kashf al-ghiṭāʾʿan mubhamāt al-sharīʿa al-gharrāʾ*. 4 vols. Mashhad: Maktab al-Iʿlām al-Islāmī, 1380sh.

Al-Khann, Muṣṭafā, al-Bughā, Muṣṭafā, al-Sharbjī, ʿAlī. *al-Fiqh al-manhajī ʿalā madhhab al-imām al-Shafiʿī*. 8 vols. Damascus: Dār al-Qalam li-l-Ṭibāʿa wa-l-Nashar wa-l-Tawzīʿ.

Al-Khānsārī, Āqā Ḥusayn. *Takmīl mashāriq al-shumūs fī sharḥ al-Durūs*. Qum: Muʾassasat Āl al-Bayt li Iḥyāʾ al-Turāth, 1311.

Kohlberg, Etan. "Al-Uṣūl al-Arbaʿumi'a." in *Jerusalem Studies in Arabic and Islam: Jahiliyya and Islamic Studies in Honour of M. J. Kister: Septuagenarian (II)*. 10 (1987): 128–66.

Kohlberg, Etan. "Shiʿa Ḥadīth: Introduction." in *The Study of Shiʿi Islam: History, Theology and Law*. edited by Farhad Daftary and Gurdofarid Miskinzoda. London: I.B. Tauris Publishers and Co. Ltd and the Institute of Ismaili Studies, 2014: 165–79.

Al-Kulaynī, Muḥammad b. Yaʿqūb. *al-Kāfī fī ʿilm al-dīn*. edited by ʿAlī Akbar Ghaffārī. 8 vols. Tehran: Dār al-Kutub al-Islāmiyya, 1407/1367sh.

Makkī al-ʿĀmilī, Shams al-Dīn Muḥammad. *al-Durūs al-sharʿiyya fī fiqh al-imāmiyya*. 3 vols. Qum: Muʾassasat al-Nashr al-Islāmī, 1417.

Makkī al-ʿĀmilī, Shams al-Dīn Muḥammad. *al-Lumʿa al-dimashqiyya fī fiqh al-imāmiyya*. Qum: Dār al-Fikr, 1411.

Al-Marāghī, Mīr ʿAbd al-Fattāḥ al-Ḥusaynī. *al-ʿAnāwīn al-fiqhiyya*. 2 vols. Qum: Muʾassasat al-Nashr al-Islāmī, 1417.

Al-Marghīnānī, ʿAlī b. Abī Bakr b. ʿAbd al-Jalīl. *al-Hidāya fī sharḥ Bidāyat al-mubtadī*. edited by Ṭalāl Yūsuf. 4 vols. Beirut: Dār Iḥyāʾ al-Turāth al-ʿArabī, 2010.

Marmon, Shaun. *Eunuchs and Sacred Boundaries in Islamic Society*. Oxford: Oxford University Press, 1995.

Al-Māwardī al-Baṣrī, Abū l-Ḥasan ʿAlī b. Muḥammad. *al-Ḥāwī l-kabīr fī fiqh madhhab al-imām al-Shāfiʿī*. 18 vols. Beirut: Dār al-Kutub al-ʿIlmiyya, 1419/1999.

Meera, Ahamed Kameel Mydin. "Islamic Gold Dinar: The Historical Standard." *International Journal of Islamic Economics and Finance (IJIEF)* 1, no.1 (2018): 109–22.

Monro, Surya et al. "Intersex: Cultural and Social Perspectives." *Culture, Health and Sexuality* 23, no. 4 (2021): 431–40.

Al-Mufīd, Muḥammad b. Muḥammad b. Nuʿmān al-ʿUkbarī. *al-Iʿlām bi-mā ittafaqat ʿalayhi l-imāmiyya min al-aḥkām*. edited by Muḥammad al-Ḥassūn. Qum: al-Muʾtamar al-ʿĀlamī li-Alfiyyat al-Shaykh al-Mufīd, 1413.

Al-Mufīd, Muḥammad b. Muḥammad b. Nuʿmān al-ʿUkbarī. *al-Muqniʿa*. Qum: al-Muʾtamar al-ʿĀlamī li-Alfiyyat al-Shaykh al-Mufīd,1413.

Multiple unknown authors. *al-Mawsūʿa al-Fiqhiyya al-Kuwaytiyya*. 45 vols. Kuwayt: Wazārat al-ʾAwqāf wa-l-Shuʾūn al-Islāmiyya, 1404–1427.

Al-Muqaddas al-Ardabīlī, Aḥmad. *Majmaʿ al-fāʾida wa-l-burhān fī sharḥ Irshād al-adhhān*. edited by Mujtabā al-ʿIrāqī, ʿAlīpanāh al-Ishtihārdī, and Ḥusayn al-Yazdī. 14 vols. Qum, Iran: Muʾassasat al-Nashr al-Islāmī, 1422.

Al-Najafī, Muḥammad Ḥasan. *Jawāhir al-kalām fī sharḥ Sharāʾiʿ al-islām*. edited by ʿAbbās al-Qūchānī. 43 vols. Beirut: Dār Iḥyāʾ al-Turāth al-ʿArabī,1981.

Al-Narāqī, Aḥmad b. Muḥammad. *Mustanad al-shīʿa*. 19 vols. Qum: Muʾassasat Āl al-Bayt li-Iḥyāʾ al-Turāth, 1415.

Al-Narāqī, Aḥmad. *al-Ḥāshiya ʿalā l-Rawḍa al-bahiyya fī sharḥ al-Lumʿa al-dimashqiyya fī fiqh al-imāmiyya*. Qum: Muʾassasat al-Nashr al-Islāmī, 1425.

Nasr et al. *The Study Quran: A New Translation and Commentary*. San Francisco: HarperOne, 2015.

Al-Nawawī, Yaḥyā b. Sharaf. *al-Majmūʿ Sharḥ al-Muhadhdhab*. 20 vols. Beirut: Dār al-Fikr, 1990.

Nezhad, Zarra M. "A Brief History of Money in Islam and Estimating the Value of Dirham and Dinar." *Review of Islamic Economics* 8, no. 2 (2004): 51–65.

OHCHR, *Background Note on Human Rights* (United Nations: Human Rights Office of the High Commissioner, 2019). 2, Accessed March 2024: https://www.ohchr.org/en/documents/tools-and-resources/background-note-human-rights-violations-against-intersex-people.

Al-Qāḍī al-Nuʿmān, *Daʿāʾim al-islām*. 2 vols. Cairo: Dār al-Maʿārif, 1383/1963.

Al-Qudūrī, Abū l-Ḥusayn Aḥmad b. Muḥammad. *Mukhtaṣar al-Qudūrī fī l-fiqh al-Ḥanafī*. edited by Muḥammad Muḥammad ʿAwīḍa. Beirut: Dār al-Kutub al-ʿIlmiyya, 1418/1997.

Al-Rāzī, Muḥammad b. Zakariyyā. *al-Ḥāwī fī l-ṭibb*. 7 vols. Beirut: Dār Iḥyāʾ al-Turāth al-ʿArabī, 1422/2002.

Rowson, Everett K. "The Effeminates of Early Medina." *Journal of the American Oriental Society* 111, no. 4 (1991): 671–93.

Al-Ṣadr, Sayyid Ḥasan. *Faṣl al-qaḍāʾ fī l-kitāb al-mushtahar bi-Fiqh al-Riḍā*. edited by Riḍā Ustādī. Qum: Muʾassasat al-Nashr al-Islāmī, 1373sh.

Al-Ṣadūq, Muḥammad b. ʿAlī b. Bābawayh. *al-Muqniʿ*. Qum: Muʾassasat al-Imām al-Hādī, 1415.

Al-Ṣadūq, Muḥammad b. ʿAlī b. Bābawayh. *Man lā yaḥḍuruhu l-faqīh*. edited by ʿAlī Akbar Ghaffārī. 4 vols. Qum: Muʾassasat al-Nashr al-Islāmī, 1404.

Sallār al-Daylamī, Ḥamaz b. ʿAbd al-ʿAzīz. *al-Marāsim al-ʿalawiyya fī l-fiqh wa-aḥkām al-nabawiyya*. editd by Muḥsin al-Ḥusaynī al-Amīnī. Qum: al-Majmaʿ al-ʿĀlamī li-Ahl al-Bayt, 1414.

Al-Sarakhsī, Muḥammad b. Aḥmad. *al-Mabsūṭ*. 30 vols. Beirut: Dār al-Maʿrifa, 1414/1993.

Al-Sāwujī, Niẓām al-Dīn. *Jāmiʿ ʿabbāsī (takmila)*. 2 vols. Tehran: Farāhānī, 1350sh.

Sears, Stuart D. "An ʿAbbasid Revolution Hoard from the Western Jazira (AL-RAQQA?)." *American Journal of Numismatics* (1989–) vol. 12 (2000): 171–93.

Al-Sharīf al-Murtaḍā, Abū l-Qāsim ʿAlī b. al-Ḥusayn. *al-Intiṣār fī infirādāt al-imāmiyya*. Qum: Muʾassasat al-Nashr al-Islāmī, 1415.

Al-Sharīf al-Murtaḍā, Abū l-Qāsim ʿAlī b. al-Ḥusayn. *Rasāʾil*. Qum: Dār al-Qurʾān al-Karīm, 1405.

Al-Sughdī, Abū l-Ḥusayn ʿAlī b. al-Ḥusayn b. Muḥammad. *al-Nutaf fī l-fatāwā*. edited by Ṣalāḥ al-Dīn al-Nāhī. 2 vols. Amman: Dār al-Furqān/Beirut: Muʾassasat al-Risāla, 1404/1984.

Al-Suyūrī al-Ḥillī (al-Fāḍil al-Miqdād), Jamāl al-Dīn Miqdād b. ʿAbd Allāh. *al-Tanqīḥ al-rāʾiʿ li-Mukhtaṣar al-sharāʾiʿ*. 4 vols. Qum: Maktabat Āyatallāh al-Marʿashī al-Najafī, 1404.

Al-Thaqafī, Ibrāhīm b. Muḥammad b. Saʿīd b. Hilāl. *al-Ghārāt*. 2 vols. Qum: Dār al-Kitāb al-Islāmī, 1410.

Al-Thaʿlabī, Abū Muḥammad ʿAbd al-Wahhāb b. ʿAlī. *al-Maʿūna ʿalā madhhab ʿālim al-madīna "al-Imām Mālik b. Anas."* edited by Ḥamīsh ʿAbd al-Ḥaqq. 3 vols. Makka: al-Maktaba al-Tijāriyya, 1995.

Tolino, Serena. "Eunuchs in the Sunni Legal Discourse: Reflections on the Gender of Castrated Men." *Studi Magrebini* 20, no. 2 (2022): 117–36.

Al-Ṭūsī, Muḥammad b. Ḥasan. *al-Nihāya fī mujarrad al-fiqh wa-l-fatāwā*. Beirut: Dār al-Kitāb al-ʿArabī, 1400.

Al-Ṭūsī, Muḥammad b. Ḥasan. *al-Khilāf fī l-aḥkām*. 6 vols. Qum: Muʾassat al-Nashr al-Islāmī, 1407.

Al-Ṭūsī, Muḥammad b. Ḥasan. *Tahdhīb al-aḥkām*. edited by Ḥusayn Khirsān, ʿAlī Ākhūndī, and Muḥammad Ākhūndī. 10 vols. Tehran: Dār al-Kutub al-ʿIlmiyya, 1365sh.

Al-Ṭūsī, Muḥammad Ḥasan. *al-Istibṣār fī-mā ukhtulifa min al-akhbār*. edited by Ḥasan al-Khirsān. 4 vols. Tehran: Dār al-Kutub al-Islāmiyya, 1363sh.

Al-Ṭūsī, Muḥammad Ḥasan. *al-Mabsūṭ fī fiqh al-imāmiyya*. 8 vols. Tehran: al-Maktabat al-Murtaḍawiyya li-Iḥyāʾ al-Āthār al-Jaʿfariyya, 1387.

Uncertain author. *Fiqh al-Riḍā*. Qum: Muʾassasat Āl al-Bayt li-Iḥyāʾ al-Turāth, 1406.

Al-Uṣūl al-sitta ʿashar min al-uṣūl al-awwaliyya. edited by Ḍiyāʾ al-Dīn al-Maḥmūdī. Qum: Dār al-Ḥadīth, 1423.

Wilkes, Tim. *Islamic Coins and Their Values Volume 1: The Mediaeval Period*. London: Spink and Son, Ltd, 2015.

Al-Yazdī, Sayyid Kāẓim. *Ḥāshiyat Farāʾid al-uṣūl*. compiled by Muḥammad Ibrāhīm al-Yazdī, 3 vols. Qum: Dār al-Hudā, 1426.

Al-Zahrāwī [Albucasis], Abū l-Qāsim. *Kitāb al-taṣrīf li-man ʿajaza ʿan al-taʾlīf: al-maqāla al-thalāthūn: al-Jarāḥa*. Riyadh: Maktabat al-Malik Fahd al-Waṭaniyya, 1422/2001.

Zayd b. ʿAlī. *al-Majmūʿ al-ḥadīthī wa-l-majmūʿ al-fiqhī* (*Musnad al-Imām Zayd b. ʿAlī*). edited by ʿAbdallāh b. Ḥamūd b. Dirham al-ʿAzzī. Saʿda: Dār al-Imām Zayd Ibn ʿAlī li-l-Ṭibāʿa wa-l-Nashr, 1435/2014.

CHAPTER EIGHT

The *Khunthā* in Classical Sunni Jurisprudence

Indira Falk Gesink

Abstract

This chapter summarizes the historical development of Sunni legal discourse on the *khunthā*, a person who has variations of sexual characteristics that make them difficult to categorize as either male or female. The concept of a non-binary body was present in early legal discussions via several narrations of *ḥadīth*s regarding the inheritance of persons who had both male and female genitalia or neither. The concept of the *khunthā* developed gradually, becoming an established element of Sunni juristic literature by the 1000s. The chapter traces the evolution of the discourse as elaborated chiefly in Shāfiʿi, Ḥanafi, and Ḥanbali legal manuals. Use of Qur'ān as evidence for rulings on the *khunthā* was rare. Sunni jurists struggled to reconcile a faith-based worldview of sex as binary with their social reality that included non-binary bodies. They succeeded by distinguishing conceptually between the epistemological category of *khunthā*, which existed for the purpose of accommodating people whose sex could not be discerned, and the ontological and divinely created categories of male and female. Despite their maintenance of the binary ontological framework, their legal rulings constructed a social world in which *khunthā*s were placed hierarchically and spatially between male and female.

Keywords: *khunthā*, Sunni fiqh/jurisprudence, gender and sex in Islam, legal personhood, inheritance, diya

Introduction

Khunthā is the Arabic term for a person born with variations of sexual characteristics that complicate assignment to male or female sex. The earliest appearance of the term is in an Arabic dictionary from the 700s.[1] Most classical Muslim jurists defined a *khunthā* as someone who had mixed genitalia, but they also used the term for people who matured into a sex different from that assigned at birth due to hormone changes or to development of adult sexual indicators that were absent or ambiguous during childhood.

The scholarly literature on Islamic jurisprudence and the *khunthā* up to this point has been limited and based on review on too few of the vast number of primary sources that address non-binary gender in Islamic societies. It has also been plagued by conclusions drawn without addressing the hermeneutics of different systems of Islamic legal reasoning. Sunni jurists were from the earliest generations immured in a hermeneutic system that required them to acknowledge some textual sources, particularly the Qur'an, as epistemologically certain. From within that hermeneutic framework there was no escaping the fact that the Qur'an spoke to males and females and described the creation of male and female souls. That produced a gap between the text and a social reality in which non-binary people existed. Sunni jurists tried to bridge that gap, but their bridge was under constant tension. For the most part they could acknowledge that a social and legal category for non-binary people did and should exist in order for those people to receive their human rights, but many of them separated this epistemological category from ontological status: someone might be a *khunthā* in law, but this was because human epistemology was based on imperfect knowledge due to inability to detect someone's innate maleness or femaleness, and God knew whether that person had been created male or female. Therefore, the Qur'an did not require any creative re-interpretation: humans were only created male or female (see Chapter Four by Saqer Almarri). As is discussed in Mehrdad Alipour's chapter on Shi'i law (See Chapter Seven), Shi'i jurists used different hermeneutics that enabled some of them to envision an ontological third category: *khunthā* as a distinct divine creation. Physicians and literati (see Chapters Two and Nine) could also envision God creating a third gendered type. But few Sunni jurists stated such a thing openly. However, as this chapter will show, while Sunni jurists could not openly state that a third type of creation existed, and in fact often asserted that it did not, they nevertheless constructed a third social space for people to exist legally in a gendered society with non-binary bodies.

First and foremost, we must note the lack of parallels between classical Islamic gender concepts and modern concepts of "sex" as a biological fact and "gender" as a socially constructed or internally perceived or performed identity. One of the more striking features of legal discussions of "sex" or "gender" during the formative period of the Islamic legal tradition is the absence of either of those terms. In none of the literature of the formative period do authors deploy a consistent term for a conceptual category of sexual difference. They do not employ the modern Arabic term *jins* to mean 'sexual category' in the sense that it is used now. That they functioned with a concept of sexual difference was clear: there were women and there were men and there were others who were not quite men or women, but there was no word for that difference as such. In legal discussions, the words used, such as "type" (*naw'*), referred to categorical differences that affected what rights and obligations a person had. These differences included age (being a minor vs. being of age), freedom (being a slave vs. being free), sanity (being sane vs. being insane), and so on.

A second striking feature is the tendency of late formative period authors to attribute to early formative period authors opinions that are no longer extant and therefore unverifiable. Further inquiry is needed into these chains of antecedent authority. The *extant* literature from the earliest generation of Sunni legal thinkers displays mostly binary thinking about sex, although some of the terms they used had fuzzy boundaries. Formative period thinkers, with few exceptions, wrote about human creation as male and female. Those who were not-quite-men-or-women socially were nevertheless male or female creations.

The first generation

Traditionally, historians have tended to think of Sunni legal thinking as having started with a cohort of specific named figures. First in the traditional sequence were the earliest generation of jurists and *ḥadīth* transmitters whose rulings predate the evolution of the legal schools, such as the Umayyad jurists Saʿīd b. al-Musayyib (d. 715 CE), Abū ʿAmr ʿĀmir al-Shaʿbī (d. 723 CE), Ibn Shihāb al-Zuhrī (d. 124/741), and Sufyān al-Thawrī (d. 168/771). Their ideas preceded and led to the era of the legal school (*madhhab*). The predominant scholars of the formative era of the legal schools include Abū Ḥanīfa (d. 767 CE), who along with his chief disciple Abū Yūsuf (d. 798 CE) and their student Muḥammad al-Shaybānī (d. 805 CE), founded the Ḥanafī school of law; and Mālik b. Anas (d. 795 CE), also a student of Abū Ḥanīfa and founder of the Mālikī school of law. Mālik taught al-Shāfiʿī (d. 820 CE), founder of the Shāfiʿī school of law; al-Shāfiʿī taught Aḥmad b. Ḥanbal (d. 855 CE), founder of the Ḥanbalī school of law.

This traditional rendering only sometimes acknowledges (a) that these authors drew on earlier scholars' orally transmitted reports and opinions of which we sometimes have only second-hand knowledge, (b) that Abū Ḥanīfa was himself a student of Jaʿfar al-Ṣādiq (d. 765 CE), Sixth Imam of the Twelver and Ismāʿīlī Shiʿi sects of Islam, and that therefore some of the rulings traditionally attributed to the Sunni "Imams" (founders of the law schools) can also be found in Jaʿfar al-Ṣādiq's rulings, (c) that as legal historian Norman Calder has argued, the books attributed to the Sunni founders may not represent the authentic productions of those scholars' own times but rather the accreted school consensus rulings of the subsequent century.[2]

Having reviewed the texts traditionally associated with the earliest generation as represented above, this is what I conclude: either the transmitters, copyists, and modern editors who police how we receive these texts have edited out references to intersex in some texts (possible but unlikely),[3] or the earliest generations of legal scholars had limited experience of non-binary persons.

For example, in the *Muwaṭṭa* of Mālik b. Anas as related by Muhammad al-Shaybānī, which Norman Calder has argued is a Ḥanafī refutation of Mālikī positions rather than an authentic representation of Mālik's reports,[4] the word *khunthā* does not appear at all, nor is there any discussion of persons who are neither male nor female. In the section on prayer, the question of where a non-binary person might stand during communal prayer does not come up. The word *mukhannath* (effeminate male) does not appear either, which is interesting given the amount of attention paid to *mukhannathūn* in collections of *ḥadīth* that appear after the reign of the notorious ʻAbbāsid caliph al-Amīn (809–813). The word *mukhannath* does appear in Malik's *Mudawanna*, as related by ʻAbd al-Salām b. Saʻīd al-Tanūkhī "Ṣaḥnūn" (d. 240/854), on the authority of ʻAbd Al-Raḥman b. al-Qāsim al-ʻUtaqī (d. 191/806), as a term one might use to slander someone.[5] Saḥnūn also relates that Mālik had not told him any rulings regarding the *khunthā*, that they themselves "did not dare to rule on such things" as a result, but that he recommended assigning inheritance, testimony rights, and other issues by the place of urination, as urination was located at the same place as reproduction.[6] The Shāfiʻī scholar al-Māwardī reported that Mālik had said he did not know whether a *khunthā* was male or female.[7] We may infer from this that either Mālik never encountered a *khunthā*, or that this legal category entered the Sunni legal corpus after his death.

Likewise, no extant text attributed to Abū Ḥanīfa contains either the word "*khunthā*" or "*mukhannath*" or any variation of the root "*kh-n-th*." His *Kitāb al-athār*, as narrated by early Ḥanafi jurist Muḥammad al-Shaybānī, relates a notion of conception in which "The drop [of semen] is in the womb for forty days, and then it is a clinging blood clot for forty days, then it is a morsel of flesh for forty days, and then its outward form is originated, so he [the angel] says, 'Is it male or female? Miserable or fortunate? What is its provision?'"[8] No alternative to male or female creation is considered. When Abū Ḥanīfa encounters legal problems such as female slaves who cannot be penetrated sexually because they have no vaginal opening, he considers this to be analogically similar to castration, leprosy, or madness: they are defects that render one unacceptable as a partner in marriage or as a purchased slave.[9] Absence of a vaginal opening had not yet been recognized as a sign that one might be legally categorized as something other than male or female.

As in the case of Mālik and Saḥnūn (teacher and transmitter), it is Abū Ḥanīfa's transmitter who introduces the discussion of the *khunthā*, and the transmitter attributes the discussion back to Abū Ḥanīfa and his predecessors. The text is *al-Aṣl*, sometimes also conflated with its abbreviated form, *al-Mabsūṭ*. *Al-Aṣl* is attributed to Muḥammad al-Shaybānī, who studied for two years with Abū Ḥanīfa and longer with Abū Yūsuf.[10] Al-Shaybānī's method was to state the *ḥadīth*s relevant to a particular issue, then the opinions of Abū Ḥanīfa and Abū Yūsuf and, more rarely, other jurists. If his own opinion differed, the text offered that opinion up in the third person, e.g. "Muḥammad said..., reportedly in the voice of the text's Ḥanafi transmitters, such as Abū Sūlaymān al-Jūzjānī (d. 816 CE). The author(s) relied to a great extent on juristic precedent and on analogies drawn from those precedents.

According to the *Aṣl*, ʿAlī b. Abī Ṭālib had reported that the Prophet (PBUH) was asked about an infant who had "what a male has and what a female has [*mā li-l-mar'a wa-mā li-l-rajul*]." How would the infant inherit? The Prophet (PBUH) said, "From where he urinates."[11] Abū Ḥanīfa, al-Shaybānī, and Abū Yūsuf had followed this dictum in their own rulings.[12]

The *Aṣl* also reported that the Kūfan judge al-Shaʿbī (d. 723 CE) encountered a slightly different report but had ruled similarly:

> ʿUmar bin Bashīr bin Qays al-Hamdānī informed me on the authority of ʿĀmir al-Shaʿbī that he was asked about a newborn boy, who was neither male nor female but had what a male had [*laysa bi-dhakar wa lā unthā, wa lahu mā li-l-dhakar*], and a discharge coming out of his navel that looked like thick urine. He was asked about his inheritance. ʿĀmir said: He has half the share of a male and half the share of a female. Muḥammad said: This is according to us, and the *khunthā mushkil* is the same.[13]

The adjective *mushkil* modifying the noun *khunthā* meant that the *khunthā*'s physical characteristics did not give any clue of inclination toward male or female legal categorization and was therefore "complex," or complicated. A *khunthā* whose physical characteristics inclined toward maleness or femaleness was *ghayr mushkil*, "non-complex" or "simple." A *khunthā mushkil* would have been in reality exceedingly rare, as double genitalia with two functioning urinary exits occur much more rarely than other intersex variations, and most legal cases dealt with *khunthā*s who were identified at puberty as having apparently changed sex. The *Aṣl* notes that when Abū Ḥanīfa was asked about a *khunthā* whose urine came from both male and female orifices, he'd said, "I have no knowledge of that." Abū Yūsuf had ruled that inheritance would be awarded by the orifice that emitted the most urine but that if that test failed to determine a dominant organ, he "had no knowledge" received from previous authorities. In that case, they would reason by analogy from al-Shaʿbī's ruling: half the inheritance of a man and half that of a woman.[14] Abū Yūsuf offered further guidance to help establish a gendered legal status at puberty: if the *khunthā* had insertive intercourse or a wet dream, then he was a man. If he did not have insertive intercourse but grew a beard, he was a man. If he did not either have insertive intercourse or grow a beard but developed breasts like those of women or lactated, then he was a woman. If he did not develop breasts but menstruated, then he was a woman. If he neither developed breasts nor menstruated but had receptive intercourse, then he was a woman. And, if he did not have receptive intercourse, breasts, or beard, he was, apparently by default, a man. But rest assured, the text says, puberty would resolve any remaining ambiguity by producing some sign of inclination either way. Both Abū Yūsuf and al-Shaybānī said they had no knowledge of what to do about a person who remained ambiguous despite the test of urination and who did not reach puberty. Their gender framework was binary. Their conceptual world had to be stretched to include someone in between male and female.[15]

The text then extrapolated from these principles via analogy a number of rulings that remained more-or-less standard throughout the corpus of Sunni law. Al-Shaybānī is presented in Socratic dialogue with Abū Yūsuf, asking for his opinions. How should a pre-pubertal *khunthā* be prepared for burial? In a funerary service for a man, a woman, and a *khunthā*, how would the bodies be arranged? Could a *khunthā* be buried in a common grave with a man? Would the *khunthā* wear jewelry like women, wear women's clothing on pilgrimage, pray with a veil? Would a person who had sex with the *khunthā* be eligible to marry the *khunthā*'s mother? Where would the *khunthā* stand for communal prayer? Who would circumcize the infant? And so on. It is hard to say how much of this is genuinely a product of the late 700s and how much was added by Ḥanafī redactors in the subsequent century, as much of the content is repeated by later authors.

Abū Yūsuf replied that an ambiguous body should be purified with earth (*tayammum*) rather than being washed by either a man or a woman. The body should be carried on a bier, like a woman's, but placed upside down. In the grave, the body should be shrouded like a girl's, and only a relative should enter the grave.[16] In a multi-body funerary service, the body of a man should be positioned closest to the imam, a *khunthā* second, and a woman farthest. If buried in a common grave, a barrier of earth should be placed between a *khunthā* and a male body. A *khunthā* should not wear jewelry (like a man) but should veil (like a woman) and pray in women's postures. In communal prayer, a *khunthā* should stand in between the rows of men and women. Circumcision should be delayed, and if the *khunthā* child reaches the age of circumcision before gender indicators appear, circumcision should be done by a slave woman who is trained in such things. Al-Shaybānī clarified that the state treasury should provide funds for the purchase if the *khunthā* is insolvent.[17] This establishes the principle that the ethical circumcision of a non-binary child is a public duty for which the imam must take responsibility if the family cannot afford the accommodation. We could draw the modern analogy: the ethical medical treatment of a non-binary child is a public duty for which the state or the state's religious branch must take responsibility, if the family cannot afford to do so. It also indicates that both boys and girls were circumcised; there is no discussion of excluding a *khunthā* who turns out to be a girl from circumcision.

Abū Yūsuf and al-Shaybānī both regarded the *khunthā* as pre-pubertal: in their opinions, maturity would typically clarify the *khunthā*'s male or female legal status. Children were not legally responsible. Hence *khunthās* could dress as women because children would not be legally culpable for cross-dressing if they matured as men. If they slandered someone, or were slandered, or apostacized, there would be no punishment. They could not testify in court. If enslaved, they could not inherit from masters. They could not fight, and if taken prisoner in battle, they were protected as children. If dhimmis, they were not subject to jizya.[18] If they cut off a man's or woman's hand, their kin would be responsible for paying blood money, "because [the *khunthā*] is a minor who has not yet reached puberty."[19] If the *khunthā* were accidentally killed before puberty, al-Sha'bī ruled that his heirs would receive half the blood money of a man and half that of a woman. Abū Ḥanīfa, Abū Yūsuf, and al-Shaybānī rejected that and ruled in favor of certainty: unless the heirs of the slain could provide evidence of male legal status, the compensation would be that for a female, because it was certain under the law that at least the female share was owed.[20] After puberty, however, *khunthās* would become legally culpable for crimes such as theft.[21]

In other legal matters, what comes to the forefront is the *khunthā*'s gendered uncertainty. *Khunthās*' inheritance could be delayed until puberty, on the assumption that puberty would clarify gender status.[22] If enslaved, they could not be freed under any emancipation statement that specified the gender of slaves to be freed. A man who vowed to divorce his wife if he purchased a slave, employing a word for 'slave' that implied gender, who then bought a *khunthā*, would remain married unless the *khunthā*'s status changed to that gender at puberty.[23] Fathers could not arrange *khunthā* marriages until puberty, nor could they inherit from each other.[24] If injured, they could not claim right of retaliation unless they had obtained male legal status.[25]

An adult *khunthā* did not necessarily have to undergo court examination. In fact some questions about gendered status would only arise after the *khunthā* had died, such as inheritance questions in which heirs inherit from both a father and his adult *khunthā* offspring. In such situations, Abū Yūsuf allowed a free living guardian to swear that the *khunthā* was male or female. Unless the *khunthā* urinated from both male and female organs or was otherwise known to be ambiguously sexed, that statement was sufficient to establish legal status as male or female.[26] In cases of conflicting evidence, Abū Yūsuf tended to rule in favor of the person who would gain the most from a primary claim.[27] In the absence of other evidence or testimonies, a living *khunthā* could also assert status as male or female.[28]

Al-Aṣl provided numerous hypothetical scenarios of inheritance possibilities that included *khunthās*, such as inheritance of a "*khunthā* daughter" (*ibnah khunthā*) in a household that also included a male heir, or a "known son" (*ibn*^{an} *ma'rūf*^{an}), or the *khunthā*'s own children. The contraposition of *khunthā* with "known" indicates that a *khunthā* was someone whose legal status as male or female was uncertain even though the person was performing a social role as son or daughter. According to the text, Abū Ḥanīfa preferred to award the female portion of inheritance—and we can infer from the contraposition between "*khunthā*" and "known" that he ruled thus because the female portion of the inheritance was the amount that was certain to be owed. The ruling does not construct the *khunthā* as hierarchically equivalent to a female (a binary between "male" and "not-male") but rather as an unknown, an uncertain quantity that might resolve into male or female.[29] Until the certainty resolved, the inheritance would be the smallest share that would be owed in any given situation, because the jurist could be sure that the *khunthā* would at least be due the smallest share.[30]

Abū Yūsuf asserted that puberty would resolve any ambiguity, when the *khunthā* grew a beard or breasts or some other sign by which maleness or femaleness could be claimed.[31] Nevertheless, *al-Aṣl's* rulings constructed the *khunthā* as inherently of uncertain gender. Even after puberty, uncertainty remained. Post pubertal *khunthā*s had to continue wearing a veil to pray. They could not uncover in the presence of men or women, nor could they be alone with a man or woman other than an unmarriageable relative. They required a male unmarriageable relative to travel for three or more days.[32] They could not bathe in the presence of either men or women.[33] A simple assertion of gender status, e.g. "I am a man" or "I am a woman," was at one point ruled insufficient to claim legal status and at another point ruled sufficient.[34]

Al-Shāfiʿī, eponym of the Shāfiʿī school, belonged to the same generation as the transmitters of Mālik and Abū Ḥanīfa. As such, we should not be surprised to find that he ruled on similar issues. Al-Shāfiʿī's rulings regarding the *khunthā* provide conflicting evidence. Al-Shāfiʿī's *Risāla* does not mention the *khunthā* or any gendered category other than male or female. The *Risāla* text quotes the Qur'an to show that God created everyone male or female (Qur'an 49:13).[35] It considers only male and female inheritance, male and female punishments, male and female witnesses, male and female slaves, and male and female thieves.[36] The *Kitāb al-Umm* also deals mostly in binary oppositions: male and female, mature and immature, rational and irrational.[37]

However, the edition of *al-Umm* in the recension of Rabīʿ, published by Dār al-Shaʿb in 1968, along with the *Mukhtaṣar* of *al-Umm* written by al-Shāfiʿī's disciple, Ismāʿīl b. Yaḥyā al-Muzanī (d. 878 CE), and the edition of *al-Umm* published by Dār al-Fikr in 1983, all discuss the *khunthā*. The text offers rulings regarding funerary rites, prayer positioning, breastfeeding, marriage, divorce for impotence, qiṣāṣ (retaliation), and diya (compensatory payments for injury or death) of a *khunthā*. In the 1968 edition, these rulings are in the third person as related by his student Rabīʿ, whose opinion is also sometimes appended.

According to both recensions, al-Shāfiʿī ruled that the heirs of a *khunthā mushkil* who had been intentionally killed would be entitled to *qiṣāṣ*, the right of retaliation, "because the *khunthā* can be either a man or a woman. Thus, they are entitled to *qiṣāṣ* if he is a *khunthā*. If they ask for *diya* (compensatory payment), it would be ruled as the *diya* of a woman, since that is certain. They would not be granted the *diya* of a man, nor an amount greater than the *diya* of a woman, because that would be uncertain."[38]

First, this asserts that a *khunthā* is either a man or a woman. Al-Shāfiʿī, like other formative-era jurists, understood human creation as male or female—the *khunthā* was either but could not be discerned as one or the other via visible clues.

Second, someone whose status as male or female is undetermined nevertheless possesses this right to compensation for injury or death, and from that we can infer that (a) diya is a human right and (b) people whose gendered status is indiscernible are nevertheless human. Al-Shāfiʿī then reasons that the value of the *diya* for a *khunthā's* life is that of a woman, because it is certain that his value is at least that of a woman. The *khunthā* might be male—*might*—but that outcome is subject to doubt. In al-Shāfiʿī's methodology, outcomes that are certain prevail over conditions of doubt. Therefore, if the *khunthā* could be demonstrated (*bayanā*) to be or to have been a male, the payment could then be adjusted to that of a male.[39] For demonstration of maleness, al-Shāfiʿī accepted urination from a penis or "signs (*ʿalamāt*) of the man upon him that were dominant." Menstruation, "female desire" (desire to be penetrated), or loss of hymen would confirm that the *diya* of the woman was owed. For the *khunthā* who was truly non-binary, the text's narrator, Rabīʿ, relates his own judgment: "The *khunthā mushkil* is he who has a vulva and a penis, if he urinates from both, neither preceding the other and cutting off together. If one of them preceded, the ruling would be by that which preceded. If they sustained together but one cut off before the other, the ruling would be by that which persists."[40]

The reasoning continues in the same vein throughout: if a *khunthā* is injured during commission of a crime of which he himself is innocent, he obtains an initial indemnity (*arsh*) at the female rate but can prove himself male to obtain the male rate.[41] With inheritance it is the responsibility of the heirs to bring evidence as to the maleness or femaleness of the *khunthā*. If the *khunthā* is living, "the evidence will be obvious to the eyes," but if dead, evidence must be presented. If contradictory evidence is brought, it will all be cast out.[42]

A *khunthā* could marry but had to disclose impotence to a potential wife. If the *khunthā* chose to marry a woman, he would be regarded as a man, and if the *khunthā* chose to marry a man, she'd be regarded as a woman. Inheritance rights would follow that choice, although al-Rabīʿ reported a contradictory opinion that awarded the woman's share of inheritance regardless of social role. Once a gendered legal status was adopted, however, it could not be changed in order to marry someone of the same gendered status.[43] Two rules established here persist throughout the Sunni discussions of *khunthās*: first is the predominance of masculinity in the gendered system as a whole—the male pronoun "he" is used as a default to refer to all *khunthā*s unless they had assimilated to female status. Second is the predominance of conditions of certainty over conditions of uncertainty—the jurist should make every effort to determine with some degree of certainty what legal category the person belongs to, the *khunthā's* gender being by definition uncertain—and the only awards that can be allocated with certainty are the lowest amounts in any given circumstance. These are usually but not always the amounts awarded to females.

The *diya* for injury to body parts provides an index of gendered values from the time period. The penis had more than just reproductive value for the man—the penis had intrinsic value, since al-Shāfiʿi accepts the possibility that a *khunthā* female could have a penis and ruled that the value of this penis would be determined via court deliberation (*hukūma*). This discussion also addresses the possibility that relatives of a dead *khunthā* might try to claim that the *khunthā* "became male before he died"[44] or that the agnatic relatives who would benefit from a larger share if the *khunthā* was female might claim he was female. He warns that such evidence should only be accepted if it is contrary to the group's own interest in the case, or if both interest groups claim the same category for the *khunthā* and are able to describe physically why the *khunthā* should be categorized as male or female.[45]

Al-Shāfiʿī also relates a case in which a man attacked a *khunthā mushkil* and deliberately cut off the person's penis, testicles, and eyelids. Penis and testicles were characteristics that had monetary value for male bodies, and eyelids with lashes were characteristics that had monetary value for female bodies. The identification of the claimant as a *khunthā mushkil* is interesting, because one would assume, given the criteria jurists had offered for determining sex by urination, that someone with a penis and testicles would be considered male. In the resolution of the case, however, al-Shāfiʿi writes, the leadership told the *khunthā* that if he could demonstrate maleness, they would authorize *diya* for his penis and testicles and convene a hearing to discuss the eyelids. If he could demonstrate femaleness, they would authorize *diya* for a woman's eyelids and hold a hearing to discuss the penis and testicles. And if he were to die before being able to demonstrate, he would be due at least the whole *diya* of a woman, and they would hold a hearing "out of awareness that (*ʿalā aḥāṭa min*) you are male or female."[46] Here again al-Shāfiʿī expresses his gendered assumptions. The *khunthā mushkil is either* male or female. While al-Shāfiʿī recognizes a third legal category, that legal category exists only because of a temporary condition of ambiguity that prevents human perception of the *khunthā's* underlying gendered being. Ontologically, the *khunthā* must still be either male or female.

In prayer, the main issue again arose from uncertainty of gender. Unlike a castrated man, who is unquestionably still a man and can stand with men in prayer, lead prayer, give testimony, participate in battle, and share in the spoils of war, a *khunthā* of unknown legal category must always pray behind the imam, and with a group should always stand between the men and the women.[47] Likewise, in a mixed funeral service, the *khunthā* body should be placed between that of a man and that of a woman, as men are to be placed close to the imam, and women farther away, and the *khunthā* could be either.[48] Nor was the *khunthā* required to participate in warfare, unlike men.[49] This uncertainty might resolve at puberty, but puberty in itself did not confer adult responsibility, which al-Shāfiʿī set at age fifteen for slaves and for *khunthās*. So for example, a *khunthā* who has had a wet dream or who menstruated—indicators of puberty—could still not be held responsible for a confession of apostacy.[50] Al-Shāfiʿī did not believe that ontological gender could be determined reliably via secondary sexual characteristics. For example, al-Shāfiʿī also notes that there is a *diya* for a man whose breasts lactate; if his lactating breasts are injured and dry up as a result of the injury, he is also owed *diya*.[51] Al-Shāfiʿī regards this person as ontologically and categorically male, but the typical *diya* for a male breast is less than the *diya* for a lactating breast. While other texts suggest rounded breast development and lactation in the *khunthā* as indicators of femaleness, *al-Umm* only mentions urinary exit, menstruation, and penetrative vs. insertive sex as indicators. Post-pubertal sexual characteristics, such as breasts or beards, do not contradict or change one's essential being.

The two students who related al-Shāfiʿī's rulings, Rabīʿ and al-Muzanī, died in 870 and 878. In the 900s, it is primarily Shiʿi jurists who elaborate rules for *khunthā*s (see chapter on Shīʿī jurisprudence).

These first-generation authors responded reactively to questions about *khunthās*. If a case or petition was brought to them, they addressed that particular issue. The *khunthā* was either absent in their legal reasoning or enough of an exception so as not to challenge the fundamentally binary structure of gendered categorical thinking.

The Qur'an did not play a significant evidentiary role in first generation rulings about the *khunthā*. Nor did *ḥadīth*. This is in part because the word "*khunthā*" is found rarely in *ḥadīth*. Most narrations are like those in the *Aṣl* and describe the bodily conformation but don't name it. There are a few that use the term *khunthā*; for example, in the *Sunan* of al-Dārimī (d. 255/869), which says "Abū Bakr b. Abī al-Shayba told us, Hushaym told us, on the authority of Mughīra, on the authority of Shibak, on the authority of al-Shaʿbī, on the authority of ʿAlī, about the *khunthā*: 'He inherits according to the place from which he urinates.'"[52] Al-Dārimī also reports narrations similar to those in *al-Aṣl* that describe the physical characteristics later used to categorize someone as *khunthā*: " ʿUbaydallah bin Mūsā related to us, on the authority of Isrāʾīl on the authority of ʿAbd al-Alā that he heard from Muḥammad b. ʿAlī that it was told to him on the authority of ʿAlī about a man who had had what the man has and what the woman has [and asked] by which of these does he inherit? And he said, 'by whichever one he urinates from.'"[53] The other states "Abū

Nu'aym told us, Abū Hānī told us: He said 'Āmir [al-Sha'bī] was asked about a child born neither male nor female; he had neither what males have nor what females have, and there came from his navel [something] in the form of urine and feces; he was asked about its inheritance, and he said: 'Half the share of the male, and half the share of the female.'"[54] These reports are situated in a chapter on inheritance and surrounded by rulings about children who inherit and adults who die without children or parents.

Ash Geissinger has suggested elsewhere that we can use the frequency with which a *ḥadīth* is used in Quranic interpretation as an indicator of its cultural importance at the time.[55] Extrapolating from Geissinger's methods, we can also infer cultural importance from the frequency with which jurists deploy a *ḥadīth* in legal manuals, although this will be of less utility for the early Islamic centuries when *ḥadīth*s were not yet considered to be necessary evidence. According to Almarri's analysis in Chapter Four of this volume, no Qur'an interpreters employed the terminology of *khunthā* in exegesis prior to Makkī b. Abī Ṭālib (d. 1045 CE), suggesting that the issue of non-binary embodiment was not of great cultural concern prior to the 1000s. More research is needed to see whether the reverse would be true about *mukhannaths*.

The second generation

By the 1000s, legal thinking was occurring within an imperial environment—a network of cities some of which numbered over 100,000 in which statistically the presence of *khunthās* would have been more noticeable, and there was by that time a historical legacy of precedents that acknowledged the existence of non-binary bodies. Legal thinking was no longer reactionary. It became predictive and hypothetical. Manuals from this period that described how to perform jurisprudence often included prescriptions for resolving legal questions for people who might be either male or female or, sequentially, both. Their sources are for the most part juristic precedent, with *ḥadīth* having only a secondary evidentiary role even for Ḥanbalī jurists.

Rulings on the khunthā in the Mukhtaṣar al-Qudūrī

A discussion of the legal rights of the *khunthā* appears in the legal manual of early Ḥanafī jurist Aḥmad b. Muhammad al-Qudūrī (d. 1036–7 CE), the *Mukhtaṣar al-Qudūrī*. A "*mukhtaṣar*" was an abridgment, so the text summarizes al-Qudūrī's legal conclusions but does not provide his reasoning. The *mukhtaṣar* genre evolved to provide jurists with easy references that they could consult to provide rulings consistent with luminaries within their own schools of thought. According to the judgment of later Muslim jurists, al-Qudūrī himself preferred *taqlīd*—following the precedent of scholars in his school—to resolving legal questions using his own novel reasoning.[56] As such, the text tells us the prevailing positions within the Ḥanafi school in Baghdad in the early 1000s.

Like *al-Aṣl* and unlike the works of al-Shāfiʿī, the *Mukhtaṣar* of al-Qudūrī contains a whole chapter titled "The Book of the *Khunthā*." This tells us that al-Qudūrī considered the *khunthā*'s situation unique enough that it could not be considered as a part of the chapter on, for example, prayer or circumcision, or that the organizational structure of the book was crafted considering how someone would use it. The user is likely a jurist, and a petition regarding a *khunthā* might contain questions regarding multiple topics. So, for user friendliness, all issues that the author has considered regarding *khunthās* are grouped together. This establishes a kind of paradigm or template for future legal manuals.

Identification in al-Qudūrī:

> If the infant (*mawlūd*) has a vulva (*farj*) and a penis (*dhakar*) then he is a *khunthā*. If he was to urinate from the penis, he would be a boy (*ghulām*). If he was to urinate from the vulva, then he is female (*unthā*), and if he urinates from them both and the urine precedes (*sabaqa*) from one of the two of them, he is assigned to the one that precedes, and if the two of them are equivalent, do not rule by abundance, following Abī Ḥanīfa. Abū Yūsuf ruled and Muḥammad [al-Shaybanī] assigned [legal category] by abundance [of urine]....[57]

This method of identification by place of urination is here clearly identified as being for infants. An infant cannot express a gender identity, and as legal categorization was assigned by appearance of infant genitalia at birth, just as it generally is now, an infant with variations of genital characteristics might be difficult to categorize. Al-Qudūrī follows precedent established by formative-era scholars of the Ḥanafi school.

Al-Qudūrī does not consider the possibility of a child born without genitalia at all (what Shiʿi jurists called *mamsūḥ*) or a child whose genitalia or urination cannot conclusively categorize them as male or female. Maturation introduces the possibility of change from one category to another:

> And when the *khunthā* reaches puberty and there comes out to him a beard, or he approaches women [i.e., is capable of insertive sex], then he is a man. And if there appear to him breasts like the breasts of a woman or he lactates from his breasts or menstruates or conceives or it is possible to approach him from the vulva [is capable

> of receptive vaginal sex], then he is a woman. If there does not appear to him any of these signs, he is a *khunthā mushkil*.[58]

Al-Qudūrī differed from Shāfi'i commentaries from the same period in accepting beard growth, breast development, lactation, and menstruation as evidence that could produce or resolve ambiguity. He also expanded the *mushkil* (complex) category: whereas al-Shaybānī had held that someone who developed no adult sexual characteristics was a man, al-Qudūrī considered that person to be medial.

Prayer, circumcision, and inheritance according to al-Qudūrī

After addressing identification, al-Qudūrī then addresses three questions of public practice: Where does the *khunthā* stand during public prayer, who performs the *khunthā*'s circumcision, and what share does the *khunthā* inherit? The positions adopted are fundamentally those of *al-Aṣl*.

Al-Qudūrī does not debate whether the *khunthā* is human or deserving of rights; the jurist assumes that the *khunthā* is human and that all humans deserve rights. The question is rather how to accommodate someone who disrupts gendered legal arrangements. For example, in public prayer, men must pray with men, and women with women. Women stand behind or apart from the men. Doing otherwise can invalidate one's own prayers and those of the people around one. Some jurists would then require those whose prayers had been invalidated to repeat them. The *khunthā* potentially disrupted the neat division. What if a *khunthā* who was raised female became male at puberty? Had he been male all along? If he had been praying with the women, would that invalidate the women's previous prayers? Al-Qudūrī's solution to this was to position the *khunthā* between the men and the women. Presumably this applied to the prepubescent *khunthā* whose adult categorization had not yet been determined and might change, and to the mature *khunthā muskhil*, but not to the mature *khunthā* who could be legally categorized as male or female.

As for circumcision, there the conundrum was that men usually circumcised men, and women circumcised women.[59] The solution, here again as described in *al-Aṣl*, was to have the *khunthā* purchase a female slave (*ama*) to perform the circumcision, if he could afford to do so. The reasoning—still unstated in this *mukhtaṣar* format—was that if the *khunthā* turned out to be a woman, there was no legal violation, and if the *khunthā* turned out to be a man, then a slave looking upon his genitals was legal. If the *khunthā* did not have means sufficient to purchase the slave, the imām would arrange for the purchase of a slave with funds from the Bayt al-Māl (Central Treasury), then sell the slave back and return the funds when the deed was done.[60]

On the question of inheritance, al-Qudūrī relates differences of opinion that he attributes to the founders of the Ḥanafī legal school:

> And if his father dies and leaves behind a son and a *khunthā*, Abū Ḥanīfa rules that two shares go to the son and one to the *khunthā*, so he is female (*unthā*) in terms of inheritance unless he can prove otherwise ... And Abū Yūsuf and Muḥammad said the *khunthā* has half the inheritance of the male and half the inheritance of the female, and this is the dicta of al-Sha'bī, and the two of them differ in *qiyās* of his dicta and Abū Yūsuf said the property is divided between them into seven shares, to the son four shares and to the *khunthā* three, and Muḥammad said the property is divided between them into twelve shares, to the son seven and to the *khunthā* five.[61]

These divergent opinions, originally expressed in *al-Aṣl*, then formed the two poles of the debate over *khunthā* inheritance: either the *khunthā* is at least a woman and always due at least the woman's share, or the *khunthā* is positioned between a man and a woman, due half the man's share and half the woman's. Scholars developed various iterations of these rulings, but they remained philosophically divided between two patterns of legal reasoning. The ruling that the *khunthā* is at least a woman prioritizes certainty as the primary point of consideration: the inheritance given is the amount that is certain, for the *khunthā* is at least due the smallest amount. The ruling that the *khunthā* inherits half a man's and half a woman's share prioritizes the *khunthā's* medial social position and the possibility that the *khunthā* may need more inheritance than a woman. More investigation is needed to explore the social contexts in which such variant rulings emerge and what they may tell us about gender relations in those contexts.

Rulings on the khunthā in a Shāfi'ī commentary

Al-Māwardī was a near-contemporary of al-Qudūrī who was also active in Baghdad legal circles. Following al-Shāfi'ī's organizational model, al-Māwardī integrated rulings on the *khunthā* into all parts of his manual. While some of what he related was already part of the corpus of legal precedent as related by al-Qudūrī, al-Shāfi'ī, and Shi'i legal scholars, al-Māwardī delved into areas of law that had not yet been explored for their implications for non-binary people and were not part of the standard concerns of Ḥanafīs.[62] His commentary on al-Shāfi'ī states that his books mentioned *khunthās* frequently, and at the same time that a *khunthā* was purely a legal construction that existed to accommodate people with non-binary genitalia, for all souls were created either male or female.

Al-Māwardī on the khunthā milk-mother and self-gendering

For example, al-Māwardī considered breastfeeding and its impact on marriageability. Al-Shāfi ʿī had considered whether a *khunthā* who breastfeeds a child was subject to the same marriage prohibitions as a woman. A woman who breastfed a child was considered to become its mother after five feedings. A man whose sibling had been breastfed by a woman could not marry any of her children, because they had become his siblings. Al-Māwardī took up this topic from an explicitly binarist perspective:

> God Almighty created animals male and female, joining them together in similarity so that males may be intimate with females, and distinguishing them by their reproductive organs. He made for the man a penis and for the woman a vagina so that they may come together, overcome by the desire for intercourse that he has set into their natures. Thus the two semens [*al-manīyān*] mix in the repose of the womb, the site of conception, in order to preserve through procreation the continuity of creation.[63]

He then described the distinguishing feature of maleness as possession of a penis, and that of femaleness possession of a vagina. Anyone who combined these two features in one being was a *khunthā*, an admixture, so named after a saying that food and drink become indistinguishable from one another (*takhannatha*) if they are too similar. Because God's Creative model was one that required reproduction, all beings had to be either male or female: "If two organs come together in one person, and he has a penis and a vagina, it is not possible for him to be male and female, and it is not possible for him to be neither male nor female, and it is not possible for some of him to be male and some of him to be female, because that would violate the custom He has established for His Creation that preserves the world through reproduction."[64] Al-Māwardī then recited a litany of methods then in practice for assigning a legal category to a non-binary body: the test of urination recommended in the *ḥadīths*, counting of ribs—based on the story of Eve's creation from Adam's rib and the assertion that men would all be missing one rib—the ability to direct a stream of urine, the emission of semen from the penis or from the vaginal canal. He also reported—in contradiction to al-Qudūrī—that some scholars did not consider menstruation to be a reliable indicator of femaleness, although menstruation, unlike urination and emission of sexual fluids, only occurred in women. It could be used to distinguish women but not as a test of manliness. It was however an imperfect tool for distinguishing women, because one could bleed from causes other than menstruation. Growth of a beard was also considered an unreliable indicator, because some women grew beards. Likewise, lactation could occur in men: hence they discussed whether a man or a *khunthā* who lactated should pass to their milk-children the prohibition of marriage. Following the Shāfiʿī preference for Qur'anic evidence as epistemologically certain, al-Māwardī turned to the Qur'an for evidence, which only mentioned women as milk-mothers. Men who lactated, he concluded, and *khunthās* who identified as men, did not become milk-parents, so the prohibition on marriage did not extend to the children they nursed. However, if a *khunthā* who breastfed developed a sign indicating femaleness (other than lactation), such as a desire to marry a man, any previous marriages would be annulled and the prohibition of marriage would extend to their milk children. If a *khunthā* who breastfed and identified as a female developed signs of maleness, such as desire to marry a woman, any previous marriages would be annulled and the prohibition of marriage to their milk children would be dropped.[65] Physical indicators not being present, the *khunthā's* inclination toward being male or female was the best way to establish a legal category.[66] Al-Māwardī and al-Shāfiʿī both warned, however, that after a *khunthā* had made such a deliberate choice of gender, they could not then reverse it. The *khunthā*'s choice revealed whether God had created them male or female.[67]

Al-Māwardī on diya, "touching," and funerals

Al-Māwardī's strident binary stance appears to have been influenced by the scientific spirit of the ʿAbbāsid-era intellectuals. He rejected rib-counting as a means of resolving a *khunthā's* ambiguity, stating that the "practitioners of dissection" had observed that all humans had twelve ribs on each side regardless of sex, five in the front that were attached to the breastbone, and seven that were unattached. This led him to dismiss as fabricated the reports of ʿAlī using rib-counting to adjudicate a *khunthā*'s case.[68] However, this same scientific spirit also led him to echo ʿAbbāsid-era physicians who regarded any genital features that were contrary to one's legal category to be "extraneous." If a *khunthā* who identified as female were to lose a penis or testicle, she would not receive *diya* for them—they were unnecessary.[69] Likewise, if a man were to touch a *khuntha's* vulva, this would not invalidate his ritual ablutions. Ablution is only invalidated when one is certain that an event conferring impurity has occurred, such as a man touching a woman's body, or a woman touching a man's penis. Because a *khunthā* may be a man, his vulva may be an extraneous organ, and therefore touching it would not confer impurity. A condition of uncertainty exists, so ablution is not invalidated. However, if a man were to touch a *khunthā's* penis, he does invalidate his ablution, because if the *khunthā* is a man, he has touched a penis, and if the *khunthā* is a woman, he has touched her body. If a *khunthā* touches his own penis, his ablution is not invalidated, because he may be a man. If he touches both his penis and his vagina, then his ablution is invalidated.[70]

This uncertainty also affected al-Māwardī's rulings on preparation of the *khunthā* body for burial. Abū ʿAbdullah al-Zubayrī had narrated that the *khunthā mushkil* body should be cleansed via *tayammum* rather than washed, and that a man could not do the cleansing because the body might be female, nor could a woman, because the body might be male. Al-Māwardī opposed this ruling, arguing that washing (*ghusl*) was obligatory for all bodies and that *tayammum* involved no less difficulty than washing, because *tayammum* required touching the body's arms, and if the *khunthā* was a woman, a male washer would be prohibited from touching her arms. Because tayammum was no less problematic than washing, there was no reason to prefer *tayammum*. He advised washing the *khunthā* body in a shirt, in a darkened setting, by trustworthy men and women.[71]

Al-Māwardī on khunthā manumission and inheritance

Shāfiʿī scholars such as al-Nawawī were prolix in their efforts to elaborate all possible scenarios in which a *khunthā* might inherit.[72] Al-Māwardī insisted that al-Shāfiʿī had regarded all *khunthās* as fundamentally either male or female.[73] Furthermore, in many legal settings, such as custody, he advised that a *khunthā's* own testimony as to gender identity should be accepted as the most reliable indicator of legal category.[74]

The binarism, however, only extended so far. Juridically, al-Māwardī clearly still considered the *khunthā* a third category. This is clearest in his refusal to consider a *khunthā* slave's emancipation from a slave owner's statement that a male slave or female slave should be freed. Such a statement would not free a *khunthā*—hence a *khunthā*, while ontologically male or female, was legally neither.[75] And because *khunthā*s were legally neither, their inheritance shares were always calculated as if they might turn out to be either.[76]

Eleventh-century elaboration of Ḥanafī positions on the khunthā: al-Sarakhsī

Al-Māwardī's Ḥanafī contemporary, Muḥammad b. Aḥmad b. Abī Sahl al-Sarakhsī, known as "Shams al-A'imma" (d. 483/1090), wrote about the *khunthā* in his massive tome of commentary on Muḥammad al-Shaybānī's *Aṣl*, the *Kitāb al-mabsūṭ*. Al-Sarakhsī lived in Khurasan, an intellectual center that rivaled Baghdad, and wrote the book while in prison for questioning the validity of the ruler's marriage to a slave woman. His position on the *khunthā* marked a shift in religious scholarship to rely more on textual evidence, such as Qur'an and recorded *ḥadīth* reports, which further strengthened the binary argument. Al-Qudūrī had been willing to define the *khunthā* as potentially ambiguous in legal category after maturity, if they did not develop mature signs of inclination either way. Al-Sarakhsī, in contrast, followed the Shāfiʿī line that *khunthās* must be created either male or female and cannot be both:

> Know that God the Most High created the children of Adam males and females, as God the Most High said: "And He dispersed from them many men and women" (Al-Nisa': 1) and He the Most High said: "He gives to whom He wills females and He gives to whom He wills males" (Al-Shūrā: 49). Therefore He explained the rules for males and the rules for females in His Book, and He did not explain the rules for a person who is male and female. Thus, we know from this that the two characteristics [*al-waṣfān*] cannot be combined in one person. How can they be combined when between them there is such difference as to be opposition?[77]

It would seem therefore that al-Sarakhsī is denying the existence of a *khunthā*—except that he then proceeds to comment on both of *al-Aṣl*'s chapters on the *khunthā* and *khunthā* inheritance. He therefore acknowledges—perhaps is forced by the commentary format—that people who had male and female characteristics existed in the social world and that, as human beings, they were deserving of rights. It was the jurist's duty to determine to the best of his ability what those rights were.

Al-Sarakhsī on khunthā identification

Al-Sarakhsī, like the jurists before him, acknowledged that a child could be born without genitalia or with genitalia that were ambiguous.[78] He cited the *ḥadīth*s provided in *al-Aṣl*, adding that ʿUmar (b. al-Khaṭṭāb) had ruled that such an infant was due half the share of a male and half the share of a female. Al-Shaybānī had said that this was the ruling "among us" and that a *khunthā mushkil* should receive the same share if he were to die before puberty, when the appearance of a beard or breasts would "clarify his condition."[79] To distinguish male and female in a *khunthā* infant that had ambiguous genitalia, al-Sarakhsī followed juristic precedent in using urination to assign a legal category for rearing.[80] For this he adduced as evidence *ḥadīth*s and provided an account of a case not discussed by the jurists considered here previously:

> It was mentioned on the authority of Abū Yūsuf, on the authority of al-Kalbī, on the authority of Abū Ṣāliḥ, on the authority of Ibn ʿAbbās—may God be pleased with him—"On the authority of the Messenger of God—may God bless him and grant him peace—that he was asked about a child born among a people who had what a woman had and what a man had, how would it inherit? The Prophet—may God bless him and grant him peace—said: 'From where it urinates.'" And this is how it was narrated on the authority of ʿAlī—may God be pleased with him—and this is how it was narrated

> on the authority of Jābir b. Zayd, Qatāda and Saʿīd b. al-Musayyib—may God be pleased with him—that one inherits from where one urinates. This is a ruling that the Arabs used to follow in the pre-Islamic era, as it is narrated that a judge among them was brought to adjudicate such an occurrence, and he kept saying that [the child] is a man and a woman. His people thought that was unlikely, so he became confused and entered his house to rest, but kept tossing and turning on his bed and could not sleep because of his confusion regarding this circumstance. He had a daughter [*bunayyyat*^{an}] who nudged his legs and asked him about his thoughts. He told her about that and she said, "Forget the condition and investigate the urination" [*daʿ al-ḥāl wa-abtagh*^{i} *al-mabāl*]. So he went out to his people and ruled accordingly. They approved of that from him. And so we know that his ruling was from the pre-Islamic era and that the Messenger of God—may God bless him and grant him peace—decreed it.[81]

So it was, he wrote, with all humans (*fī l-ādamiyy*) and other animals—the genital organs had a primary purpose, which was urination, and so functioning urination indicated the legal category of the person, any other organs being "additional" rather than necessary. If urine were to come from two organs, then the jurist should rule by precedence—which organ expels the urine first.[82] Furthermore, once this ruling had been made, if the place of urination were to change, the ruling would not change. A court ruling fixed one's legal categorization. Al-Sarakhsī determined this by analogy with other legal situations, such as that of a man who claims to have married a woman and presents evidence of it and obtains a ruling in his favor: the ruling does not change if a second man appears claiming to have married the same woman, even if he also presents evidence. Likewise, once the paternity of a child has been decided, the evidence of any other claimants is ignored.[83] Nevertheless, his Ḥanafī predecessors had disagreed about the test of urination: Muḥammad al-Shaybānī and Abū Yūsuf had both said they knew of no precedents by which they could rule in the case of a *khunthā* who urinated from both organs. They both opted to rule by the abundance [*kathra*] of urine rather than by precedence, on the argument that strength of urination is a better indicator of which genital system is more functional. Al-Sarakhsī argued that the urinary meatus of a woman is wider than that of a man and so quantity or strength of urination is not a good indicator. Abū Ḥanīfa, upon hearing Abū Yūsuf's argument, said that no judge would measure the quantity of urine exiting an infant's body using vessels—this would create an "ugly" display—and he could find no text that spoke to this issue, so he felt obliged to refrain from ruling on it.[84]

Al-Sarakhsī was certain that puberty in the *khunthā* would clear up any ambiguity: "doubt about it does not persist after puberty."[85] If the *khunthā* developed a beard, experienced nocturnal emissions, or was able to have penetrative sex with the phallus, he was a man. If the *khunthā* developed breasts, menstruated, lactated, proved capable of receptive vaginal intercourse, or became pregnant, he was a woman.[86] The *khunthā*'s own assertion that these things had happened would be acceptable to the court, as they are private occurrences, and "the statement of a person is legally acceptable regarding what he tells about that is within him that no one else knows."[87] However, al-Sarakhsī also contradicted the Shāfiʿī position on self-gendering: he argued that a *khunthā* who has been determined to be *mushkil* cannot simply assert "I am a man" or "I am a woman"—such a statement would not be accepted, because "he is distorting what he is reporting about himself, as he does not know anything about that except what others know."[88] These two statements are mutually contradictory—in one, the *khunthā* knows best and can attest to the court as to his internal state and private developments, and in the other, the *khunthā* cannot know his internal state except what is apparent to others and cannot attest to the court. The text also offers a third opinion: that a *khunthā's* father or guardian could state to the court that the *khunthā* is a boy or a girl.[89] Such logical contradictions—common in *tafsīr* and in legal manuals—could result from accreted editing or simply from a desire for comprehensive coverage of precedents that themselves differed. Al-Sarakhsī also followed al-Shaybānī's ruling that a *khunthā* who developed none of these signs was a man, "because the lack of breast growth is legal evidence that he is a man."[90] This contradicted al-Qudūrī's ruling that such a person remained *mushkil*; al-Sarakhsī had asserted that puberty would erase all ambiguity, so he could not explicitly acknowledge ambiguity's continuation. Because a *khunthā* may be born without any genitalia, al-Sarakhsī's ruling allowed for such a person to be declared a man without having a penis.[91]

Al-Sarakhsī on khunthā inheritance

Al-Sarakhsī reported on the formative-era scholars' disagreement over the *khunthā* inheritance share. Abū Ḥanīfa had ruled, as reported by Muḥammad al-Shaybānī, that the *khunthā* should receive the woman's portion except in circumstances where being a male would result in the smallest portion of inheritance.[92] Al-Sarakhsī suggests that this could occur in a case in which a woman dies leaving behind a husband, a full sister, and a half-sibling *khunthā* related to her father. If the half-sibling *khunthā* were male, he would not receive a share, but if the *khunthā* were female, the husband and full-sister would sacrifice a share to a half-sister. Likewise, if a woman were to die leaving behind a husband, a mother, a maternal brother, and a *mushkil* full-sibling, and the *mushkil* sibling is treated as male, then the husband gets half, the mother gets a sixth, and the maternal brother gets a third, and there is nothing left for the male full-sibling. Abū Yūsuf had ruled that a *khunthā* inherits half the share of a man and half the share of a woman,[93] but al-Sarakhsī explains away this ruling as the product of uncertainty, saying that such cases should be adjudicated in a manner that is analogical to that of an ambiguous divorce or ambiguous emancipation of a slave, in which the ruling is made by considering the circumstances (for example, if a man dies after divorcing one of four wives before consummating the marriage, half of the dowry of the divorced wife gets distributed among the remaining wives "according to circumstances").[94] The big difference he perceives is that the *khunthā's* underlying ontological state is uncertain, and in inheritance, one's gender must be known with certainty in order to distribute the shares lawfully: "one is only given the amount that one is certain is due."[95] Thus the allocation of the smallest portion of inheritance to the person of uncertain gender is not due to some kind of inherent gender prejudice nor to assumptions about what role the *khunthā* will play in a family but rather to the understanding that the *khunthā* person is at least male or female—therefore human—and therefore deserving *at least* whatever legal portion of inheritance can be allocated with certainty, which in every case will be the smallest share or no share at all. The smallest share is the certain share.[96] Al-Sarakhsī also balks at arbitrarily ruling a *khunthā* to be male or female: "for how can one rule on that in the absence of evidence?"[97] However, if witnesses testify that the *khunthā* is a boy, and other witnesses testify at the same time that the *khunthā* is a girl, and the *khunthā* is seeking inheritance, al-Sarakhsī said he would accept the evidence of maleness because it provides more inheritance. If the *khunthā* is not seeking inheritance and a man claims the *khunthā* is his wife, al-Sarakhsī said he would rule that she is a girl.[98]

If a man bequeathed a thousand dirhams to an unborn child on condition that it be born a boy, and five hundred if it is a girl, and the child is born a *khunthā*, five hundred should be granted and the remaining five hundred withheld until the *khunthā* reaches puberty. If this were to be decided by analogy to the report from al-Sha'bī, the payment would be seven hundred.[99]

Al-Sarakhsī on purification of the deceased khunthā

If the *khunthā* died before signs of inclination toward male or female appeared, his body would not be washed by a man or a woman, because viewing the private parts is forbidden even after death, and adolescents, like adults, must cover the private parts. "If he is a *mushkil* in whom no type (*jins*) is apparent or his type is not known—whether he is among the men or among the women—then he is excused from it, because of the lack of someone to wash him, and it is like it is impossible to wash him because there is nothing to wash him with, so [the washer] should perform ritual purification with clean earth (*tayammum*), similar to a woman who dies among men with no woman with them, so she should be purified with earth...."[100] Here al-Sarakhsī uses *jins* to indicate sexual type, but the word does not yet have that general meaning, so we still render it "type" rather than "sex." The body should be carried on a bed face down and should be buried by an unmarriageable relative, shrouded like a woman's body, out of caution in case he was a woman, for "whatever is closer to concealment...is more appropriate."[101]

Al-Sarakhsī on khunthā marriage

If a man kisses the *khunthā* with lust, the man is prohibited from marrying the *khunthā's* mother until his situation clarifies (for "to not marry a woman who is permissible is more appropriate than marrying a woman who is forbidden").[102] Curiously, al-Sarakhsī evinces no concern that the man may have been kissing a boy with lust; his only concern is whether the kissing then makes the mother of the *khunthā* off-limits to the man. Marriage arrangements should be suspended until puberty, "because the male enters into marriage as owners [*mālikīn*], and the female becomes property [*mamlūka*] through marriage"[103] and it would not be clear which the *khunthā* would be. If the *khunthā* has an arranged marriage to a woman and turns out to be a man, the marriage is valid. If he is unable to consummate the marriage, the marriage is annulled ("postponed"), just as it would be for someone who was impotent. If the *khunthā* has an arranged marriage to a man and turns out to be a man, the marriage is invalid.[104] Until puberty, the marriage contract is neither approved nor annulled.[105]

Al-Sarakhsī on khunthā dress

A *khunthā* should observe the most restrictive rulings for men and for women in attire: no gold jewelry or silk, in case he turns out to be a man.[106] However, the dress of ritual purity worn during the pilgrimage, *iḥrām*, posed a unique problem, as the requirements for men and women were mutually exclusive. A man cannot wear clothing with sewn seams during *iḥrām*; he must wear ritual garb called *izār* and *riḍā'*. A woman cannot wear *izār* and *riḍā'* but must wear sewn clothing in order to ensure she is properly covered. According to al-Sarakhsī, this contradiction led Abū Yūsuf to refrain from ruling; he said only that he had no knowledge of what should be worn. But Muḥammad al-Shaybānī had ruled that the *khunthā* should wear women's clothing, because the body would be covered in case the *khunthā* was female, and the wearing of female dress in *iḥrām* for a man would be permissible if he had an excuse, and also because the rules for children are not as strict as for mature men.[107] Likewise, the *khunthā* should cover and use the postures of a woman for prayer.[108] Again, al-Sarakhsī accommodates the non-binary body in his adjudication of social rules, but he still understands the body to have an underlying created nature that is male or female. All accommodations for dress are intended to address the uncertainty of the *khunthā* and the possibility that he may be—or may become—male or female.

Al-Sarakhsī's positioning of the khunthā in communal prayers

Likewise, when al-Sarakhsī positioned the *khunthā* for public prayer, he advised the *khunthā* to stand in front of the row of women and behind the last row of men, as had all jurists before him. He explained that this was the most cautious positioning, for

> If he is a man, then his standing in the women's row invalidates his prayer, and if she is a woman, then her standing with the men invalidates the prayer of those to her right, to her left, and behind her, parallel to her. Adolescents are like adults in this case. So if he stands in the men's row in front of the women's row, we are certain that his prayer and the prayers of all the people are permissible. But if he stands in the women's row, I prefer that he repeat the prayer. Because the reason for the obligation of prayer upon him is known, and the waiver of this performance is doubtful, and taking precautions in the matter of worship is more preferable to me....[109]

If the *khunthā* were to stand in the men's row, his own prayer would be valid, but the men to his right, left, and behind would have to repeat their prayers.[110] This consistent positioning would mark the *khunthā* as a nonbinary person. If there were only one *khunthā* praying at a small mosque, that person would always be in a line alone behind the men and in front of the women.[111] This positioning might have operated to encourage pre-pubescent nonbinary people to choose a legal category and assimilate, which would have permitted them to pray with the men or with the women.

If the *khunthā* were to die and be prayed over in a ceremony in which there were also a male and a female corpse, al-Sarakhsī placed the man's body closest to the imam, then the *khunthā* behind the man, and the woman behind the *khunthā*, "as in life," for the row of men in communal prayer is closer to the imam than the row of *khunthā*s. For this ruling, al-Sarakhsī added evidence to the discussion, adducing a Prophetic *ḥadīth* that said, "Let those who are closest among you to dreams and prohibition be closest to me, then those who come after them," and so the Prophet (PBUH) had ordered that those who were more preferred should be closer to him. Al-Sarakhsī also noted that the Qur'an acknowledged men to have an edge over women. By analogy, the funerary placement of a man should be closer to the imam than that of the woman or the *khunthā*. And if they were all buried together in a single grave, then a barrier of earth should be placed between them and the man's body should be placed on the side facing the *qibla*, the *khunthā* next to him, and then the woman, "because the direction of the *qibla* is more honorable and the man is more deserving of being close to it."[112] This positioning confirmed the gender hierarchy in which men were socially superior to women. It also confirmed the social positioning of the *khunthā* as a third legal category between men and women,[113] such that the socio-legal status of a *khunthā* was different from the ontological status as a male or female creation. This point is of critical importance for contemporary law: the *khunthā* body, whether *mushkil* or assimilated to the gender binary, was of uncertain legal status. It was mutable. It was evidence that bodily conformation was not perfect evidence of one's created sex. In al-Sarakhsī's rulings, as in those of jurists before him, the *khunthā* constituted a third gender epistemologically, while ontologically the *khunthā* remained a male or female creation.

Al-Sarakhsī: the khunthā in criminal law

Al-Sarakhsī's rulings substantially follow those of al-Shaybānī. For crimes such as slander or theft, the *khunthā* is subject to the same punishments as men and women but is not subject to retaliation because al-Sarakhsī assumes all *khunthās* are pre-pubescent and thus not legally liable.[114] If someone slanders the *khunthā*, no punishment can be carried out against the slanderer because the punishment would depend on whether the victim is male or female. Male or female identification being indiscernible, no punishment can be carried out.[115] Similarly, the right of retaliation for injury cannot be granted a *khunthā*, because crimes of women against men and vice versa do not entail retaliation, and retaliation is a punishment that can be averted when there is a state of doubt. However, retaliation for loss of life does not differ whether the victim is male or female, so if a *khunthā* is killed, retaliation can be granted.[116]

Al-Sarakhsī also denies the *khunthā* the right of testimony, since he believes that a *khunthā* must always be pre-pubescent, and only adults can give testimony.[117] If the *khunthā* apostatizes, he is not subject to the death penalty. The death penalty is a punishment that is averted by doubts; furthermore, the *khunthā* is assumed to be a child and cannot be subjected to legal punishments.[118] If a non-Muslim believer (*dhimmi*), he is not subject to jizya.[119]

The compiler of the text noted that al-Sarakhsī also ruled that if the *khunthā* is an adult and prays without a veil, "she" must repeat the prayer, but if an adolescent, she does not. This contradicts al-Sarakhsī's premise that *khunthā* ambiguity always resolves after puberty; he nevertheless offers a resolution for that situation: "…it is inconceivable that he would remain *mushkil* after reaching puberty" but "if it is conceivable," then the ruling requiring a non-veiled *khunthā* to repeat the prayer covers that eventuality.[120] He also notes that a *khunthā* must remain covered in the presence of men or women and cannot be alone with either a male or female who is not an unmarriageable relative.[121] Nor did he allow the *khunthā* to travel alone or with a female *maḥram*, for if the *khunthā* were female, then that would be two women traveling alone together, which was forbidden.[122] These rulings suggest al-Sarakhsī implicitly acknowledged the possibility of a *khunthā* whose status remained ambiguous after reaching puberty.

Al-Sarakhsī on hypotheticals relating to manumission

The issue of uncertainty also plays a significant role in al-Sarakhsī's discussion of hypotheticals related to divorce and manumission. If a man swears to divorce his wife if she births a boy, or if he tells a slave girl that she is manumitted if she births a girl, but the woman births a *khunthā*, then, in al-Sarakhsī's judgment, neither divorce nor manumission could occur until the child's condition clarifies itself.[123] Al-Sarakhsī explains that this is drawn from analogy to a case in which a man swore that if he did not enter a person's house, he would free his slave. He then died without anyone knowing whether the condition for manumission had been fulfilled: the slave is not freed due to the uncertainty.[124] Likewise, if a man states that every male slave of his is free, or every female slave of his is free, any *khunthā* slaves he has will not be freed. This again points to the epistemological distinction between a *khunthā* and a man or woman: a *khunthā* is neither but potentially either. Ontologically, the *khunthā* is one or the other, but which one is uncertain. Therefore one cannot be certain that the *khunthā* is either male or female, so the *khunthā* cannot be freed if "male" or "female" is specified in the manumission document. But if the slave owner were to say "all my male and female slaves are free," then *khunthā* slaves are freed on the assumption that they will turn out to be either male or female.[125] If a man swore to divorce his wife if he owned a male slave, and he bought a *khunthā*, the wife is not divorced. If on the other hand he swore to divorce his wife if he owned male or female slaves, and he bought a *khunthā*, she would be divorced because it is certain that the *khunthā* is one or the other.[126]

Al-Sarakhsī on circumcision and khilāf al-jins

Al-Sarakhsī followed precedent on the circumcision of the *khunthā*, but again his reasoning is interesting. A *khunthā's* private parts were unviewable until he matured into male or female identity, except in the case of a slave girl purchased by the *khunthā*. Al-Sarakhsī ruled that it was forbidden for one type (*jins*) to view the genitals of the opposite type (*khilāf al-jins*) outside of legitimate sexual relationships. Before al-Sarakhsī in this debate, the idea of male and female as opposites had not yet been broached. Male and female were paired; they were complementary. That did not mean they were opposites. Al-Sarakhsī says in the section on identification that males and females are so different as to be opposites; here he uses a phrase that is equivalent to the modern expression, "the opposite sex."

The slave girl provided a solution to the dilemma entailed: If the *khunthā* were female, then the slave girl is a female looking at a female, which was permissible. If the *khunthā* were male, then the slave girl is a female slave looking at her owner. This was also permissible. Al-Sarakhsī is here following the earlier ruling of al-Shaybānī, for although al-Sarakhsī does not explicitly say "viewing" is related to circumcision or change of legal category, he adds that if the *khunthā* is insolvent, the imām must buy a female slave from the treasury, who then looks at him, and is then resold and the money returned to the treasury—for the money in the public treasury is to be used for the interests of Muslims, "and this is part of it."[127] Thus al-Sarakhsī both asserts that male and female bodies are binary opposites and upholds the principle that care of non-binary bodies is a public duty.

After al-Sarakhsī: Ḥanafī consensus and points of debate

All subsequent discussions of the *khunthā* in Ḥanafī law respond implicitly to these arguments. For example, the Ḥanafī jurist al-Marghīnānī (d. 593/1196–7 CE), who studied with one of al-Sarakhsī's students, recapitulates almost completely the rulings of al-Sarakhsī on identification, prayer positioning, veiling and prayer posture, not wearing jewelry or silk, covering in the company of men and women, traveling with a male *maḥram*, manumission, washing of the body with earth, funeral prayer, and burial in a common grave.[128] He repeats al-Sarakhsī's rulings but excises the lengthy rationales, even retaining the order in which al-Sarakhsī, and before him al-Shaybānī, discussed the subjects. He clarifies that the slave woman to be bought either from the *khunthā*'s own funds or from the public treasury is for the purposes of circumcision (as al-Qudūrī had ruled), and he resolves the dispute over what the *khunthā* should wear for *iḥrām* by ruling that the *khunthā* must wait until after puberty to enter *iḥrām*, by which time the ambiguity should have resolved.[129] Al-Marghīnānī also excises al-Sarakhsī's long discussion of the various inheritance possibilities and offers up without rationale only his own preference for Abū Ḥanīfa's ruling: the *khunthā* receives the female's inheritance portion.[130] As for the *khunthā's* authority to assert his own maleness or femaleness, al-Marghīnānī allows it for all *khunthā*s except those who have previously been designated as *mushkil*. He does not provide any other detail, so the question of whether a court investigation could allow a *mushkil* child to prove the development of pubertal sex characteristics is left open.[131] Al-Marghīnānī offers no rulings on *khunthā* marriage: if the *khunthā's* uncertainty resolves at puberty, then presumably adult marriage is permitted. Al-Marghīnānī's "Chapter on the *Khunthā*" is also positioned at the very end of his book, almost like an appendix, along with advice on other disabilities, such as muteness.

From the 1300s, we have two more Ḥanafī contributions: the *Kanz al-Daqā'iq* by al-Nasafī (d. 1310 CE), which became the quasi-official legal manual of the early Ottoman empire, and the *Tatarkhaniyya* by Indarpati (d. 1381 CE) of the Delhi Sultanate. Al-Nasafī, however, only echoed positions that had been argued by al-Sarakhsī. Only a person with mixed genitalia could be identified as a *khunthā*. Urination from a penis meant the *khunthā* was a boy; urination from a vulva meant a conclusive female designation. Only simultaneous urination from both would result in the identification of a person as truly non-binary (*mushkil*). At puberty, growth of a beard or sexual relations with women were indicators of maleness; breasts, lactation, menstruation, pregnancy, or receptive intercourse were indicators of femaleness. In communal prayer, the non-binary *khunthā* stands between the men and women; the *khunthā* is circumcised by a female slave, to be bought with public funds if necessary; in inheritance matters, the non-binary *khunthā* inherits the woman's share. However, al-Nasafī contradicted al-Sarakhsī on one important point: he held that at puberty, it was possible that no indicators of inclination to male or female would appear or that indicators would continue to be contradictory, such that a *khunthā* could remain non-binary in maturity.[132] The *Tatarkhaniyya* also echoed al-Sarakhsī's rulings, but unlike al-Nasafī, it upheld al-Sarakhsī's argument that a *khuntha's* ambiguity only persisted until puberty.[133]

Ibrahīm al-Ḥalabī (d. 956/1549), the Ottoman jurist whose *Multaqā l-abhur*, written in 1517, replaced al-Nasafī's manual as official reference for Ottoman Ḥanafīs, made some subtle changes to legal interpretation. Much of what he wrote appears at first to be standard Sunni rulings on identification of an infant gender of rearing and criteria for *mushkil* legal status.[134] Appearance of a beard, nocturnal emissions, or ability to perform insertive sex means the *khunthā* can adopt male categorization—but the text stops short of saying the *khunthā is* a man because of these things. Likewise, menstruation, pregnancy, breast development, lactation, or receptive vaginal sex mean the *khunthā can be a* woman but not that the *khunthā* necessarily *is* a woman. And, most critically, al-Ḥalabī broke with the rulings offered by al-Shaybānī, al-Sarakhsī, and the *Tatarkhaniyya* on the question of adult *khunthās* and followed al-Nasafī: he ruled that indicators of legal category may continue to conflict after puberty.[135] Then al-Ḥalabī wrote: "When one confirms that there is uncertainty, proceed with caution (*akhadha fīhi bi-l-aḥwaṭ*)." If the legal category remains uncertain, then: "he prays with a veil and stands between the rows of the men and the women, for if he were to stand in their line, the [men] standing beside him and women behind him would have to repeat [their prayers], and if he is with the women, he would have to repeat [his prayers]."[136] The way al-Ḥalabī words his explanation indicates subtle shifts in intent: he wants to ensure that those who pray together in the mosque do not have to repeat their prayers. His concern is for their salvation and their comfort, and to protect the community from any *fitna* (social disorder) that might result from resentment of a person whose gendered presence invalidates prayers.

Al-Ḥalabī's understanding that ambiguity might resolve in adulthood also subtly affected his ruling on manumission. Whereas previously, scholars had agreed that a slave owner's statement that "every male" or "every female slave should be freed" would not apply to a *khunthā*, al-Ḥalabī allowed for a *khunthā* slave to be emancipated after "his circumstance has been clarified (*yastabin*)."[137]

In all other rulings, al-Ḥalabī chose for the *khunthā* the path that observed the strictest precautions: in dress, veiling, travel, and circumcision. This protected the *khunthā's* own hope of salvation. Like al-Sarakhsī, al-Ḥalabī did not forbid a *khunthā* from marrying. The text specifies the presence of an "unmarriageable relative" to accompany the *khunthā* to the marriage, as though in case the *khunthā* turns out to be a woman.[138] Nevertheless, while appearing to follow established precedent, his rulings diverge in significant ways from previous Sunni rulings. For example, al-Ḥalabī followed precedent on positioning of the *khunthā* body in a multi-gender funerary service, but specified that a *khunthā* corpse purified by *tayammum* should also be wrapped in five winding sheets, and that neither male nor female should lament at the tomb.[139] Al-Ḥalabī also reported the same divergent rulings on inheritance as had his predecessors, but instead of following Abū Ḥanīfa's ruling that due to the uncertainty of the *khunthā's* status, a *khunthā* was due at least a woman's share, he followed al-Sha'bī's ruling that the *khunthā* should inherit half of the male portion and half the female portion.[140] Here al-Ḥalabī departed from the ruling that was legally certain and chose the ruling that affirmed the *khunthā* as non-binary, between male and female.

Al-Ḥalabī also departed from previous Ottoman practice by ruling that a *khunthā* could present to a court and declare a male or female legal category.[141] Al-Marghīnānī had previously ruled that a court should not accept a *khunthā's* assertion of legal category unless there were some physical signs present to provide evidence for the claim.[142] A footnote clarifies that in a *khunthā mushkil*, there would be no physical signs of male or female inclination, so the individual would have to be certain of this "in his own self" (*amīn fī ḥaqq nafsihi*). Al-Ḥalabī asserts: the *khunthā's* statement of legal category "will be accepted."[143] However, if the uncertainty of legal category had already been resolved, and the *khunthā* were to reverse course, the court would not accept the reversal. Once again, the courts fixed one's legal category.

Ḥanbali rulings on the khunthā

Unlike the jurists previously discussed, the Ḥanbali jurist Ibn Qudāma (d. 620H/1223 CE), author of *al-Mughnī*, the most influential Ḥanbali legal manual of its era, considered the *khunthā* as a possible legal category on almost every issue for which gender would be relevant. His rulings on *khunthā*s appear throughout the text, similar to the Shāfiʿī organizational scheme, rather than collected for easy reference in a single chapter as was the Ḥanafī preference. The impact of this socially would therefore be much greater, as a person would not just encounter the possibility of medial gender when dealing with a petition related to a case of gender ambiguity but also when looking up information about, for example, whether one could pray behind a female imām or characteristics that affect the value of slaves.

Ibn Qudāma on identification

On the issue of how to legally categorize someone with ambiguous genitalia, he wrote that a *khunthā* had either both a penis and a vulva or no genitalia except a vulvar urinary exit. A *khunthā* who exhibited signs of masculinity or femininity *was* a man or a woman, but a man or woman "in whom there is an extra feature."[144] He noted that "among us privilege (*mazya*) goes to one of the two indicators," meaning genital indicators of sex; if genitalia were ambiguous, then the test of urination would be used to assign a gender of rearing. Only if the urine issuing from both exits were equal would a person be assigned *khunthā mushkil* legal status.[145]

As a Ḥanbalī, Ibn Qudāma took pains to adduce narrated evidence for this practice, first to previous Sunni scholars and through them to reports from the Prophet. His proximate source was Abū Bakr Muḥammad b. al-Mundhir of Nishapur, a third-generation Shāfiʿī, but he noted that those who narrated the same precedent included "ʿAlī, Muʿāwiya, Saʿīd b. al-Musayyab, Jābir b. Zayd, the people of Kufa, and all the scholars," and then he appended al-Kalbī's narration of the Prophetic tradition—the same used by the Ḥanafīs—but on the authority of Ibn al-Labbān.[146] He preferred precedence of urine to abundance, because this preference had been narrated by Ibn al-Musayyib and because this, he claims, had been the "explicit" ruling of Aḥmad b. Ḥanbal. Ibn Ḥanbal, he said, had only used abundance if the urine came at the same time from both organs, as narrated by al-Awzāʿī (d. 774 CE.).[147] Ibn Qudāma also explained why the urinary exit was so prominent in legal reasoning: "because it is found in the young and the old. All other signs only occur after adulthood, such as the growth of a beard, the development of breasts, the emission of semen, menstruation, and pregnancy."[148] Urination was also a determiner of legal personhood, according to another Prophetic ḥadīth that said a *khunthā* from the Anṣār of Medina had been brought to Muḥammad (PBUH) and he had told them that inheritance from the infant would commence the first time it urinated.[149]

Ibn Qudāma also elaborated on the second method of legal categorization, narrated on the authority of ʿAlī and al-Ḥassan, that of counting ribs. Ibn al-Labbān had pointed out that ribs were as much a permanent part of the body's structure as was the urinary meatus, so if men and women had unequal numbers of ribs, then there would be no need to examine urination.

Jābir bin Zayd had suggested the third mechanism of distinction. He argued that ability to direct a stream of urine is what distinguished men from women, so that a *khunthā* should be made to urinate next to a wall. If the *khunthā* can urinate on the wall, the *khunthā* is a man. If the urine dribbles between the thighs, the *khunthā* is a woman.[150] This method, said Ibn Qudāma, was insufficiently reliable.[151] Consequently, jurists preferred the test of urination.

Ibn Qudāma on khunthā inheritance

On the question of inheritance, Ibn Qudāma reported disagreement among jurists. He reported that "the majority said" that the "matter is stopped until he reaches maturity," when signs of maleness or femaleness would appear. There are three implications of this: first, that he believed in the 1200s that the majority of jurists to that point held puberty would resolve all ambiguity; second, the existence of a majority meant there also existed a minority who held ambiguity persisted after puberty, i.e., there was no consensus; third, that inheritance portions could not be fully distributed until ambiguity had been resolved. Ibn Qudāma said that the correct ruling on inheritance would be to award the share of inheritance that is certain, which is the woman's share, and pay out to all the other heirs what they would have received had the *khunthā* been unambiguously male, and withhold the difference until the *khunthā* matures, and then to spend some significant effort on the determination of legal category. If the *khunthā* matures as a female, that remainder can be paid out to the heirs; if the *khunthā* matures as a male, the remainder can be paid to him.[152]

Unlike the jurists previously discussed, Ibn Qudāma tells us that he had personal experience with two petitioners who had neither male nor female genitalia.[153] Thus he knew from his own experience that it was possible for a *khunthā* to remain *mushkil* after puberty. This would occur if "there do not appear on him any signs."[154] One petitioner described to him a vulval area with nothing present but "protruding flesh like a hill, from which urine constantly leaks." The second had a single hole used for both urination and defecation, something that can happen when the embryonic cloaca does not develop into separate urinary, vaginal, and digestive canals.[155]

Ibn Qudāma asked the first person how he dressed (using male pronouns). "He told me that he only wears women's clothing, mixes with them, flirts with them, and considers himself a woman."[156] In considering these cases, Ibn Qudāma also made reference to a story he had heard: "I was told that in some Persian countries there is a person who has no exit at all, neither a vagina nor anus, and he only vomits what he eats and drinks."[157] These people were also *khunthā mushkil*, he decided, the only distinction being that there was no way to categorize them by urination. If no other signs appeared to distinguish them legally, they would remain *mushkil* beyond puberty.[158]

Ibn Qudāma ruled in these cases that:

> he inherits half the inheritance of a man and half the inheritance of a female as transmitted by Aḥmad and this is the ruling of ['Abd Allāh] b. 'Abbās [d. 687]; al-Sha'bī; Ibn Abī Laylā [d. 83 /702–3]; "the people of Medina and Mecca," [Sufyān] al-Thawrī [d. 778]; Hasan b. Ziyad al-Lu'lu'ī; Shārik [b. 'Abdullah b. Abi Namir]; Ḥasan bin Ṣāliḥ; Abī Yūsuf; Yaḥyā b. Ādam [d.818]; Ḍarār b. Ṣard and Na'īm b. Ḥamād. And Abū Ḥanīfa allotted him the inheritance of the worst of his condition and gave the rest to the other heirs. And al-Shāfi'ī and those with him gave the certain and kept the remainder until his condition clarified itself or they were generally recognized.[159]

Abū Ḥanīfa bequeathed only what was certain (the woman's share), while al-Shāfi'ī and those who followed him bequeathed what was certain and withheld the rest until the *khunthā* matured.[160]

Ibn Qudāma then devoted a whole chapter to the problem of the inheritance of the *khunthā mushkil* and the various arguments about how to divide the shares when the *khunthā* is receiving half the male and half the female share. He preferred the argument of the "*madhhab al-Munazzalīn*," which he says is also preferred by his associates. In this method, the inheritance is calculated once as if the *khunthā* is male, and once as if female, or the female share is calculated and multiplied by two to get the male share. The shares are then divided by two and that number added to each of the male and female shares to get the amount to distribute to the *khunthā*.[161] According to Ibn Qudāma, this method is derived from a ruling of al-Thawrī and al-Lu'lu'ī on an inheritance in which there was a son, a daughter, and a child *khunthā*: the son would receive four shares, the *khunthā* three, and the daughter two. So, the son receives twice that of the daughter, and the *khunthā* half of both. He pronounced this solution "acceptable."[162]

There might also be situations in which a *khunthā* is either responsible for or is the recipient of maintenance funds. If the *khunthā* is the responsible party, the responsibility varies by amount of inheritance received. If he matures as female and is therefore not responsible for maintenance, the *khunthā* is eligible for return of funds that he had paid out prior to demonstrating femaleness. If he matures as male and is responsible for a greater share of maintenance, others may be able to claim funds from him.[163]

Ibn Qudāma on qiṣāṣ and diya

On matters of injury and *diya* payments, Ibn Qudāma ruled that any injury incurs payment.[164] However, if a *khunthā mushkil* loses a penis, testicles, or labia, retaliation cannot be awarded immediately, because if the injury is to penis or testicles and the *khunthā* matures as female, or if the injury is to labia and the *khunthā* matures as male, the injured organs would be judged as superfluous. If the *khunthā* chooses *diya*, compensatory payment, then the certain payment can be awarded, which is the smallest amount, and a ruling will be made for the other parts. If all genitalia are severed, then the *diya* for the labia is awarded—because it is the least amount and therefore certain—and a ruling will be made on the penis and testicles. But "if he despairs of his condition being revealed," the *khunthā* should be awarded half the *diya* for the penis and testicles, and half the *diya* for the labia, and a ruling should be rendered on the remaining half.[165] The phrase "if he despaired of his condition being revealed" suggests that a *khunthā* was not automatically isolated by medial positioning in a mosque. Most *khunthā*s would probably live assimilated to either binary legal category, unrevealed. That being revealed might cause despair also suggests that designation as *khunthā* was, at least in Ibn Qudāma's context, socially undesirable.

Ibn Qudāma states that "scholars of opinion" had ruled that a murdered *khunthā* is due half the diya for a male and half that for a female. He relates al-Shāfiʿī's ruling that the only obligatory payment is that due to a female, because that is certain, and that the doubts about maleness make any further payment optional. However, Ibn Qudāma wrote, "He is potentially masculine and feminine in a single potentiality [*annahu yaḥtamil*ᵘ *al-dhukūriyya wa-l-unūthiyya iḥtimāl*ᵃⁿ *wāḥid*ᵃⁿ], and we have despaired of revealing his condition, so it is necessary to mediate between them and act according to both potentialities."[166] This, I think, expresses the *khunthā*'s status most clearly: the *khunthā* legal category is a category whose essence is uncertainty and potentiality. The *khunthā* is either male or female but discernible as neither and therefore potentially either. The *khunthā* is the classical Islamic version of Schrodinger's cat. Like a cat trapped in a box with a radiation-triggered poison, which one cannot know to be dead or alive until the box is opened, a *khunthā* is potentially both male and female until observation proves the *khunthā* to be one or the other. Just as for the quantum physicist the cat is simultaneously dead and alive, for the jurist the *khunthā* is both male and female. And just as the quantum physicist knows that the cat cannot in our reality be both dead and alive at the same time, the jurist's binary gender references do not permit him to imagine a *khunthā* who is actually both male and female.

Ibn Qudāma on manumission

Ibn Qudāma's discussion of manumission highlights the ambiguity of juridical reasoning on the *khunthā*. He addressed situations in which a will specifies that a slave be freed after its owner's death. If the will specifies freeing *aḥd raqīqī* ("one of my slaves"), then the general practice was to cast lots to determine which slave should be freed. But if the will says to free *aḥd ʿabīdī* ("one of my slaves," grammatically male), the assumption is that the slave should be male, so neither a female nor a *khunthā* may be freed. Likewise, if a will says to free *aḥd ama* ("one female slave") neither a male nor a *khunthā* may be freed. This is because the *khunthā* is not known to be either a male or a female. Ibn Qudāma clarifies that if the *khunthā* is not *mushkil*, then male *khunthā*s can be freed with male slaves, and female *khunthā*s with female slaves.[167] This is interesting because the wording displays how the *khunthā* who has assimilated into male or female legal status is still carrying the sublimated status of *khunthā*; they *are* male or female but at the same time are also still *khunthā*. There is only one reason for *khunthā* categorization to persist as a sublimated identity after someone has been categorized as male or female: recognition that *khunthā* sex is malleable. Although jurists try to limit changes of legal category, literary accounts (see chapter two) testify that they happened.

Conclusion

The earliest generation of Sunni Muslim legal scholars wrote little if anything about intersex. It was the second generation, the transmitters, those who elaborated law in the years while the legal schools were still developing, who first confronted a sufficient number of cases or petitions regarding non-binary bodies such that they had to elaborate rules to accommodate them. This happened in the context of the ʿAbbāsid imperium, in population centers where, given even a low occurrence rate of 1 visibly intersex birth in every 1,500, there could still be perhaps 50–70 intersex people.

By the 1000s, Sunni legal manuals typically paid at least cursory attention to the existence of non-binary bodies and the need to accommodate them. Shāfiʿī manuals exhibit somewhat different concerns than Ḥanafī and Ḥanbalī manuals. Shāfiʿīs focused on categorical reasoning, in which certain sets of rules applied to "men" and others to "women," and those categories were assumed to entail fundamentally different social roles.[168] This led al-Shāfiʿī to argue, based on Qur'anic text, that every *khunthā* was in fact male or female, even if there was no means by which a human could discern sex. Ideally, some physical sign would appear, but if none did, a person's internal inclinations could serve as indicators. Such statements became embedded in Shāfiʿī discourse on the *khunthā* and influenced some Ḥanafī jurists as well, notably al-Sarakhsī. Ḥanafī jurists tended to focus their concern on issues that would affect social functioning, such as the positioning of a *khunthā* for congregational prayer where they would not accidentally invalidate others' prayers. Shāfiʿī jurists exhibited more concern for the protection of certainty as a guarantor of rights, such as in the disallowance of menstruation, ejaculation, beard development, and lactation as indicators of puberty on the grounds that both sexes could exhibit these indicators. Ḥanbalī jurists sought textual evidence in the form of *ḥadīth*s. Underlying these slight differences was a shared notion, either explicit or implicit, that the existence of an epistemological category for non-binary persons did not imply its ontological existence. The existence of non-binary bodies in the social world did not mean God created them to be non-binary.

The fact remained that non-binary bodies required accommodation so that they could fulfil their religious obligations and receive their rights, so jurists developed elaborate rules that constructed the *khunthā* as a medial being in a social world in which bodies were gendered along a hierarchically arranged spectrum from male to female. In this arrangement, men were protectors, owners, providers; women were protected, owned, maintained.[169] In the mosque, the *khunthā* stood behind the men and boys and in front of the women. In funerary rites, a *khunthā* body was placed between a body of a man and that of a woman, with the men closest to the imām. *Khunthā*s observed the most restrictive form of dress for either sex: veiling and no gold jewelry or silk, and sewn clothing for pilgrimage. Regarding issues of inheritance and compensation for injury or death, attention had to be paid to the possibility that the *khunthā* could change from uncertain to male or female: only what was certain could be granted. Likewise, a *khunthā mushkil* slave would not be freed by emancipatory clauses in wills that used gendered words for "slave" such as *ʿabīd* or *ama*, because a *khunthā mushkil* might be, but could not be proved to be, male or female. The Qur'an may have told believers that they were created male or female, but a non-binary person entangled in such a network of rulings, would have experienced gender as neither male nor female, but somewhere in between.

Notes

1 See Chapter Two of this volume, entitled "The Intersex Character (*al-khunthā*) in Classical Arabic Lexicography and Literature."

2 Norman Calder, *Studies in Early Muslim Jurisprudence* (Oxford: Clarendon Press, 1993).

3 Ash Geissinger, *Gender and Muslim Constructions of Exegetical Authority*: A Rereading of the Classical Genre of Qur'ān Commentary (Leiden: Brill, 2015), 4, 14–15.

4 Calder, Early Muslim Jurisprudence," 55.

5 Mālik b. Anas, *al-Mudawwana* (Beirut: Dār al-Kutub al-'Ilmiyya, 1994 ed.), 4: 448, 530.

6 Mālik b. Anas, *al-Mudawwana*, 2: 173; Idem, *al-Mudawwana* (Dār al-Buḥūth al-Islāmiyya, 1423/2002 ed.), 4: 9–10.

7 Abū al-Ḥasan 'Alī b. Muḥammad b. Muḥammad b. Ḥabīb al-Baṣrī al-Baghdādī al-Māwardī, *Kitāb al-ḥāwī l-kabīr fī fiqh madhhab al-Imām al-Shāfi'i wa-huwa sharḥ Mukhtaṣar al-Muzanī*, ed. 'Alī Muḥammad Mu'awwaḍ and 'Ādil Aḥmad 'Abd al-Mawjūd (Beirut: Dār al-Kutub al-'Ilmiyyah, 1419/1999), 8:168, 12:211.

8 Abū Ḥanīfa, *Kitāb al-Āthār of Imām Abū Ḥanīfa: The Narration of Imam Muhammad b. al-Hasan ash-Shaybani.* ed. Ibn Rajab al-Ḥanbali, Yahya and Safira Batha, Shams al-Ḍuḥā Muḥammad. English translation by 'Abdaṣṣamad Clarke, 223–4, no. 389. Muḥammad comments that the person who is miserable is "miserable in his mother's womb," i.e., born to misery, whereas someone who is fortunate "draws admonition from others," i.e., learns from experience. He does not comment on male/female.

9 Abū Ḥanīfa, *Kitāb al-Āthār*, 231, no. 402.

10 Questions have been raised about the authenticity of this attribution (Calder, *Early Muslim Jurisprudence*, 39), but Mehmet Boynukalın argues that much of the writing bears characteristic phraseology, such as "This is in analogy to the saying of x." Analogies drawn from al-Sha'bī's ruling are mentioned twenty-four times in the *Book of the Khunthā*, according to Boynukalın ("Introduction," Muḥammad al-Shaybānī, *al-Aṣl*, ed. Mehmet Boynukalın, 13 vols. (Beirut: Dār Ibn Ḥazm li-l-Ṭibā'a wa-l-Nashr wa-l-Tawzī', 2012), 1: 66–7). The phrasing and terminology are also distinctively different from other, later versions (113). The *Book of the Khunthā* is mentioned by early authors as having been one of the original books that al-Shaybānī later edited to appear as a single unit (106, 115, 120).

11 Al-Shaybānī, *al-Aṣl*, 9:321.

12 Ibid

13 Ibid., 9: 322, 335. Likewise, the 'Ibāḍī theologian Jābir bin Zayd (d. 711) and the Medinan jurist Sa'īd bin al-Musayyab (d. 715) are both reported to confirm these rulings (9: 322).

14 Ibid., 9: 322.

15 Ibid., 9: 322–323, 325 (lactation), 334, 342. Abū Yūsuf asserted that any khunthā who reached puberty would not remain *mushkil*. Absence of any signs of gendered status would result in the khunthā being declared male (329).

16 Ibid., 9: 323.

17 Ibid., 9: 322–325, 327.

18 Ibid., 9: 322–5.

19 Ibid., 9: 325.

20 Ibid., 9: 327.

21 Ibid., 9: 324.

22 Ibid., 9: 325.

23 Ibid., 9: 326.

24 Ibid., 9: 327. In a hypothetical scenario in which two *khunthā mushkil*s marry one another on the grounds that one must be male and the other female, Abū Yūsuf said he would neither permit nor invalidate the marriage, because he would not know if the marriage was impermissible until their statuses were clarified. Prior to maturity, neither could inherit from the other. If they died and their parents were also all dead, and the heirs presented evidence that their own relative was male and the other female, Abū Yūsuf considered all the evidence to be contradictory and invalid, even if a prior ruling approving one set of evidence existed (9: 333).

25 Ibid., 9: 325.

26 Ibid., 9: 330–2. In cases where sworn statements conflicted, they were held to nullify each other. Prior evidence that elicited a ruling took precedence over later conflicting evidence, but if no jurist had yet ruled, the later evidence nullified both. If a *khunthā* died and the mother and guardian claimed he was male, but the heirs claimed the *khunthā* was a girl, the female share would be awarded unless the mother and guardian provided evidence of their claim (331). If a *khunthā* self-asserted male or female status, but someone claimed the contrary, e.g. the *khunthā* claimed male status that would lessen the shares of heirs who claim he is a girl, he would need to provide evidence, e.g., prior marriage to a girl (332).

27 Ibid., 9: 333–4. For example, if a *khunthā* adolescent of uncertain age has witnesses swearing that he is a boy and witnesses swearing that he is a girl, and there are no signs on him that a judge would recognize as male or female, Abū Yūsuf said he would rule that the *khunthā* was a boy if he was a claimant to an inheritance, and invalidate the contrary evidence. But if there were a man claiming the *khunthā* as his wife, then he would rule that the *khunthā* is a girl, make her his wife, and invalidate the other evidence (333–334). If then a woman comes forward and says he is her husband and the evidence is invalid, then the matter would be postponed until his legal status is clarified. If nothing was at stake, Abū Yūsuf would postpone hearing any evidence until the *khunthā*'s status clarified (334). If he were to mature with a beard and breasts, with ambiguous genitalia, then legal status would be determined by place of urination (334).

28 Ibid., 9: 331.

29 al-Shaybānī, *al-Aṣl*, 9: 335–7. The inclusion of the *khunthā*'s children, such as "the *khunthā* son's daughter" (337) also suggests that the category *khunthā* was not the same as modern "intersex," as most of the genetic mutations that result in intersex also reduce or eliminate fertility. XY males with hypospadias would be fertile and yet be categorized as *khunthā* due to the location of the urinary outlet; we would not today consider such a person to be intersex.

30 Ibid., 9: 346.

31 Ibid., 9: 327, 329, 342.

32 Ibid., 9: 323–5.

33 Ibid., 9: 333.

34 Ibid., 9: 327 (insufficient), 331 (sufficient). Inconsistencies like this are among the factors that Calder used to judge *al-Aṣl* a multi-author book (*Early Muslim Jurisprudence*, 39 49).

35 Al-Shāfiʿī, *Risāla*, trans. Majid Khadduri as *Treatise on the Foundations of Islamic Jurisprudence*. 2nd ed. (Cambridge: Islamic Texts Society, 1987 [Johns Hopkins, 1961]), 98.

36 Ibid., 103, 105, 247, 305, 311, 325.

37 Muḥammad b. Idrīs al-Shāfiʿī, *Kitāb al-Umm*, ed. Rifa'at Fawzī ʿAbd al-Muṭṭalib (Mansura: Dār al-Wafā', 2001), see for example 2: 151.

38 Abū Abdullah Muḥammad b. Idrīs al-Shāfiʿī, *al-Umm*, 2nd edition (Beirut: Dār al-Fikr, 1403/1983), 6:26–27; Abū Abdullah Muḥammad b. Idrīs al-Shāfiʿī, *al-Umm*, with *al-Mukhtaṣar* by Abū Ibrahīm

Ismā'īl bin Yaḥyā al-Muzanī. With an introduction by Ḥasan 'Abbās Zakī (N.p.: Dār al-Sha'b, 1968), 6: 21.

39 Al-Shāfi'ī, *al-Umm*, 1968, 6: 22; 1983, 6: 114–115, 131.

40 Ibid., 1968, 6: 22; 1983, 6: 26–27.

41 Ibid., *al-Umm*, 1968, 6: 22.

42 Ibid

43 Ibid., *al-Umm*, 1983, 5: 43. Contradictory urination evidence could lead to the marriage being annulled. Someone who married a *khunthā* who asserted female status but urinated like a man, or one who asserted male status but urinated like a woman, could have their marriage annulled.

44 Ibid., *al-Umm*, 1968, 6: 22.

45 Ibid

46 Ibid

47 Ibid., *al-Umm*, 1983, 1: 198.

48 Ibid., 1: 314.

49 Ibid., 4: 172.

50 Ibid., 3: 239.

51 Ibid., *al-Umm*, 1968, 6:114; 1983, 5:38, states that a *khunthā* who lactates is "most likely a woman." The 1983 edition is also uncertain about the ontological status of a man who breastfeeds: "(Al-Shāfi'ī—may God Almighty have mercy on him—said): I do not think that a man should have milk. If he has milk and breastfeeds a female child with it, I would dislike him marrying her, and if his son marries her, I would not annul it, because God Almighty mentioned the breastfeeding of mothers, and mothers are females, and parents are not mothers" (5:38). These two categories, "mothers" and "fathers," were binary opposites in his reasoning: "It is not permissible for the ruling of fathers to be the ruling of mothers, nor for the ruling of mothers to be the ruling of fathers. God Almighty has distinguished between their rulings" (5:38).

52 Abdullah b. 'Abd al-Raḥmān al-Dārimī, *Sunan al-Dārimī*, Book 21, *ḥadīth* no. 2881.

53 *Sunan al-Dārimī*, Book 21, *ḥadīth* no. 2880; listed as *ḥadīth* no. 3012.

54 Ibid., *ḥadīth* no. 2882.

55 Geissinger, *Gender and Muslim*, 9.

56 Ibn Kamāl Pasha, *Sharḥ tajwīd al-tajrīd fī majmū' rasā'il 'allāma Ibn Kemāl Bāshā*, ed. Ḥamza el-Bekrî (Istanbul: Dār al-Lubāb, 2018), 1: 18.

57 Ahmad ibn Muhammad al-Quduri, *Le statut personnel en droit musulman hanefite*. Trans. Georges Henri Bousquet, Leon Bercher (Paris: Recueil Sirey, 1953), Arabic text on pp. 213; Arabic text also available with an outdated English translation as *The Mukhtasar Al-Quduri: A Manual of Islamic Law According to the Hanafī School*, under author's name Imam Abu'l Husayn Ahmad Ibn Muhammad Ibn Ahmad Ibn Ja'far Ibn Hamdan al Baghdadi, translated by Taher Mahmood Kiana (London: Ta-Ha Publishers, Ltd., 2010).

58 Al-Quduri, *Le statut*, 213.

59 Women were circumcised: all the earliest texts refer to the necessity of ablutions after "the two circumcised parts" meet, but the fact that women *were* circumcised does not tell us *how* they were circumcised. Given that prevailing theories of conception in 'Abbāsid medical texts held that a woman had to orgasm in order to conceive, one hopes that circumcision practices did not damage clitoral functioning. The question then is whether those who performed circumcisions were aware of the connection between clitoris to orgasmic ability.

60 Al-Quduri, *Le statut*, 215.

61 Al-Quduri, *Le statut*, 215–7.

62 There is more similarity between Ḥanafī and Ḥanbalī areas of concern than between either of them and Shāfiʿī areas of concern. The one point on which the *madhāhib* agreed was that a *khunthā mushkil* should stand between lines of men and women in the mosque (Al-Māwardī, *Kitāb al-ḥāwī al-kabīr*, 2:174), although al-Māwardī also specified that boys should stand behind men, and *khunthā*s after the boys, and the women behind them (2:340).

63 Al-Māwardī, *Kitāb al-ḥāwī al-kabīr*, 11: 410. I owe thanks to Kecia Ali for pointing me to Shāfiʿīs' discussion of "the khunthā who lactates."

64 Al-Māwardī, *Kitāb al-ḥāwī al-kabīr*, 11: 410. One wonders what al-Māwardī would make of someone with mosaic XX/XY karyotype who is part male and part female on the cellular level, or of species that are all female and reproduce parthenogenically. The natural world is demonstrably not as binary as he thought.

65 Al-Māwardī, *Kitāb al-ḥāwī al-kabīr*, 9: 380–2; 11: 411–3.

66 Ibid., 9: 383–4.

67 Ibid., 9: 380; 11: 410. Al-Māwardī did not permit a *khunthā mushkil* who has not yet declared an inclination toward either male or female to have sexual relationships (9: 389).

68 Ibid., 9: 382. For accounts of this case, see Saqer Almarri, in "You Have Made Her a Man Among Men: Translating the Khuntha's Anatomy in Fatimid Jurisprudence," *Transgender Studies Quarterly* 3, nos. 3-4 (2016):578–86, and Indira Falk Gesink, "Intersex in Islamic Medicine, Law, and Activism," in *The Routledge Handbook on Islam and Gender*, ed. Justine Howe (London: Routledge, 2020), 119.

69 Al-Māwardī, *Kitāb al-ḥāwī al-kabīr*, 12: 91.

70 Ibid., 1: 96.

71 Ibid., 3: 18.

72 Abū Zakāriyā Muhyī al-Dīn Yaḥyā bin Sharaf al-Nawawī, *Rawdat al-Ṭālibīn wa Umdat al-Muftīyīn*. 3rd. ed. 12 vols. ed. Zuhair al-Shāwīsh (The Islamic Office, 1412 AH / 1991), 6:42.

73 Al-Māwardī, *Kitāb al-ḥāwī al-kabīr*, 8: 168.

74 Ibid., 11: 520.

75 Ibid., 18: 290.

76 Ibid., 8:168–70.

77 Muḥammad b. Aḥmad b. Abī Sahl Shams al-A'imma al-Sarakhsī, *Kitāb al-mabsūṭ*. 31 vols. (Egypt: Maṭba'at al-Saʿāda, 1906–1913), "Kitāb farā'iḍ al-khunthā," 30:91. This chapter title only appears in the Arabic-language version.

78 Al-Sarakhsī, "Kitāb farā'iḍ al-khunthā," *Kitāb al-mabsūṭ*, 30: 92.

79 Ibid

80 Ibid., 30: 92, 93.

81 Ibid., 30: 103.

82 Ibid., 30: 103.

83 Ibid., 30: 104. A less coherent version of the same argument is given on 30: 112.

84 Ibid., 30: 104

85 Ibid

86 Ibid., 30: 105. The pronoun disagreement is in the original: *fa huwa imra'at*un.

87 Ibid., 30: 104.

88 Ibid., 30: 110. This point is reiterated less coherently on 30: 114. If a *khunthā* has previously gone to the court to declare himself *mushkil* but later claims to have become male or female, the second presentation of evidence will not be accepted. This seems to contradict the passage on secondary sexual development at puberty, in which al-Sarakhsī asserts that a *khunthā*'s gender must clarify at puberty. This would require that the *khunthā* be determined *mushkil* in childhood, and would permit a second presentation of evidence at puberty. Therefore we should understand this passage

to mean that an adult *khunthā* would not be permitted to declare themselves *mushkil* and later change their mind.

89 Ibid., 30: 112.

90 Ibid

91 This implies that in medical practice it is unnecessary to assign an XY infant born without a penis to female gender. A penis is not essential for male rearing. Compare Alireza Mirshemirami, et al., "Penile Agenesis: Report on 8 Cases and Review of Literature," *Iranian Journal of Pediatrics* 19, no. 2 (2009): 173–9.

92 Al-Sarakhsī, "Kitāb farā'iḍ al-khunthā," *Kitāb al-mabsūṭ*, 30: 92.

93 Ibid

94 Ibid., 30: 93.

95 Ibid

96 Al-Sarakhsī spends several pages outlining hypothetical inheritance situations involving *khunthā*s and what the *khunthā* share would be using either method of calculation (30: 93–102), and the option to withhold part of the inheritance until the *khunthā* attains puberty (30: 93–94). He also explains further some of the disagreement: that Muḥammad disagreed with the division of property that would result from al-Sha'bī's ruling, whereas Abū Yūsuf interpreted al-Sha'bī's ruling as equating the *khunthā* either with two-thirds a son or one-and-one-half a daughter (30:94) and therefore plausible from the point of certainty. I have read modern medical cases in which multiple children from the same family inherit intersex variations, so I no longer regard these as impossible occurrences and therefore hypothetical circumstances.

97 Al-Sarakhsī, "Kitāb al-khunthā," *Kitāb al-mabsūṭ*, 30: 101.

98 Ibid., 30: 114.

99 Ibid., 30: 109.

100 Ibid., 30: 105. He details under what conditions the washer should use a rag or not.

101 Ibid., 30:105–6.

102 Ibid., 30: 106.

103 Ibid

104 Ibid. A third party comments that the shaykh (al-Sarakhsī) could have also used rules about looking at genitals to discuss marriage. If the *khunthā* is a woman and marries a woman, looking at the genitals is legal but the marriage is invalid (30: 110).

105 Ibid., 30:113. The guardians have the right to contract the marriage, but the *khunthā* must be mature for the marriage to be approved, and the married parties could turn out to be two males, or two females, or if both parties are *khunthā*, the bride and groom might be reversed. If the *khunthā* is not *mushkil*, the marriage is permissible (30: 114).

106 Ibid., 30: 106.

107 Ibid

108 Ibid., 30: 106–107.

109 Ibid., 30: 106.

110 Ibid., 30: 107.

111 Saqer Almarri, "Non-binary sexual and gender identities in the community: the khuntha as an isolated being in the mosque," *Body and Religion* 3, no. 2 (2020):166–87.

112 Al-Sarakhsī, "Kitāb al-khunthā," *Kitāb al-mabsūṭ*, 30: 107.

113 Indira Gesink, "Intersex Bodies in Premodern Islamic Discourse: Complicating the Binary," *Journal of Middle East Women's Studies* 14, no. 2 (2018): 152–73, at 164–5.

114 Al-Sarakhsī, "Kitāb al-khunthā," *Kitāb al-mabsūṭ*, 30:108.

115 Ibid

116 Ibid
117 Ibid., 30:109.
118 Ibid
119 Ibid
120 Ibid., 30:108.
121 Ibid
122 Ibid., 30:109.
123 Ibid
124 Ibid
125 Ibid., 30:110.
126 Ibid
127 Ibid
128 ʻAlī b. Abī Bakr b. ʻAbdul Jalīl al-Farghānī al-Marghīnānī, *Kitāb bidāyat al-mubtadī* (Cairo: Muhammad Ali Subh Library and Printing Press, n.d.), 266–7.
129 Ibid., 266. This edition has a misprint in the text, *ummuhu* for *ama*, so that it reads as if it says his mother buys for him a circumciser instead of a slave girl being bought to circumcise him, but the next line clarifies that the imām buys an "ama."
130 Ibid., 267.
131 Ibid
132 Abū al-Barakāt ʻAbdullah bin Aḥmad Al-Nasafī. *Kanz Al-Daqā'iq*. ed. Sāʻid Bakdāsh (N.p.: Dar Al-Bashair Al-Islamiyyah, Dar Al-Siraj, 1432/2011), 684.
133 Khayr al-Dīn Al-Ramlī, *al-Fatāwā al-khayriyya li-naf al-bariyya ʿalā madhhab al-Imām al-Aʿzam Abī Ḥanīfa al-Nuʿmān* (Beirut: Dār al-Maʿrifa, 1974–), 2: 205–8.
134 All citations in this chapter unless otherwise noted are from Ibrāhīm bin Muḥammad bin Ibrāhīm al-Ḥalabī, "Kitāb al-khunthā," *Multaqā l-abḥur*, annotated by Wahbī Sulaymān Ghāwjī Al-Albānī, vol. 1 (Beirūt: Mu'assasat al-Risāla, 1989), 334–6. A cut-down version, text stripped of its commentary and/or footnotes (and that there was commentary is evident from the amount of text per page), is available at al-Maktaba al-Shamila: Ibrāhīm al-Ḥalabī, *Majma' al-anhur fī sharḥ Multaqā l-abḥur*, ed. Khalīl Imran al-Mansur, Beirut: Dār al-Kutub al-ʻIlmiyya, 1998; The English version by E. Abu Bakr, Mia Brandel-Syrier, and Ibrāhīm M. Ḥalabī, *The Religious Duties of Islam As Taught and Explained by Abu Bakr Effendi*, Leiden: Brill, 1971, does not include the chapter on the *khunthā*, only a statement that "hermaphrodites" must stand behind the boys and in front of the women during prayer (67).
135 Al-Ḥalabī, *Multaqā*, 1:335. It will be important for a future scholar to assemble multiple manuscripts of this ruling to assess whether this interpretation is borne out across different versions.
136 For an example of such resentment, see the story in which ʻAbbāda the *mukhannath* struck an imām because he made the congregants repeat the prayers after leading them while in a state of ritual impurity (Abū Saʻīd Manṣūr bin al-Husayn Al-Ābī, *Nathr al-durr*, ed. Munīr Muḥammad al-Madanī, [Cairo: al-Hi'a al-Miṣriyya al-ʻAmma lil-Kitāb, 1990], 7:313–4). The story is intended as a humorous anecdote but still illustrates the point. Having to repeat prayers because a *khunthā* was discovered to have changed gender would be annoying at the least.
137 Al-Ḥalabī, *Multaqā*, 1:336.
138 Ibid., 1:335. Note too that this ruling on circumcision is present in al-Nasafī.
139 Ibid
140 Ibid., 1:336.
141 I want to make clear: al-Ḥalabī was departing from Ottoman practice as represented in al-Nasafī's legal manual. The precedents for courts changing a person's gendered legal category by decree

stretch all the way back to the earliest years of the Islamic state. Al-Qāḍī al-Nu'man (d. 974) records the earliest case, attributed to the reign of 'Alī, in which a wife enters the court of the judge Shurayḥ and demands separation from her husband on grounds of having fathered a child with a slave girl (Abū Hanīfa al-Nu'mān, *Da'ā'im al-islām wa-dhikr al-ḥalāl wa-l-ḥarām wa-l-qaḍāyā wa-l-aḥkām 'an ahl bayt Rasūl Allāh* [Cairo: Dar al-Ma'ārif, 1969], 1/2: 387–90).

142 Al-Marghīnānī, *Bidāyat al-mubtadī*, 267.

143 Al-Ḥalabī, *Multaqā*, 1: 336.

144 Abū Muḥammad 'Abd Allah bin Aḥmad ibn Qudāma, *al-Mughnī. Mukhtasar by Abū Al-Qāsim 'Umar bin Ḥusayn bin 'Abdullah bin Aḥmad Al-Kharqī*. ed. Ṭaha Al-Zaynī, Maḥmūd 'Abd al-Wahhāb Fāyed, 'Abd al-Qādir 'Aṭṭa, and Maḥmūd Ghānem Ghaith. 10 vols. (Maktabat Al-Qāhira, 1968), 6:336.

145 Ibn Qudāma, *al-Mughnī*, 6:336.

146 Ibid

147 Ibid

148 Ibid

149 Ibid

150 Ibid

151 Ibid

152 Ibid

153 Ibid., 6:339.

154 Ibid., 6:336.

155 Ibid., 6:339–40.

156 Ibid., 6:640.

157 Ibid

158 Ibid

159 Ibid., 6:336. Restated on 6:337. He also mentioned a report by Abū Thawrūdārdū Ibn Jarīr on a ruling that he considered "invalid": in Basra, some people determined the inheritance of a *khunthā* by allocating first what was certain—the woman's share—and then making a legal claim (*al-da'wā*) on what remained, but among those who made claims were some who were "originally slaves" (6:336).

160 Ibid., 6: 337. On this point, Ibn Qudāma notes ambiguously "Abū Thawra, Dawūd, and Ibn Jarīr said the same" (6: 337).

161 Ibid

162 Ibid. He then works out a number of permutations with different numbers and gender distributions of heirs (6: 337–8) and for situations where gender makes a difference between inheriting and not inheriting (6: 338–9), which he said he derived from Abū al-Khaṭṭāb's "Al-Hidāya" (6: 338).

163 Ibid., 8: 220.

164 Ibid., 8: 328.

165 Ibid

166 Ibid., 8: 486.

167 Ibid., 10: 462.

168 Kecia Ali, *Marriage and Slavery in Early Islam* (Cambridge: Harvard, 2010), 15.

169 Ibid

Bibliography

Al-Ābī, Abū Sa'īd Manṣūr b. al-Ḥusayn. *Nathr al-durr*. Vol. 7. edited by Munīr Muḥammad al-Madanī. Al-Hi'a al-Miṣriyya al-'Amma lil-Kitāb, 1990.

Abu Bakr, E., Mia Brandel-Syrier, and Ibrāhīm M. Ḥalabī. *The Religious Duties of Islam As Taught and Explained by Abu Bakr Effendi*. Leiden: Brill, 1971.

Abū Ḥanīfa. *Kitāb al-Athār of Imām Abū Ḥanīfa: The Narration of Imam Muhammad ibn al-Hasan ash-Shaybani*. edited by Ibn Rajab al-Ḥanbali, Yaḥyā and Safīra Batha, Shams aḍ-Ḍuḥā Muḥammad. English translation by 'Abdaṣṣamad Clarke. Turath Publishing, 2007.

Ali, Kecia. *Marriage and Slavery in Early Islam*. Harvard, 2010.

Almarri, Saqer. "Non-binary Sexual and Gender Identities in the Community: the *Khunthā* as an Isolated Being in the Mosque." *Body and Religion* 3, no. 2 (2020): 166–187.

Almarri, Saqer. "You Have Made Her a Man Among Men: Translating the *Khunthā*'s Anatomy in Fatimid Jurisprudence." *Transgender Studies Quarterly* 3, nos. 3–4 (2016): 578–586.

Calder, Norman. *Studies in Early Muslim Jurisprudence*. Clarendon Press, 1993.

Al-Dārimī, 'Abdullah b. 'Abd al-Raḥman. *Sunan al-Dārimī*, Book 21. https://sunnah.com/

Geissinger, A. *Gender and Muslim Constructions of Exegetical Authority: A Rereading of the Classical Genre of Qur'ān Commentary*. Leiden: Brill, 2015.

Gesink, Indira Falk. "Intersex Bodies in Premodern Islamic Discourse: Complicating the Binary." *Journal of Middle East Women's Studies* 14, no. 2 (2018): 152–173.

Gesink, Indira Falk. "Intersex in Islamic Medicine, Law, and Activism." Chapter in *The Routledge Handbook on Islam and Gender*, 116–129. Edited by Justine Howe. Routledge, 2020.

al-Ḥalabī, Ibrāhīm. *Majma' al-Anhar fī sharḥ Multaqā l-abḥur*. edited by Khalīl Imran al-Mansur. Dār al-Kutub al-'Ilmiyya, 1998. https://shamela.ws/book/6185/2013 pp. 467-472.

Al-Ḥalabī, Ibrāhīm b. Muḥammad b. Ibrāhīm. "Kitāb al-*khunthā*." Chapter in *Multaqā l-abḥur*, annotated by Wahbī Sulaymān and Ghāwjī Al-Albānī. Vol. 1. Mu'assasat al-Risāla, 1989.

Ibn Anas, Mālik. *Al-Mudawwana*, 4 vols. Dār al-Kutub al-'Ilmiyya, 1994. https://shamela.ws/book/587

Ibn Anas, Mālik. *Al-Mudawwana*. Dār al-Buḥūth al-Islāmiyya, 1423/2002.

Ibn Ḥanbal, Aḥmad. *Musnad of Imām Aḥmad b. Ḥanbal*. Edited by Shu'ayb al-Arna'ūt, 'Adel Murshid, supervised by 'Abdullah ibn 'Abdul Moḥṣen al-Turkī. Al-Risala Foundation, 2001.

Ibn Kamāl Pasha. *Sharḥ Tajwīd al-Tajrīd in Majmū' rasā'il 'allāma Ibn Kemāl Bāshā*. edited by Ḥamza el-Bekrî. Istanbul: Dār al-Lubāb, 2018.

Ibn Qudāma, Abū Muḥammad 'Abd Allah b. Aḥmad. *Al-Mughnī. Mukhtasar by Abū Al-Qāsim 'Umar b. Ḥusayn b. 'Abdullah b. Aḥmad Al-Kharqī*. edited by Ṭaha Al-Zaynī, Maḥmūd 'Abd al-Wahhāb Fāyed, 'Abd al-Qādir 'Aṭṭa [d. 1403 AH], Maḥmūd Ghānem Ghaith. 10 vols. Maktabat Al-Qāhira, 1968. https://shamela.ws/book/8463/2658#p1.

Al-Marghīnānī, 'Alī b. Abī Bakr b. 'Abdul Jalīl al-Farghānī. *Kitāb bidāyat al-mubtadī*. Muhammad Ali Subh Library and Printing Press, n.d., https://shamela.ws/book/6170/265.

Al-Māwardī, Abū Al-Ḥassan 'Alī b. Muḥammad b. Muḥammad b. Ḥabīb Al-Baṣrī Al-Baghdādī. *Kitāb al-ḥāwī al-kabīr fī fiqh madhhab al-Imām al-Shāfi'ī wa huwwa sharḥ al-Muzanī*. 19 vols. edited by 'Alī Muḥammad Mu'awwaḍ and 'Adel Aḥmed 'Abd al-Mawjūd. Dār Al-Kutub Al-'Ilmiyya, 1419 AH/1999. https://shamela.ws/book/6157.

Mirshemirani, Alireza, Ahmad Khaleghnejad, Hoshang Pourang, Naser Sadeghian, Mohsen Rouzrokh, Shadab Salehpour. "Penile Agenesis: Report on 8 Cases and Review of Literature." *Iranian Journal of Pediatrics* 19, no. 2 (June 2009): 173–179.

Al-Nasafī, Abū al-Barakāt ʿAbdullah b. Aḥmad. *Kanz Al-Daqā'iq*. edited by Sāʿid Bakdāsh. Dar Al-Bashair Al-Islamiyyah, Dar Al-Siraj, 1432/2011 https://shamela.ws/book/14262/549

Al-Nawawī, Abū Zakāriyā Muhyī al-Dīn Yaḥyā b. Sharaf. *Rawdat al-Ṭālibīn wa Umdat al-Muftīyīn*. 3rd. ed. 12 vols. Edited by Zuhair al-Shāwīsh. The Islamic Office, 1412 AH / 1991.

Nuʿmān b. Muḥammad, Abū Ḥanīfah (Al-Qāḍī al-Nuʿmān). *Daʿā'im al-Islām wa-dhikr al-ḥalāl wa-al-ḥarām wa-al-qaḍāyā wa-al-iḥkām ʿan ahl bayt Rasūl Allāh*. 2 vols. Dār al-Maʿārif, 1389 [1969].

Al-Quduri, Ahmad ibn Muhammad. *Le statut personnel en droit musulman hanefite*. Translated by Georges Henri Bousquet and Leon Bercher, with Arabic text. Recueil Sirey, 1953.

Al-Quduri, Ahmad ibn Muhammad. *The Mukhtasar al-Quduri: A Manual of Islamic Law According to the Hanafī School*. edited by Imam Abu'l Husayn Ahmad Ibn Muhammad Ibn Ahmad Ibn Ja'far Ibn Hamdan al Baghdadi. Translated by Taher Mahmood Kiana. With Arabic text. Ta-Ha Publishers, Ltd., 2010. https://www.kalamullah.com/mukhrasar-al-qudri.html.

Al-Ramlī, Khayr al-Dīn. *Al-Fatāwā al-khayriyya li-nafʿ al-bariyya ʿalā madhhab al-Imām al-Aʿzam Abī Ḥanīfa al-Nuʿmān*. Dār al-Maʿrifa, 1974.

Al-Sarakhsī, Muḥammad b. Aḥmad ibn b. Sahl Shams al-A'immah. *Kitāb al-mabsūṭ*. 31 vols. Maṭba'at al-Saʿāda, 1906-1913. https://shamela.ws/book/5423/6059

Al-Shāfiʿī, Muḥammad b. Idrīs. *Kitāb al-Umm*. Edited by Rifa'at Fawzī ʿAbd al-Muṭṭalib. Dār al-Wafā', 2001. Al-Shafiʿī, Muhammad b. Idris. *Treatise on the Foundations of Islamic Jurisprudence*. Translated by Majid Khaddouri. 2nd ed. Islamic Texts Society, 1987; Johns Hopkins, 1961.

Al-Shāfi'ī, Abū Abdullah Muḥammad b. Idrīs. *al-Umm*. 2nd edition. Eight parts in five volumes. Beirut: Dar al-Fikr, 1403/1983. https://shamela.ws/book/1655

Al-Shāfiʿī, Abū Abdullah Muḥammad b. Idrīs. *al-Umm*, with *al-Mukhtaṣar* by Abū Ibrahīm Ismā ʿīl bin Yaḥyā al-Muzanī. With an introduction by Ḥasan ʿAbbās Zakī. Dār al-Shaʿb, 1968.

Al-Shaybānī, Muḥammad. *Al-Aṣl*. edited by Mehmet Boynukalın. 13 vols. Dār Ibn Ḥazm li-l-Ṭibāʿa wa-l-Nashr wa-l-Tawzīʿ, 2012.

CHAPTER NINE

Tracing Difference: Zakariyyā l-Rāzī and the Intersex Body in Classical Persian Medical Discourse*

Mehrdad Alipour

Abstract

In this chapter, I examine how classical Persian medical discourse addressed human diversity through the writings of Abū Bakr Muḥammad b. Zakariyyā l-Rāzī (d. 313/925). Focusing on his conception of how the embryo is shaped and differentiated, I show that he proposed five "sex" and/or "gender" categories of human being: male, female, *khunthā* (roughly intersex), *mukhannath* (effeminate), and *mutarajjil* (mannish). I argue that al-Rāzī diverged from the binary notion of humanity commonly accepted in his time by presenting a biologically grounded, non-hierarchical model of human variation. He identifies five categories without reinforcing a male–female binary or privileging masculinity. Although he medicalizes certain behaviors, such as the connection between effeminacy and male sexual passivity, he refrains from moral judgement and surgical intervention. Finally, I discuss the reception of al-Rāzī's non-binary conception in the legal, medical, and literary discourses of Muslim culture.

Keywords: Persian medicine, classical typology of human being, intersex person (*khunthā*), effeminate (*mukhannath*), mannish (*mutarajjil*), Zakariyyā l-Rāzī

Introduction

In recent decades, while modern scholarship on intersex topics has gradually advanced in the West through medical, gender, and religious studies, Islamicists have largely overlooked this topic.[1] Nonetheless, a few scholars have begun to address Islamic juristic traditions related to intersex laws over the past decade,[2] with an even smaller number investigating Muslim medical and bioethical discussions.[3] Notably, two recent studies by Scalenghe and Gesink have specifically examined classical Muslim medical discourse on this subject. Scalenghe analyzed the perspectives of the Andalusian medical expert Khalaf b. ʿAbbās al-Zahrāwī, also known as Abū l-Qāsim or Albucasis (d. 403–4/1013), the author of the thirty-volume medical encyclopedia *Kitāb al-taṣrīf li-man ʿajaza ʿan al-taʾlīf* (The Arrangement of

Medical Knowledge for One Who is Not Able to Compile a Book for Himself), commonly referred to as *The Method of Medicine*.[4] Gesink, on the other hand, studied the Persian physician Ibn Sīnā (d. 438H/1037), the author of *al-Qanūn fī l-ṭibb* (The Canon of Medicine).[5]

Gesink, in particular, contends that, unlike Sanders,[6] classical Muslim scholars perceived biological sex as existing on a spectrum ranging from all-male/protectors to all-not-male/protected. According to this view, intersex individuals occupy a "medial" category.[7] Through an analysis of Ibn Sīnā's medical texts and several Sunni legal works, Gesink challenges Sanders's argument on binary categories and shows that a group of classical Muslim thinkers, including Ibn Sīnā, perceived sex as malleable.[8] According to her, "rather than 'protecting' male privilege, the authors of these texts largely served an individual's health and religious needs."[9]

Nevertheless, these studies are insufficient to fully represent a holistic view of classical Muslim medical experts. Suffice that there were several physicians prior to al-Zahrāwī and Ibn Sīnā, whose scholarships are yet to be explored in this regard, such as the following Persian medical experts: ʿAli b. Sahl Rabban al-Ṭabarī (d. between 240/855 and 250/864) the composer of *Firdaws al-ḥikma* (the Paradise of Wisdom), Abū Bakr Muḥammad b. Zakariyyā l-Rāzī (d. 313/925) the author of *Kitāb al-ḥāwī fī l-ṭibb* (the Comprehensive Book on Medicine) and "*Risāla fī l-ubna*" (A Treatise on Male Passivity) or "*Maqāla fī l-dāʾ al-khafī*" (An Essay on the Hidden Illness), and ʿAlī b. al-ʿAbbās al-Majūsī al-Ahwāzī (d. c. 384/994) the author of *Kitāb kāmil al-ṣināʿa al-ṭibbiyya* (The Complete Book of the Medical Art), also known as *al-Kitāb al-malakī* (The Royal Book). In this chapter I will examine al-Rāzī's medical opinion on intersexuality.

Intersex conceptualization

In classical Muslim discourse, a group of people whose biological appearance and (often) sexual anatomy did not fit the definition of male or female bodies—those who are currently classed as intersex—were commonly referred to as *khunthā* (pl. *khanāthā* or *khināth*), derived from the same root—*kh-n-th*—as *mukhannath* (effeminate, a different category of humankind in Muslim culture).[10] Al-Khalīl b. Aḥmad al-Farāhīdī (d. 175/790–1) defined *khunthā* as individuals who are neither males nor females. This definition implies that such persons are in a separate category from males and females, or that they may be a combination of both. By contrast, al-Jawharī (d. 393/1003) defined *khunthā* as male and female persons who have both female and male sexual organs or genitalia.[11]

These definitions underscore the controversies on the conceptualization of *khunthā*: Does the term denote a male, a female, a blend of both, or neither? Although al-Jawharī's definition prevailed among lexicographers, al-Khalīl's definition has sparked extensive discussion in Islamic medical and juristic literature.[12] Due to limitations on medical knowledge, classical Muslim medical experts were only able to assign a sex to those individuals whose visible sex characteristics, including sexual anatomy and reproductive organs, differed from the norm. Those with different hormonal or chromosomal patterns that had no physical manifestations were categorized as male or female based on their visible sex characteristics. Therefore, classical discussions of *khunthā* did not encompass every individual who at present would be classified as intersex.[13] For example, Ibn Sīnā introduce *khunthās* as those who have neither male nor female sexual organs or those who have both.[14] Al-Zahrāwī on the other hand only refers to those who were born with both genitalia as *khunthās*.[15] According to these experts, the medical treatment for *khunthās* was often to remove the non-functioning/unremarkable organ or, as Albucasis remarks, to carefully remove the extra flesh (*al-luḥūm al-zāʾida*).

Although al-Zahrāwī and Ibn Sīnā refer to some anecdotal marvelous stories about *khunthās*, they have expressed no moral judgment or repulsion or contempt towards intersex people. However, it seems that they both see intersex conditions as types of deformity or disability that needed to be cured. In relation to the typological classification of intersex individuals, al-Zahrāwī's engagement with the topic appears to be markedly minimal. His scholarly focus is predominantly on the application of surgical techniques aimed at enabling intersex individuals to conform to the functional roles of either male or female.

However, as Gesink notes, Ibn Sīnā's surgical recommendations for intersex people, in contrast to Sanders' views,[16] were not intended to protect "real men" from the presence of those considered incomplete.[17] This is evident in Ibn Sīnā's focus on the treatment of women's sexual organs and the excision of "extra flesh" from the uterine opening, as his aim was to achieve alignment between a woman's sexual perception and her physical appearance. This approach sought to enhance psychological well-being and sociosexual function, while also providing relief from pain upon request. Gesink further concludes that Ibn Sīnā did not adhere to a rigid binary conception of sex.[18]

It is accurate that Ibn Sīnā sought to align an individual's sexual perception with their physical characteristics to enhance psychological well-being and sociosexual functioning. His concerns, however, extend beyond merely the removal of excess flesh from a woman's uterine opening or the excision of additional sexual organs in individuals with intersex characteristics (*khunthās*). Following his discussion on *khunthās*, Ibn Sīnā devotes several chapters to the sexual organs of both males and females, examining their deficiencies, sizes, and possible remedies. He advises physicians to be proactive in helping individuals optimize their sexual pleasure and function. Ibn Sīnā also proposes various treatments, including penile enlargement, vaginal narrowing, and the removal of excess flesh.[19]

However, Gesink may overinterpret Ibn Sīnā's text regarding *khunthā*, where she suggests that Ibn Sīnā recommended surgery for those seeking relief. The text does not clarify whether such surgery was intended only for adults or if it was also performed on infants at their parents' request. It is plausible that such surgeries might have been carried out during infancy, without the *khunthā*'s consent or opportunity to request relief. This is particularly relevant today, as similar surgeries are still performed on infants at their parents' request in many parts of the world, including Muslim-majority countries. Furthermore, while parents often seek medical assistance for their children, it remains unclear whether their primary motivation is to find relief for the child or to avoid social stigma, shame, and ambiguity.[20]

Regarding the typology of *khunthā*, my examination of Ibn Sīnā's texts does not provide evidence that he categorizes *khunthā*s as a distinct category of humanity—neither male nor female. At most, his writings remain ambiguous or silent on whether, following surgery, *khunthā*s would be classified as male or female based on the organ that was removed or retained, or if they would be considered a separate category of human being.

In contrast to Ibn Sīnā and al-Zahrāwī, al-Rāzī does not view surgery as the sole solution for *khunthā*s. Instead, he addresses *khunthā*s by elaborating on the biological factors that lead to an infant becoming a *khunthā*, and he further develops a typology of intersex individuals among other categories of humanity. In the remainder of this chapter, I will examine al-Rāzī's perspective on this topic.

Al-Rāzī's position on *khunthā*

Al-Rāzī does not address *khunthā*s in his masterpiece *al-Ḥāwī*, except for where he briefly references a scholar named al-Hindī, who offers an explanation for why an embryo might be born as a girl, a boy, or a *khunthā*.[21] According to this view, the amount of semen (*manī*) released by a male and female during sexual intercourse is considered the crucial factor in determining the embryo's sex. By calculating the amount of semen released by each partner, based on the timing of the end of the previous menstruation period and the start of the new one, one can speculate whether the embryo will be male or female. If both the male and female release equal amounts of semen, the embryo would be classified as a *khunthā*. This perspective seems to align with views attributed to classical Greek physicians. Al-Rāzī does not further elaborate on this issue or provide a positive or negative assessment of this position. I will come back to this point later in this chapter.

However, in a treatise titled *Risāla fī l-ubna* (A Treatise on Male Passivity, also known as *Maqāla fī l-dā' al-khafī*: An Essay on the Hidden Illness), al-Rāzī extensively addresses issues related to *khunthās*. He categorizes three distinct categories apart from the male and female categories: *khunthā* (intersex), *mukhannath* (effeminate), and *mutarajjil* (mannish), describing these as variations on a spectrum between purely masculine male and purely feminine female. Thus, moving beyond a binary framework, he conceptualizes five distinct categories of humans as follows (see figure: 6):

1. Purely masculine male/man
2. Purely feminine female/woman
3. Effeminate (*mukhannath*)
4. Mannish (*mutarajjil*)
5. Intersex (*khunthā*)

In the remainder of this chapter, I will examine al-Rāzī's perspective as presented in this treatise. The discussion will be structured into three sections. First, I will elaborate on the various manuscripts of the treatise that have been discovered to date. Next, I will outline the content of the treatise. Finally, I will analyze al-Rāzī's position as reflected in the text and conclude with remarks drawn from this examination.

The manuscripts

It was known to scholars that al-Rāzī had a treatise called *risāla fī l-ʾubna* (A Treatise on Male Passivity), also known as *Maqāla fī l-dāʾ al-khafī* (An Essay on the Hidden Illness), because classical bibliographers such as Ibn al-Nadīm (d. c. 380/990) in his *Fihrist*, al-Bīrūnī (d. after 443/1050) in his *Bibliography of al-Rāzī's Books*, and Ibn Abī Uṣaybiʿa (d. 668/1270) in *ʿUyūn al-anbāʾ* mentioned this treatise.

However, the treatise was not discovered or debated by modern scholars until the mid-20th century. The late Iranian bibliographer ʿAbdul-Ḥusayn Hāʾirī (d. 1394sh/2015) expressed considerable excitement upon locating a manuscript containing several medical treatises, including this one, in the Library of Majlis in Iran, describing it as a significant discovery.[22] Similarly, the late orientalist Franz Rosenthal (d. 2003) was equally enthusiastic when he encountered a manuscript that included this treatise in the General Library of Rabat in Morocco.[23]

Currently, several manuscripts of this treatise have been located:

Three manuscripts in the Majlis and Sinā (now Mūza) Libraries in Tehran:

- Majlis, no. 352, Ṭabāṭabāʾī (registration 31059/4679).[24]
- Majlis, no. 6201 (registration 7179/61805).[25]
- Sinā (now Mūza), no. 360 (registration 3258).[26]

One manuscript in the General National Library in Rabat:
- II, 332, no. 2641, shelf-no. 1588d.[27]

Also, an excerpt of this treatise survived in *Bustān al-aṭibbā' wa-rawḍat al-alibbā'* (The Orchard of the Physicians and Garden of the Wise) of Ibn al-Maṭrān (d. 587/1191). Two manuscripts of *Bustān al-aṭibbā'* are found in the following libraries:
- Majlis, no. 3821 (registration 3821/26085).[28]
- kitāb-khāna-yi Malik, no. 94/1.

Furthermore, Shahāb al-Dīn Aḥmad al-Tīfāshī (d. 651/1253) has inserted this treatise in his book entitled *Nuzhat al-albāb fī-mā lā yūjad fī kitāb* (Delight of the hearts regarding what is not to be found in any book), chap.12: *fī l-khināth wa-l-mukhannathīn.*[29] This version is almost identical to the Rabat manuscript, trusting Franz Rosenthal's translation of the manuscript.[30]

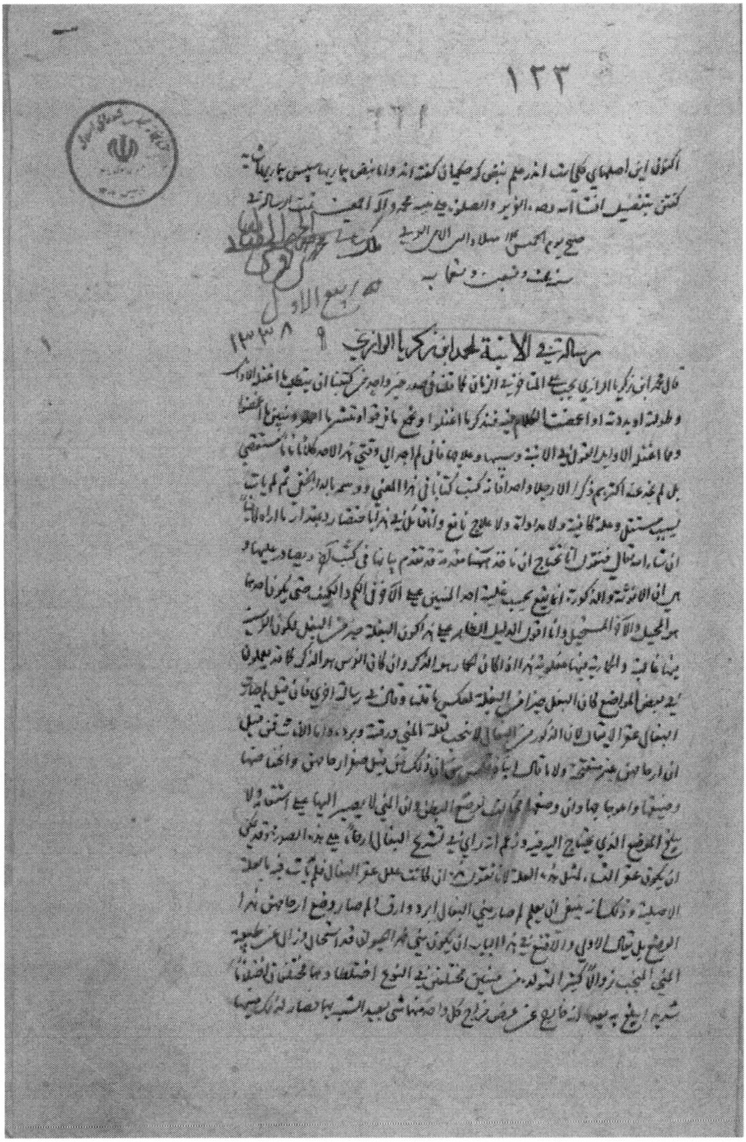

Figure 9.1: Ms. Majlis, no. 352 Ṭabāṭabāʾī, fol. 63v/p. 123

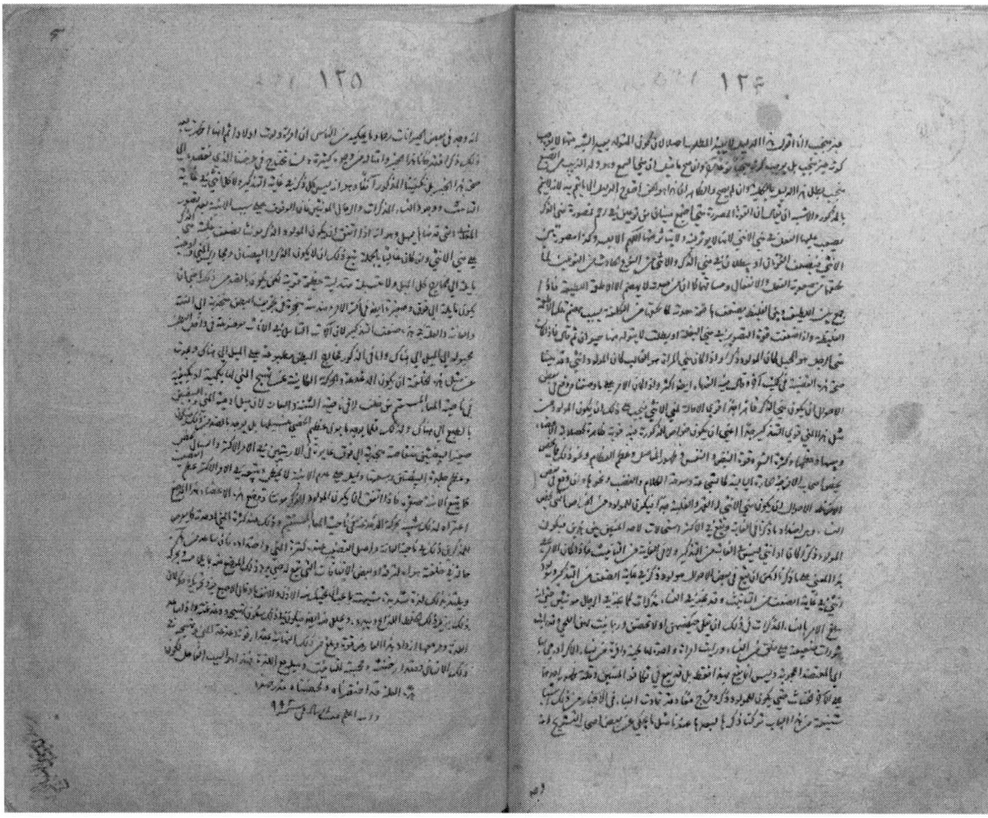

Figure 9.2: Ms. Majlis, no. 352 Ṭabāṭabāʾī, fol. 64r–v/pp. 124–5

Figure 9.3: Ms. Sinā, no. 360, fol. 382r–v

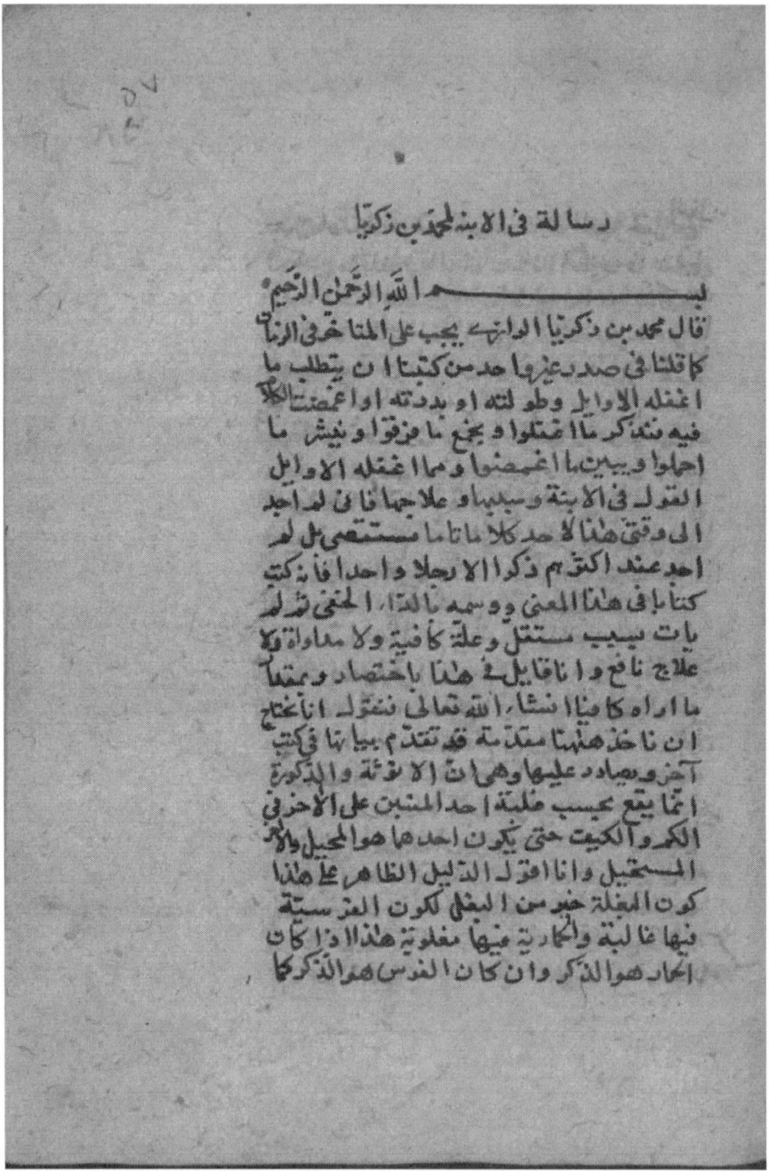

رسالة في الابنة لمحمد بن زكريا

بسم الله الرحمن الرحيم

قال محمد بن زكريا الرازي يجب على المتاخر في الزمان
كما قلنا في صدر غير واحد من كتبنا ان يتطلب ما
اغفله الاوايل وطولته او بددته او اغمضته
فيه فيذكر ما اغفلوا و يجمع ما فرقوا و يبسط ما
اجملوا و يبين ما اغمضوا و مما اغفله الاوايل
القول في الابنة وسببها و علاجها فاني لم اجد
الى وقتي هذا لاحد كلاما تاما مستقصى بل لم
اجد عند اكثرهم ذكرا الا رجلا واحدا فانه كتب
كتابا في هذا المعنى و وسمه بالداء الخفي ثم لم
يات بسبب مستقل و علة كافية ولا مداواة ولا
علاج نافع وانا قايل في هذا باختصار و مبين
ما اراه كافيا ان شاء الله تعالى فنقول انا نحتاج
ان ناخذ ههنا مقدمة قد تقدم بيانها في كتب
آخر و نصادر عليها وهي ان الانوثة والذكورة
انما يقع بحسب غلبة احد المنيين على الآخر في
الكم والكيف حتى يكون احدهما هو المحيل والآخر
المستحيل وانا اقول الدليل الظاهر على هذا
كون البغلة خيرا من البغل لكون الفرسية
فيها غالبة والحمارية فيها مغلوبة هذا اذا كان
الحمار هو الذكر وان كان الفرس هو الذكر كما

Figure 9.4: Ms. Majlis, no. 6201, fol. 30v/p. 57

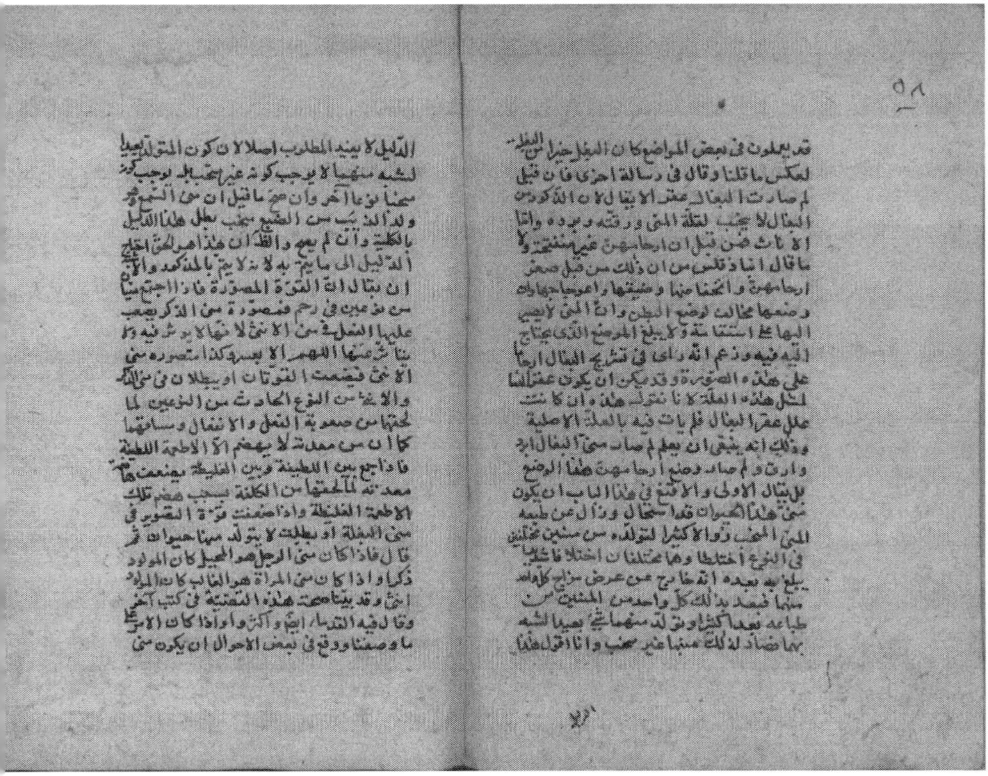

Figure 9.5: Ms. Majlis, no. 6201, fol. 31r–v/pp. 58–9

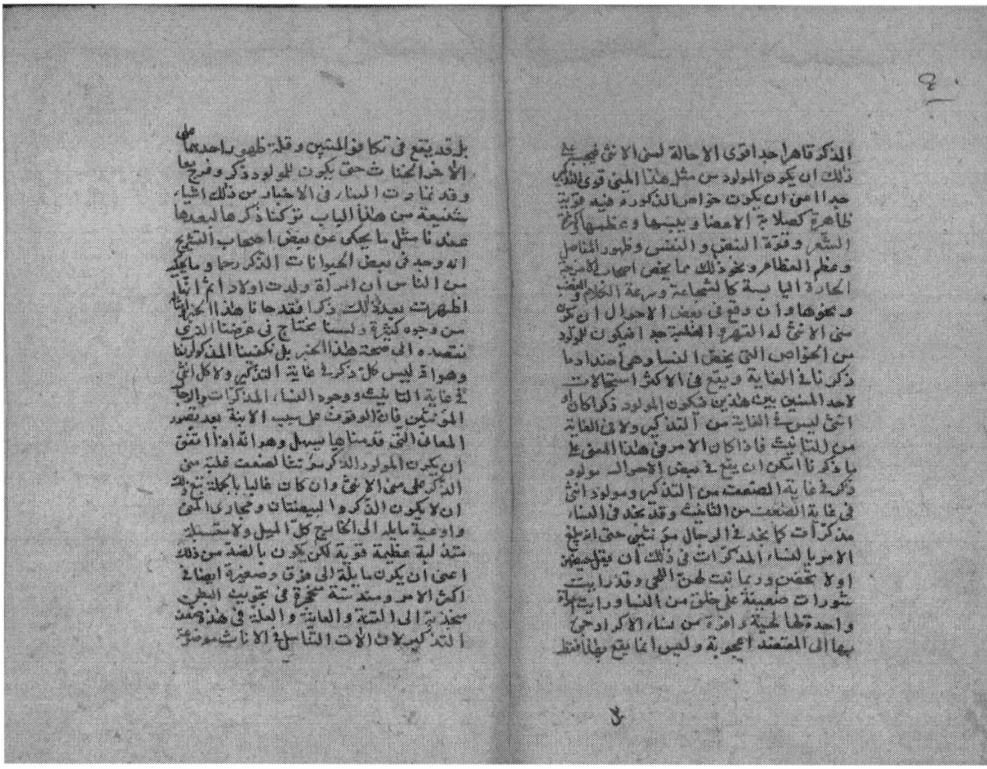

Figure 9.6: Ms. Majlis, no. 6201, fol. 32r–v/pp. 60–1

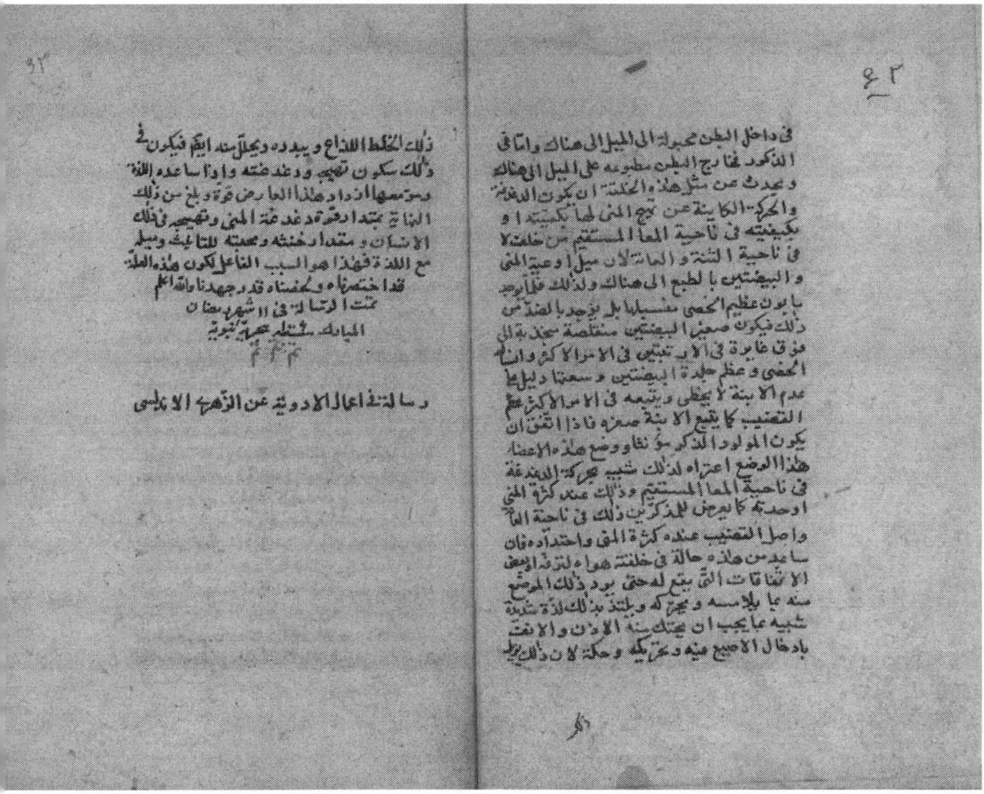

Figure 9.7: Ms. Majlis, no. 6201, fol. 33r–v/pp. 62–3

(ومنهـا):

علیك بزبٍّ وافـرٍ ذي صلابةٍ   ودعْ قولَ ارباب السّفاهةِ واللغو
فما الفرقُ بين اللّذتين لعاقلٍ   وكلتاهما مِنْ حَكِّ عضوٍ على عضوٍ؟

النـوع الثامـن
في سبب الخُناث وعلاجه
على رأي محمّد بن زكريّا الرازيّ

قال مصنّف الكتاب: انا ناقل ههنا مقالةً وجدتها لأبي بكر محمد بن زكريّا الرازيّ في الأُبْنة، بنصّها حرفاً بحرف، ليكون هذا الكتاب بها آخذاً بحظّه من الجدّ والهزل، كاملاً في الاحتواء على طرفي الكلام، الرقيق والجزل.

قال أبو بكر محمد بن زكريّا الرازيّ:

يجب على المتأخّر في الزمان، كما قلنا في صدر غير واحد من كتبنا، أن يطلب ما أغفلته الأوائل أو طوّلته أو أغمضت الكلام فيه، فيذكر ما أغفلوه ويجمع ما فرّقوه ويشرح ما أجملوه ويبيّن ما أغمضوه. وممّا أغفلته الأوائل القول في الأُبنة وسببها وعلاجها، فإني لم أجد فيها لأحد كلاماً مستقصى بل لم أجد عند أحد ذكراً لها إلّا رجلاً واحداً، فإنه كتب كتاباً في هذا المعنى وسَمَه بـ (الداء الخفيّ) ثم لم يأت فيه بسبب ولا علّة كافية ولا مداواة ولا علاج نافع، وأنا قائل في ذلك باختصار وبمقدار ما أراه كافياً إن شاء الله تعالى.

فنقول: إنّا نحتاج أن نأخذ ههنا مقدمة قد تقدم بيانها في كتب أُخَر وهي الأنوثة والذكورة، فإنها إنّما تقع بحسب غلبة المنيين أحدهما على الآخـر في الكمّ والكيف، حتى يكون أحدهما هو المُحيل. فإذا كان منّي الرجل هو المحيل، كان المولود ذكراً. وإذا كان منيُّ المراة هو المُحيل، كان المولود انثى. وقد بينّا صحّة هذه القضية في كتب أُخر وقال فيه القدماء أيضاً وأكثروا. وإذا كان الامر على ما وصفنا وقع في بعض الأحوال أن يكون منيُّ الرجل قاهراً جداً، قويُّ الاحالة لمنيّ الأنثى، فيجب على ذلك أن

Figure 9.8: al-Tīfāshī's insertion of the Treatise (first page of the Treatise)

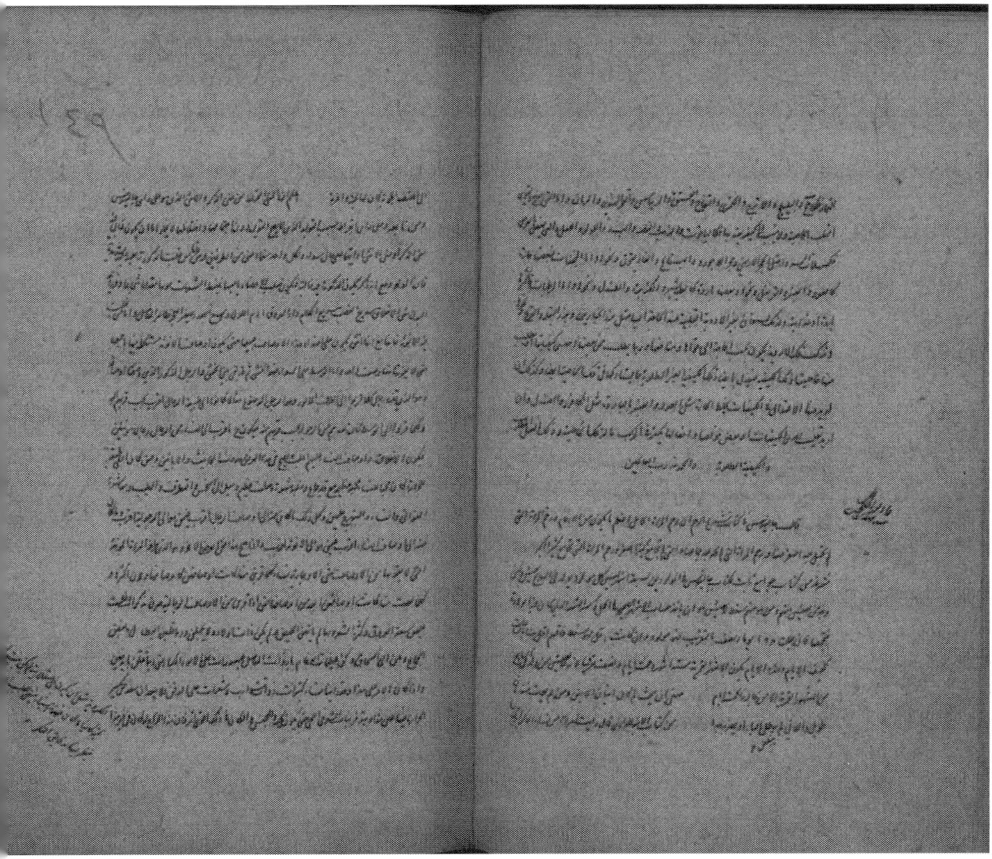

Figure 9.9: Ibn al-Maṭrān's excerpt of the Treatise: Majlis, no. 3821, fol. 149r–v.

The question remains whether we can confidently assert that these manuscripts correspond to the treatise attributed to al-Rāzī. Rosenthal, who produced a critical English edition of the treatise, maintains that its attribution to al-Rāzī is beyond question. Furthermore, as noted, scholars such as Ibn al-Maṭrān in the twelfth century, who excerpted this treatise in his own work, and al-Tīfāshī in the thirteenth century, who incorporated it into his writings, both accepted al-Rāzī's authorship without doubt. These versions closely resemble the manuscripts preserved in Rabat and Tehran.

Name and contents

The treatise has been referred to by slightly different names. In Ms. Rabat, the title appears as "The Essay (*maqāla*) of Abū Bakr al-Rāzī on the Hidden Illness (*al-dāʾ al-khafī*)." Al-Tifāshī identifies it as "An Essay on *Ubna* by Abū Bakr Muḥammad b. Zakariyyā al-Rāzī." The Mss. Majlis, no. 352 Ṭabāṭabāʾī and Majlis, no. 6201/5 refer to it as "A Treatise (*risāla*) on *Ubna* by Muḥammad b. Zakariyyā al-Rāzī," while Ms. Sinā describes it as "On *Ubna*, also one of his compositions and monographs written for some of his friends." Ibn al-Nadīm, al-Bīrūnī, and Ibn Abī Uṣaybiʿa all mention variations of a similar title concerning a treatise on *ubna* and its cure.[31] Unlike others, Ibn Maṭrān refers to it as "The Book on *Ubna* by al-Rāzī," which is unusual, given that the surviving portions of this work can scarcely be classified as a book.

It remains uncertain whether al-Rāzī himself assigned any of these titles to the treatise. However, both terms—"the hidden illness" (*al-dāʾ al-khafī*) and "male passivity" (*ubna*)—originate from al-Rāzī, as he refers to them at the beginning of the treatise:

> One topic that early scholars have largely neglected is the discussion of "male passivity" (*ubna*), along with its causes and treatments… I have found hardly any mention of it by these scholars, except for one man who wrote a book on the subject, which he titled *The Hidden Illness* (*al-dāʾ al-khafī*). However, in it, he neither identified a specific cause nor provided a satisfactory explanation, nor did he offer any medication or useful treatment.

This treatise consists of three sections:
- On typology of humans and the reason behind the birth of different infants.
- On *ubna* and the reason behind it.
- On the medical treatment of *ubna*.

While the Rabat manuscript and al-Tīfāshī's insertion include all the three sections, the Tehran manuscripts contain only the first two parts, omitting the part concerning treatments for *ubna*. Conversely, the Tehran manuscripts feature a lengthy addition not found in either the Rabat manuscript or *Nuzhat al-albāb* of al-Tīfāshī. The passage explores explanations for mule sterility, focusing on physiological and structural theories that al-Rāzī critiques for not addressing root causes. He attributes sterility to *istiḥāla* (transformation), where the mixing of horse and donkey sperm creates incompatible sperm due to deviation from the natural temperament (*mizāj*) of each species. Al-Rāzī further argues that the mutual weakening of formative power in combined sperms leads to sterility, drawing analogies to weakened digestion caused by incompatible food combinations. This addition seems unrelated to the main topic of the treatise, which focuses on the emergence of various types of infants and the cause of *ubna*.[32] According to Rosenthal, much of this addition may not be original to the treatise but instead extracted from other works by al-Rāzī, and incorporated by the compilers of the Tehran manuscripts. However, this observation may not extend to the initial lines of the addition. If these lines were indeed part of the original text, it suggests that both the Rabat manuscript and al-Tīfāshī's insertion might also be excerpts, with a complete version of the treatise still to be found.[33]

It is, however, important to note that the absence of the third section in the Tehran manuscripts does not pose an issue for this study, as the focus is primarily on the first section. The second and third sections are not critical to the objectives of this chapter.

Examination and analysis

Since its translation into English, this treatise has garnered significant attention in academic scholarship. However, most studies have primarily focused on the second and third sections, where al-Rāzī provides an intricate analysis of male passivity (*ubna*). The scholars' focus on these sections of the treatise is well justified, as the title indicates that it primarily aims to address a hidden disease known as *ubna* and its treatment. Unlike the second and third parts, the first section, which addresses various categories of human being and explores the underlying causes that result in embryos being born with differing physical and behavioral traits, has been largely overlooked. To my knowledge, this section represents a distinctive contribution to Islamic medical discourse, offering notable insights into classical understandings of human categories. In this study, I will concentrate exclusively on this section of the treatise, providing a detailed examination of its content and situating it within the broader context of Islamic medical thought.

Pre-modern Muslim medical discourse, influenced in part by Greek physicians,[34] provides an account of sex differences based on the contributions of both males and females to the formation of embryos. This discourse identifies two critical factors in determining fetal sex: (a) the predominance of the male or female seed; and (b) the location within the uterus where the seed is deposited; and (c) the environmental conditions of heat and cold at the time of conception. According to this model, if the male seed predominates and is deposited in the right side of the uterus under conditions of greater heat, the embryo developes as male. Conversely, if the female seed predominates and is deposited in the left side under cooler conditions, the embryo developes as female. If neither seed predominates and the deposition occurs in the central region of the uterus—where the temperature was believed to be moderate or mixed—the resulting child exhibits characteristics of *khunthā*. In this view, sexual differentiation is not fixed solely by divine will or anatomical clarity, but rather emerges from a complex interplay of physical, environmental, and anatomical factors at the moment of conception. This multifactorial framework reflects a broader epistemology in pre-modern Islamic medicine, where bodily states were understood as dynamic and contingent, rather than binary or absolute.

Al-Rāzī elucidates his view by addressing the same concept that femaleness (*unūtha*/roughly, "femininity") and maleness (*dhukūra*/roughly, "masculinity") result from the predominance of one sexual partner's semen over the other in both quantity and quality. Thus, one partner's semen ultimately becomes the transformative agent (*muḥīl*), while the other's is transformed (*mustaḥīl*). If the semen of the man is the transformative agent, the infant will be male; conversely, if the semen of the woman predominates and transforms, the infant will be female.

Thus, al-Rāzī offers a spectrum of humanity (see figure 6): at one end, there is a purely masculine male, who exemplifies all properties of masculinity (*maleness/tadhkīr/dhukūra*), such as robust and well-defined limbs, abundant body hair, a strong pulse and breath, and thick bones, along with behavioral traits typical of individuals with a hot and dry temperament, such as courage, rapid speech, and quickness to anger. This represents a condition where the male semen is entirely dominant and effective in transforming the female semen. Conversely, at the other end of the spectrum, there is a purely feminine female, who exhibits all properties of femininity, with physical and behavioral characteristics that are the direct opposite of those associated with males by al-Rāzī.

However, al-Rāzī continues, in most instances, one of the two semen sources undergoes transformation between the two extreme poles. In these situations, the resulting infant is neither masculine in the extreme nor feminine in the extreme, albeit biologically seems to have male sexual organs or female sexual organs respectively. Occasionally, the masculinity of a male-born child or the femininity of a female-born child may be markedly diminished, leading to the emergence of two new categories of individuals: masculine women/females (*nisā' mudhakkarāt*), known as *mutarajjilāt* in classical Muslim culture, and feminine men/males (*rijāl mu'annathūn*), known as *mukhannathūn* in classical Muslim culture.

According to al-Rāzī, there are various biological and behavioral characteristics associated with feminine men and masculine women that distinguish them from the first two categories—namely, purely masculine male and purely feminine female. For example, masculine women may exhibit biological traits such as minimal or absent menstruation and facial hair growth, while behaviorally, they may display what have traditionally been perceived as masculine traits, such as being courageous and temperamental. Al-Rāzī notes his own observations of such masculine women, who had beards and sparse moustaches. He also recalls an occasion when he was present at the court of the ʿAbbāsid caliph al-Muʿtaḍid, where a Kurdish woman was presented as a wondrous phenomenon (*uʿjūba*) due to her abundant beard.

On the other hand, feminine men exhibit soft and calm behaviors, along with biological characteristics that distinguish them from purely masculine males. In the second section of the treatise, al-Rāzī draws a connection between the biological traits of effeminate males (*mukhannathūn*) and their sexual behavior, particularly the desire to be penetrated by another man. He endeavors to provide a biological explanation for this so-called deviant sexual inclination. According to him, the diminished dominance of male sperm over female sperm in *mukhannathūn* results in underdeveloped male reproductive organs, including the testicles and sperm ducts, which remain small and tend to retract into the abdomen. This inward orientation is analogous to the female reproductive system, which is situated internally within the body. Consequently, stimulation occurs near the rectum rather than in the hypogastric and pubic regions. Those *mukhannathūn* affected by *ubna* typically possess small, wrinkled testicles that retract into the groin instead of hanging low.

Finally, al-Rāzī describes a condition in which the contributions of the two semen sources appear to be equal, with neither exerting significant dominance over the other. In such cases, the resulting infant is classified as intersex (*khunthā*).[35] This situation is characterized by the presence of both penile and vulval anatomy and exhibits moderate behavioral traits, displaying neither distinctly masculine nor feminine attributes

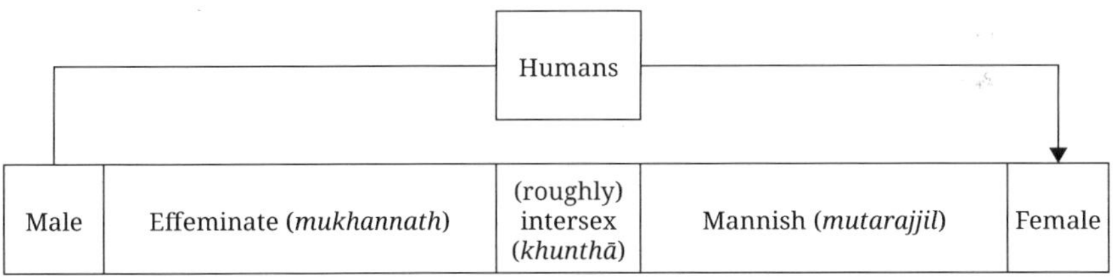

Figure 9.10: al-Rāzī's typology of human being

Al-Razı does not provide further clarification in this treatise on how the timing of sexual intercourse causes an infant to become a *khunthā*. However, if one assumes that what al-Rāzī cites in *al-Ḥāwī* from *al-Hindī* concerning the quantity of semen released by males and females during sexual intercourse reflects his own perspective as well, then this may introduce nuance regarding when an infant is determined to be male, female, *mukhannath*, *mutarajjil*, or *khunthā* based on the day of legal purity (*ṭuhr*). Given that the quantity of semen is significant, the timing of the sexual intercourse—specifically after the female partner's menstruation period ends and her legal purity begins—becomes important in this context. Al-Rāzī reports the following from al-Hindī:

> [The embryo would develop as] a boy due to the abundance of male semen or as a girl due to the abundance of female semen. According to this view, if intercourse occurs on the first day after she completes her menstrual purification (when the period of legal purity begins), she will conceive a boy. On the fifth day, it would result in a girl; on the sixth day, a boy; on the seventh day, a girl; on the eighth day, a boy; on the ninth day, a girl; on the tenth day, a boy; and on the eleventh day, the child would be *khunthā*.[36]

According to this report, although al-Hindī refers to the quantity of semen released by each sexual partner, it seems perplexing—and remains unexplained by al-Hindī—why, on these alternate days, either the male or female releases more semen. However, there is another account of this approach by Ibn Sīnā, in which he cites a scholar without specifying his name. This account differs somewhat from what Al-Rāzī attributed to al-Hindī:

> Pregnancy will result in a boy if conception occurs from the first day of the period of legal purity up until the fifth day. From the fifth to the eighth day, it would result in a girl. If conception occurs between the eighth and eleventh day, it will again result in a boy. After the eleventh day, the child will be a *khunthā*.[37]

Thus, according to this account, during the first five days of the period of legal purity, the embryo would be a boy because the man was believed to release more semen than the woman. From the fifth to the eighth day, the embryo would be a girl, as the woman was thought to release more semen. If conception occurs between the eighth and eleventh day, the embryo would again be a boy, as the man was believed to release more semen during this period. After the eleventh day, the embryo would be a *khunthā*, as both partners were considered to release an equal amount of semen, with no predominance.

Although al-Rāzī mentions encountering astonishing and (occasionally) repulsive narratives about *khunthā*s, he deliberately refrains from elaborating on these accounts, dismissing them as absurd and unworthy of serious consideration. For example, one account reports that a surgeon discovered a uterus in certain male animals, or many others speak of a woman who bore children and subsequently developed male genitalia. Such stories, he remarks, have been relayed from various sources. For the purposes of his discussion, al-Rāzī asserts that verifying the accuracy of these accounts is unnecessary. Rather, what has been previously mentioned—that not every male is fully masculine, nor every female fully feminine, and that there are categories such as "mannish" and "effiminate"—is sufficient to advance the conversation. By this, he aims to draw a connection between effeminates (*mukhannathūn*) and the desire to be penetrated by another man. In the second and third sections of the treatise, he endeavors to provide a biological explanation for this deviant sexual inclination of *ubna*, categorizing it as a disease, and subsequently offering medical treatments aimed at curing it.[38]

Concluding remarks

This study confirms that, akin to al-Zahrāwī and Ibn Sīnā, al-Rāzī, as a physician, does not morally judge individuals who do not conform to traditional male and female categories, such as *khunthā*, *mutarajjil*, and *mukhannath*. He neither addresses them with repulsion nor contempt. Al-Rāzī exhibits skepticism towards the sensational narratives surrounding these individuals, regarding them absurd and unworthy of belief. However, in contrast to al-Zahrāwī and Ibn Sīnā, he does not perceive intersexuality as a form of deformity or disability that can be medically treated. This perspective likely extends to the bodies of *mukhannath* and *mutarajjil* as well. Nevertheless, in instances where *mukhannathūn* express a desire to be penetrated, he categorizes this desire—aligning with the prevailing perceptions of his time—as a disease known as *ubna*, which he believes requires certain forms of treatment, though not surgical intervention.

The study further elucidates that al-Rāzī identifies five categorical variants of infants, including *khunthā*s, which arise from one of several naturally occurring combinations of the sexual partners' semen. These combinations are influenced by various factors, including the time, place, and other biological and environmental conditions surrounding the act of sexual intercourse. The identified sex variants include purely feminine female/woman, purely masculine male/man, *mutarajjil*, *mukhannath*, and *khunthā*.

In addition, unlike the two categories of *mutarajjil* and *mukhannath*, al-Rāzī does not assign maleness or femaleness to *khunthā*, neither in this context nor in *al-Ḥāwī*. However, one could reasonably argue that, according to al-Rāzī's logic, a *khunthā* ought to be considered equally a combination of both male and female.

It is convincing to conclude that for al-Rāzī being a pure masculine male and a pure masculine female are only two categories of humanity, there are other natural/biological types as well, such as the three categories of *khunthā*, *mukhannath*, and *mutarajjil*. Clearly, by holding such a position, al-Rāzī transgresses from the binary norm of male and female sex and or gender categories.

It is important to note that al-Rāzī's categorization of human being is not hierarchical; the male category is not positioned at the apex, nor the female category at the base, with the other three categories placed in between. Consequently, the diagram is arranged horizontally rather than vertically (see Figure 9.10). This model contrasts with the notion of a spectrum of humanity that extended from maleness to various degrees of non-maleness in some classical Muslim cultures. In that model, free males were considered the complete expression of humanity—physically, intellectually, and spiritually—while other groups, such as *mukhannath*s and females, were perceived as representing lesser, imperfect degrees of humanity.[39] In contrast, al-Rāzī's figure refrains from assigning value to these categories, avoiding any implication of superiority or inferiority. Instead, it primarily addresses the biological and environmental factors that contribute to the diversity of human categories.

While the prevalent modern discourse tends to distinguish between the two concepts of sex and gender, by claiming that the former refers to biological matter and the latter is a socially constructed phenomenon, principally grounded in nurture, not nature, in al-Razi's scholarship, we do not find such terms and distinction. Instead, acknowledging biological features and behavior characteristics of these groups, he holds that these two aspects of an individual are intertwined and essentially grounded in biological determination and natural circumstances, including geographical regions, rather than cultural or social circumstances.

Reception

Al-Rāzī's categorization within Islamic medical discourse appears to be distinctly his own. Although Ibn Sīnā alludes to this perspective, he does so anonymously, failing to credit al-Rāzī as the principal advocate of this approach in the Islamic medical tradition.[40] Ibn Sīnā seems to regard the opinion as unworthy of serious examination; consequently, he neither endorses nor critiques this approach, thereby effectively sidelining it within the broader discourse.

In *ḥadīth* literature, the term *khunthā* is frequently discussed, with various physical indicators, such as the mode of urination and the number of ribs, being suggested to determine the sex of these individuals. The primary concern of the *ḥadīth* tradition regarding *khunthā*s stems from the fact that legal rights and responsibilities differ based on one's sex classification. *Mukhannath*s are also mentioned in some *ḥadīth* sources as individuals who could freely be in the company of Muslim women, including the wives of the Prophet in his household. However, there are other *ḥadīth*s recording that the Prophet later banished *mukhannath*s from the city of Medina or prohibited them from entering the female quarters of mosques and Muslim homes. Some studies have concluded that Muslims, including the Prophet, initially perceived *mukhannath*s as people who lacked sexual desire, perhaps analogous to asexual individuals in modern terms. However, it was reported that the Prophet later came to understand that *mukhannath*s did, in fact, experience sexual desire, particularly towards women, indicating that they were like other Muslim males.[41] Moreover, references to *mutarrajjil*s also occasionally appear in *ḥadīth* literature; however, these reports provide limited details about this group, primarily suggesting a prohibition against women adopting masculine behavior due to its association with resembling men.

The controversies about these two groups continued in Muslim societies and have been reflected in Muslim literature, particularly Arabic and Persian. As various studies note, *mukhannath*s and *mutarrajjil*s were distinct groups within early and medieval Muslim societies who, despite being born with a penis (i.e., a *mukhannath*) or vulva (i.e., a *mutarrajjil*), consistently presented, moved, and adorned themselves in behavioral manners typically associated with the opposite gender.[42] However, *mukhannath*s and *mutarrajjil*s did not identify as female and male, respectively, nor were they categorized as such by others.[43]

It is important to emphasize that effeminacy and mannishness were more about the reversal of gender roles or behaviors than about sexual orientation or biological sex. These traits were often employed to gain social privileges that were otherwise restricted. For example, mannish women could gain access to male privileges within the new Islamic patriarchal community or compete with men in a heavily masculinized society—possibly by engaging in warfare or working on farms—to demonstrate that Arab and Persian women could be as masculine as men, if not stronger, and thus should not be considered inferior to Muslim males. In the case of effeminate males, they could sing, access women's quarters (where other men were not permitted), and be exempt from military service due to their perceived softness and feminine attitudes.

Arabic and Persian literature did not address *khunthā*s as frequently as the categories of *mukhannath* and *mutarrajjil*. However, *khunthā*s, as Scalenghe also notes, are occasionally depicted as having astonishing features. Biographers often associate stories with *khunthā*s as marvels or oddities, though these accounts were generally not conveyed with contempt or condemnation.[44]

The terms *khunthā*, *mukhannath*, and *mutarrajjil* also feature in Muslim legal discourse. Jurists have extensively examined the category of *khunthā*, exploring its nature and the legal rights and responsibilities associated with intersex individuals. They have debated the classification of these individuals: while some jurists have classified them as either male or female, others have identified them a distinct category that is neither male nor female.[45] However, due to the lack of definitive evidence, it remains uncertain whether those jurists who classified *khunthā*s as a third sex category were influenced by al-Rāzī.

Drawing upon the aforementioned *ḥadīth*s, jurists often hold that *mukhannath*s are prohibited from entering the women's quarters of mosques and *mutarrajjil*s are prohibited from entering the men's section. Moreover, they forbid male and female beautifications intended to resemble the opposite group. The reasoning behind these rulings can be understood by noting that these jurists maintain that *mukhannath*s are, in fact, (biologically) male and *mutarrajjil*s are (biologically) female. Consequently, they are expected to act according to the sex or nature they are inherently assigned.

Furthermore, in juristic contexts, there are no references to these two groups as disputed categories who have legal rights and responsibilities distinct from those of men and women. For instance, jurists extensively outline Islamic law regarding inheritance shares of various categories of people. While they carefully delineate the rights of men, women, and intersex individuals (*khunthā*s), there are no discussions concerning the inheritance shares of *mukhannath*s and *mutarrajjil*s. Similarly, when determining where an individual should pray in a mosque based on their category/nature/sex, jurists engage in extended debates, typically asserting that men should stand at the front, women at the back, and intersex individuals in the middle, yet there is hardly any discussion or disputes regarding the placement of *mukhannath*s and *mutarrajjil*s. These examples demonstrate that, in the view of Muslim jurists, *mukhannath*s and *mutarrajjil*s were understood as males and females, respectively.

Notes

* This chapter is part of the project Beyond Binaries: Intersex in Islamic Legal Tradition (Project Number: vi.Veni.211F.093), funded by the Dutch Research Council (NWO) under the Veni Talent Programme.

1 The application of contemporary terms such as "sex," "gender," and "intersex," to classical Muslim medical contexts requires careful consideration to avoid anachronistic interpretations. It is crucial to differentiate between our modern discourse on sex and gender and the categories or behaviors that existed in historical contexts. In this chapter, I employ the terms "sex" in conjunction with "category" and "nature" to denote primarily the biological or sexed body of individuals, as well as their behavioral traits, with the aim of rendering the discussion accessible to a contemporary audience. Furthermore, my use of the term "intersex" should be interpreted within the same framework and considerations. Undoubtedly, the application of these modern terms differs significantly from their historical precedents. For additional clarification on terminology, please refer to the introduction of this book.

2 See, for example, Mehrdad Alipour, "Navigating Body Politics in Shiʿi Legal Tradition: Examining Sayyid Kāẓim al-Yazdī's Account of Non-Binary Intersex," *Islamic Law and Society* 32, no. 3 (2025): 262–315; idem, "Transgender Identity, The Sex-Reassignment Surgery Fatwās and Islāmic Theology of a Third Gender," *Religion and Gender* 7, no. 2 (2017): 164–79; Ash Geissinger, "Islam and Discourses of Same-Sex Desire," in *Queer Religio: Homosexuality in Modern Religious History*, eds. Donald L. Boisvert and Jay E. Johnson, 2 vols. (Santa Barbara: Praeger, 2012), 1: 69–90, at 72–3; Indira Falk Gesink, "Intersex Bodies in Premodern Islamic Discourse: Complicating the Binary," *Journal of Middle East Women's Studies* 14, no. 2 (2018), 152–73; Ani Amelia Zainuddin and Zaleha Abdullah

Mahdy, "The Islamic Perspectives of Gender-Related Issues in the Management of Patients with Disorders of Sex Development," *Archives of Sexual Behavior* 46 (2017): 353–60.

3 See, for example, Nasir Malim and Aasim I. Padela, "Islamic Bioethical Perspectives on Gender Identity for Intersex Patients," *Journal of the British Muslim Medical Association* 5, no. 2 (2020): 19–25; Inas A. Mazen, "Clinical Management of Gender in Egypt: Intersexuality and Transsexualism," *Archives of Sexual Behavior* 46 (2017): 369–72; Mohd Salim Mohamed and Siti Nurani Mohd Noor, "Islamic Bioethical Deliberation on the Issue of Newborns with Disorders of Sex Development," *Science and Engineering Ethics* 21 (2015): 429–40. On the correlation between the medicalization of intersex people and Islamic law or legal *fatwā*s, see Mehrdad Alipour, "The Nexus between Gender-Confirming Surgery and Illness: Legal-Hermeneutical Examinations of Four Islamic Fatwas," *Journal of Middle East Women's Studies* 18, no. 3 (2022): 359–86; Muhammad Afif Mohd Badrol, Abdul Bari Awang, and Sayed Sikandar Shah Haneef, "Intersex Gender Determination in Classical Islamic Law and Modern Medicine: An Analysis for Integration," *Al-Shajarah: Journal of the International Institute of Islamic Thought and Civilization* (ISTAC) 23, no. 2 (2018): 469–96; Taqwa Zabidi, "Analytical Review of Contemporary Fatwas in Resolving Biomedical Issues over Gender Ambiguity," *Journal of Religion and Health* 58, no. 1 (2019): 153–67.

4 Sara Scalenghe, *Disability in the Ottoman Arab World, 1500–1800* (Cambridge: Cambridge University Press, 2014), 124–62.

5 Indira Falk Gesink, "Intersex in Islamic Medical, Law and Activism," in *The Routledge Handbook of Islam and Gender*, ed. Justine Howe (London: Routledge, 2020): 116–29, at 121–2; idem, "Intersex Bodies in Premodern Islamic Discourse," 160–3.

6 Paula Sanders, "Gendering the Ungendered Body: Hermaphrodites in Medieval Islamic Law," in *Women in Middle Eastern History: Shifting Boundaries in Sex and Gender*, eds. Beth Baron and Nikki Keddie (New Haven: Yale University Press, 1991): 74–95.

7 Gesink, "Intersex Bodies," 153.

8 Sanders later modified her earlier claims. Addressing Everett Rowson's thesis concerning the "penetrator" versus "penetrated" dichotomy in Arabic literary texts, she wrote, "One of the most important conclusions resulting from this body of work is that male/female was not the only gender dichotomy in medieval Islamic societies; there was also male/not male." (Paula Sanders, "Hermaphrodites Revisited: A Reconsideration," *Academia* [2008, unpublished], Accessed October 2023: https://www.academia.edu/35003377/Hermaphrodites_revisited_a_reconsideration_1. Also, see Sanders's contribution to this volume, chapter 1).

9 Gesink, "Intersex Bodies," 153.

10 See Abū ʿAbd al-Raḥmān al-Khalīl b. Aḥmad al-Farāhīdī, *Kitāb al-ʿayn*, eds. Mahdī al-Makhzūmī and Ibrāhīm al-Sāmarrāʾī, 8 vols. (Baghdad: Dār al-Rashād, 1980), 4: 248; Abū Naṣr Ismāʿīl al-Jawharī, *al-Ṣiḥāḥ tāj al-lugha wa-ṣiḥāḥ al-ʿarabiyya*, ed. Aḥmad ʿAbd al-Ghafūr ʿAṭṭār, 6 vols. (Beirut: Dār al-ʿIlm li-l-Malāīīn, 1407/1986–7), 1: 281; Muḥammad b. al-Ḥasan b. Durayd al-Azdī, *Jamharat al-lugha*, ed. Ramzī Munīr Baʿlbkī, 3 vols. (Beirut: Dār al-ʿIlm li-l-Malāīīn, 1987), 1: 418; Muḥammad b. Aḥmad al-Azharī, *Tahdhīb al-lugha*, 15 vols. (Beirut: Dār Iḥyāʾ al-Turāth al-ʿArabī, 2001), 7: 145; Aḥmad b. Muḥammad b. ʿAlī al-Fayyumī, *al-Miṣbāḥ al-munīr fī gharīb al-sharḥ al-kabīr, 2 vols. (*Beirut: al-Maktaba al-ʿIlmiyya, 1994*)*, 1: 183*;* Muḥammad b. Mukarram b. Manẓūr, *Lisān al-ʿarab*, 15 vols. (Beirut: Dār Ṣādir li-l-Ṭibāʿa wa-l-Nashr, 1414), 2: 145; Muḥammad Murtaḍā al-Zabīdī, *Tāj al-ʿarūs min jawāhir al-Qāmūs*, ed. ʿAbd al-ʿAzīz Maṭar, 40 vols. (Kuwait: Maṭbaʿat Ḥukūmat al-Kuwait, 1414/1994), 5: 240–2.

11 Al-Jawharī, *al-Ṣiḥāḥ*, 1: 281.

12 For example, al-Azharī (d. 370/980) repeats al-Jawharī's definition of *khunthā* (al-Azharī, *Tahdhīb al-lugha*, 7: 145). Al-Fayyūmī (d. 770/1368), however, describes a *khunthā* as a person who has both a vulva (*farj al-marʾa*) and a penis (*farj al-rajul*) (al-Fayyūmī, *al-Miṣbāḥ al-munīr*, 1: 183). Like al-Khalīl,

Ibn Manẓūr (d. 711/1311–2) defines *khunthā* as a person who is not exclusively a female or a male, which suggests that *khunthās* cannot always be categorized as male or female: in some cases, they belong to a distinct category separate from both male and female. Ibn Manẓūr also explains that the term *khunthā* can be applied either as an adjective (and thus it makes sense to say a "*khunthā* man", which means a male individual who has both male and female sexual organs) or as a noun without qualification, namely, using *khunthā* alone, which implies a person who has biological signs of a male and female, such as a beard and breasts (Ibn Manẓūr, *Lisān al-ʿarab*, 2: 145). This last point refers to a legal debate concerning *al-khunthā al-mushkil* (a difficult-to-determine intersex condition/complicated intersex) and *al-khunthā ghayr al-mushkil* (an easily recognizable intersex condition/uncomplicated intersex). By the latter condition, namely a *khunthā* without qualification, Ibn Manẓūr perhaps intends to refer to *al-khunthā al-mushkil* whose nature is unknown or cannot be assessed, and by the former—a *khunthā* man—he probably refers to *al-khunthā ghayr al-mushkil* whose nature can be determined through markers.

13 See, for example, Muḥammad b. Zakariyyā l-Rāzī, *al-Ḥāwī fī l-ṭibb*, 7 vols. (Beirut: Dār Iḥyāʾ al-Turāth al-ʿArabī, 1422/2002), 3: 192; Ibn Sīnā, *al-Qānūn fī l-ṭibb*, 4 vols. (Beirut: Dār Iḥyāʾ al-Turāth al-ʿArabī, 2005), 3: 449; Abū l-Qāsim al-Zahrāwī [Albucasis], *Kitāb al-taṣrīf li-man ʿajaza ʿan al-taʾlīf: al-maqāla al-thalāthūn: al-Jarāḥa* (Riyadh: Maktabat al-Malik Fahd al-Waṭaniyya, 1422/2001), 306. For secondary sources, see Gesink, "Intersex Bodies," 160–3; Scalenghe, "Disability in the Ottoman Arab World," 132–6.

14 Ibn Sīnā, *al-Qānūn fī l-ṭibb*, 4 vols. (Beirut: Dār Iḥyāʾ al-Turāth al-ʿArabī, 2005), 3: 449.

15 Abū l-Qāsim al-Zahrāwī [Albucasis], *Kitāb al-taṣrīf li-man ʿajaza ʿan al-taʾlīf: al-maqāla al-thalāthūn: al-Jarāḥa* (Riyadh: Maktabat al-Malik Fahd al-Waṭaniyya, 1422/2001), 306. It is worth noting that jurists also often describe *khunthā* as those who possess both male and female sexual organs or lack distinct male or female genitalia: See, for example, Yaḥyā b. Sharaf al-Nawawī (d. 676/1277), *al-Majmūʿ Sharḥ al-Muhadhdhab*, 20 vols. (Beirut: Dār al-Fikr, 1990), 2: 46–7; Muḥammad b. Aḥmad al-Sarakhsī (d. 483/1090), *al-Mabsūṭ*, 30 vols. (Beirut: Dār al-Maʿrifa, 1414/1993), 30: 91; Abū al-Ḥusayn ʿAlī b. al-Ḥusayn b. Muḥammad al-Sughdī, *al-Nutaf fī l-fatāwā*, ed. Ṣalāḥ al-Dīn al-Nāhī, 2 vols. (Amman: Dār al-Furqān/Beirut: Muʾassasat al-Risāla, 1404/1984), 2: 857–8; Abū l-Ḥasan ʿAlī b. Muḥammad al-Māwirdī al-Baṣrī, *al-Ḥāwī l-kabīr fī fiqh madhhab al-imām al-Shāfiʿī*, 18 vols. (Beirut: Dār al-Kutub al-ʿIlmiyya, 1419/1999), 8: 108. However, several legal experts only refer to *khunthā* as people with both male and female genitalia: see, for example, Abū Muḥammad ʿAbd al-Wahhāb b. ʿAlī al-Thaʿlabī, *al-Maʿūna ʿalā madhhab ʿālim al-madīna "al-Imām Mālik b. Anas"*, ed. Ḥamīsh ʿAbd al-Ḥaqq, 3 vols. (Makka: al-Maktaba al-Tijāriyya, 1995), 3: 657; Abū l-Ḥusayn Aḥmad b. Muḥammad al-Qudūrī al-Ḥanafī, *Mukhtaṣar al-Qudūrī fī l-fiqh al-Ḥanafī*, ed. Muḥammad Muḥammad ʿAwīḍa (Beirut: Dār al-Kutub al-ʿIlmiyya, 1418/1997), 137; ʿAlī b. Abī Bakr b. ʿAbd al-Jalīl al-Marghīnānī, *al-Hidāya fī sharḥ Bidāyat al-mubtadī*, ed. Ṭalāl Yūsuf, 4 vols. (Beirut: Dār Iḥyāʾ al-Turāth al-ʿArabī, 2010), 4: 546.

16 Sanders, "Gendering the Ungendered Body," 81.

17 Gesink, "Intersex Bodies," 162–3.

18 Ibid

19 Ibn Sīnā, *al-Qānūn*, 3: 426–34.

20 Nevertheless, as Gesink noted in response to an earlier draft of this chapter, certain questions remain that merit further critical examination. Given the state of medical technology at the time, one must ask whether it was technically feasible to perform such a surgical intervention on an infant. If so, and if such a procedure had indeed been undertaken, it would plausibly have been recorded and celebrated as a noteworthy medical accomplishment. While this observation is reasonable, it is not conclusive; rather, it underscores the need for further inquiry and corroborating historical evidence.

21 Al-Rāzī, *al-Ḥāwī*, 3: 192.

22 ʿAbdul-Ḥusayn Hāʾirī, "Muʿarrafī-yi Yakī az Āthār-i Bāz-Yāfta-yi Muḥammad b. Zakariyyā-yi Rāzī," *Waḥīd*, no. 14 (1343sh/1965): 78–80.

23 Franz Rosenthal, "Ar-Razi on the Hidden Illness," *Bulletin of the History of Medicine* 52, no. 1 (1978): 45–60, at 45–6.

24 The treatise on *ubna* appears on fols. 63v–64v/pp. 123–5 (modern pencil pagination). It was copied in 993/1585, though the identity of the scribe remains unknown. Notably, another treatise within the same manuscript, focused on maintaining health and well-being, includes the copyist's name at the end of the treatise, Muḥammad Amīn b. Maḥmūd Dastjirdānī (fol. 83r/p. 162), with the copying date of Rabīʿ I 993/March 1585. However, the handwriting of this latter treatise differs from that of the treatise in question.

25 The treatise on *ubna* appears on fols. 30v–33v/pp. 57–63 (modern pencil pagination). It was copied on 11 Ramadan 1006/17 April 1598. The manuscript includes various classical Muslim medical works, all transcribed by the same hand, though the scribe remains unidentified.

26 The treatise on *ubna* is found on fol. 382r–v (in modern pencil pagination 371 and 377, recto–verso numbering offset by six pages; it should be noted that this page numbering is unusually low for f. 382, which would normally correspond to pages 763–764. Furthermore, the blank folios preceding this leaf are not included in the modern pagination). This treatise was copied in 12 Muharram 1007/14 August 1598, but the identity of the scribe remains unknown. My detailed comparison of the three Tehran Mss. demonstrates that they are nearly identical, with only minor textual discrepancies. This high degree of similarity suggests a common origin. In contrast, when compared with Ms. Majlis, no. 6201—regarded as the most reliable of the three—the Mss. Majlis, no. 352 and Sinā exhibit omissions that, as Rosenthal suggests, are due to homoioteleuton.

27 I. S. Allouche and A. Regragui, Catalogue des manuscrits arabes de Rabat, II, 332, no. 2641, shelf-no. 1588d (Paris, 1954, and Rabat, 1958, Pubi, de l'Institut des Hautes Études Marocaines, 58, 63). The treatise is found on fols. 44v–49r of the manuscript. The consistent handwriting throughout indicates that the manuscript was produced by a single scribe, identified as Abū al-Qāsim ʿAbdallāh b. Muḥammad b. Muḥammad b. Ibrāhīm b. ʿAbd al-Salām al-Asadī al-Andalusī. While this treatise is undated, a copying date of Muharram 917/April 1511, found at the end of an entry on fol. 145v, likely applies to the entire manuscript.

28 The excerpted text is found on fol. 149r–v.

29 See Shahāb al-Dīn Aḥmad al-Tīfāshī, *Nuzhat al-albāb fī-mā lā yūjad fī kitab*, ed. Jamāl Jumʿa (London: Riaḍ El-Royyes Books, 1992): 251–308, at 302–8. It appears that Rosenthal was unaware of this version while translating the treatise.

30 Currently, I do not have access to the Rabat manuscript.

31 For these last three sources, see Rosenthal, "Ar-Razi on the Hidden Illness," 45.

32 Here is a detailed summary of the passage: it discusses various explanations for the sterility of mules. Initially, some theories attribute the sterility to physiological factors such as the scarcity, thinness, or coldness of mule sperm, or the structural issues in the female mule's uterus, such as its size, narrowness, or placement. However, al-Rāzī critiques these explanations, arguing they fail to address the root causes of sterility. A more plausible explanation, according to him, is based on the concept of *istiḥāla* (transformation), which posits that mule sperm undergoes a significant deviation from the nature of reproductive sperm. This transformation is attributed to the mixing of sperm from two distinct species—horse and donkey—resulting in sperm that is incompatible with reproduction due to its removal from the natural "temper" (*mizāj*) of each parent species. Al-Rāzī also critiques another proof, which suggests sterility results simply because the offspring of two different species is inherently different from both parents. This reasoning is dismissed as

incomplete and lacking depth. Instead, he argues that when the sperms of two species combine, the formative power of each sperm weakens, making it difficult for the sperm to act upon or influence the other effectively. This mutual weakening leads to sterility. Analogies are drawn to digestion, where combining incompatible foods weakens the digestive power, illustrating the challenges of combining distinct reproductive materials.

33 Rosenthal, "Ar-Razi on the Hidden Illness," 46. Rosenthal contends that "If the text available to us at this time is an excerpt, it represents one that omits nothing essential." (Ibid., 47).

34 Ibn al-Maṭrān in his excerpt of the treatise in *Bustān al-aṭibbā'* attributes this point to Hippocrates and Galen. See Galen, *On Semen/De semine*. Edition, translation, and commentary by Philipp de Lacy (Berlin: Akademie Verl., 1992), 291 S. (Corpus medicorum Graecorum V3,1); Hippocrates, "On Generation (*De Genitura*)," in *Hippocrates*, vol. 6, translated by Philip J. Potter (Cambridge: Harvard University Press, 1998): 235–65; Hippocrates, "On Generation (*De Genitura*)," translated by Francis Adams, in *The Genuine Works of Hippocrates* (London: Sydenham Society, 1849): 367–90.

35 All Tehran manuscripts record the term *khināth* in this context, which is the plural form of *khunthā*. Following Rosenthal's translation, the Rabat manuscript also contains the term *khināth*. However, in this instance, al-Tīfāshī's version uses the noun form of the term, namely *al-khunth*, referring to the state or condition of being a *khunthā*. He states: "But a condition of *khunth* (ambiguity; literally, bending or softness) may also occur—when the two seminal fluids are equivalent and neither predominates over the other—to the extent that the newborn may have both a penis and a vulva" (al-Tīfāshī, *Nuzhat al-albāb*, 303).

36 Al-Rāzī, *al-Ḥāwī*, 3: 192.

37 Ibn Sīnā, *al-Qānūn*, 3: 449.

38 On *ubna*, see Khaled El-Rouayheb, *Before Homosexuality in the Arab-Islamic World, 1500–1800* (Chicago: University of Chicago Press, 2005), 19–25; Mehrdad Alipour, *Negotiating Homosexuality in Islam: A Legal-Hermeneutical Examination of Modern Shi'i Discourse* (Leiden: Brill, 2024), 125–30.

39 Geissinger, "Islam and Discourses of Same-Sex Desire," 72–3.

40 Ibn Sīnā, *al-Qānūn*, 3: 449.

41 Everett K. Rowson, "The Effeminates of Early Medina," *Journal of the American Oriental Society* 111, no. 4 (1991): 671–93, at 672–5; Alipour, *Negotiating Homosexuality in Islam*, 107–8 and 110, n.87.

42 Rowson, "The Effeminates of Early Medina," 672–5; Alipour, *Negotiating Homosexuality in Islam*, 107–13.

43 Ash Geissinger, "Applying Gender and Queer Theory to Pre-modern Sources," in *The Routledge Handbook of Islam and Gender*, ed. Justine Howe (London: Routledge, 2021): 101–15, at 103.

44 Scalenghe, *Disability in the Ottoman Arab World*, 131–2.

45 See Alipour, "Navigating Body Politics;" Gesink, "Intersex Bodies;" Sanders, "Gendering the Ungendered Body."

Bibliography

Alipour, Mehrdad. "Navigating Body Politics in Shi'i Legal Tradition: Examining Sayyid Kāẓim al-Yazdī's Account of Non-Binary Intersex." *Islamic Law and Society* 32, no. 3 (2025): 262–315.

Alipour, Mehrdad, "Transgender Identity, The Sex-Reassignment Surgery Fatwās and Islāmic Theology of a Third Gender." *Religion and Gender* 7, no. 2 (2017): 164–79.

Alipour, Mehrdad. *Negotiating Homosexuality in Islam: A Legal-Hermeneutical Examination of Modern Shi'i Discourse*. Leiden: Brill, 2024.

Alipour, Mehrdad. "The Nexus between Gender-Confirming Surgery and Illness: Legal-Hermeneutical Examinations of Four Islamic Fatwas." *Journal of Middle East Women's Studies* 18, no. 3 (2022): 359–86.

Allouche, I. S. and Regragui, A., Catalogue des manuscrits arabes de Rabat, II, 332, no. 2641, shelf-no. 1588d, Paris, 1954, and Rabat, 1958 (Pubi, de l'Institut des Hautes Études Marocaines, 58, 63).

Al-Azdī, Muḥammad b. al-Ḥasan b. Durayd. *Jamharat al-lugha*. edited by Ramzī Munīr Baʿlbkī. 3 vols. Beirut: Dār al-ʿIlm li-l-Malāīīn, 1987.

Al-Azharī, Muḥammad b. Aḥmad. *Tahdhīb al-lugha*. 15 vols. Beirut: Dār Iḥyāʾ al-Turāth al-ʿArabī, 2001.

Badrol, Muhammad Afif Mohd, Awang, Abdul Bari, and Haneef, Sayed Sikandar Shah. "Intersex Gender Determination in Classical Islamic Law and Modern Medicine: An Analysis for Integration." *Al-Shajarah: Journal of the International Institute of Islamic Thought and Civilization* (ISTAC) 23, no. 2 (2018): 469–96.

Al-Baṣrī, Abū l-Ḥasan ʿAlī b. Muḥammad al-Māwirdī. *al-Ḥāwī l-kabīr fī fiqh madhhab al-imām al-Shāfiʿī*. 18 vols. Beirut: Dār al-Kutub al-ʿIlmiyya, 1419/1999.

El-Rouayheb, Khaled. *Before Homosexuality in the Arab-Islamic World, 1500–1800*. Chicago: University of Chicago Press, 2005.

Al-Farāhīdī, Abū ʿAbd al-Raḥmān al-Khalīl b. Aḥmad. *Kitāb al-ʿayn*. edited by Mahdī al-Makhzūmī and Ibrāhīm al-Sāmarrāʾī. 8 vols. Baghdad: Dār al-Rashād, 1980.

Al-Fayyumī, Aḥmad b. Muḥammad b. ʿAlī. *al-Miṣbāḥ al-munīr fī gharīb al-sharḥ al-kabīr*. 2 vols. Beirut: al-Maktaba al-ʿIlmiyya, 1994.

Galen, *On Semen/De semine*. Edition, translation, and commentary by Philipp de Lacy, Berlin: Akademie Verl., 1992, 291 S. (Corpus medicorum Graecorum V3,1).

Geissinger, Ash. "Applying Gender and Queer Theory to Pre-modern Sources." in *The Routledge Handbook of Islam and Gender*. edited by Justine Howe. London: Routledge, 2021: 101–15.

Geissinger, Ash. "Islam and Discourses of Same-Sex Desire." in *Queer Religio: Homosexuality in Modern Religious History*. edited by Donald L. Boisvert and Jay E. Johnson. 2 vols. Santa Barbara: Praeger, 2012: 1: 69–90.

Gesink, Indira F. "Intersex Bodies in Premodern Islamic Discourse: Complicating the Binary." *Journal of Middle East Women's Studies* 14, no. 2 (2018): 152–73.

Gesink, Indira F. "Intersex in Islamic Medical, Law and Activism." in *The Routledge Handbook of Islam and Gender*. edited by Justine Howe. London: Routledge, 2020: 116–29.

Hāʾirī, ʿAbdul-Ḥusayn. "Muʿarrafi-yi Yakī az Āthār-i Bāz-Yāfta-yi Muḥammad b. Zakariyyā-yi Rāzī." *Waḥīd*, no. 14 (1343sh/1965): 78–80.

Hippocrates. "On Generation (*De Genitura*)," in *Hippocrates*. vol. 6. translated by Philip J. Potter. Cambridge: Harvard University Press, 1998: 235–65.

Hippocrates. "On Generation (*De Genitura*)." in *The Genuine Works of Hippocrates*. translated by Francis Adams. London: Sydenham Society, 1849: 367–90.

Ibn Manẓūr, Muḥammad b. Mukarram. *Lisān al-ʿarab*. 15 vols. Beirut: Dār Ṣādir li-l-Ṭibāʿa wa-l-Nashr, 1414.

Ibn al-Maṭrān. *Bustān al-aṭibbāʾ wa-rawḍat al-alibbāʾ*. Ms. Tehran, Majlis Library, no. 3821 (registration 3821/26085) and kitāb-khāna-yi Malik, no. 94/1.

Ibn Sīnā. *al-Qānūn fī l-ṭibb*. 4 vols. Beirut: Dār Iḥyāʾ al-Turāth al-ʿArabī, 2005.

Al-Jawharī, Abū Naṣr Ismāʿīl. *al-Ṣiḥāḥ tāj al-lugha wa-ṣiḥāḥ al-ʿarabiyya*. edited by Aḥmad ʿAbd al-Ghafūr ʿAṭṭār. 6 vols. Beirut: Dār al-ʿIlm li-l-Malāīīn, 1407/1986–7.

Malim, Nasir and Padela, Aasim I. "Islamic Bioethical Perspectives on Gender Identity for Intersex Patients." *Journal of the British Muslim Medical Association* 5, no. 2 (2020): 19–25.

Al-Marghīnānī, ʿAlī b. Abī Bakr b. ʿAbd al-Jalīl. *al-Hidāya fī sharḥ Bidāyat al-mubtadī.* edited by Ṭalāl Yūsuf. 4 vols. Beirut: Dār Iḥyāʾ al-Turāth al-ʿArabī, 2010.

Mazen, Inas A. "Clinical Management of Gender in Egypt: Intersexuality and Transsexualism." *Archives of Sexual Behavior* 46 (2017): 369–72.

Mohamed, Mohd Salim and Noor, Siti Nurani Mohd. "Islamic Bioethical Deliberation on the Issue of Newborns with Disorders of Sex Development." *Science and Engineering Ethics* 21 (2015): 429–40.

Al-Nawawī, Yaḥyā b. Sharaf (d. 676/1277). *al-Majmūʿ sharḥ al-Muhadhdhab.* 20 vols. Beirut: Dār al-Fikr, 1990.

Al-Qudūrī al-Ḥanafī, Abū l-Ḥusayn Aḥmad b. Muḥammad. *Mukhtaṣar al-Qudūrī fī l-fiqh al-Ḥanafī.* edited by Muḥammad Muḥammad ʿAwīḍa. Beirut: Dār al-Kutub al-ʿIlmiyya, 1418/1997.

Al-Rāzī, Muḥammad b. Zakariyyā. *al-Ḥāwī fī l-ṭibb.* 7 vols. Beirut: Dār Iḥyāʾ al-Turāth al-ʿArabī, 1422/2002.

Al-Rāzī, Muḥammad b. Zakariyyā. *Risāla fī l-ubna.* in MS. Tehran, Majlis Library, no. 6201 (registration 7179/61805): fols. 30v–33v/pp. 57–63 (modern pencil pagination).

Al-Rāzī, Muḥammad b. Zakariyyā. *Risāla fī l-ubna.* in MS. Tehran, Majlis Library, no. 352, Ṭabāṭabāʾī (registration 31059/4679): fols. 63v–64v/pp. 123–5 (modern pencil pagination).

Al-Rāzī, Muḥammad b. Zakariyyā. *Fī l-ubna.* in MS. Tehran, Sinā (now Mūza) library, no. 360 (registration 3258): fol. 382r–v (in modern pencil pagination 371 and 377, recto–verso numbering offset by six pages).

Rosenthal, Franz. "Ar-Razi on the Hidden Illness." *Bulletin of the History of Medicine* 52, no. 1 (1978): 45–60.

Rowson, Everett K. "The Effeminates of Early Medina." *Journal of the American Oriental Society* 111, no. 4 (1991): 671–93.

Sanders, Paula, "Gendering the Ungendered Body: Hermaphrodites in Medieval Islamic Law." in *Women in Middle Eastern History: Shifting Boundaries in Sex and Gender.* edited by Beth Baron and Nikki Keddie. New Haven: Yale University Press, 1991: 74–95.

Sanders, Paula. "Hermaphrodites Revisited: A Reconsideration." *Academia* (2008, unpublished), Accessed October 2023: https://www.academia.edu/35003377/Hermaphrodites_revisited_a_reconsideration_1.

Al-Sarakhsī, Muḥammad b. Aḥmad (d. 483/1090). *al-Mabsūṭ.* 30 vols. Beirut: Dār al-Maʿrifa, 1414/1993.

Scalenghe, Sara. *Disability in the Ottoman Arab World, 1500–1800.* Cambridge: Cambridge University Press, 2014.

Al-Sughdī, Abū al-Ḥusayn ʿAlī b. al-Ḥusayn b. Muḥammad. *al-Nutaf fī l-fatāwā.* edited by Ṣalāḥ al-Dīn al-Nāhī. 2 vols., Amman: Dār al-Furqān/Beirut: Muʾassasat al-Risāla, 1404/1984.

Al-Thaʿlabī, Abū Muḥammad ʿAbd al-Wahhāb b. ʿAlī. *al-Maʿūna ʿalā madhhab ʿālim al-madīna "al-Imām Mālik b. Anas."* edited by Ḥamīsh ʿAbd al-Ḥaqq. 3 vols. Makka: al-Maktaba al-Tijāriyya, 1995.

Al-Tīfāshī, Shahāb al-Dīn Aḥmad. *Nuzhat al-albāb fī-mā lā yūjad fī kitab.* edited by Jamāl Jumʿa. London: Riaḍ El-Royyes Books, 1992.

Al-Zabīdī, Muḥammad Murtaḍā. *Tāj al-ʿarūs min jawāhir al-Qāmūs.* edited by ʿAbd al-ʿAzīz Maṭar. 40 vols. Kuwait: Maṭbaʿat Ḥukūmat al-Kuwait, 1414/1994.

Zabidi, Taqwa. "Analytical Review of Contemporary Fatwas in Resolving Biomedical Issues over Gender Ambiguity." *Journal of Religion and Health* 58, no. 1 (2019): 153–67.

Al-Zahrāwī [Albucasis], Abū l-Qāsim. *Kitāb al-taṣrīf li-man ʿajaza ʿan al-taʾlīf: al-maqāla al-thalāthūn: al-Jarāḥa.* Riyadh: Maktabat al-Malik Fahd al-Waṭaniyya, 1422/2001.

Zainuddin, Ani Amelia and Mahdy, Zaleha Abdullah. "The Islamic Perspectives of Gender-Related Issues in the Management of Patients with Disorders of Sex Development." *Archives of Sexual Behavior* 46 (2017): 353–60.

Conclusion

Indira Falk Gesink and Mehrdad Alipour

This volume has aimed to examine classical Islamic engagements with intersex bodies across literary, legal, and medical discourses, predominantly situated within Arabic and Persian historical, cultural, and intellectual traditions. These sources—ranging from lexicographical works, biographical collections, prose and poetic literature, and the scriptural corpus (Qur'ān and *ḥadīth* traditions) to juristic texts and medical treatises—offer a complex and contested array of perspectives on bodily ambiguity and gender differentiation of intersex individuals. By tracing these discourses, the study highlights how classical Muslim scholars developed nuanced, often highly technical frameworks to address questions of legal responsibility, ritual practice, and bodily classification. In doing so, it foregrounds the ways in which the intersex body became a site for legal reasoning and epistemological negotiation. Importantly, the study limits itself to classical sources and conceptual frameworks, intentionally excluding later ethical, political, legal, or biomedical developments.

As noted, this work is situated within the field of religious studies, with particular attention to its intersection with the study of sex and gender. This disciplinary lens enables a critical interrogation of how religious traditions—and, in this case, Islam—have historically constructed, regulated, or contested bodily categories and identities, including those that resist prevailing binaries. Religious studies, moreover, is not confined to abstract theological claims or legal pronouncements; it is equally attentive to lived belief, ritual practice, and the diffuse structures of religious authority that shape everyday life. As such, it provides a productive framework for considering how intersex persons and their families have engaged, and may continue to engage, with religious norms and institutions, whether through negotiation, adaptation, or resistance.

Modern scholarly discussions of non-binary individuals in Islamic societies have, until recently, focused predominantly on the perspectives of jurists and physicians. Yet even within this context, such individuals were not comprehensively studied. This selectivity of sources has contributed to a modern understanding of Islamic societies as rigidly structured around binary sex and gender norms. Such an understanding has been shaped in part by Orientalist assumptions that religious texts, especially the Qur'ān, constitute the sole or ultimate source of social values in Muslim contexts, coupled with the observation that the Qur'ān refers to the creation of "male" and "female" but does not clearly articulate a third or other category(ies). Equally influential has been the global diffusion of nineteenth-century European ideals of binary sex and gender, which have exerted normative force across diverse cultural contexts. Against this backdrop, the present volume seeks to move scholarly inquiry beyond these inherited frames, opening new avenues for examining how classical Islamic traditions negotiated bodily and gendered difference.

Finding the discursive evolution of *khunthā* in classical Islamic thought

The contributors to this volume have examined the topic of *khunthā* and its relation to sex and gender norms within the classical Arabic and Persian traditions across a range of disciplines, including lexicography, literature, scripture, law, and medicine. To avoid merely repeating the contents of each chapter, we have grouped them here thematically, focusing on recurring tensions and points of intersection. We also highlight where the various disciplines converged or contradicted one another. The main themes that are debated and traced in their evolution, along with shifts in approach, are as follows.

a. Scant appearance of the *khunthā* in the scriptural text

Although one might expect the *khunthā* to feature prominently in the Islamic scriptural corpus—given that it was a matter of biological traits that would have been clearly visible to the Prophet Muḥammad and his companions—it is striking that the Qurʾān does not explicitly mention this group. In Chapter Four, Almarri demonstrates that, due to this silence, classical Qurʾānic commentators treated the *khunthā* as an ambiguity of human perception rather than as a distinct, divinely created category. In doing so, they sought to defend a binary gender order rooted in the belief that every person has a 'true' nature in God's knowledge. Paradoxically, this approach institutionalized the *khunthā* within the exegetical tradition, framing it as a liminal subject positioned between male and female.

It is also notable that the early extant *ḥadīth* literature paid relatively little attention to the *khunthā*, despite its later prominence in Muslim legal discourse. As Alipour has shown, early Shiʿi *ḥadīth* compilations, prior to the production of the major *ḥadīth* collections—the so-called Four Books (*al-kutub al-arbaʿa*)—contain only a handful of narrations referring to the *khunthā* and addressing its legal status. Yet in later compilations—whether in the Sunni context (Chapter Eight by Gesink), the Ismāʿīlī context (Chapter Six by Almarri), or the Twelver Shiʿi context (Chapter Seven by Alipour)—the *khunthā* is treated extensively. These later *ḥadīth* collections sought to define the *khunthā*'s legal status and to provide indicators for its classification, focusing on primary signs observed before puberty and secondary signs that emerged around or after puberty. While many of these *ḥadīth* concentrated on questions of inheritance, others addressed ritual obligations, prayer, and related areas of devotional and legal practice.

b. *Khunthā* and *mukhannath*: between legal and moral neutrality and social stigma

This study shows that while Arabic lexicographical dictionaries gave equal attention to both *khunthā* and *mukhannath*, and distinguished between the two—the former defined primarily by bodily and biological characteristics, and the latter articulated largely through behavioral traits—the Arabic literary, biographical, and anecdotal traditions, as Gesink and Alipour demonstrate in Chapter Two, were more preoccupied with the figure of the *mukhannath* than with the *khunthā*. Nevertheless, instances of the *khunthā* can be found within these texts, and narratives about such individuals often expressed curiosity and wonder yet were generally devoid of contempt or harsh language directed solely at their being *khunthā*. By contrast, as Seyed-Gohrab argues in Chapter Three, in Persian literature both terms were used in a range of contexts. Whereas the *mukhannath* was sometimes associated with brothels and gendered stigma, the *khunthā* emerged as a figure imbued with spiritual or moral resonance. Through narratives such as ʿAṭṭār's account of Shiblī and Rūmī's depiction of a *khunthā* character, we encounter a nuanced interplay between gender, spirituality, and social norms, highlighting the era's worldview while challenging superficial judgements about gender and corporeality.

The same approach—namely, treating the *khunthā* with no contempt or moral censure—is evident within the classical Islamic legal context. Alipour's examination of the classical Shiʿi legal school in Chapter Seven, and Gesink's investigation of the Sunni legal traditions in Chapter Eight, both indicate that the *khunthā* was approached with neither disdain nor opprobrium. Similarly, as Alipour argues in Chapter Nine, this neutral stance is also reflected within classical Muslim medical discourse. The work of the Persian physician Zakariyyā l-Rāzī provides a notable example: he refrained from expressing any sense of distaste or contempt towards the *khunthā*, and where astonishing accounts about such cases circulated, he expressed doubt, urging that such reports be treated critically and verified before being deemed credible. Significantly, al-Rāzī never classified the *khunthā* as a 'disabled' or 'diseased' person. By contrast, when discussing the *mukhannath*, al-Rāzī associated this figure with a desire for being sexually penetrated, identifying it as the medical condition of *ubna* and proposing therapeutic interventions, yet even he stopped short of characterizing the *mukhannath* or other gender-variant individuals as morally deficient. In this way, the literary, legal, and medical discourses of the period demonstrate a measured and neutral stance towards the *khunthā*, grounded more in inquiry and classification than in judgement.

c. Gender and sex ambiguity in the classical Islamic traditions

The complexity and ambiguity of sex, with due reservations about the anachronistic application of these terms, was not treated as a deficiency within the Islamic tradition, but rather as a recognized and accommodated condition. In this regard, as Gesink and Alipour note in Chapter Two, the lexicons reveal two distinct approaches to the *khunthā*. Lexicographical sources reflect significant variation in how the *khunthā* was understood. On the one hand, al-Khalīl b. Aḥmad al-Farāhīdī (d. between 160/777–8 and 175/790–1), for instance, defined the *khunthā* as an individual who is neither male nor female, suggesting the possibility of a third category or a liminal state that resists binary sex or gender classification. By contrast, al-Jawharī (d. 393/1003) characterized the *khunthā* as someone possessing both male and female genitalia, presenting the *khunthā* as potentially a composite of both sexes. These definitions underscore the debates surrounding the conceptualization of the *khunthā*: does the term denote a male, a female, a blend of both, or neither? They also raise the question of whether the *khunthā* can be both male and female at once, or whether the *khunthā* is, in fact, male or female but with 'extra appendages.' The former position supports the view of sex as a spectrum, whereas the latter supports a binary gender paradigm. Although al-Jawharī's definition came to prevail among lexicographers, al-Khalīl's earlier formulation sparked extensive discussion in literary, medical, and juristic texts. Yet certain literary figures, such as Muḥammad al-Muḥibbī (d. 1111/1699), and many jurists, such as al-Sarakhsī (d. 483/1090), used the term in yet another way: to describe people who appeared to develop or change sex at puberty.

Islamic *ḥadīth* literature and its commentaries, as Geissinger argues in Chapter Five, display shifts in gender categorization that arise from a complex interplay of textual, interpretive, and social factors, ultimately serving commentators' aims to affirm elite masculine authority and marginalize certain gendered persons, thereby reinforcing—and simultaneously exposing the fragility of—normative gender boundaries. This is evident, for example, in the case of a *ḥadīth* about Anjasha, a camel-driver for the Prophet, which later commentators framed differently—some presenting him as a *mukhannath*, making the story a warning about gender boundaries. Through such reinterpretation, *ḥadīth* literature came to depict *mukhannath*s as morally suspect, while treating *khunthā*s as morally neutral, although early *ḥadīth* literature mentions *mukhannath*s far more frequently than *khunthā*s.

Literary sources, by contrast, clearly distinguished between the *khunthā*, a person with physical or biological characteristics that could not be easily classified as male or female in general or in a legal context, and the *mukhannath*, whose behavior was effeminate but whose personhood was legally male. *Mukhannath*s were more commonly mentioned in literature and sometimes stigmatized, whereas *khunthā*s were not—as observed both in Chapters Two and Three. Early literary usage of the term *khunthā* often referred to non-human subjects such as plants, and in the lengthy narrative of the *Kitāb al-aghānī*, a *khunthā* horse is described as possessing distinctive, almost magical, agility and speed.

Over the span of the classical era, Muslim jurists extended use of the term to apply to human bodies. Modern scholars have debated what underlying arguments motivated these jurists. Sanders previously argued that jurists have traditionally sought to determine the 'true nature' of the *khunthā*, and when this was not feasible, legal authorities typically assigned the individual a male or female status, as one could not be left legally undetermined. In Chapter One, she now suggests that this position needs critical reassessment, arguing that Muslim legal discourse has evolved towards a more nuanced consideration of sex and gender ambiguity and its implications for a non-binary legal framework, especially in light of advances in scholarship and an expanded understanding of different Islamic legal and cultural traditions.

Sanders now advocates for a more biologically sound understanding of sex and for closer attention to newer theoretical perspectives on intersex and non-binary existence. She draws on a robust foundation of biological research that demonstrates how intersex can be understood as a natural outcome of genetic mutations that arise from time to time, allowing species to adapt to changing environments. Non-human species have benefitted from such mutations, which enable their survival even after, for example, the complete disappearance of the Y-chromosome from their genome. For a believing Muslim, this reopens the question: Are *khunthā*s a 'disorder' in need of 'treatment,' or are they a deliberate creation—a part of the divine plan? The Y-chromosome is currently losing genetic material at the rate of ten genes per million years and could degrade entirely in another forty-five million years.[1] What, then, might be the role of intersex within that evolutionary context? As Susannah Cornwall has recently proposed, intersex can be conceived within an Abrahamic religious context as a gift—and understood as a gift, an intersex body would not require alteration.[2]

On the other hand, Almarri, in Chapter Six, explores the case of sex or gender ambiguity within the Ismāʿīlī *ḥadīth* corpus, showing how this posed significant challenges for Muslim communities, their interpersonal relations, and their juridical institutions. Gesink (in the Sunni context) and Alipour (in the Shiʿi context) further highlight that the ambiguous nature of certain *khunthā* cases, even if temporary or context-dependent, has long been recognized within the legal tradition as falling between established sex classifications. This is evident in cases related to inheritance, blood money, and the rules of congregational prayer, where individuals classified as *khunthā mushkil* or *mamsūḥ* were treated as occupying a medial or liminal legal status—one that was neither exclusively male nor exclusively female.

Moreover, as Alipour has demonstrated in his earlier publication, bodily ambiguity served as a catalyst for deeper debates in the classical Islamic context—debates that transcended the purely legal sphere and opened up ontological questions regarding the actual nature of intersex people.[3] Gesink, in Chapter Eight, confirms that the discourse changed over time. Early Sunni jurists often sought to integrate the *khunthā* into a binary ontological system of male and female, treating intersex variations as temporary states that would ultimately resolve into one or the other by puberty. As the legal discourse evolved to better accommodate those with non-binary bodies, jurists such as al-Sarakhsī (d. 483/1090) and al-Marghīnānī (d. 593/1196–7), along with Qurʾānic exegetes such as Makkī b. Abī Ṭālib (d. 437/1045) and Ibn ʿAṭiyya (d. 542/1148), increasingly grappled with the possibility that intersex people might constitute a distinct category of humankind created by God—although this line of inquiry often resulted in a denial of any ontological category beyond the male–female binary.[4]

By contrast, in the Twelver Shiʿi context, as Alipour shows in Chapter Seven, jurists prior to the twelfth century do not appear to have explicitly addressed the ontological status of intersex people. It seems to have been generally assumed that such a person was ultimately either male or female. As a result, the possibility that an intersex person might be neither male nor female, but rather belong to a third or distinct category, was not considered. In the late twelfth century, Ibn Idrīs al-Ḥillī became the first Shiʿi jurist to raise the question of a binary versus non-binary status for the *khunthā mushkil*. Ever since, Shiʿi legal discourse has been divided between two opposing positions: one group of jurists rejecting the notion of a third ontological category, and another arguing for its possibility and legitimacy as a distinct category of human being.[5]

In the medical context too, as al-Rāzī's work (discussed in Chapter Nine) suggests, acknowledging sex and gender ambiguity went hand in hand with accepting a diversity of human creation. Al-Rāzī's recognition of five human categories, all created by God, underscores an expansive understanding of human sex and gender that goes well beyond simplistic binary classifications.

Implications for law and medical practice

The implications of a historical examination of the *khunthā* in classical Islamic societies are manifold. First, those born with variations of sex characteristics may be regarded as part of the natural order or, if one prefers, as creations of God.

In certain instances, their sex may be ascertained through specific often physical indicators. However, there are cases where external observation is insufficient, and only the person themselves may truly know their sex, often due to internal sexual inclinations or orientation. In such circumstances, as several classical Muslim jurists acknowledged, the individual would be afforded the right to determine whether to assimilate into the male or female category. Should they be unable or unwilling to do so, the choice to remain non-binary does not diminish their humanity, nor does it exclude them from the community or justify the denial of their rights within an Islamic framework. More importantly, there is also a position within Islamic legal discourse that allows intersex individuals to move beyond the male–female categorization and to be categorized as a third human category. All of this suggests that the male–female binary framework, which many contemporary traditional Muslim scholars present as the sole authentic Islamic view, is both historically and intellectually contested. Moreover, it demonstrates that alternative and more inclusive positions have long been present within the classical Muslim cultural heritage. By gaining awareness of such precedents, contemporary Muslim communities could be better positioned to engage in constructive dialogue with traditional scholars and religious authorities, seeking greater recognition and protection for intersex persons—particularly in instances where their sex cannot be definitively classified, or where they do not wish to be assigned exclusively as male or female.

Second, although advances in modern medical technology now enable physicians to conduct a range of sophisticated investigations—including chromosomal analyses, genetic profiling, and hormonal assessments—far beyond the characteristics that defined the *khunthā* in the classical Islamic legal context, this study suggests that an individual born with a variation of sex development may not necessarily evolve into a clearly male or female identity. In fact, a number of recent medical studies have cautioned against relying exclusively on chromosomal or genital appearances to predict the adult sex or gender identity of a person born with such a variation.[6] Within an Islamic legal framework, there is scope for a distinct, non-binary category of national identification. Such a designation might be configured to acknowledge the status of an individual as *khunthā*, while also allowing for their legal classification as male or female if required. This approach encompasses the possibility that the sex assigned to a *khunthā* at birth may require revision at puberty. It should therefore be feasible for a person categorized as intersex, male, or female at birth to change their registered sex in late adolescence or early adulthood, ensuring that their legal status reflects their lived reality and affirms their dignity and rights.

The court cases examined in this volume further demonstrate that Islamic courts possessed the authority to amend a *khunthā*'s legal sex or gender status.

This contradicts the assertion, sometimes made from the mid-twentieth century onwards, that God had assigned every individual a fixed and universally evident sex or gender that could never be altered. Furthermore, several classical Muslim jurists, notably among the Shāfiʿīs and Ḥanafīs, accepted an adult's own assertion of their sexual identity as valid grounds for a court to categorize a change of sex. While medical evidence of a genetic variation can be submitted where available, making such proof a requirement would unfairly privilege those with access to costly medical diagnosis, undermining the Islamic ideal of social equity. A state grounded in the Islamic legal heritage can justifiably take pride in its historic recognition of the diverse manifestations of God's creation.

Third, the category of *khunthā* is far more expansive than the conventional juristic definition, which is often confined to an individual presenting both a penis and a vagina or neither. In fact, it can be extended to encompass those whose sex characteristics appear to shift at puberty, those born without a penis, and other conditions historically described as *khunthā*. For example, as Gesink notes in Chapter Eight, the Sunni jurist al-Sarakhsī offers two formal explanations for how someone comes to be categorized as *khunthā*: an infant may be born with both male and female genital features or without any genitalia at all.[7] However, his legal rulings also address other possibilities; for example, a person could be reared as one legal category but mature as another,[8] or could have an internal sense of their sex at odds with their external characteristics.[9] One could persuasively argue that this category should also apply to individuals whose atypical sex characteristics led their parents or medical practitioners to subject them to non-consensual sex-assignment surgeries during childhood. Such alternative legal positions have significant ramifications—not only for legal scholars addressing the public and personal rights of such individuals, but also for medical practitioners grappling with the ethical and clinical dimensions of their care.

Fourth, historically, a *khunthā* was categorized as a human being entitled to legal and social rights. In some Christian contexts, intersex individuals have argued that ecclesiastical authorities denied them a complete human existence, on the grounds that God created only male and female—a stance that barred them from baptism, confirmation, and full belonging within the religious community.[10] In the Islamic tradition, no jurist, physician, or Qurʾānic exegete ever asserted that a *khunthā* who could not be classified as male or female was thereby less than human, or undeserving of inheritance, compensation, or other legal rights. Instead, jurists sought ways to accommodate such individuals so that their rights and obligations could be properly categorized and fulfilled. This issue presents a significant challenge within the traditional Islamic legal framework when it comes to approving marriage for intersex individuals, especially those whose sex transcends or cannot be definitively classified within the male–female binary.

Nonetheless, as demonstrated in this study, there are documented instances—albeit contested—within both *ḥadīth* literature and the classical legal discourse where one party to a marriage was a *khunthā*.

Importantly, this challenge is not unique to Islam. In many parts of the world, the right to marry for people with variations of sex characteristics (VSCs) remains ambiguous, contested, or effectively denied.[11] Even in jurisdictions where marriage has been extended to same-sex couples, intersex people—especially those whose sex cannot be definitively classified or who reject assignment exclusively as 'male' or 'female'—continue to face legal and social hurdles. If the right to marry is to be treated as a fundamental human right, it would seem logical that it be granted clearly and unequivocally to intersex people. Conversely, where states restrict marriage to male–female couples, it would still be incumbent upon them to provide legal accommodations that respect the dignity and civil rights of those with variations of sex characteristics.

In the context of the Islamic tradition, this issue is further compounded. The dominant position within classical Muslim jurisprudence opposed the marriage of intersex individuals when their sex was ambiguous. Yet this was never an absolute or uniform stance. Certain texts and juristic discussions contemplated, and at times sought to clarify, the status and rights of the *khunthā*. These contested spaces reveal an internal diversity and a latent potential for reinterpretation. The central question, then, is how intersex people and their advocates might draw upon this contested heritage to engage with, and challenge, contemporary conservative Muslim scholars and authorities. In doing so, it may be possible to rethink, expand, and ultimately secure the right to marry for intersex people—both within Muslim-majority contexts and within Muslim communities in the West.

Finally, a key implication of this study for medical practitioners serving Muslim families is that the treatment of intersex variations should not be regarded as an immediate Islamic legal or social necessity requiring urgent surgical or medical intervention. Historically, Muslims approached intersex individuals with a relatively accepting attitude, and within this context there was no widespread pressure for surgical intervention. Moreover, the Islamic legal tradition historically does not prescribe surgery as a religious obligation. Although Muslim surgeons have performed surgeries on intersex individuals for life-saving treatments and gender confirmation, such variations were not universally treated as pathological conditions requiring surgical correction.

Today, the pressure to treat intersex births as medical emergencies often stems from conservative scholars, from parents unfamiliar with the historical legal discourse on intersex individuals, and from communities demanding strict gender conformity. While this pressure is genuine, so too is the risk of significant physical and psychological harm caused by unnecessary surgical interventions.

As this study suggests, there is ample discursive space within the classical Islamic tradition to justify limiting the practice of genital examinations in childhood, and to prohibit the involvement of multiple practitioners, given the risk of psychological trauma. If Muslim intersex individuals and activists were to draw upon such classical positions, they could advocate for restricting medical intervention to instances where variations affect vital bodily functions—such as salt-wasting congenital adrenal hyperplasia. They could also insist that irreversible hormonal or surgical procedures be deferred until the person is able to give informed consent, with parental consent never acting as a substitute for the person's own. In this regard, the surgical alteration of prepubescent genitalia ought to be treated analogously to female genital mutilation (FGM), a practice that recent Muslim jurists have ruled impermissible. Moreover, a person with variations of sex characteristics (VSC) should be afforded the right to seek legal redress or claim *diya* if their sexual or reproductive function is impaired by medical treatment administered without their adult consent.

Limits and silences

This volume is intentionally confined to the classical period and does not explore modern and contemporary discourse related to intersex matters. As a result, it does not engage with evolving debates and reinterpretations that emerged in later historical periods. The absence of such inquiry leaves open a significant area for future research that can illuminate how intersex people have been treated and represented within shifting socio-legal, religious, and medical landscapes beyond the classical era.

Moreover, this study has not entered the scholarly discussion of the ethical or political terrains of present-day intersex activism or biomedical intervention. Although this study, as indicated, provides foundational bases for Muslims in general and for intersex individuals and activists in particular to open constructive negotiations with religious and legal authorities of their respective society to enhance the rights of people with VSCs, the questions that animate contemporary discourse—such as medical practices, gender assignment, human rights, and the role of state and civil institutions—fall beyond the scope of the present examination. This limitation is deliberate, ensuring a concentrated focus on the formative texts and classical interpretative traditions. Nonetheless, this creates an evident lacuna for scholars interested in tracing continuity and rupture between pre-modern discussions and their modern counterparts.

A further limitation lies in the restricted examination of legal traditions. The present volume draws extensively upon dominant Sunni and Twelver Shiʿi and Ismāʿīlī sources, but it does not incorporate analyses of the Zaydī and ʿIbādī legal schools. These traditions, rich and complex in their own right, have developed nuanced treatments of sex and gender ambiguity that deserve closer examination. Their absence here means that the present study cannot claim comprehensive coverage of the diverse landscape of Islamic legal thought.

Finally, the medical discourse underpinning classical treatments of the *khunthā* remains far from fully explored. This study primarily engages with al-Rāzī's contributions, leaving a substantial body of medical manuscripts—both those preceding him, such as the Persian physician ʿAlī b. Sahl Rabban al-Ṭabarī (d. between 240/855 and 250/864), and those succeeding him, including ʿAlī b. al-ʿAbbās al-Ahwāzī (d. 384/994 [?])—largely unexamined. While prior scholarship has addressed the works of al-Zahrāwī (Albucasis) (d. 403–4/1013) and Ibn Sīnā (d. 438/1037), a focused examination of the lesser-studied texts by these aforementioned figures promises to enrich our understanding of the dynamic relationship between medical theory, legal reasoning, and gender categorization. The limited scope of the current study reflects its focus and methodological boundaries, making this an inviting area for future research and critical inquiry.

Final remark

Studies have demonstrated that debates on sex and gender ambiguities in Muslim societies have been diverse, yielding a range of perspectives. In relation to sexuality, for example, scholars have shown that while classical Islamic law predominantly prohibited male active pederasty or sodomy (*liwāṭ*), Muslim culture—whether in the context of the Ṣūfī gaze or in vernacular settings—sometimes embraced expressions of romantic affection towards boys. At the same time, these settings generally refrained from openly legitimizing sexual involvement between adult men and boys, although this does not mean that such practices never occurred.[12] A similar dynamic applies to gender diversity. Although effeminate individuals (*mukhannath*s) and mannish women (*mutarajjil*s) were not treated as distinct legal entities—being classified under the categories of male and female respectively—their distinct social role or category was largely acknowledged within classical Muslim culture.[13]

With regard to binary and non-binary bodies, a similar contestation emerges. In examining intersex embodiment in Islam, it is evident that the binary classification of human beings was a position embraced by many classical Muslim scholars of exegesis (*tafsīr*), law (*fiqh*), and medical discourse (*ṭibb*). According to this approach, a *khunthā* was to be classified as either male or female, and when ambiguity remained, jurists would still assign a legal sex—male or female—to that person. Part of the reason for this was the preservation of the patriarchal order, in which masculinity played a pivotal role and the existence of a liminal entity such as the *khunthā* was perceived as a potential challenge to that structure. However, this was not the sole consideration. As Gesink has convincingly argued, "Intersex persons could be assigned or could adopt a legal sex of male, female, or neither. Rather than 'protecting' male privilege, the authors of these texts largely served an individual's health and religious needs."[14]

Nevertheless, as previous studies have demonstrated[15]—and as this study further confirms—there were always alternative attitudes towards this matter. In the classical Islamic context, alongside the binary position, there existed legal, medical, and ontological categories that acknowledged persons who were almost-but-not-quite men, almost-but-not-quite women, and neither-male-nor-female but potentially either. The point that this study advances is that diverse attitudes towards sex and gender were present within the classical Islamic tradition. To be clear, this is not to assert that Islam possessed a monolithic gender-pluralist social structure. Rather, a binary gender ontology coexisted with non-binary legal categories, and, to date, very little evidence has surfaced to suggest that this coexistence was contested or treated as problematic. It is true that instances of discrimination existed, and we have identified a handful of records referring to abuse of a person claiming to be *khunthā*—though these appear to relate to a single case (see Chapter Two). Moreover, certain periods, such as the Mamluk era, witnessed heightened gender policing, including a shift towards more binary-focused jurisprudence and a tendency to prioritise *ḥadīth* interpretations that enforced gender binaries. Yet such episodes should be understood within their specific historical and local contexts, and must not be taken as evidence of a universally monolithic Islam.

Despite such a diverse view, surprisingly, since the twentieth century, traditional Muslim scholars have largely advocated a rigid, binary understanding of Islamic conceptions of sex and gender—one that expressly excludes any recognition of non-binary classifications. This stance reflects prevailing Muslim cultural idealism and has been articulated through authoritative legal opinions and fatwas. Within this framework, the birth of an intersex infant is typically treated as a problem to be resolved through assignment to one of the two normative categories, male or female. As a result, Muslim parents—both in Muslim-majority contexts and in Muslim minority communities in the West—have often opted for gender-affirming surgery (GAS) to "fix" the child's sex, generally based on personal or cultural considerations and conducted without the child's assent or regard for their future autonomy. Such decisions are commonly made in the absence of historically-grounded legal, ethical, or medical guidance. Hence, the pivotal question emerges: What historical and intellectual shifts have led to the widespread perception that "Islam" exclusively accommodates a binary conception of gender in the modern and contemporary period?

Afsaneh Najmabadi has argued that, in the context of modern Iran, the translation of Western sexological texts into Persian from the Qajar era onwards—including Sylvanus Stall's *What a Young Husband Ought to Know* (1897), translated in 1929, and Freud's works in the 1930s—contributed to a shift towards a stricter gender binary.[16] A similar trend can be observed in Arab Middle Eastern sources associated with late nineteenth-century reformers. Most of these Arab Middle Eastern societies had been subjected to Western colonial domination, and as a result inherited a complex legacy of legal, political, and cultural influences.

Although reformers such as Rifāʿa al-Ṭahṭāwī, Muḥammad ʿAbduh, Rashīd Riḍā, and Shāh Walī Allāh advocated a return to the original sources of 'pure' Islam, drawing extensively upon the *ḥadīth* literature as a hermeneutic aid for interpreting the Qurʾān, it is difficult to imagine that the Western colonial discourse of strict gender binaries did not play a significant role in shaping their outlook. The *ḥadīth* corpus itself, compiled in an era when *mukhannath*s were increasingly marginalized and the category of *khunthā* remained relatively obscure, tended to project a strongly binary model of gender. In this way, European texts and ideas about sex and gender came to corroborate and intensify the reformers' evolving vision of a world sharply divided along binary sex and gender lines.

These were the same reformers who dominated the Arabic print sphere. By the turn of the twentieth century, reformist authors writing in Arabic and Persian had largely erased the normative presence of non-binary sex and gender categories. Later in the twentieth century, when jurists, particularly in the Sunni context, were confronted with cases involving transgender women seeking gender-affirming medical treatments, their responses—exemplified by the 1989 ruling of the Islamic Fiqh Council of the Muslim World League—declared such alterations forbidden as changes to what God had created. On the other hand, the same legal statement allows the parents of intersex infants to request GCS, on the grounds that they regard the intersex condition as a medical disorder necessitating treatment.[17] In issuing these rulings, the jurists were either unaware that they were entrenching a binary gender discourse that had only recently achieved cultural dominance, or they deliberately overlooked the historical Muslim legal debates that recognized the possibility of a non-binary framework.

Consequently, further research is required to investigate the political, cultural, and theological factors that have contributed to the resistance within modern traditional Islamic legal and social contexts to recognizing non-binary sex and gender categories in Islamic legal and cultural reasoning since the early modern period. This remains an open and pressing subject in need of thorough scholarly attention.

Notes

1 Lucy Cooke, *Bitch: On the Female of the Species* (New York City: Basic Books, 2022; Audiobook, 2022), 16–17.

2 Susannah Cornwall, "Bodily Rights and Gifts: Intersex, Abrahamic Religions and Human Rights," *Culture, Health, and Sexuality* 23, no. 4 (2021): 533–47.

3 Mehrdad Alipour, "Navigating Body Politics in Shiʿi Legal Tradition: Examining Sayyid Kāẓim al-Yazdī's Account of Non-Binary Intersex," *Islamic Law and Society* 32, no. 3 (2025): 262–315.

4 Also, see Alipour, "Navigating Body Politics in Shiʿi Legal Tradition," 285–7, n.64; Almarri, Chapter Four of this volume.

5 See Alipour, "Navigating Body Politics in Shiʿi Legal Tradition."

6 Suzanne Kessler, "The Medical Construction of Gender: Case Management of Intersexed Infants," *Signs Journal of Women in Culture and Society* 16, no.1 (1990): 3–26; Ursula Kuhnle and Wolfgang Krahl, "The Impact of Culture on Sex Assignment and Gender Development in Intersex Patients," *Perspectives in Biology and Medicine* 45, no. 1 (2002): 85–103; A. I. Lev, "Intersexuality in the Family: An Unacknowledged Trauma," *Journal of Gay & Lesbian Psychotherapy* 10, no. 2 (2006): 27–56; Mohd Salim Mohamed and Siti Nurani Mohd Noor, "Islamic Bioethical Deliberation on the Issue of Newborns with Disorders of Sex Development," *Science and Engineering Ethics* 21 (2015): 429–40; Martina Cools et al., Anna Nordenström, Ralitsa Robeva, Joanne Hall, Puck Westerveld, Christa Flück, Birgit Köhler, Marta Berra, Alexander Springer, Katinka Schweizer, Vickie Pasterski; on behalf of the COST Action BM1303 working group 1, "Caring for Individuals with a Difference of Sex Development (DSD): A Consensus Statement," *National Review of Endocrinology* 14, no. 7 (2018): 415–29.

7 Muḥammad b. Aḥmad al-Sarakhsī, *Kitāb al-mabsūṭ*, 30 vols. (Beirut: Dār al-Kutub al-ʿIlmiyya, 2001), 30: 92.

8 Al-Sarakhsī, *al-Mabsūṭ*, 30: 114–5, describes a hypothetical arranged marriage in which two *khunthā*s are married to one another in childhood with the understanding that one is male and the other female. Al-Sarakhsī ruled such a marriage invalid because the gender of rearing might not match the adult gender, and the marriage would potentially unite two males or two females. (See Chapter Eight).

9 Al-Sarakhsī, *al-Mabsūṭ*, 30:104–5.

10 Stephanie Budwey, *Intersex and Religion* (Routledge, 2023), 51–88 and 127–67.

11 See for example Julie A. Greenburg, "Can I Marry a Man, Woman, Either, or Neither?" in *Intersexuality and the Law: Why Sex Matters* (New York University Press, 2012): 51–64.

12 See Khaled El-Rouayheb, *Before Homosexuality in the Arab-Islamic World, 1500–1800* (Chicago: University of Chicago Press, 2005), Chapter Three.

13 See Everett K. Rowson, "The Effeminates of Early Medina." *Journal of the American Oriental Society* 111, no. 4 (1991): 671–93; Ash Geissinger, "Islam and Discourses of Same-Sex Desire," in *Homosexuality in modern religious history*. eds. Boisvert, Donald. L., and Johnson, Jay. E. (Santa Barbara, Calif: Praeger, 2012): 69–90. Also, see Chapter Five of this volume.

14 Indira Falk Gesink, "Intersex Bodies in Premodern Islamic Discourse: Complicating the Binary," *Journal of Middle East Women's Studies* 14, no. 2 (2018): 152–73, at 153.

15 Alipour, "Navigating Body Politics in Shiʿi Legal Tradition;" Gesink, "Intersex Bodies in Premodern Islamic Discourse."

16 Afsaneh Najmabadi, *Women with Mustaches and Men Without Beards: Gender and Sexual Anxieties of Iranian Modernity* (Berkeley: University of California Press, 2005), Chapters Two and Three.

[17] Mehrdad Alipour, "The Nexus between Gender Confirmation Surgery and Illness: Legal-Hermeneutical Examinations of Four Islamic Fatwās," *Journal of Middle East Women's Studies*, 18(3), 2022, 359–86, at 366–68, 378–79.

Bibliography

Alipour, Mehrdad. "Navigating Body Politics in Shi'i Legal Tradition: Examining Sayyid Kāẓim al-Yazdī's Account of Non-Binary Intersex." *Islamic Law and Society* 32, no. 3 (2025): 262–315.

Alipour, Mehrdad. "The Nexus between Gender-Confirming Surgery and Illness: Legal-Hermeneutical Examinations of Four Islamic Fatwas." *Journal of Middle East Women's Studies* 18, no 3 (2022): 359–86.

Budwey, Stephanie A. *Religion and Intersex: Perspectives from Science, Law, Culture, and Theology*. London: Routledge, 2023.

Cooke, Lucy. *Bitch: On the Female of the Species*. New York City: Basic Books, 2022; Audiobook, 2022.

Cools, Martina, Anna Nordenström, Ralitsa Robeva, Joanne Hall, Puck Westerveld, Christa Flück, Birgit Köhler, Marta Berra, Alexander Springer, Katinka Schweizer, Vickie Pasterski; on behalf of the COST Action BM1303 working group 1. "Caring for Individuals with a Difference of Sex Development (DSD): A Consensus Statement." *National Review of Endocrinology* 14, no. 7 (2018): 415–29.

Cornwall, Susannah. "Bodily Rights and Gifts: Intersex, Abrahamic Religions and Human Rights." *Culture, Health, and Sexuality* 23, no. 4 (2021): 533–47.

El-Rouayheb, Khaled. *Before Homosexuality in the Arab-Islamic World, 1500–1800*. Chicago: University of Chicago Press, 2005.

Geissinger, Ash. "Islam and Discourses of Same-Sex Desire." in *Homosexuality in Modern Religious History*. edited by Donald L. Boisvert and Jay E. Johnson. Santa Barbara: Praeger, 2012: 69–90

Gesink, Indira Falk. "Intersex Bodies in Premodern Islamic Discourse: Complicating the Binary." *Journal of Middle East Women's Studies* 14, no. 2 (2018): 152–73.

Greenburg, Julie A. "Can I Marry a Man, Woman, Either, or Neither?" in *Intersexuality and the Law: Why Sex Matters*. New York University Press, 2012: 51–64.

Kessler, Suzanne. "The Medical Construction of Gender: Case Management of Intersexed Infants." *Signs Journal of Women in Culture and Society* 16, no. 1 (1990): 3–26. DOI:10.1086/494643.

Kuhnle, U. and W. Krahl. "The Impact of Culture on Sex Assignment and Gender Development in Intersex Patients." *Perspectives in Biology and Medicine* 45, no. 1 (2002): 85–103.

Lev, A. I. "Intersexuality in the Family: An Unacknowledged Trauma." *Journal of Gay & Lesbian Psychotherapy* 10, no. 2 (2006): 27–56.

Mohamed, Mohd Salim and Siti Nurani Mohd Noor. "Islamic Bioethical Deliberation on the Issue of Newborns with Disorders of Sex Development." *Science and Engineering Ethics* 21 (2015): 429–40.

Najmabadi, Afsaneh. *Women with Mustaches and Men Without Beards: Gender and Sexual Anxieties of Iranian Modernity*. Berkeley: University of California Press, 2005.

Rowson, Everett K. "The Effeminates of Early Medina." *Journal of the American Oriental Society* 111, no. 4 (1991): 671–93.

Al-Sarakhsī, Muḥammad b. Aḥmad. *Kitāb al-mabsūṭ*. 30 vols. Beirut: Dār al-Kutub al-ʿIlmiyya, 2001.

Index of Names

Note: In the index of names below, the Arabic definite article *al-* has been omitted so that names are listed alphabetically under the principal element.

Index of Terms

Iranian Studies Series

H. Baghaei-Abchooyeh
Beyond Orientalism: Sir William Jones (1746–1794), A Journey of Understanding
ISBN 978 90 8728 447 3

J.T.P. de Bruijn
Pearls of Meanings: Studies on Persian Art, Poetry, Ṣūfism and History of Iranian Studies in Europe
ISBN 978 90 8728 348 3

J.C. Bürgel & C. van Ruymbeke (eds.)
Nizāmī: A Key to the Treasure of the Hakim
ISBN 978 90 8728 097 0

J. Coumans
The Rubáiyát of Omar Khayyám: An Updated Bibliography
ISBN 978 90 8728 096 3

D. Farhosh-van Loon
Ayatollah Khomeini's Mystical Poetry and Its Reception in Iran and the Diaspora
ISBN 978 90 8728 401 5

B.M. Fomeshi
The Persian Whitman: Beyond a Literary Reception
ISBN 978 90 8728 335 3

N. Fozi
Reclaiming the Faravahar: Zoroastrian Survival in Contemporary Tehran
ISBN 978 90 8728 214 1

A. Ghajarjazi
Irrationalities in Islam and Media in Nineteenth-Century Iran: Faces of Modernity
ISBN 978 90 8728 398 8

R. Harris & M. Afsharian (eds.)
A Journal of Three Months' Walk in Persia in 1884 by Captain John Compton Pyne
ISBN 978 90 8728 262 2

A. Karimi-Hakkak
A Fire of Lilies: Perspectives on Literature and Politics in Modern Iran
ISBN 978 90 8728 329 2

M.M. Khorrami & A. Moosavi (eds.)
Losing Our Minds, Coming to Our Senses: Sensory Readings of Persian Literature and Culture
ISBN 978 90 8728 368 1

F. Lewis & S. Sharma (eds.)
The Necklace of the Pleiades: 24 Essays on Persian Literature, Culture and Religion
ISBN 978 90 8728 091 8

S. McGlinn (ed.)
Principles for Progress: Essays on Religion and Modernity by Abdu'l-Bahā
ISBN 978 90 8728 307 0

M.A. Nematollahi Mahani
The Holy Drama: Persian Passion Plays in Modern Iran
ISBN 978 90 8728 115 1

Z. Noorian
Parvin Etesami in the Literary and Religious Context of Twentieth-Century Iran: A Female Poet's Challenge to Patriarchy
ISBN 978 90 8728 412 1

C. Pérez González
Local Portraiture: Through the Lens of the 19th-Century Iranian Photographers
ISBN 978 90 8728 156 4

S. Rafiee Rad
Expeditions in Persia: Exploring Qajar Persia in two 19th-Century Diaries
ISBN 978 90 8728 468 8

L. Rahimi Bahmany
Mirrors of Entrapment of Emancipation: Forugh Farrokhzad and Sylvia Plath
ISBN 978 90 8728 224 0

R. Rahmoni & G. van den Berg
The Epic of Barzu as Narrated by Jura Kamal
ISBN 978 90 8728 116 8

A. Sedighi
Agreement Restrictions in Persian
ISBN 978 90 8728 093 2

A. Sedighi
Persian in Use: An Elementary Textbook of Language and Culture
ISBN 978 90 8728 217 2

A.A. Seyed-Gohrab
Courtly Riddles: Enigmatic Embellishments in Early Persian Poetry
ISBN 978 90 8728 087 1

A.A. Seyed-Gohrab (ed.)
The Great Umar Khayyam: A Global Reception of the Rubáiyat
ISBN 978 90 8728 157 1

A.A. Seyed-Gohrab (ed.)
Sufi Non-Conformism: Antinomian Trends in the Persianate Cultural Traditions
ISBN 978 90 8728 454 1

A.A. Seyed-Gohrab (ed.)
Gender and Sexuality in Persian Literary and Religious Traditions: Embodied Encounters
ISBN 978 90 8728 5005

A.A. Seyed-Gohrab & S.R.M. McGlinn (eds.)
One Word – Yak Kaleme: 19th-Century Persian Treatise Introducing Western Codified Law
ISBN 978 90 8728 089 5

A.A. Seyed-Gohrab & S.R.M. McGlinn (eds.)
Safina Revealed: A Compendium of Persian Literature in 14th-Century Tabriz
ISBN 978 90 8728 088 8

A.A. Seyed-Gohrab, F. Doufikar-Aerts & S. McGlinn (eds.)
Embodiments of Evil: Gog and Magog. Interdisciplinary Studies of the 'Other' in Literature & Internet Texts
ISBN 978 90 8728 090 1

P. Shabani-Jadidi
Processing Compound Verbs in Persian: A Psycholinguistic Approach to Complex Predicates
ISBN 978 90 8728 208 0

B. Solati
The Reception of Ḥāfiẓ: The Sweet Poetic Language of Ḥāfiẓ in Nineteenth and Twentieth Century Persia
ISBN 978 90 8728 197 7

R. Tabandeh
The Rise of the Niʿmatullāhī Order in 19th-Century Persia: Shi'ite Sufi Masters and Their Battle against Islamic Fundamentalism
ISBN 978 90 8728 367 4

S. Tabatabai
Father of Persian Verse: Rudaki and his Poetry
ISBN 978 90 8728 092 5

K. Talattof & A.A. Seyed-Gohrab (eds.)
Conflict and Development in Iranian Film
ISBN 978 90 8728 169 4

M. Van Zutphen (ed.)
A Story of Conquest and Adventure: The Large Farāmarznāme
ISBN 978 90 8728 272 1

R. Zipoli
Irreverent Persia: Invective, Satirical and Burlesque Poetry from the Origins to the Timurid Period (10th to 15th century)
ISBN 978 90 8728 227 1